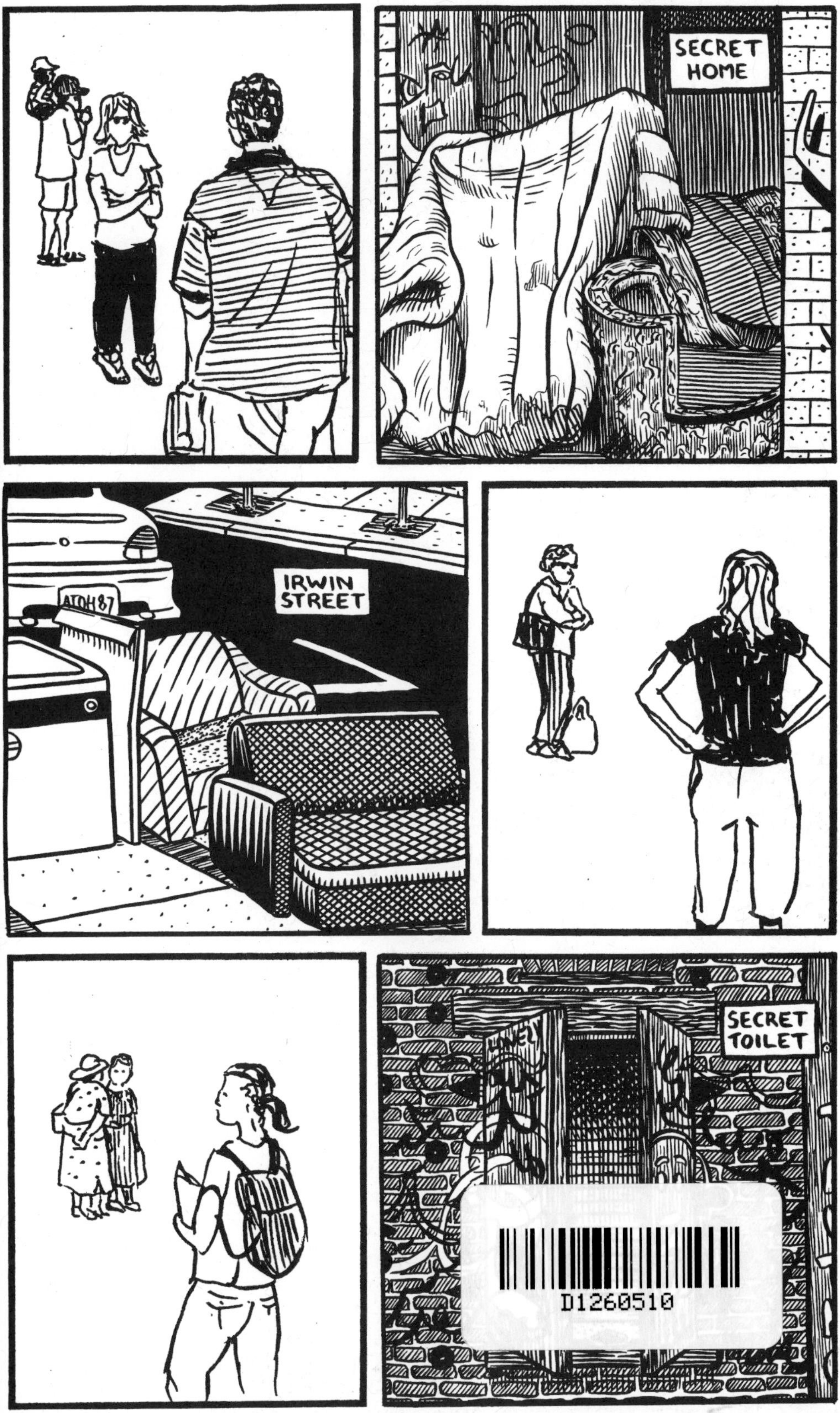
SECRET HOME
IRWIN STREET
ATOH87
SECRET TOILET

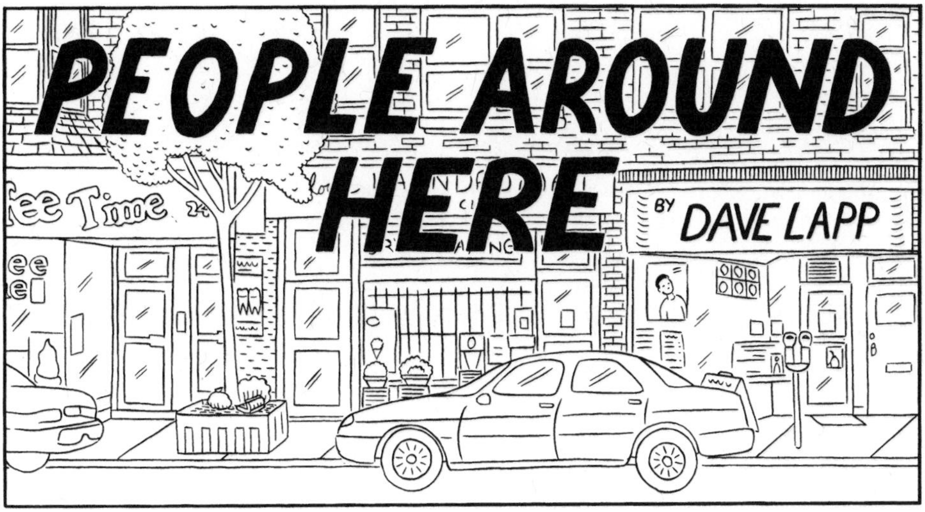
PEOPLE AROUND HERE
BY DAVE LAPP

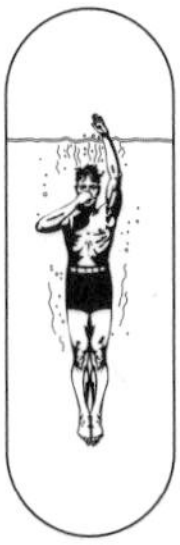

Printed at Gauvin Press, Gatineau, Quebec
First Edition

Dave Lapp would like to thank: Conan Tobias, Alan Hunt, Brian Burchell, Jason Kieffer, Chester
Brown, Lydia Chao, Cary Chao, Alison Payne, Jordan Bursach, Dalton Sharp, Kerby Waud,
Walter Dickinson, Dean Tweed, Sarah Penturn, Stacy Tang, Sam Feldman, John Booth, Brett Lamb,
Nadia Halim, Greg Lapp, Donna Stevenson, Julie Lapp, Carl Lapp, Greg Baker, and especially
Andy Brown for publishing all my books!

Library and Archives Canada Cataloguing in Publication

Lapp, Dave, 1965-
     People around here / Dave Lapp.

ISBN 978-1-894994-59-0

     1. Graphic novels. I. Title.

PN6733.L36P46 2012          741.5'971          C2012-900451-0

Conundrum Press
Greenwich, Nova Scotia, Canada
www.conundrumpress.com

MIX
Paper from
responsible sources
FSC
www.fsc.org    FSC® C100212

Conundrum Press acknowledges the financial support of the Canada Council for the Arts and the
Government of Canada through the Canada Book Fund toward its publishing activities.

Canada Council    Conseil des Arts
for the Arts      du Canada

Canada

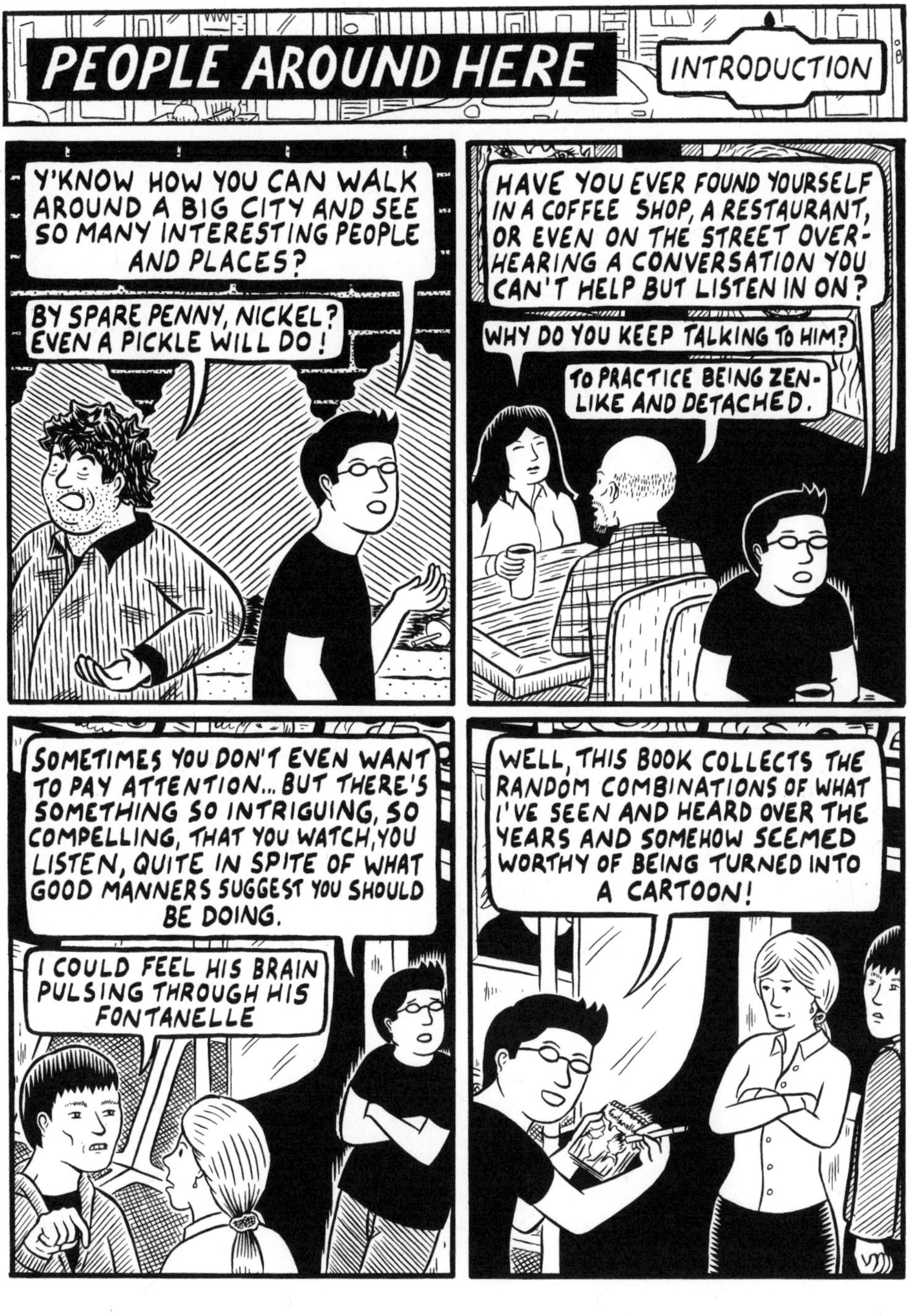
PEOPLE AROUND HERE
INTRODUCTION
Y'KNOW HOW YOU CAN WALK AROUND A BIG CITY AND SEE SO MANY INTERESTING PEOPLE AND PLACES?
BY SPARE PENNY, NICKEL? EVEN A PICKLE WILL DO!
HAVE YOU EVER FOUND YOURSELF IN A COFFEE SHOP, A RESTAURANT, OR EVEN ON THE STREET OVER-HEARING A CONVERSATION YOU CAN'T HELP BUT LISTEN IN ON?
WHY DO YOU KEEP TALKING TO HIM?
TO PRACTICE BEING ZEN-LIKE AND DETACHED.
SOMETIMES YOU DON'T EVEN WANT TO PAY ATTENTION... BUT THERE'S SOMETHING SO INTRIGUING, SO COMPELLING, THAT YOU WATCH, YOU LISTEN, QUITE IN SPITE OF WHAT GOOD MANNERS SUGGEST YOU SHOULD BE DOING.
I COULD FEEL HIS BRAIN PULSING THROUGH HIS FONTANELLE
WELL, THIS BOOK COLLECTS THE RANDOM COMBINATIONS OF WHAT I'VE SEEN AND HEARD OVER THE YEARS AND SOMEHOW SEEMED WORTHY OF BEING TURNED INTO A CARTOON!

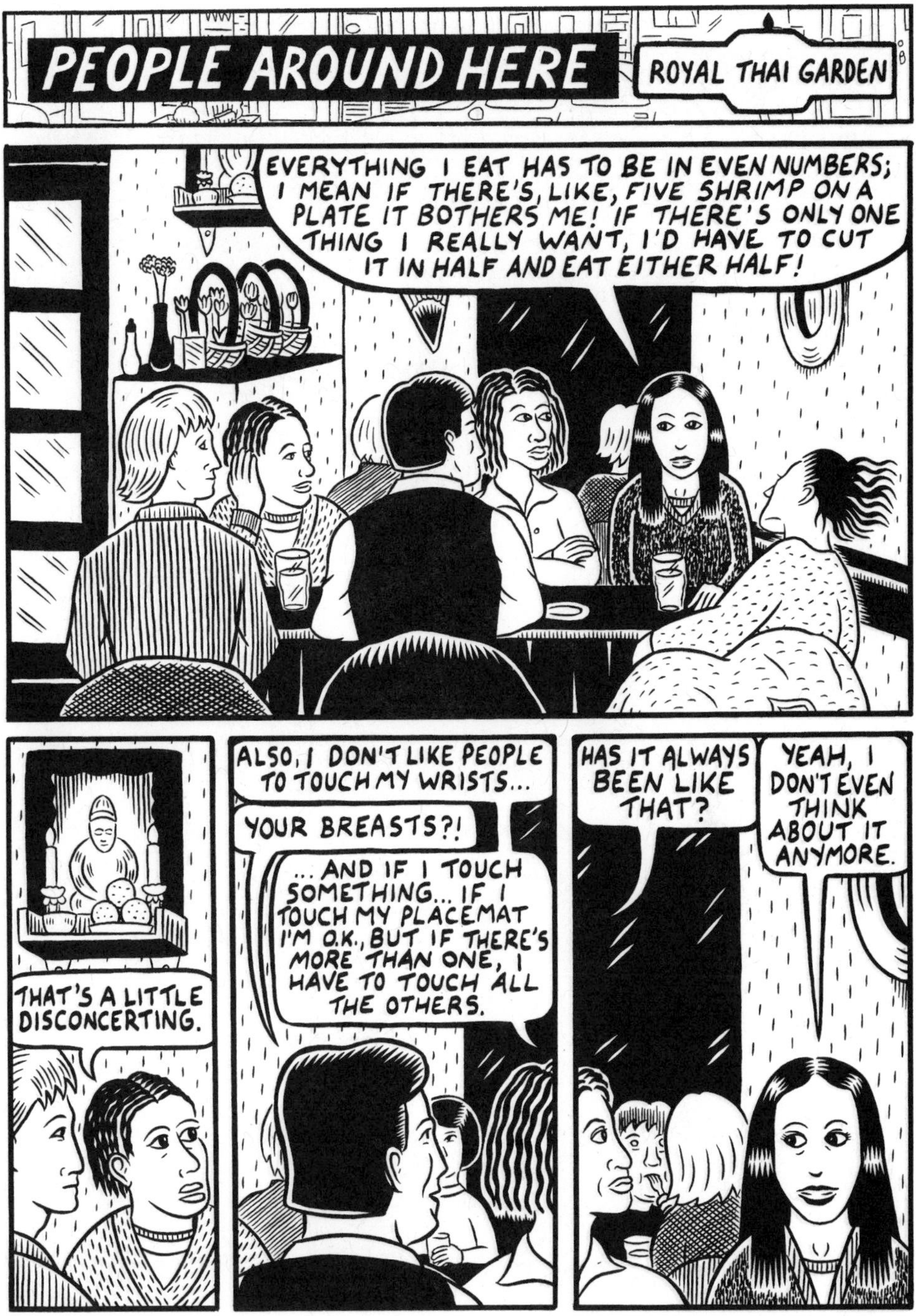
PEOPLE AROUND HERE
ROYAL THAI GARDEN
EVERYTHING I EAT HAS TO BE IN EVEN NUMBERS; I MEAN IF THERE'S, LIKE, FIVE SHRIMP ON A PLATE IT BOTHERS ME! IF THERE'S ONLY ONE THING I REALLY WANT, I'D HAVE TO CUT IT IN HALF AND EAT EITHER HALF!
THAT'S A LITTLE DISCONCERTING.
ALSO, I DON'T LIKE PEOPLE TO TOUCH MY WRISTS...
YOUR BREASTS?!
... AND IF I TOUCH SOMETHING... IF I TOUCH MY PLACEMAT I'M O.K., BUT IF THERE'S MORE THAN ONE, I HAVE TO TOUCH ALL THE OTHERS.
HAS IT ALWAYS BEEN LIKE THAT?
YEAH, I DON'T EVEN THINK ABOUT IT ANYMORE.

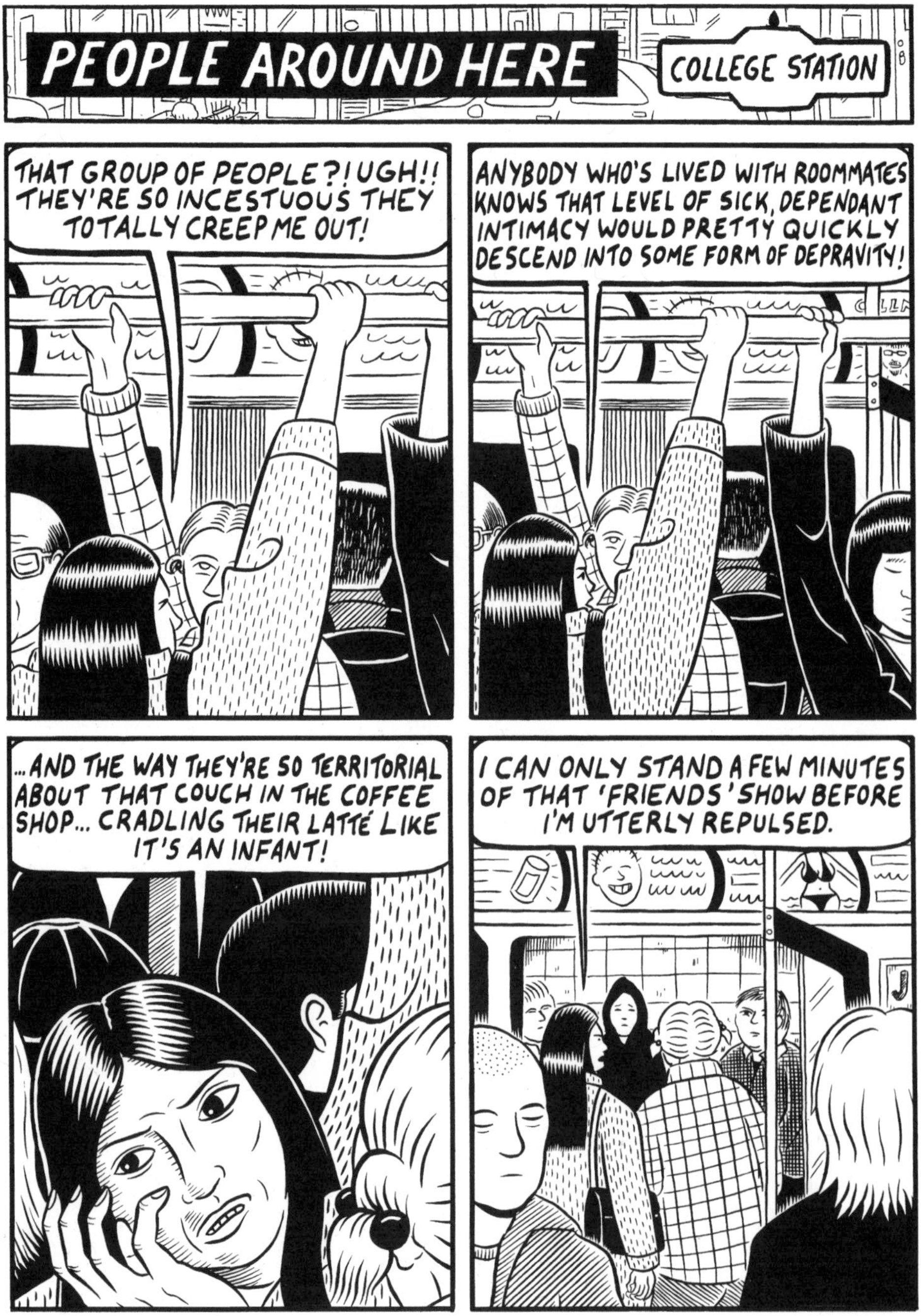
PEOPLE AROUND HERE
COLLEGE STATION
THAT GROUP OF PEOPLE?! UGH!! THEY'RE SO INCESTUOUS THEY TOTALLY CREEP ME OUT!
ANYBODY WHO'S LIVED WITH ROOMMATES KNOWS THAT LEVEL OF SICK, DEPENDANT INTIMACY WOULD PRETTY QUICKLY DESCEND INTO SOME FORM OF DEPRAVITY!
...AND THE WAY THEY'RE SO TERRITORIAL ABOUT THAT COUCH IN THE COFFEE SHOP... CRADLING THEIR LATTÉ LIKE IT'S AN INFANT!
I CAN ONLY STAND A FEW MINUTES OF THAT 'FRIENDS' SHOW BEFORE I'M UTTERLY REPULSED.

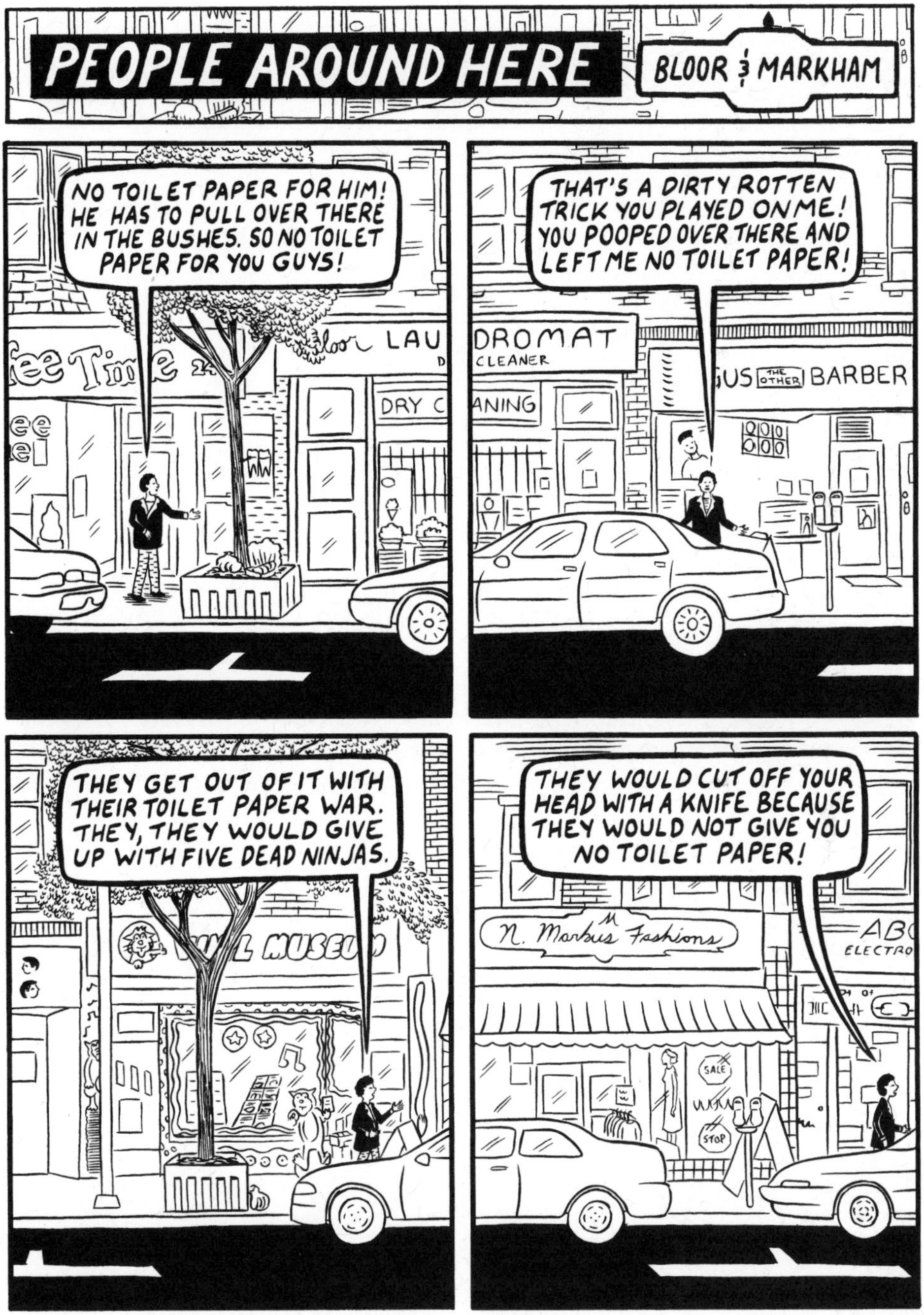
PEOPLE AROUND HERE
BLOOR & MARKHAM
NO TOILET PAPER FOR HIM! HE HAS TO PULL OVER THERE IN THE BUSHES. SO NO TOILET PAPER FOR YOU GUYS!
THAT'S A DIRTY ROTTEN TRICK YOU PLAYED ON ME! YOU POOPED OVER THERE AND LEFT ME NO TOILET PAPER!
THEY GET OUT OF IT WITH THEIR TOILET PAPER WAR. THEY, THEY WOULD GIVE UP WITH FIVE DEAD NINJAS.
THEY WOULD CUT OFF YOUR HEAD WITH A KNIFE BECAUSE THEY WOULD NOT GIVE YOU NO TOILET PAPER!

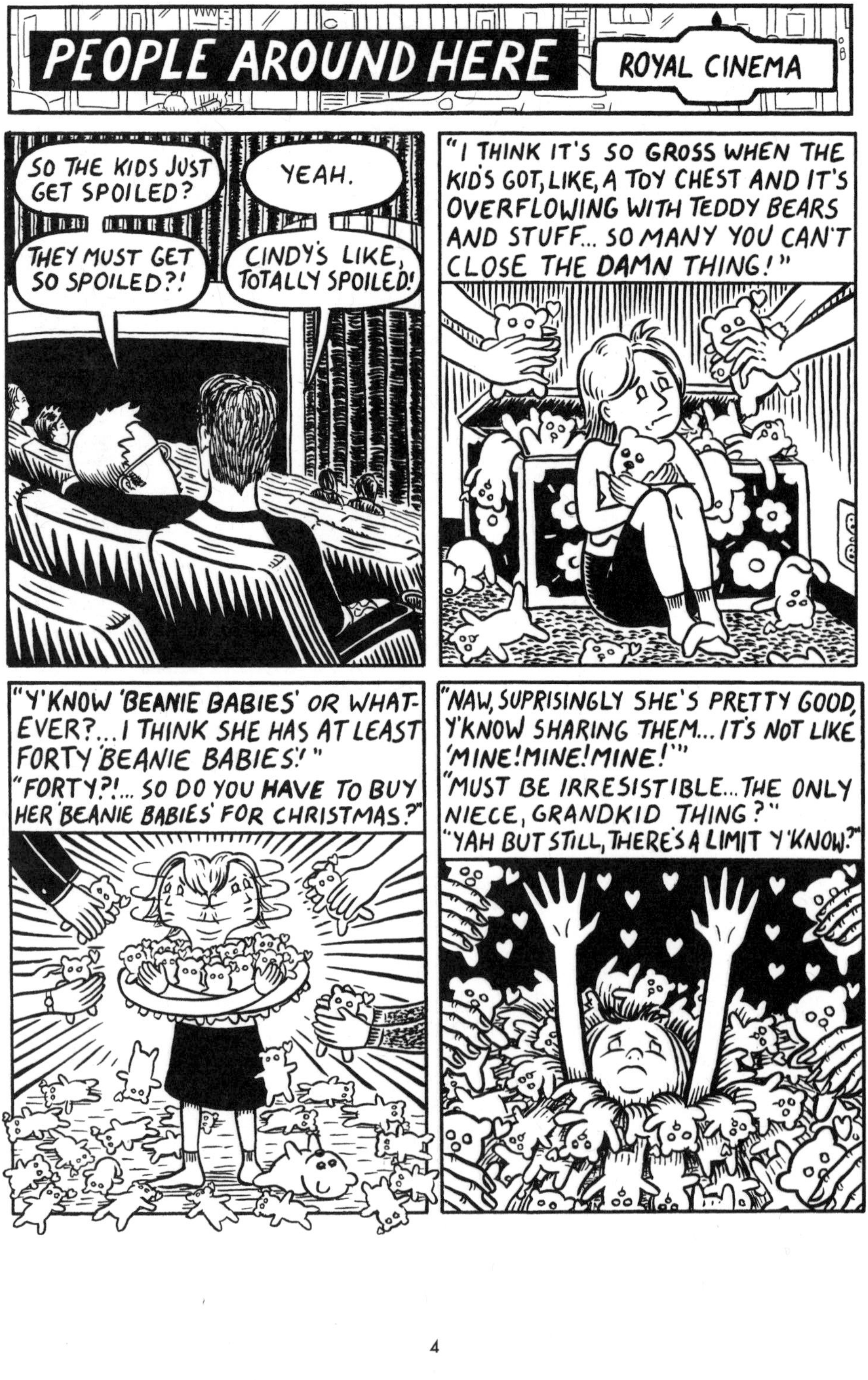
PEOPLE AROUND HERE
ROYAL CINEMA
SO THE KIDS JUST GET SPOILED?
THEY MUST GET SO SPOILED?!
YEAH.
CINDY'S LIKE, TOTALLY SPOILED!
"I THINK IT'S SO GROSS WHEN THE KID'S GOT, LIKE, A TOY CHEST AND IT'S OVERFLOWING WITH TEDDY BEARS AND STUFF... SO MANY YOU CAN'T CLOSE THE DAMN THING!"
"Y'KNOW 'BEANIE BABIES' OR WHAT-EVER?... I THINK SHE HAS AT LEAST FORTY 'BEANIE BABIES'!"
"FORTY?!... SO DO YOU HAVE TO BUY HER 'BEANIE BABIES' FOR CHRISTMAS?"
"NAW, SUPRISINGLY SHE'S PRETTY GOOD, Y'KNOW SHARING THEM... IT'S NOT LIKE 'MINE! MINE! MINE!'"
"MUST BE IRRESISTIBLE... THE ONLY NIECE, GRANDKID THING?"
"YAH BUT STILL, THERE'S A LIMIT Y'KNOW."

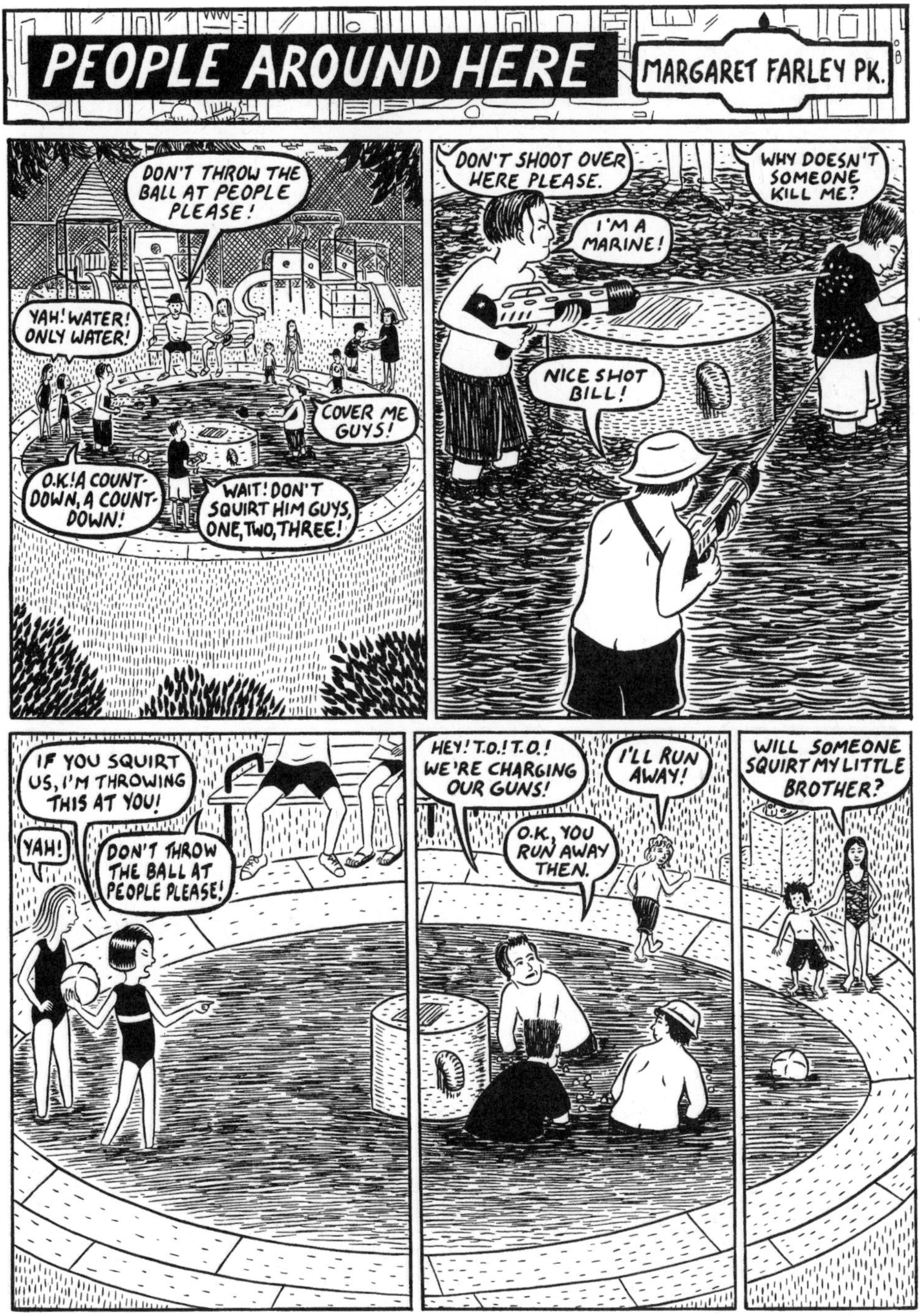
PEOPLE AROUND HERE
MARGARET FARLEY PK.
DON'T THROW THE BALL AT PEOPLE PLEASE!
YAH! WATER! ONLY WATER!
COVER ME GUYS!
O.K.! A COUNT-DOWN, A COUNT-DOWN!
WAIT! DON'T SQUIRT HIM GUYS, ONE, TWO, THREE!
DON'T SHOOT OVER HERE PLEASE.
WHY DOESN'T SOMEONE KILL ME?
I'M A MARINE!
NICE SHOT BILL!
IF YOU SQUIRT US, I'M THROWING THIS AT YOU!
YAH!
DON'T THROW THE BALL AT PEOPLE PLEASE!
HEY! T.O.! T.O.! WE'RE CHARGING OUR GUNS!
I'LL RUN AWAY!
O.K., YOU RUN AWAY THEN.
WILL SOMEONE SQUIRT MY LITTLE BROTHER?

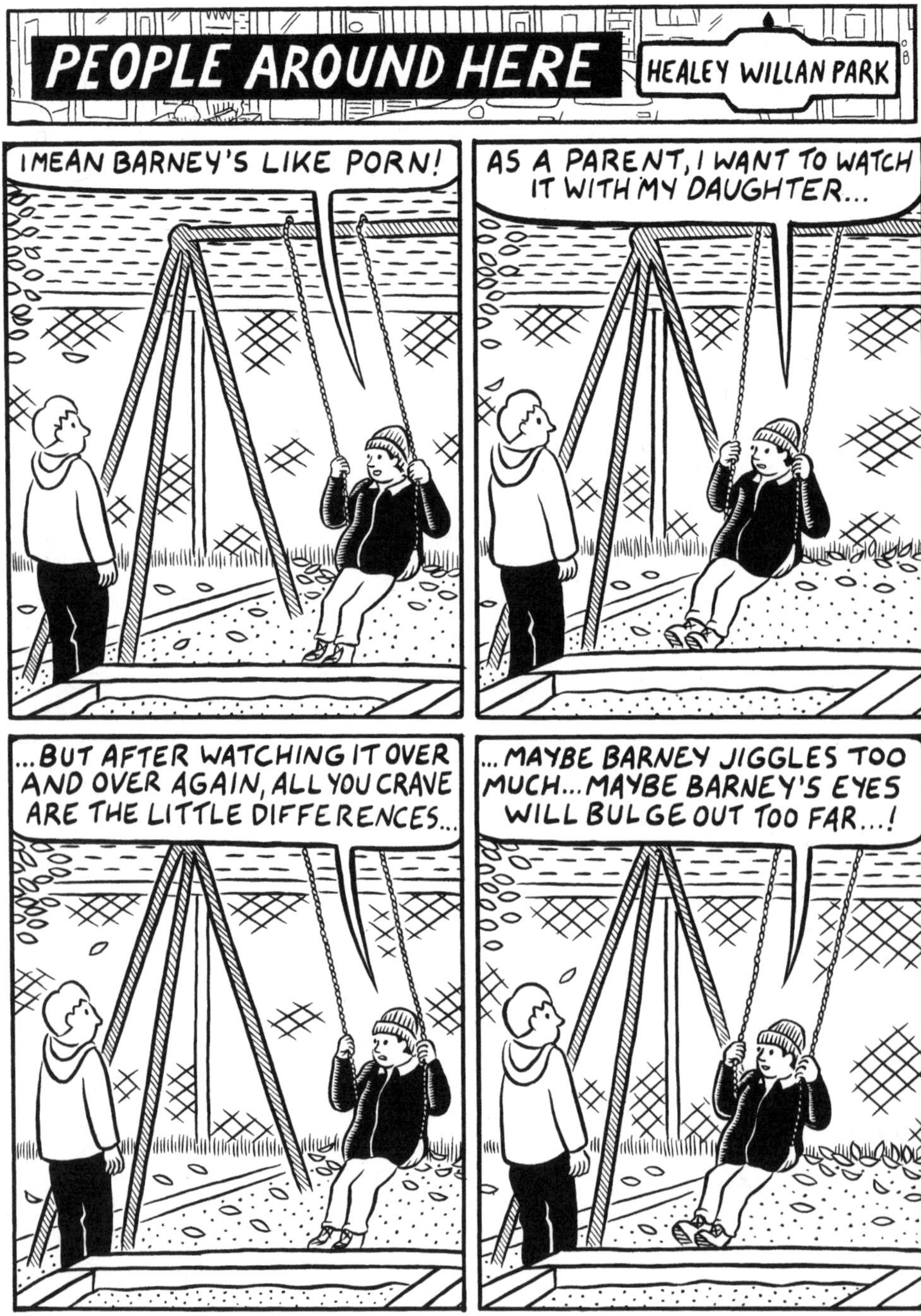
PEOPLE AROUND HERE
HEALEY WILLAN PARK
I MEAN BARNEY'S LIKE PORN!
AS A PARENT, I WANT TO WATCH IT WITH MY DAUGHTER...
...BUT AFTER WATCHING IT OVER AND OVER AGAIN, ALL YOU CRAVE ARE THE LITTLE DIFFERENCES...
...MAYBE BARNEY JIGGLES TOO MUCH...MAYBE BARNEY'S EYES WILL BULGE OUT TOO FAR...!

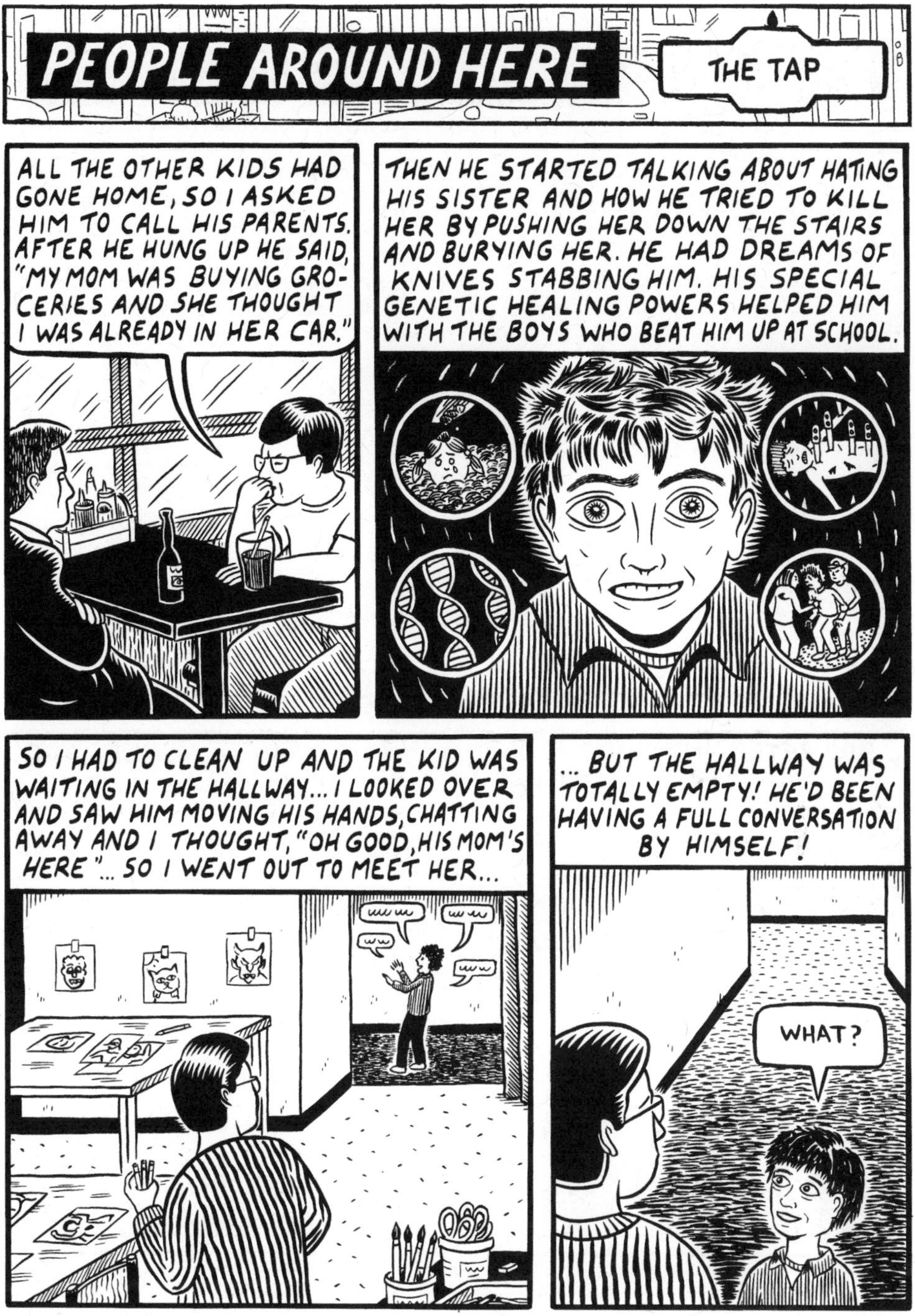
PEOPLE AROUND HERE
THE TAP
ALL THE OTHER KIDS HAD GONE HOME, SO I ASKED HIM TO CALL HIS PARENTS. AFTER HE HUNG UP HE SAID, "MY MOM WAS BUYING GROCERIES AND SHE THOUGHT I WAS ALREADY IN HER CAR."
THEN HE STARTED TALKING ABOUT HATING HIS SISTER AND HOW HE TRIED TO KILL HER BY PUSHING HER DOWN THE STAIRS AND BURYING HER. HE HAD DREAMS OF KNIVES STABBING HIM. HIS SPECIAL GENETIC HEALING POWERS HELPED HIM WITH THE BOYS WHO BEAT HIM UP AT SCHOOL.
SO I HAD TO CLEAN UP AND THE KID WAS WAITING IN THE HALLWAY... I LOOKED OVER AND SAW HIM MOVING HIS HANDS, CHATTING AWAY AND I THOUGHT, "OH GOOD, HIS MOM'S HERE"... SO I WENT OUT TO MEET HER...
... BUT THE HALLWAY WAS TOTALLY EMPTY! HE'D BEEN HAVING A FULL CONVERSATION BY HIMSELF!
WHAT?

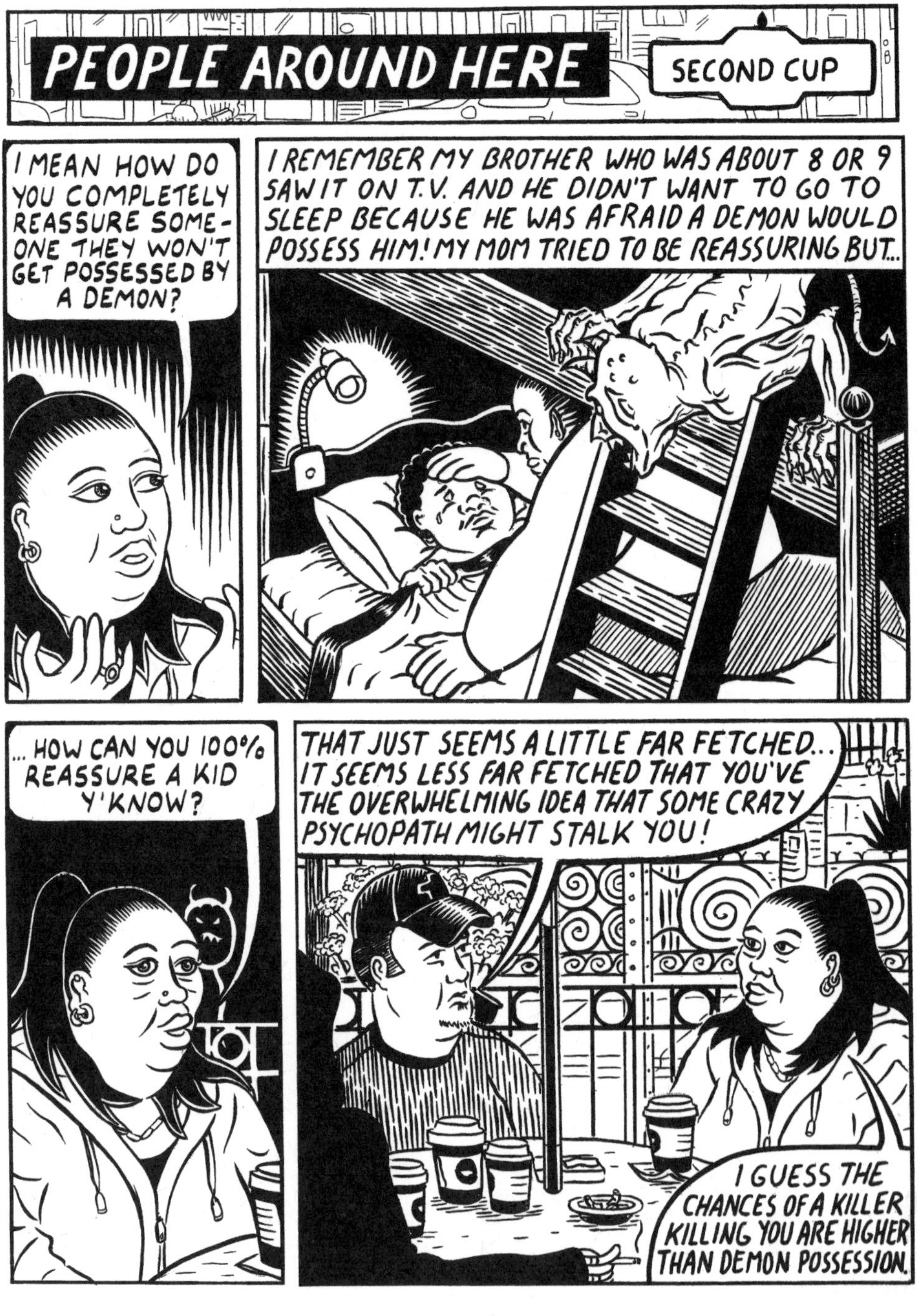
PEOPLE AROUND HERE
SECOND CUP
I MEAN HOW DO YOU COMPLETELY REASSURE SOME-ONE THEY WON'T GET POSSESSED BY A DEMON?
I REMEMBER MY BROTHER WHO WAS ABOUT 8 OR 9 SAW IT ON T.V. AND HE DIDN'T WANT TO GO TO SLEEP BECAUSE HE WAS AFRAID A DEMON WOULD POSSESS HIM! MY MOM TRIED TO BE REASSURING BUT...
...HOW CAN YOU 100% REASSURE A KID Y'KNOW?
THAT JUST SEEMS A LITTLE FAR FETCHED... IT SEEMS LESS FAR FETCHED THAT YOU'VE THE OVERWHELMING IDEA THAT SOME CRAZY PSYCHOPATH MIGHT STALK YOU!
I GUESS THE CHANCES OF A KILLER KILLING YOU ARE HIGHER THAN DEMON POSSESSION.

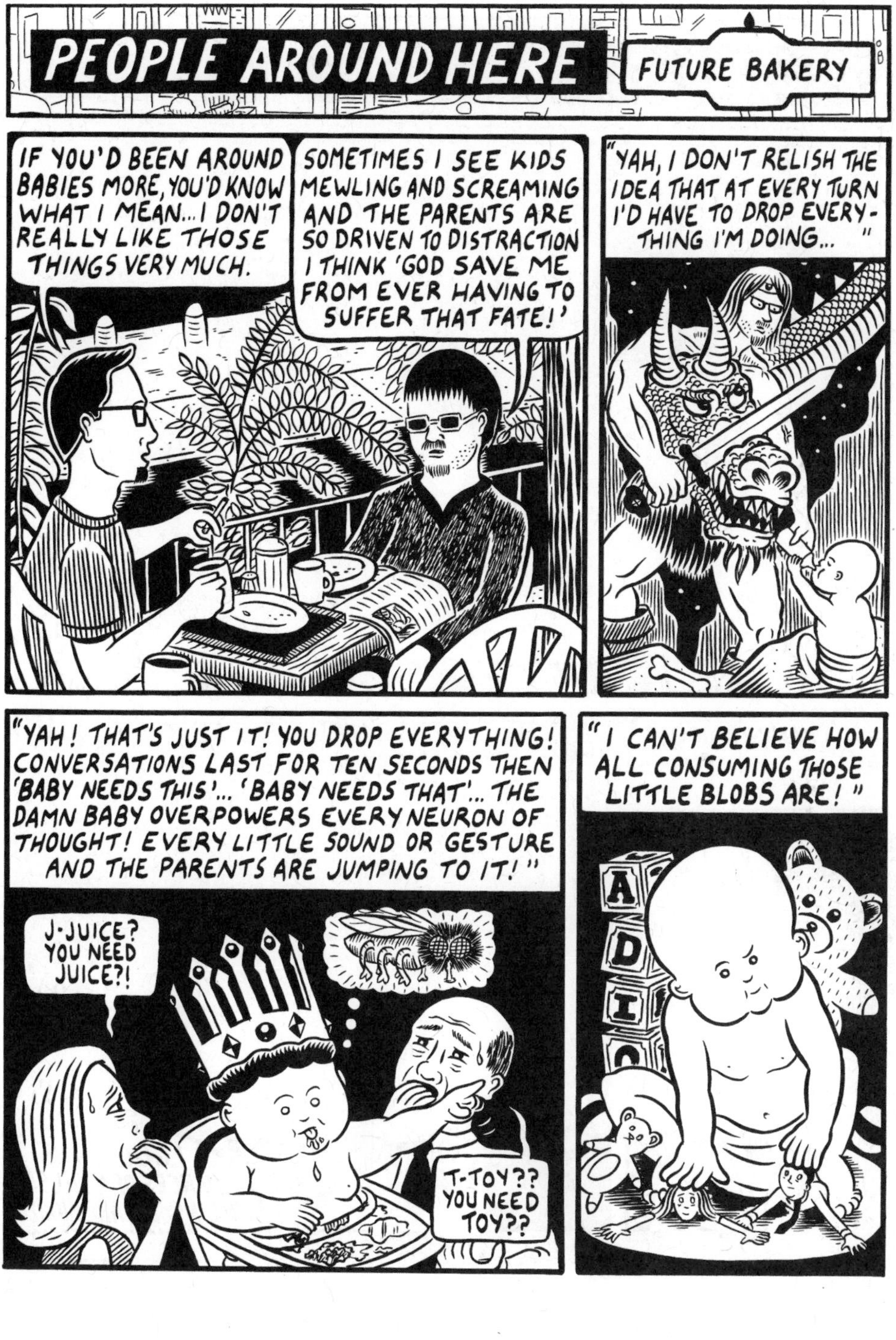
PEOPLE AROUND HERE
FUTURE BAKERY
IF YOU'D BEEN AROUND BABIES MORE, YOU'D KNOW WHAT I MEAN... I DON'T REALLY LIKE THOSE THINGS VERY MUCH.
SOMETIMES I SEE KIDS MEWLING AND SCREAMING AND THE PARENTS ARE SO DRIVEN TO DISTRACTION I THINK 'GOD SAVE ME FROM EVER HAVING TO SUFFER THAT FATE!'
"YAH, I DON'T RELISH THE IDEA THAT AT EVERY TURN I'D HAVE TO DROP EVERYTHING I'M DOING..."
"YAH! THAT'S JUST IT! YOU DROP EVERYTHING! CONVERSATIONS LAST FOR TEN SECONDS THEN 'BABY NEEDS THIS'... 'BABY NEEDS THAT'... THE DAMN BABY OVERPOWERS EVERY NEURON OF THOUGHT! EVERY LITTLE SOUND OR GESTURE AND THE PARENTS ARE JUMPING TO IT!"
J-JUICE? YOU NEED JUICE?!
T-TOY?? YOU NEED TOY??
"I CAN'T BELIEVE HOW ALL CONSUMING THOSE LITTLE BLOBS ARE!"

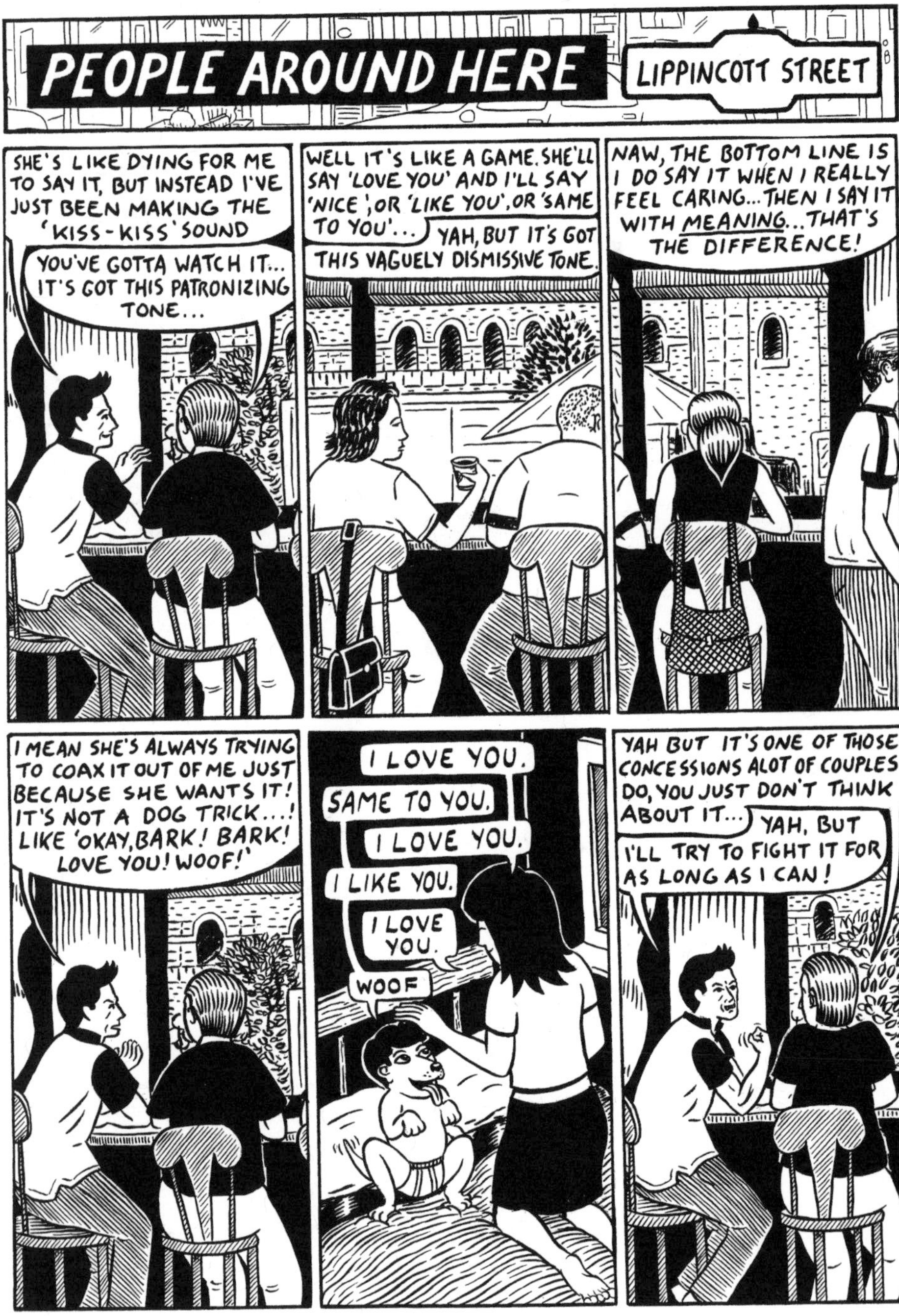
PEOPLE AROUND HERE
LIPPINCOTT STREET
SHE'S LIKE DYING FOR ME TO SAY IT, BUT INSTEAD I'VE JUST BEEN MAKING THE 'KISS-KISS' SOUND
YOU'VE GOTTA WATCH IT... IT'S GOT THIS PATRONIZING TONE...
WELL IT'S LIKE A GAME. SHE'LL SAY 'LOVE YOU' AND I'LL SAY 'NICE', OR 'LIKE YOU', OR 'SAME TO YOU'...
YAH, BUT IT'S GOT THIS VAGUELY DISMISSIVE TONE.
NAW, THE BOTTOM LINE IS I DO SAY IT WHEN I REALLY FEEL CARING... THEN I SAY IT WITH MEANING... THAT'S THE DIFFERENCE!
I MEAN SHE'S ALWAYS TRYING TO COAX IT OUT OF ME JUST BECAUSE SHE WANTS IT! IT'S NOT A DOG TRICK...! LIKE 'OKAY, BARK! BARK! LOVE YOU! WOOF!'
I LOVE YOU.
SAME TO YOU.
I LOVE YOU.
I LIKE YOU.
I LOVE YOU.
WOOF
YAH BUT IT'S ONE OF THOSE CONCESSIONS ALOT OF COUPLES DO, YOU JUST DON'T THINK ABOUT IT...
YAH, BUT I'LL TRY TO FIGHT IT FOR AS LONG AS I CAN!

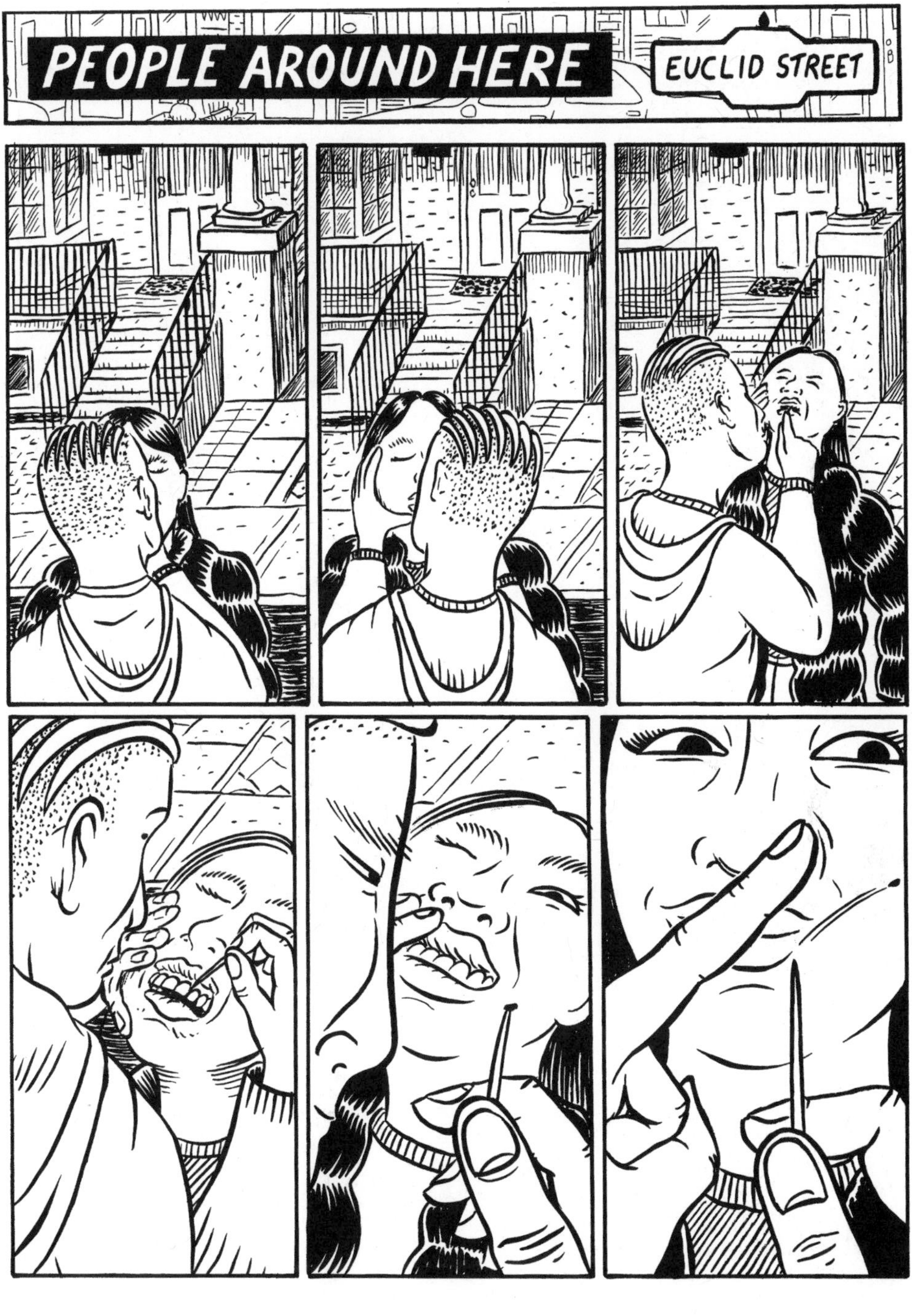
PEOPLE AROUND HERE
EUCLID STREET

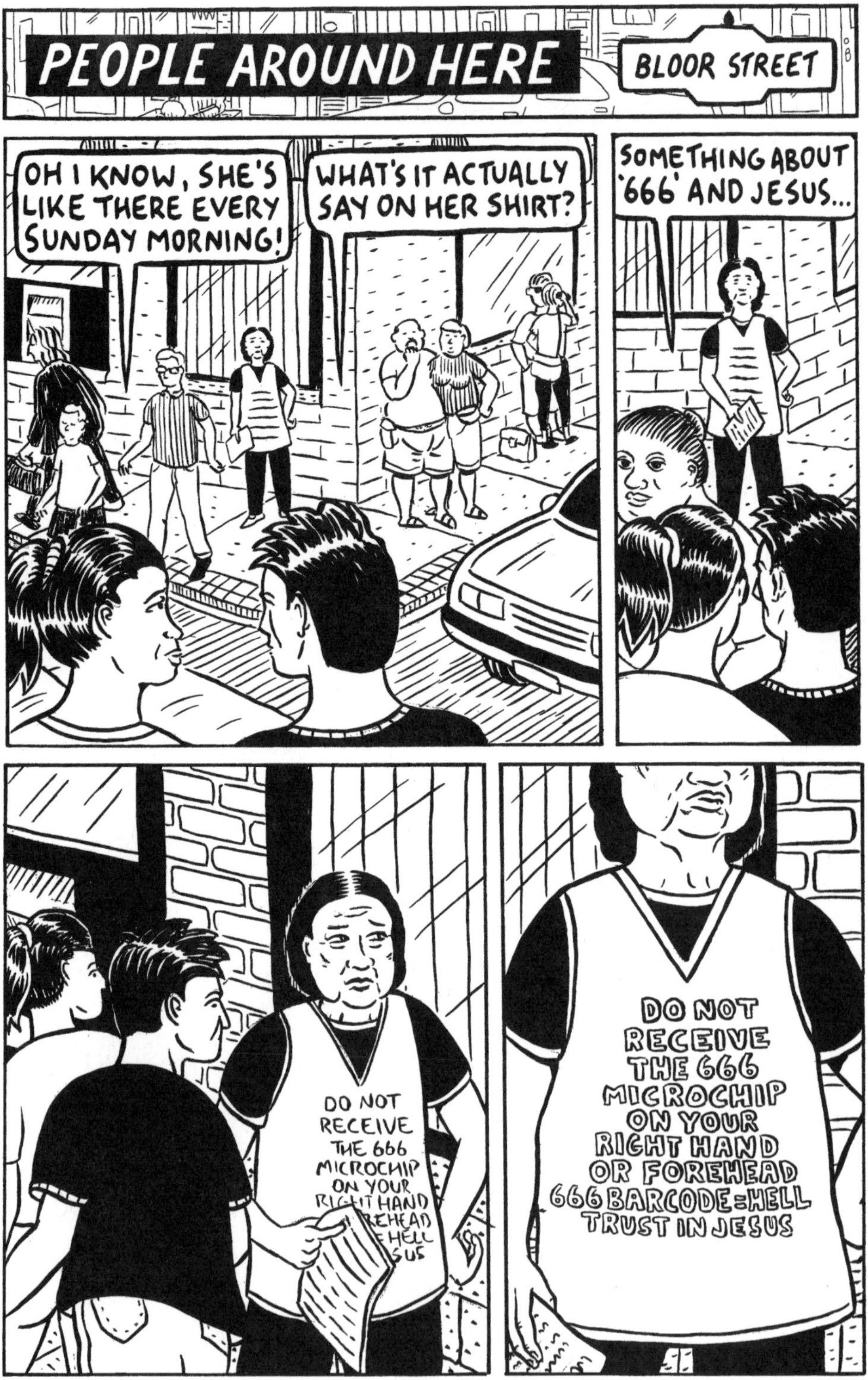
PEOPLE AROUND HERE
BLOOR STREET
OH I KNOW, SHE'S LIKE THERE EVERY SUNDAY MORNING!
WHAT'S IT ACTUALLY SAY ON HER SHIRT?
SOMETHING ABOUT '666' AND JESUS...
DO NOT
RECEIVE
THE 666
MICROCHIP
ON YOUR
DO NOT
RECEIVE
THE 666
MICROCHIP
ON YOUR
RIGHT HAND
OR FOREHEAD
666 BARCODE=HELL
TRUST IN JESUS

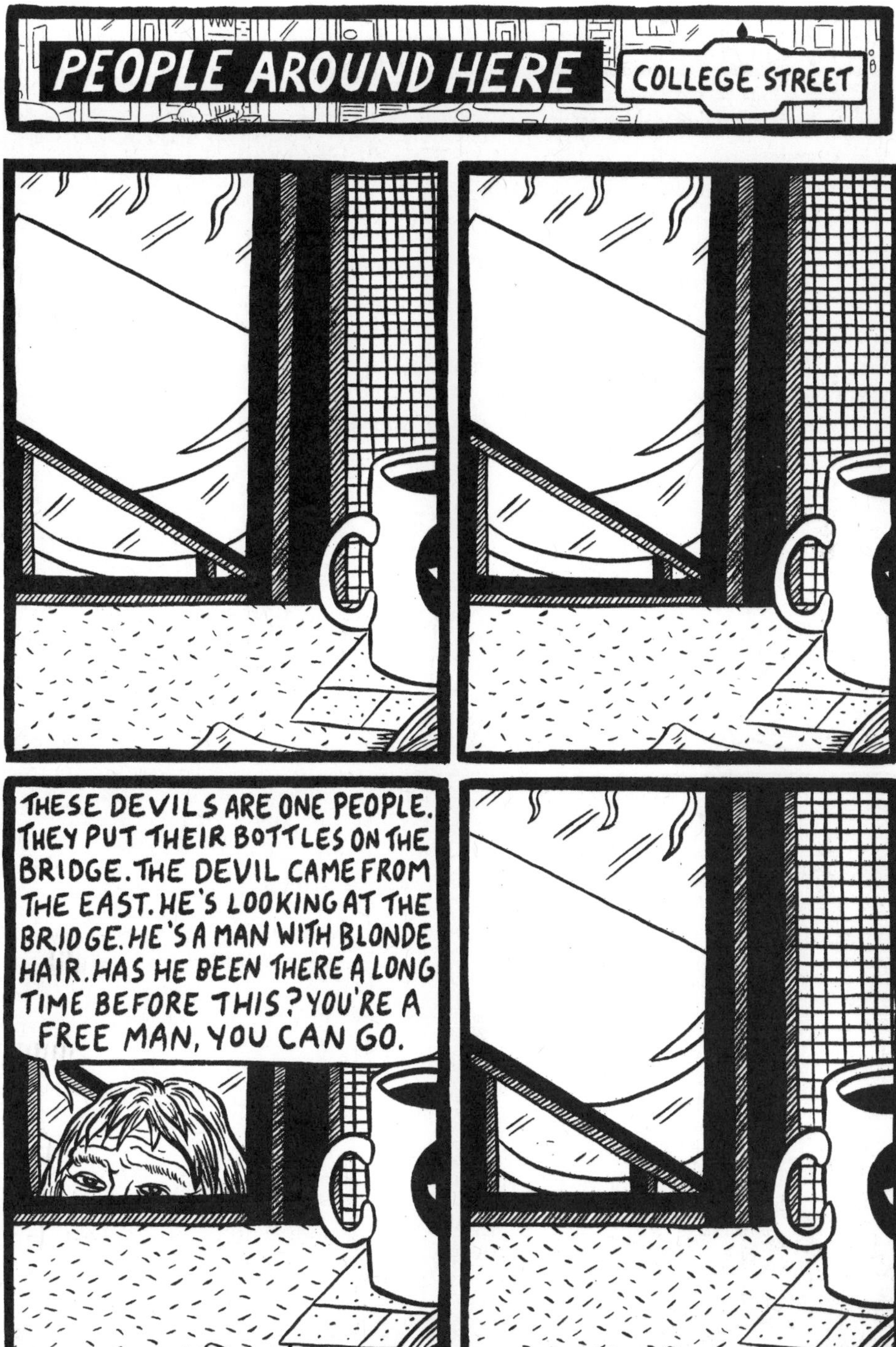
PEOPLE AROUND HERE
COLLEGE STREET
THESE DEVILS ARE ONE PEOPLE. THEY PUT THEIR BOTTLES ON THE BRIDGE. THE DEVIL CAME FROM THE EAST. HE'S LOOKING AT THE BRIDGE. HE'S A MAN WITH BLONDE HAIR. HAS HE BEEN THERE A LONG TIME BEFORE THIS? YOU'RE A FREE MAN, YOU CAN GO.

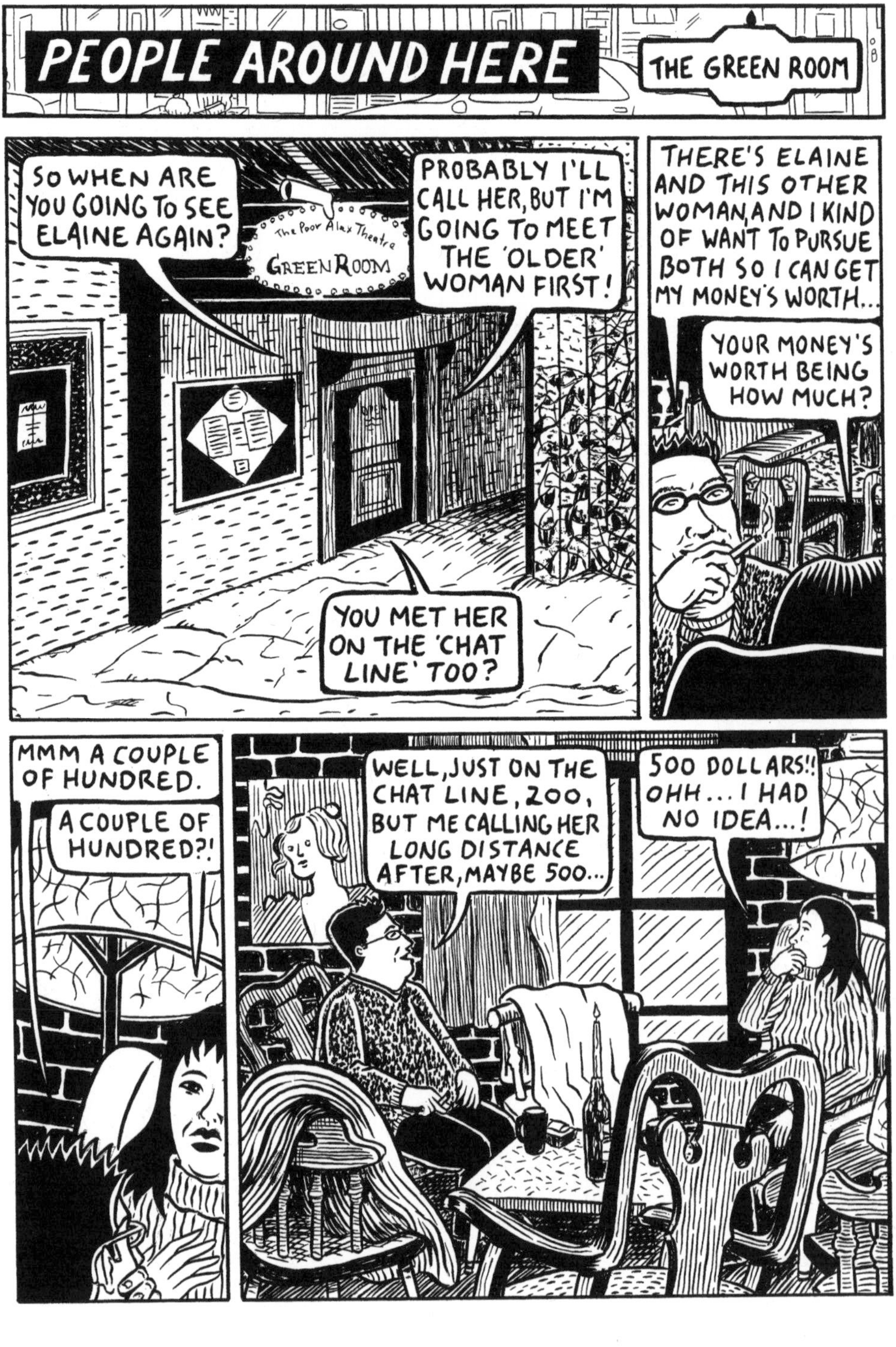
PEOPLE AROUND HERE
THE GREEN ROOM
SO WHEN ARE YOU GOING TO SEE ELAINE AGAIN?
The Poor Alex Theatre
GREEN ROOM
PROBABLY I'LL CALL HER, BUT I'M GOING TO MEET THE 'OLDER' WOMAN FIRST!
YOU MET HER ON THE 'CHAT LINE' TOO?
THERE'S ELAINE AND THIS OTHER WOMAN, AND I KIND OF WANT TO PURSUE BOTH SO I CAN GET MY MONEY'S WORTH...
YOUR MONEY'S WORTH BEING HOW MUCH?
MMM A COUPLE OF HUNDRED.
A COUPLE OF HUNDRED?!
WELL, JUST ON THE CHAT LINE, 200, BUT ME CALLING HER LONG DISTANCE AFTER, MAYBE 500...
500 DOLLARS!! OHH... I HAD NO IDEA...!

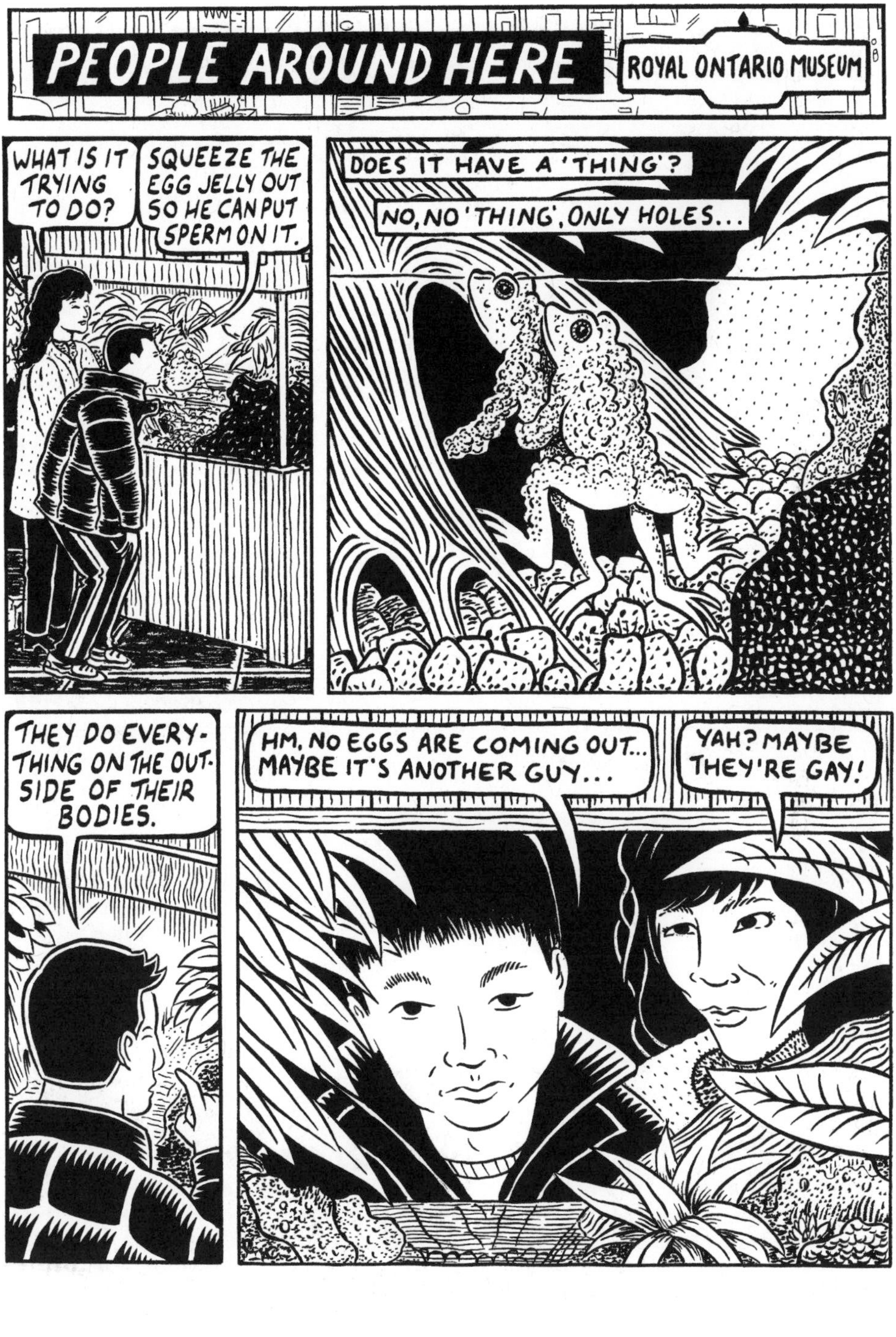
PEOPLE AROUND HERE
ROYAL ONTARIO MUSEUM
WHAT IS IT TRYING TO DO?
SQUEEZE THE EGG JELLY OUT SO HE CAN PUT SPERM ON IT.
DOES IT HAVE A 'THING'?
NO, NO 'THING', ONLY HOLES...
THEY DO EVERY-THING ON THE OUT-SIDE OF THEIR BODIES.
HM, NO EGGS ARE COMING OUT... MAYBE IT'S ANOTHER GUY...
YAH? MAYBE THEY'RE GAY!

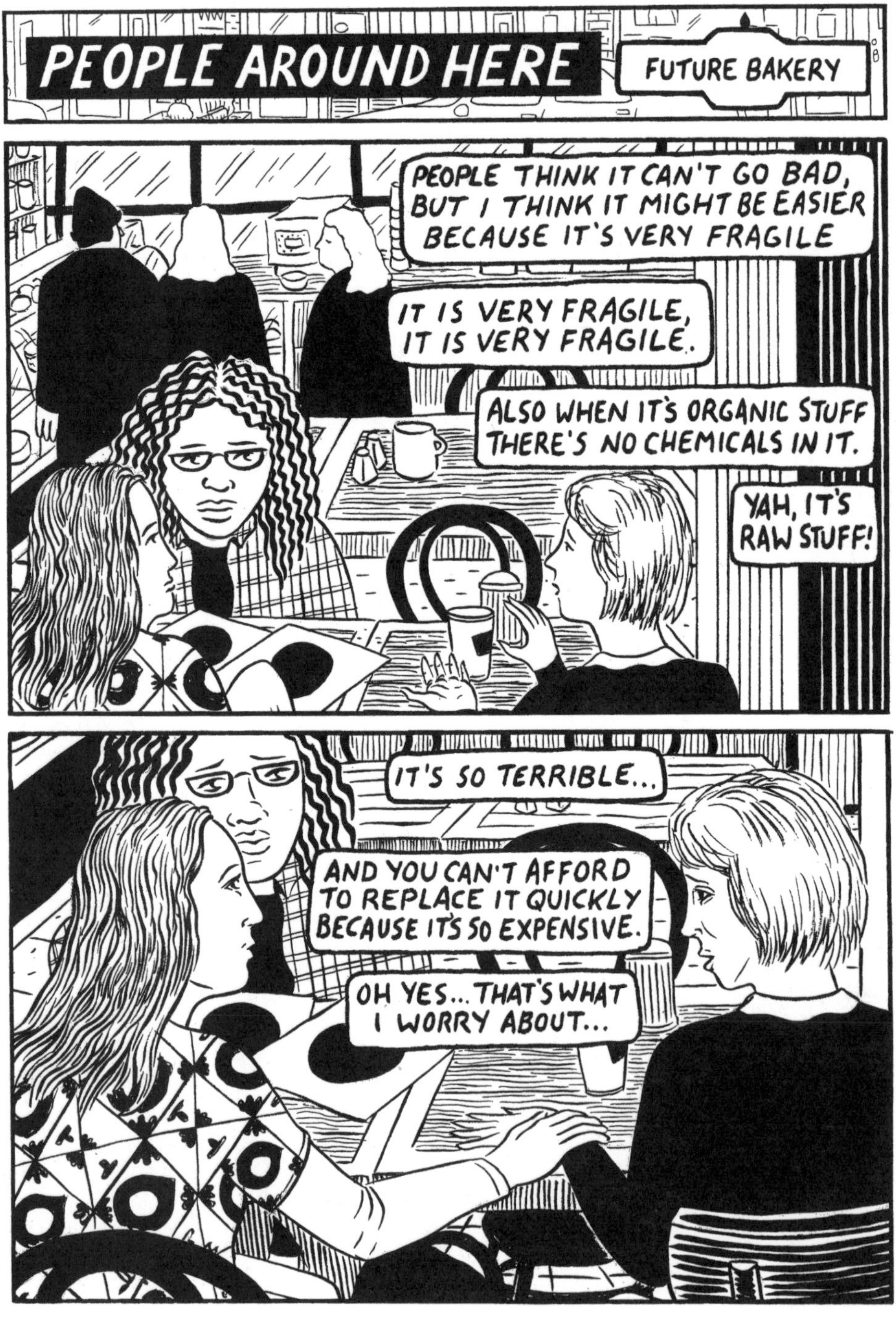
PEOPLE AROUND HERE
FUTURE BAKERY
PEOPLE THINK IT CAN'T GO BAD, BUT I THINK IT MIGHT BE EASIER BECAUSE IT'S VERY FRAGILE
IT IS VERY FRAGILE, IT IS VERY FRAGILE.
ALSO WHEN IT'S ORGANIC STUFF THERE'S NO CHEMICALS IN IT.
YAH, IT'S RAW STUFF!
IT'S SO TERRIBLE...
AND YOU CAN'T AFFORD TO REPLACE IT QUICKLY BECAUSE IT'S SO EXPENSIVE.
OH YES... THAT'S WHAT I WORRY ABOUT...

PEOPLE AROUND HERE
BAY STATION
♫ IT'S TRUE LOVE, YES TRUE LOVE, IT'S TRUE LOVE, YES IT IS! ♫ ♪ TRUE LOVE ♪
♫ TRUE LOVE, TRUE LOVE, YES IT IS! ♪ TRUE LOVE, IT'S TRUE LOVE ♫ OH YES, OH YES, YOU KNOW IT IS!... COME ON! COME ON... YOU KNOW IT IS! HA HA
YOU CAN'T ROB, YOU CAN'T ROB, YOU CAN'T ROB THE WORLD OF GOD.
HA HA HA! FOO-LISH AND FRIGH-TENED, FOO-LISH AND FRIGH-TENED. SO FOOLISH AND FRIGHTENED! FOOLISH AND FRIGHTENED.*

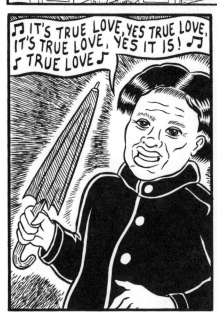

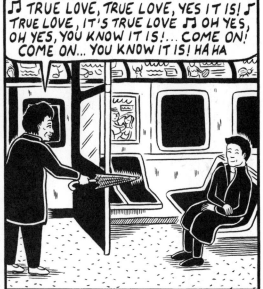

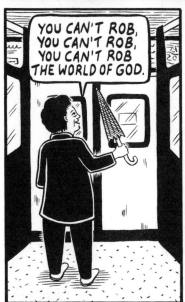

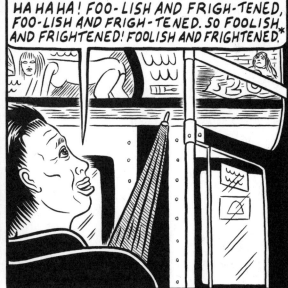

* LOOKING AT GIRL WRAPPED IN A GIANT 20 DOLLAR BILL

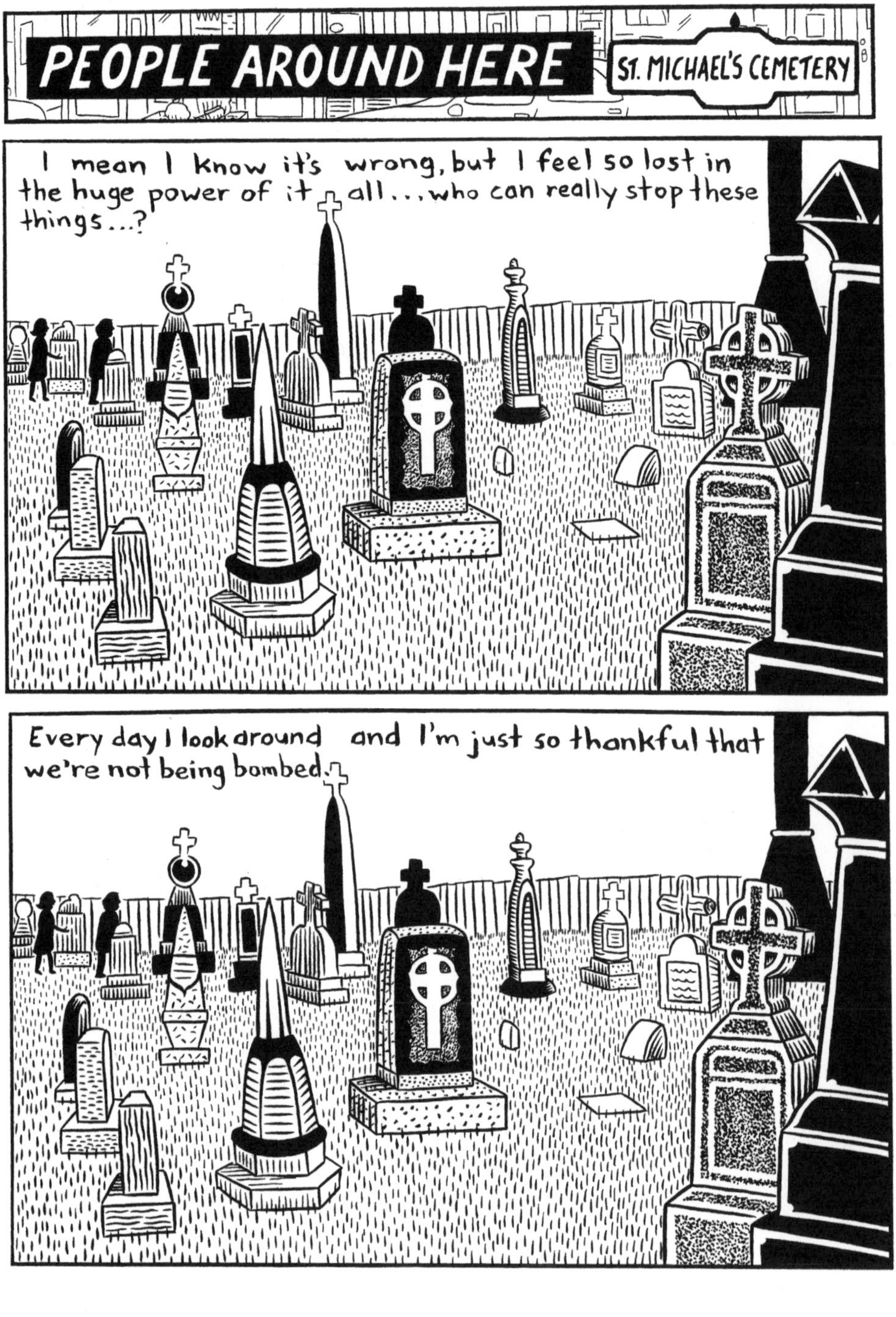
PEOPLE AROUND HERE
ST. MICHAEL'S CEMETERY
I mean I know it's wrong, but I feel so lost in the huge power of it all...who can really stop these things...?
Every day I look around and I'm just so thankful that we're not being bombed.

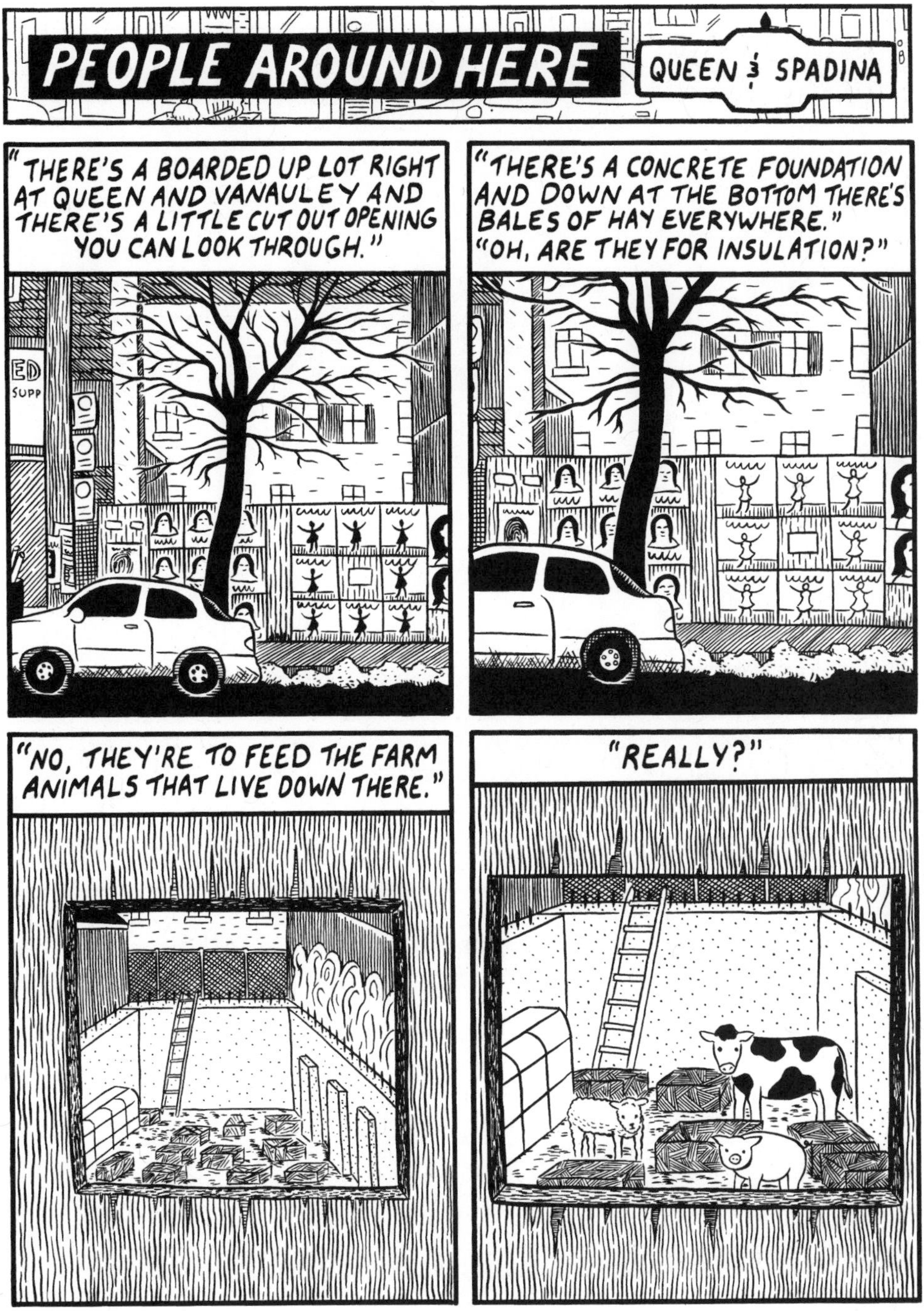
PEOPLE AROUND HERE
QUEEN & SPADINA
"THERE'S A BOARDED UP LOT RIGHT AT QUEEN AND VANAULEY AND THERE'S A LITTLE CUT OUT OPENING YOU CAN LOOK THROUGH."
ED
SUPP
"THERE'S A CONCRETE FOUNDATION AND DOWN AT THE BOTTOM THERE'S BALES OF HAY EVERYWHERE."
"OH, ARE THEY FOR INSULATION?"
"NO, THEY'RE TO FEED THE FARM ANIMALS THAT LIVE DOWN THERE."
"REALLY?"

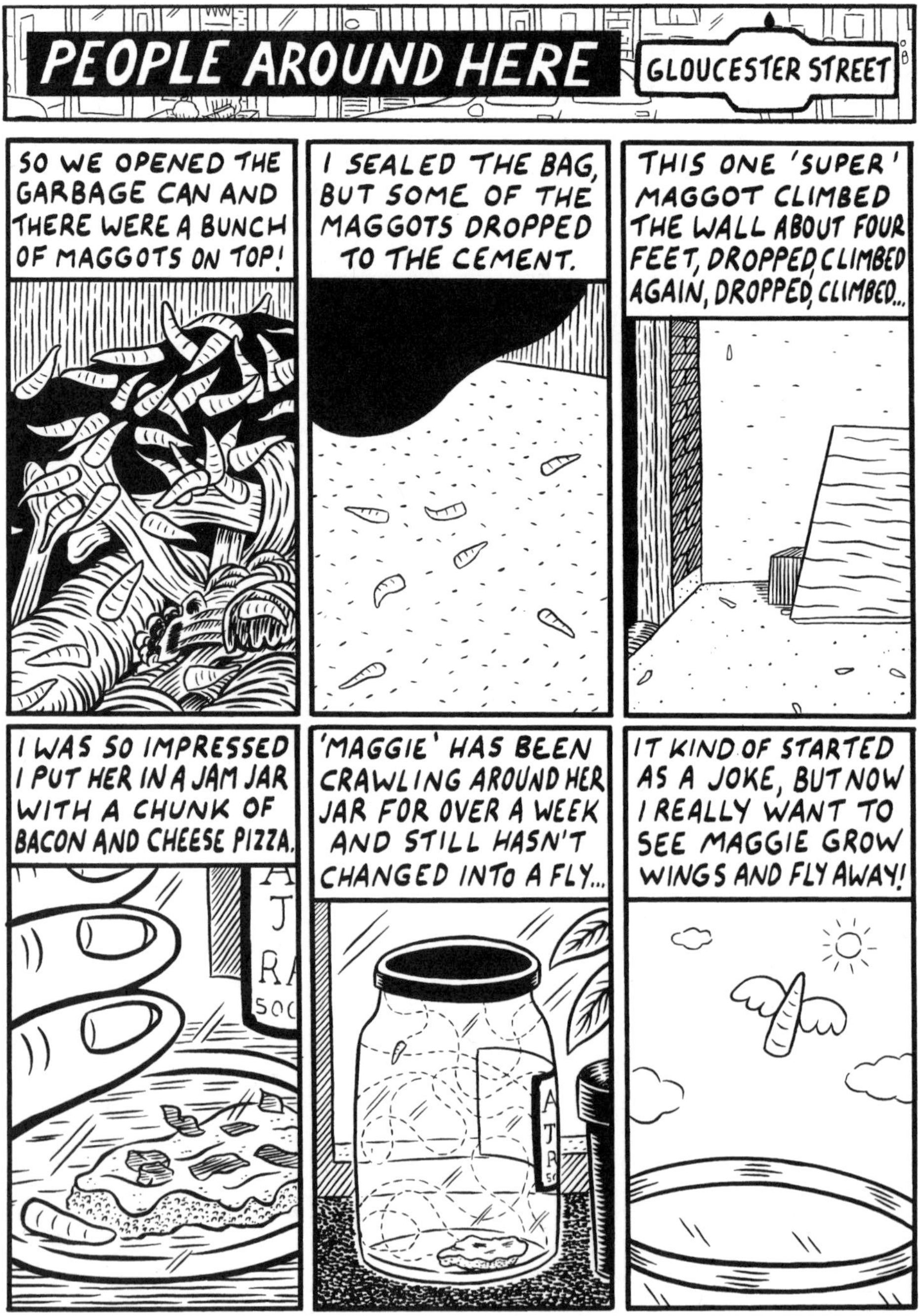
PEOPLE AROUND HERE
GLOUCESTER STREET
SO WE OPENED THE GARBAGE CAN AND THERE WERE A BUNCH OF MAGGOTS ON TOP!
I SEALED THE BAG, BUT SOME OF THE MAGGOTS DROPPED TO THE CEMENT.
THIS ONE 'SUPER' MAGGOT CLIMBED THE WALL ABOUT FOUR FEET, DROPPED, CLIMBED AGAIN, DROPPED, CLIMBED...
I WAS SO IMPRESSED I PUT HER IN A JAM JAR WITH A CHUNK OF BACON AND CHEESE PIZZA.
'MAGGIE' HAS BEEN CRAWLING AROUND HER JAR FOR OVER A WEEK AND STILL HASN'T CHANGED INTO A FLY...
IT KIND OF STARTED AS A JOKE, BUT NOW I REALLY WANT TO SEE MAGGIE GROW WINGS AND FLY AWAY!

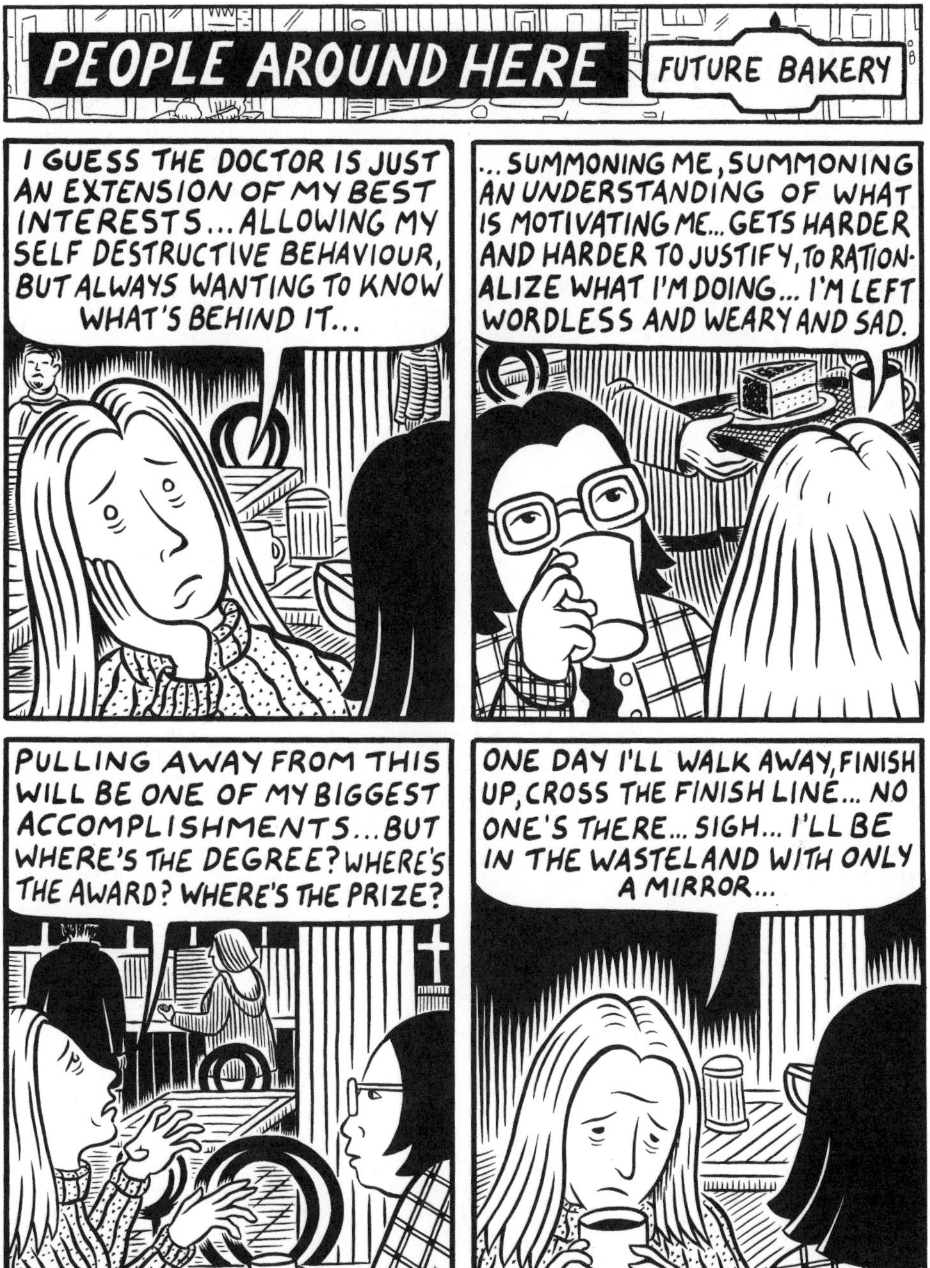
PEOPLE AROUND HERE
FUTURE BAKERY
I GUESS THE DOCTOR IS JUST AN EXTENSION OF MY BEST INTERESTS... ALLOWING MY SELF DESTRUCTIVE BEHAVIOUR, BUT ALWAYS WANTING TO KNOW WHAT'S BEHIND IT...
...SUMMONING ME, SUMMONING AN UNDERSTANDING OF WHAT IS MOTIVATING ME... GETS HARDER AND HARDER TO JUSTIFY, TO RATIONALIZE WHAT I'M DOING... I'M LEFT WORDLESS AND WEARY AND SAD.
PULLING AWAY FROM THIS WILL BE ONE OF MY BIGGEST ACCOMPLISHMENTS... BUT WHERE'S THE DEGREE? WHERE'S THE AWARD? WHERE'S THE PRIZE?
ONE DAY I'LL WALK AWAY, FINISH UP, CROSS THE FINISH LINE... NO ONE'S THERE... SIGH... I'LL BE IN THE WASTELAND WITH ONLY A MIRROR...

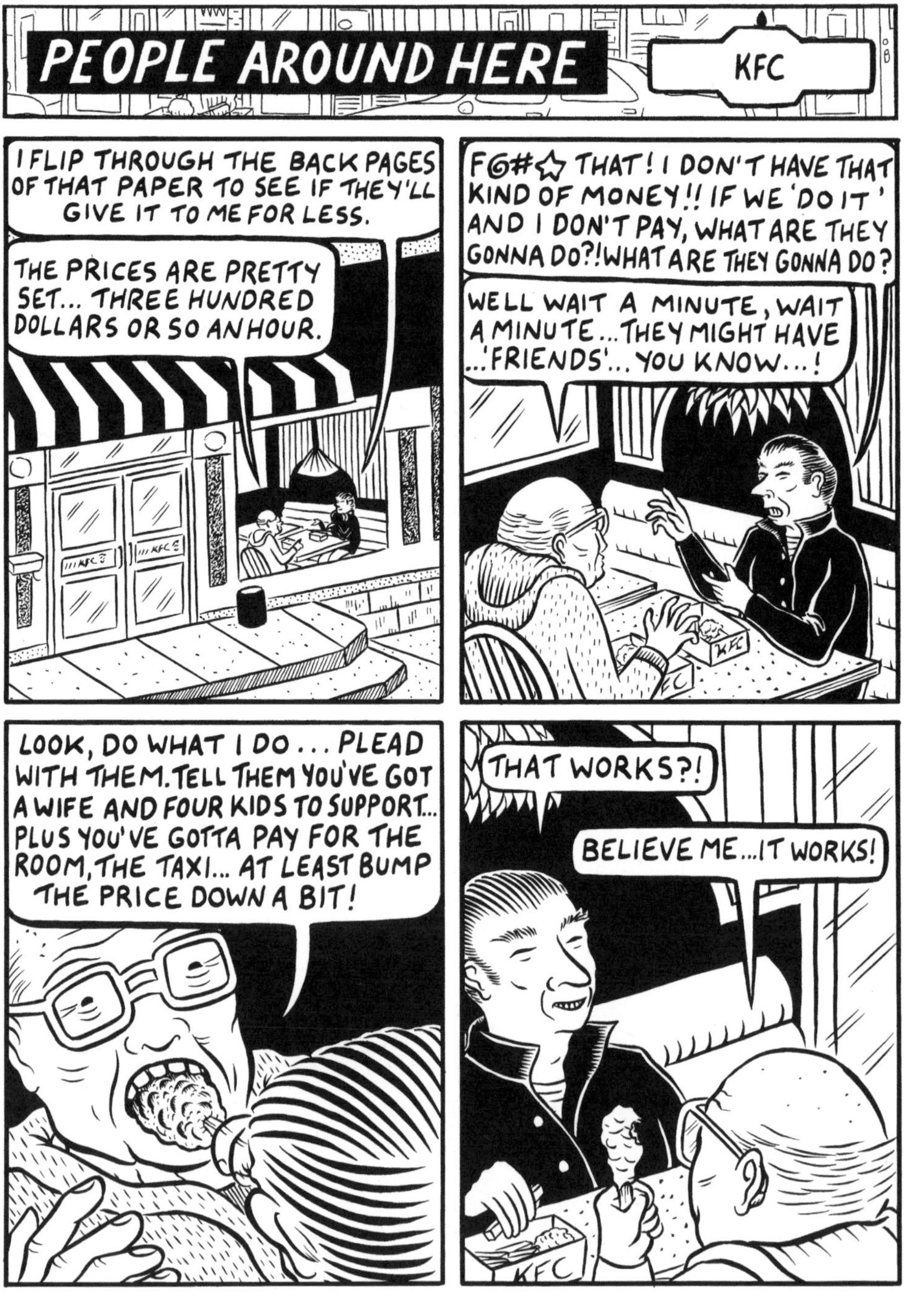
PEOPLE AROUND HERE
KFC
I FLIP THROUGH THE BACK PAGES OF THAT PAPER TO SEE IF THEY'LL GIVE IT TO ME FOR LESS.
THE PRICES ARE PRETTY SET... THREE HUNDRED DOLLARS OR SO AN HOUR.
KFC
KFC
F@#☆ THAT! I DON'T HAVE THAT KIND OF MONEY!! IF WE 'DO IT' AND I DON'T PAY, WHAT ARE THEY GONNA DO?! WHAT ARE THEY GONNA DO?
WELL WAIT A MINUTE, WAIT A MINUTE... THEY MIGHT HAVE ...'FRIENDS'... YOU KNOW...!
KFC
KFC
LOOK, DO WHAT I DO... PLEAD WITH THEM. TELL THEM YOU'VE GOT A WIFE AND FOUR KIDS TO SUPPORT... PLUS YOU'VE GOTTA PAY FOR THE ROOM, THE TAXI... AT LEAST BUMP THE PRICE DOWN A BIT!
THAT WORKS?!
BELIEVE ME...IT WORKS!
KFC

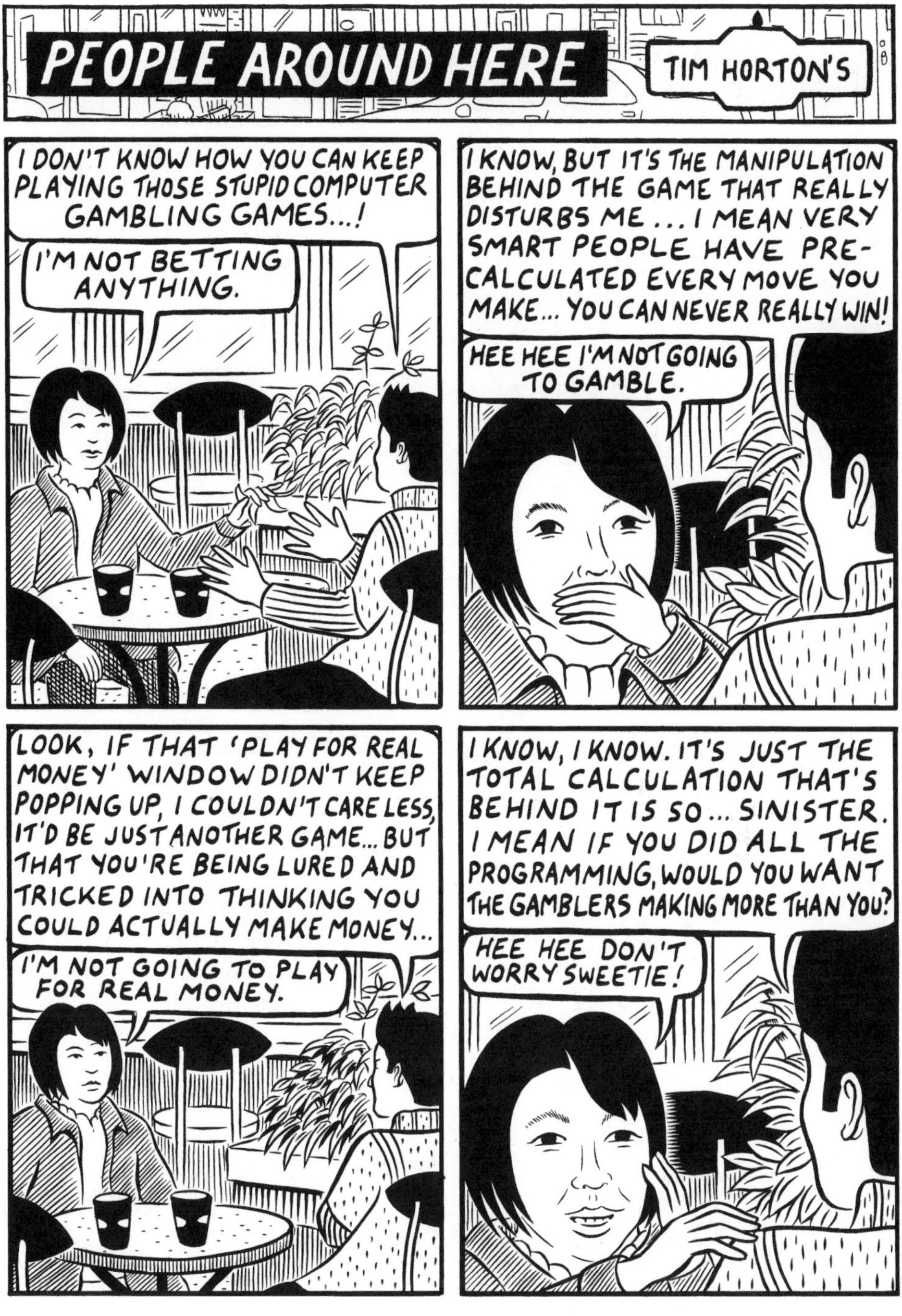

PEOPLE AROUND HERE
TIM HORTON'S
I DON'T KNOW HOW YOU CAN KEEP PLAYING THOSE STUPID COMPUTER GAMBLING GAMES...!
I'M NOT BETTING ANYTHING.
I KNOW, BUT IT'S THE MANIPULATION BEHIND THE GAME THAT REALLY DISTURBS ME ... I MEAN VERY SMART PEOPLE HAVE PRE-CALCULATED EVERY MOVE YOU MAKE... YOU CAN NEVER REALLY WIN!
HEE HEE I'M NOT GOING TO GAMBLE.
LOOK, IF THAT 'PLAY FOR REAL MONEY' WINDOW DIDN'T KEEP POPPING UP, I COULDN'T CARE LESS, IT'D BE JUST ANOTHER GAME... BUT THAT YOU'RE BEING LURED AND TRICKED INTO THINKING YOU COULD ACTUALLY MAKE MONEY...
I'M NOT GOING TO PLAY FOR REAL MONEY.
I KNOW, I KNOW. IT'S JUST THE TOTAL CALCULATION THAT'S BEHIND IT IS SO... SINISTER. I MEAN IF YOU DID ALL THE PROGRAMMING, WOULD YOU WANT THE GAMBLERS MAKING MORE THAN YOU?
HEE HEE DON'T WORRY SWEETIE!

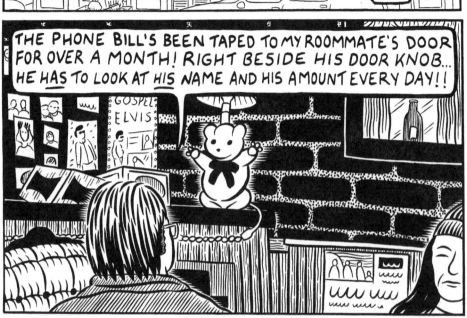

PEOPLE AROUND HERE
THE TAP
THE PHONE BILL'S BEEN TAPED TO MY ROOMMATE'S DOOR FOR OVER A MONTH! RIGHT BESIDE HIS DOOR KNOB... HE HAS TO LOOK AT HIS NAME AND HIS AMOUNT EVERY DAY!!
GOSPEL
ELVIS
SO WHEN HE FINALLY SLIDES THE MONEY UNDER MY DOOR... HE'S ONE DOLLAR SHORT!! A WHOLE MONTH LOOKING AT HIS NAME AND THE AMOUNT IN BIG BLACK LETTERS AND HE CAN'T GET IT RIGHT! UNBELIEVABLE!
ELVIS

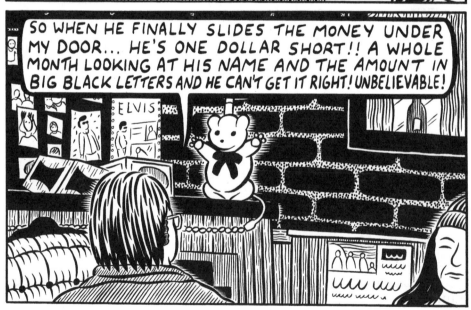

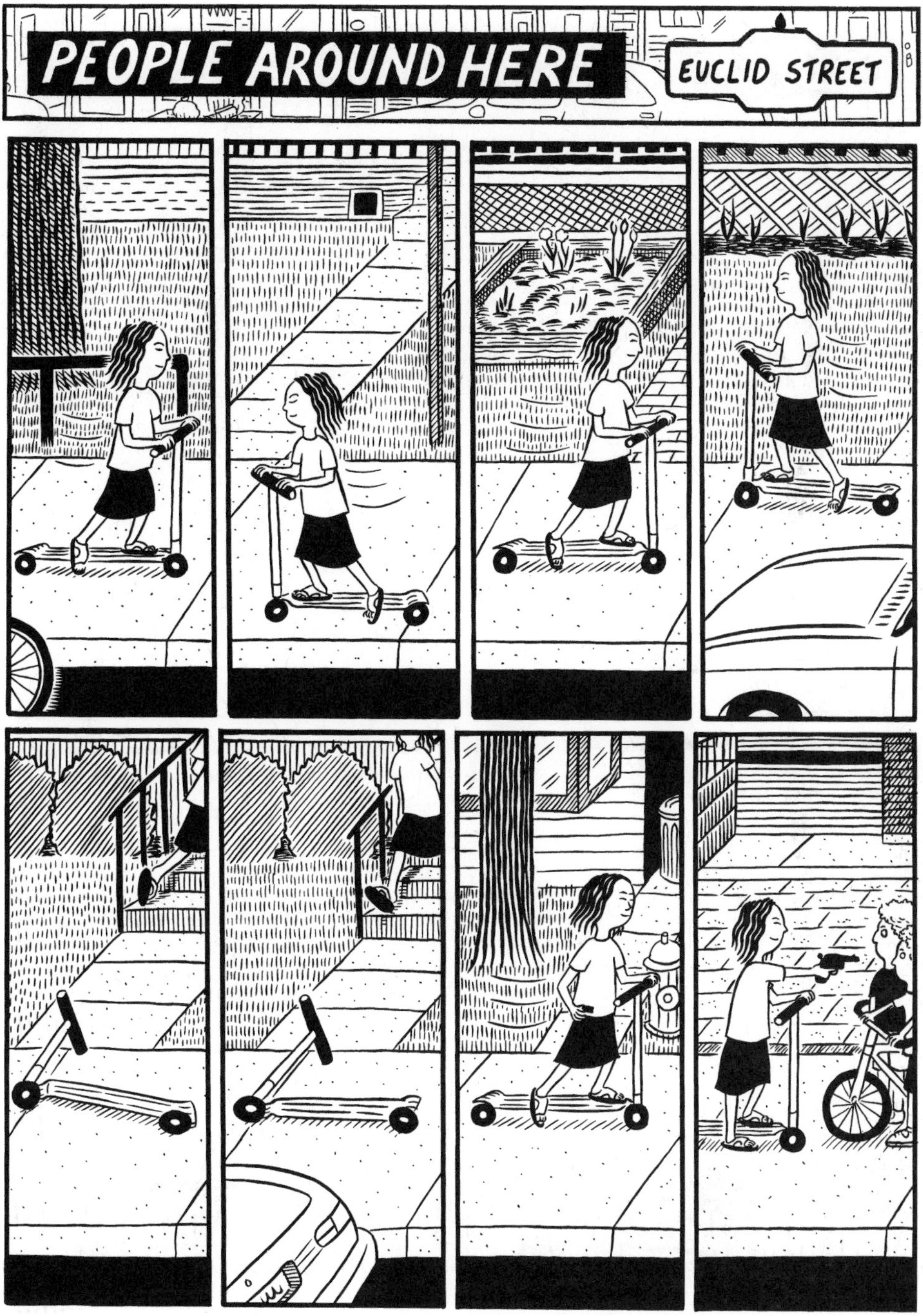
PEOPLE AROUND HERE
EUCLID STREET

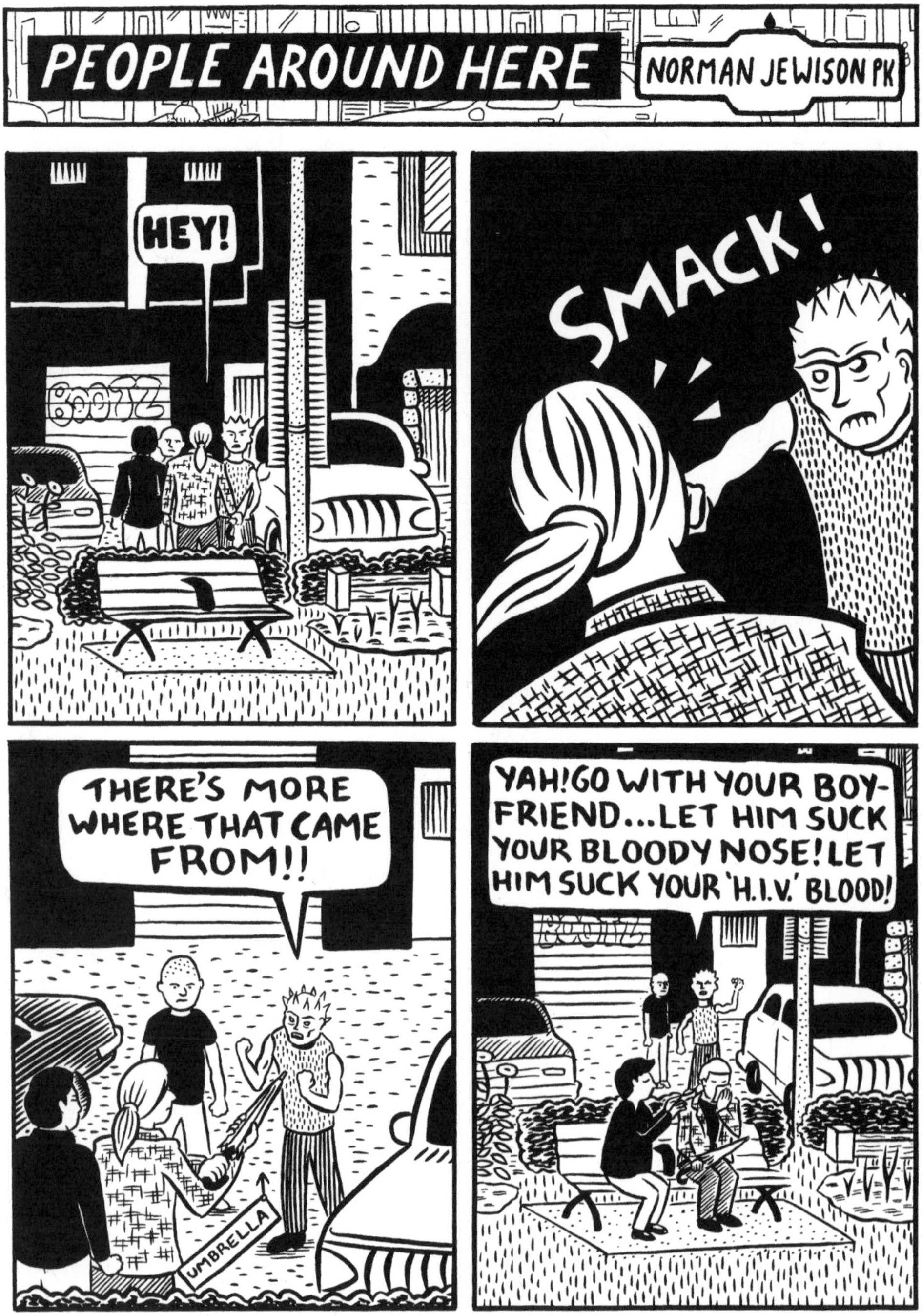
PEOPLE AROUND HERE
NORMAN JEWISON PK
HEY!
SMACK!
THERE'S MORE WHERE THAT CAME FROM!!
UMBRELLA
YAH! GO WITH YOUR BOY-FRIEND...LET HIM SUCK YOUR BLOODY NOSE! LET HIM SUCK YOUR 'H.I.V.' BLOOD!

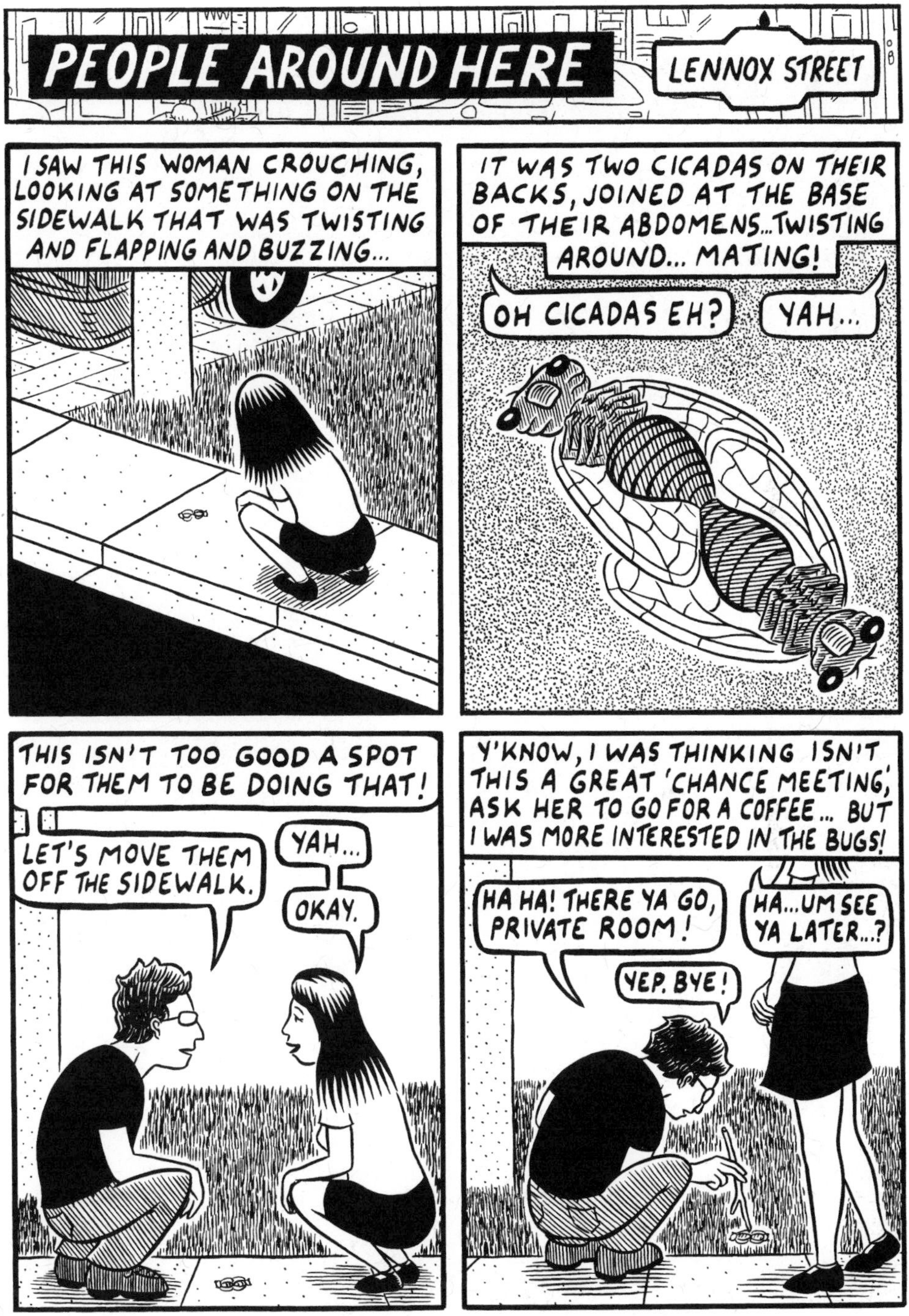
PEOPLE AROUND HERE
LENNOX STREET
I SAW THIS WOMAN CROUCHING, LOOKING AT SOMETHING ON THE SIDEWALK THAT WAS TWISTING AND FLAPPING AND BUZZING...
IT WAS TWO CICADAS ON THEIR BACKS, JOINED AT THE BASE OF THEIR ABDOMENS...TWISTING AROUND... MATING!
OH CICADAS EH?
YAH...
THIS ISN'T TOO GOOD A SPOT FOR THEM TO BE DOING THAT!
LET'S MOVE THEM OFF THE SIDEWALK.
YAH...
OKAY.
Y'KNOW, I WAS THINKING ISN'T THIS A GREAT 'CHANCE MEETING', ASK HER TO GO FOR A COFFEE... BUT I WAS MORE INTERESTED IN THE BUGS!
HA HA! THERE YA GO, PRIVATE ROOM!
HA...UM SEE YA LATER...?
YEP. BYE!

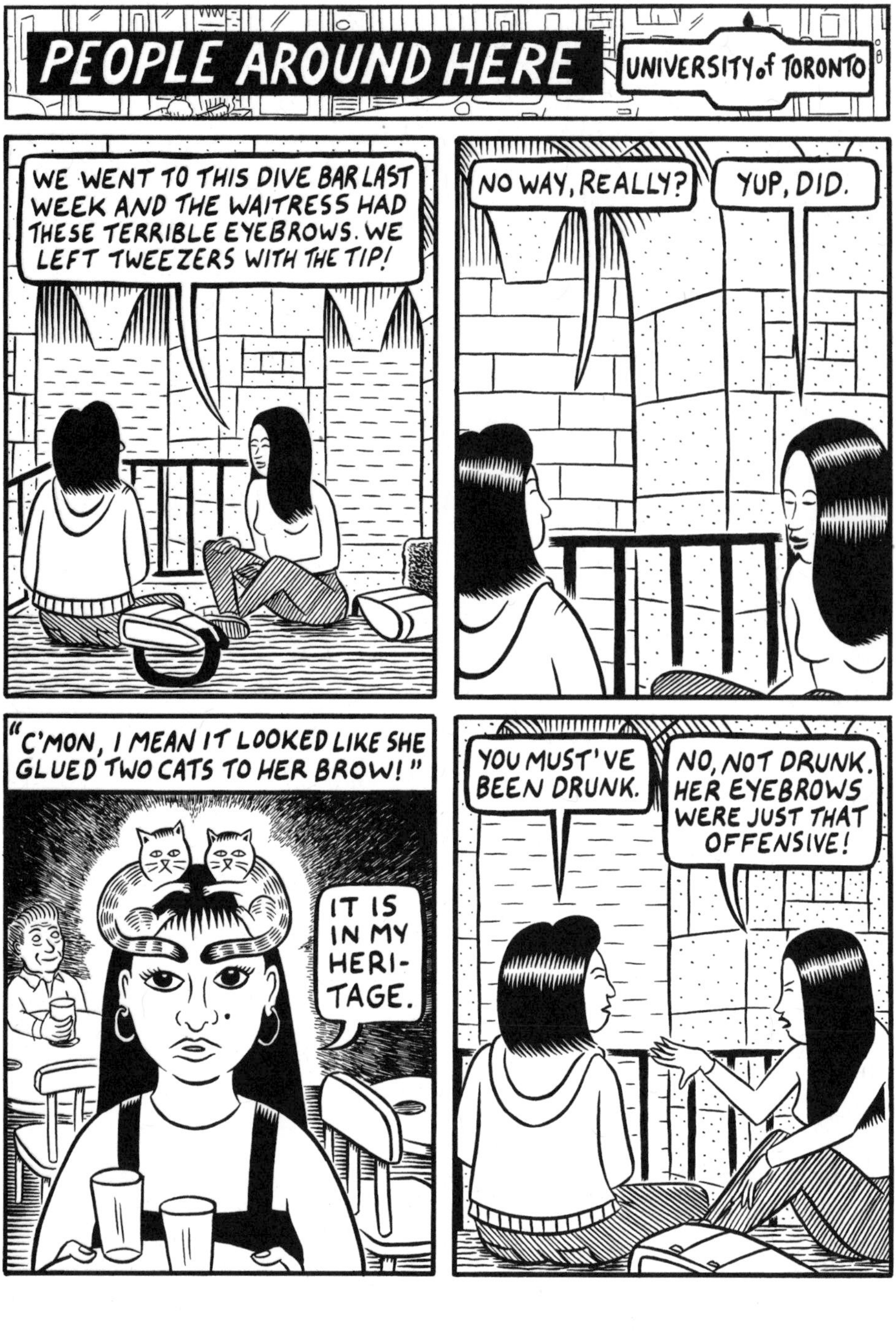
PEOPLE AROUND HERE
UNIVERSITY of TORONTO
WE WENT TO THIS DIVE BAR LAST WEEK AND THE WAITRESS HAD THESE TERRIBLE EYEBROWS. WE LEFT TWEEZERS WITH THE TIP!
NO WAY, REALLY?
YUP, DID.
"C'MON, I MEAN IT LOOKED LIKE SHE GLUED TWO CATS TO HER BROW!"
IT IS IN MY HERI-TAGE.
YOU MUST'VE BEEN DRUNK.
NO, NOT DRUNK. HER EYEBROWS WERE JUST THAT OFFENSIVE!

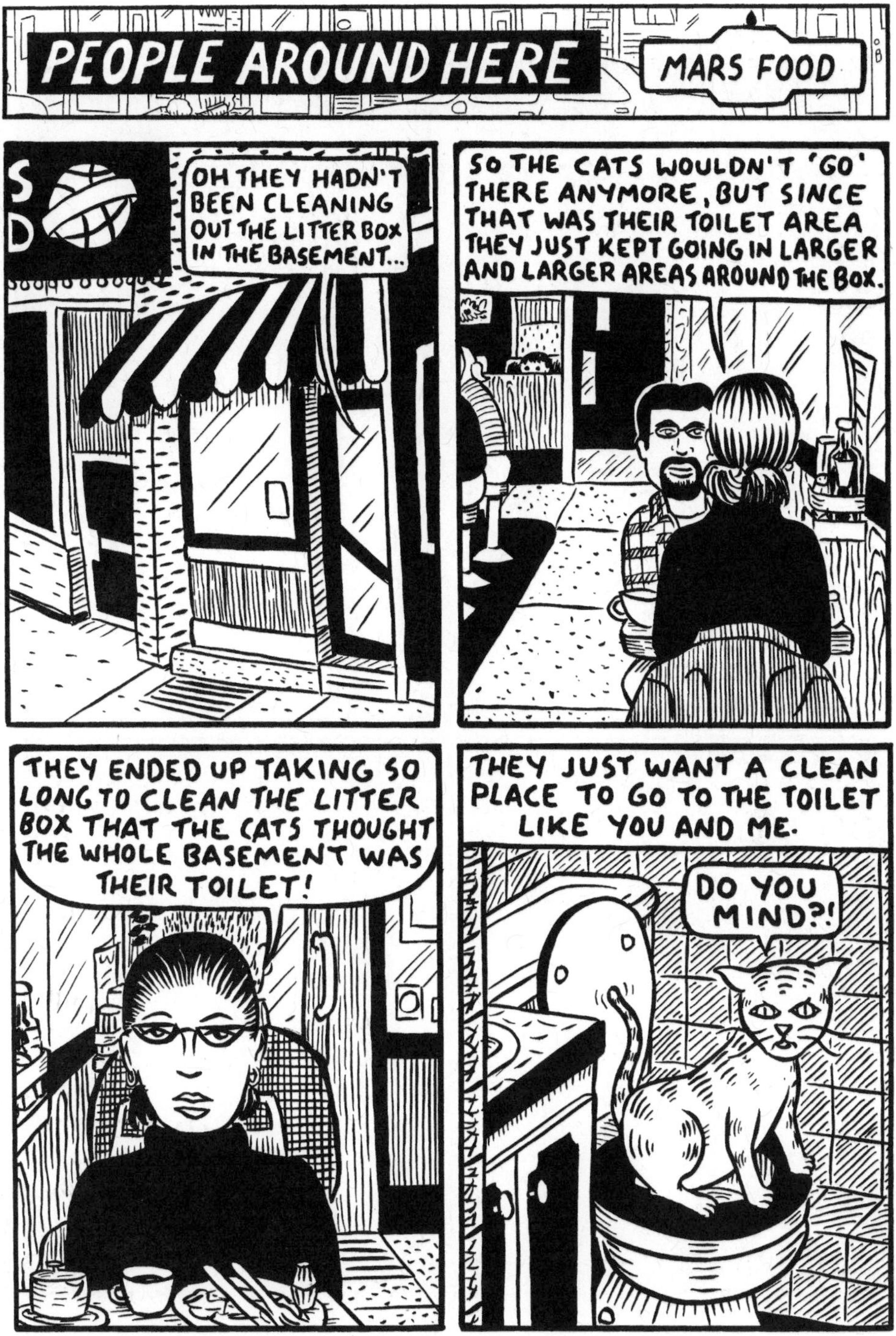
PEOPLE AROUND HERE
MARS FOOD
OH THEY HADN'T BEEN CLEANING OUT THE LITTER BOX IN THE BASEMENT...
SO THE CATS WOULDN'T 'GO' THERE ANYMORE, BUT SINCE THAT WAS THEIR TOILET AREA THEY JUST KEPT GOING IN LARGER AND LARGER AREAS AROUND THE BOX.
THEY ENDED UP TAKING SO LONG TO CLEAN THE LITTER BOX THAT THE CATS THOUGHT THE WHOLE BASEMENT WAS THEIR TOILET!
THEY JUST WANT A CLEAN PLACE TO GO TO THE TOILET LIKE YOU AND ME.
DO YOU MIND?!

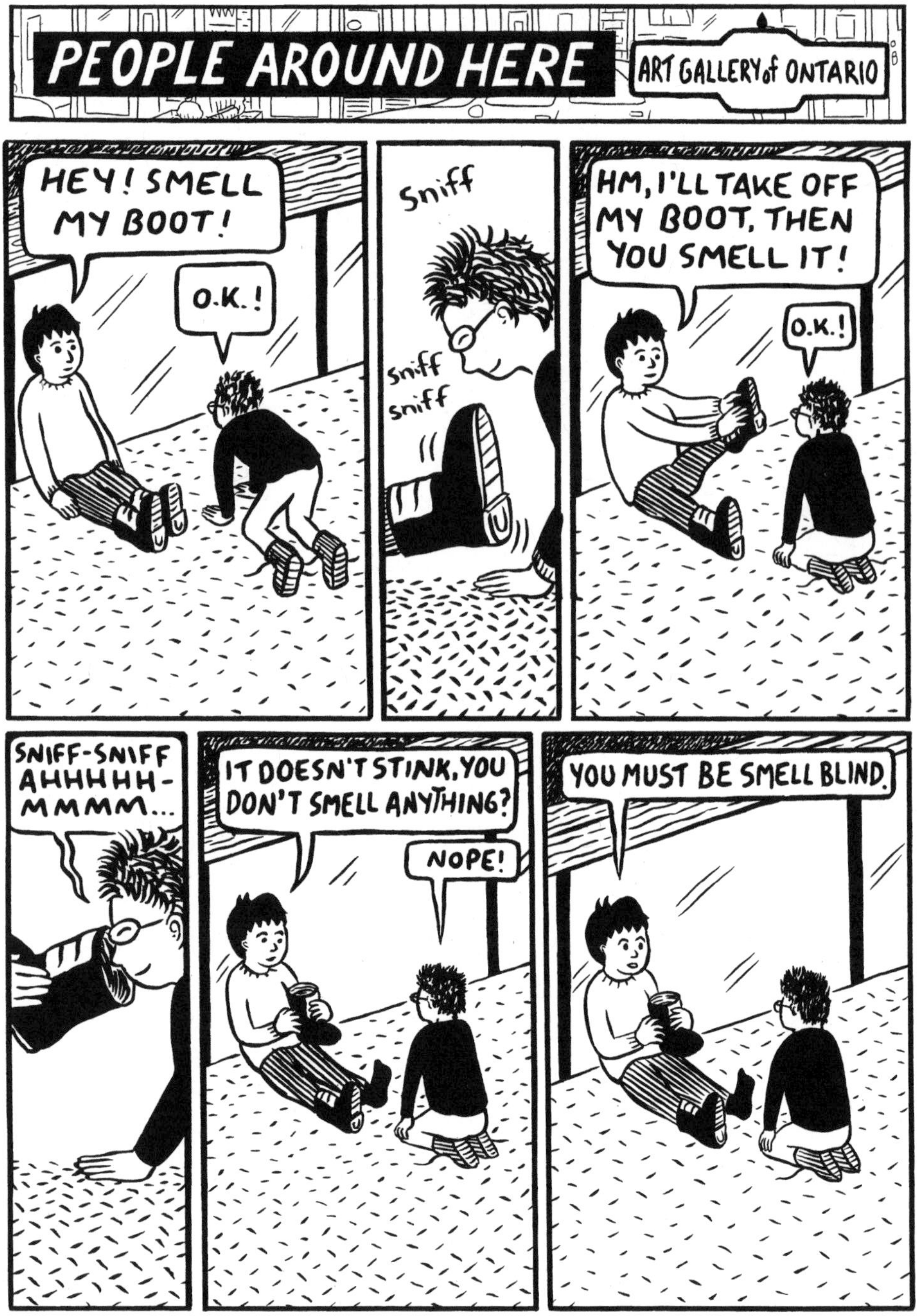
PEOPLE AROUND HERE
ART GALLERY of ONTARIO
HEY! SMELL MY BOOT!
O.K.!
Sniff
sniff
sniff
HM, I'LL TAKE OFF MY BOOT, THEN YOU SMELL IT!
O.K.!
SNIFF-SNIFF AHHHHH-MMMM...
IT DOESN'T STINK, YOU DON'T SMELL ANYTHING?
NOPE!
YOU MUST BE SMELL BLIND.

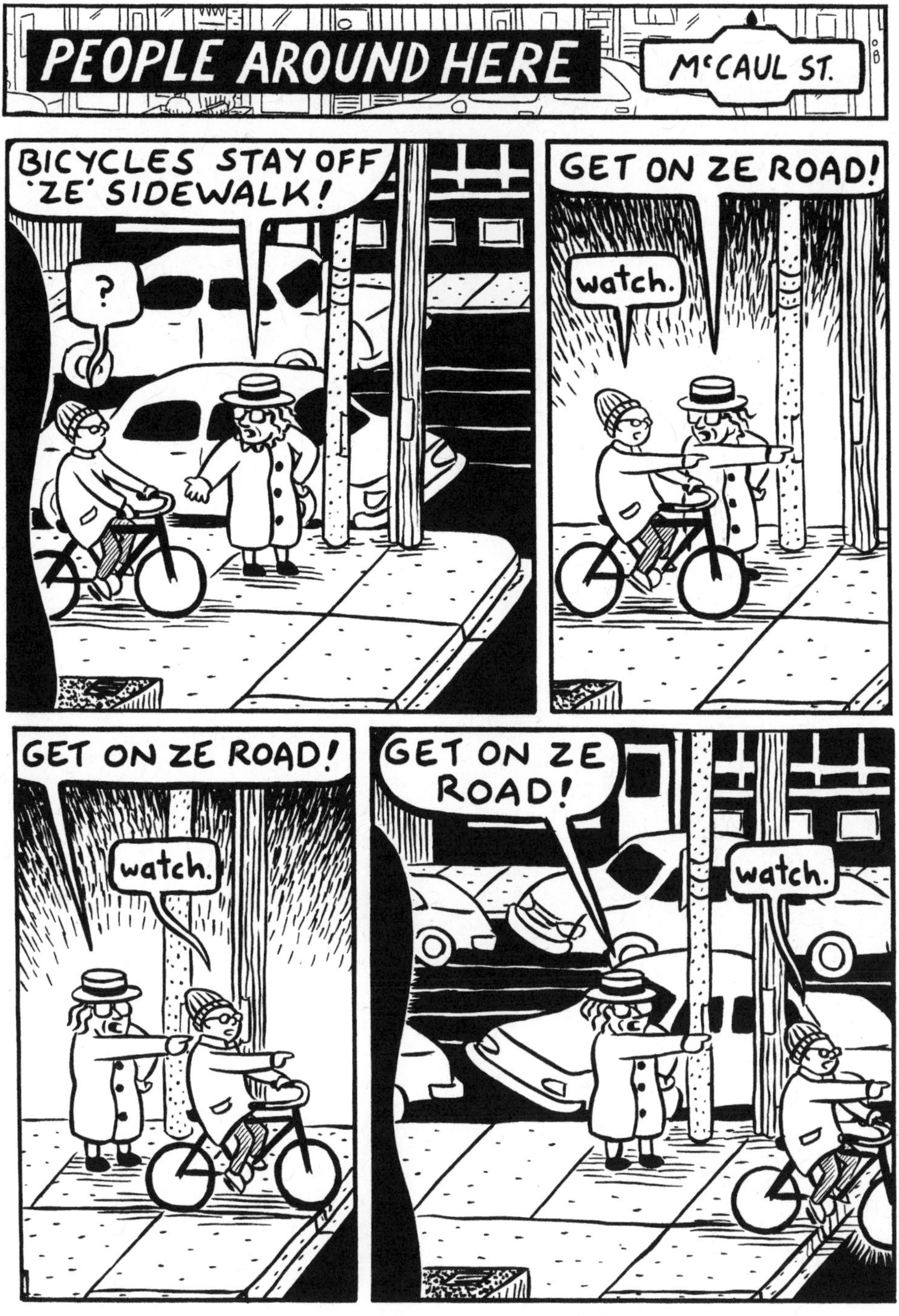
PEOPLE AROUND HERE
M^c CAUL ST.
BICYCLES STAY OFF 'ZE' SIDEWALK!
?
GET ON ZE ROAD!
watch.
GET ON ZE ROAD!
watch.
GET ON ZE ROAD!
watch.

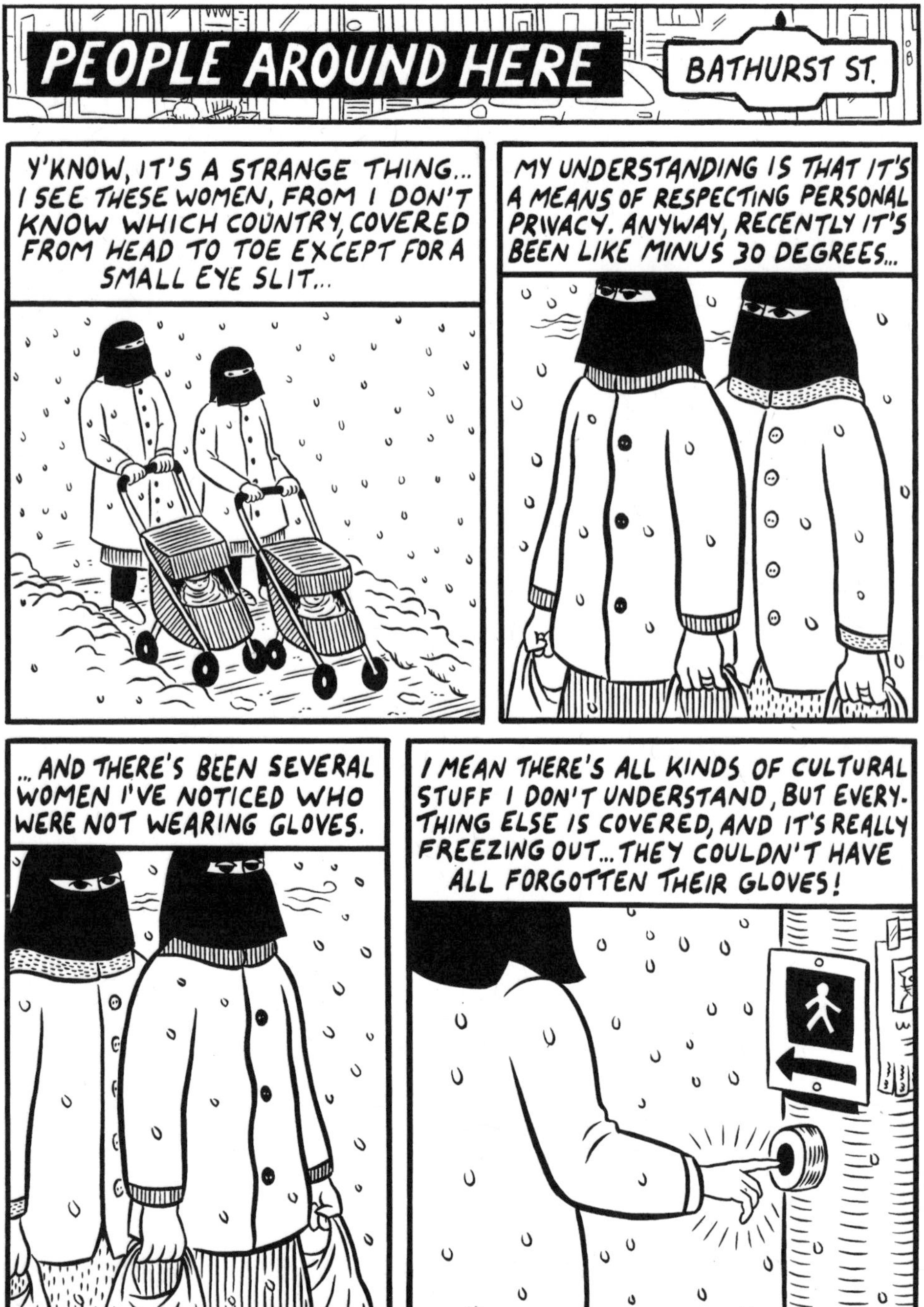
PEOPLE AROUND HERE
BATHURST ST.
Y'KNOW, IT'S A STRANGE THING... I SEE THESE WOMEN, FROM I DON'T KNOW WHICH COUNTRY, COVERED FROM HEAD TO TOE EXCEPT FOR A SMALL EYE SLIT...
MY UNDERSTANDING IS THAT IT'S A MEANS OF RESPECTING PERSONAL PRIVACY. ANYWAY, RECENTLY IT'S BEEN LIKE MINUS 30 DEGREES...
...AND THERE'S BEEN SEVERAL WOMEN I'VE NOTICED WHO WERE NOT WEARING GLOVES.
I MEAN THERE'S ALL KINDS OF CULTURAL STUFF I DON'T UNDERSTAND, BUT EVERYTHING ELSE IS COVERED, AND IT'S REALLY FREEZING OUT... THEY COULDN'T HAVE ALL FORGOTTEN THEIR GLOVES!

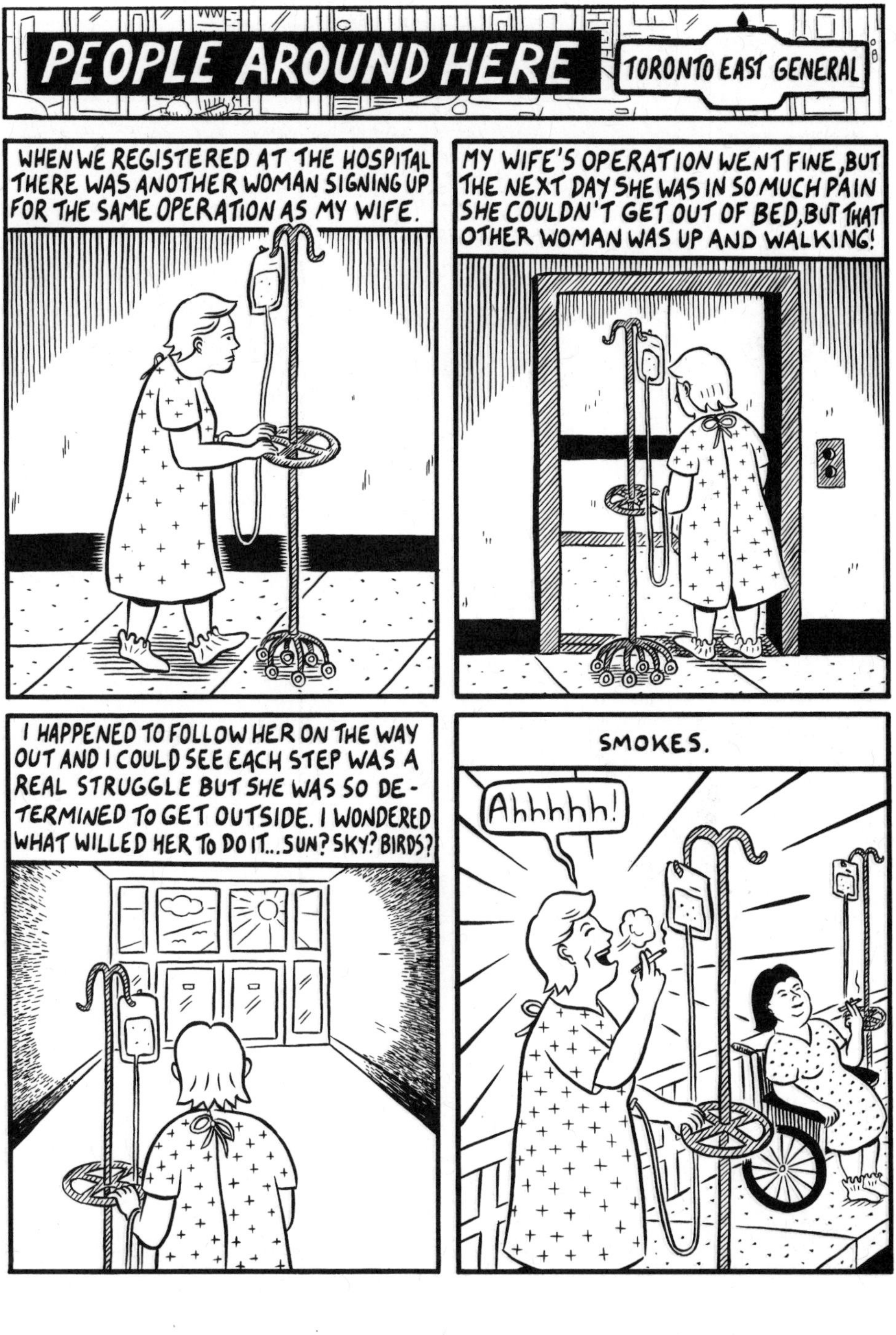
PEOPLE AROUND HERE
TORONTO EAST GENERAL
WHEN WE REGISTERED AT THE HOSPITAL THERE WAS ANOTHER WOMAN SIGNING UP FOR THE SAME OPERATION AS MY WIFE.
MY WIFE'S OPERATION WENT FINE, BUT THE NEXT DAY SHE WAS IN SO MUCH PAIN SHE COULDN'T GET OUT OF BED, BUT THAT OTHER WOMAN WAS UP AND WALKING!
I HAPPENED TO FOLLOW HER ON THE WAY OUT AND I COULD SEE EACH STEP WAS A REAL STRUGGLE BUT SHE WAS SO DE-TERMINED TO GET OUTSIDE. I WONDERED WHAT WILLED HER TO DO IT... SUN? SKY? BIRDS?
SMOKES.
Ahhhhh!

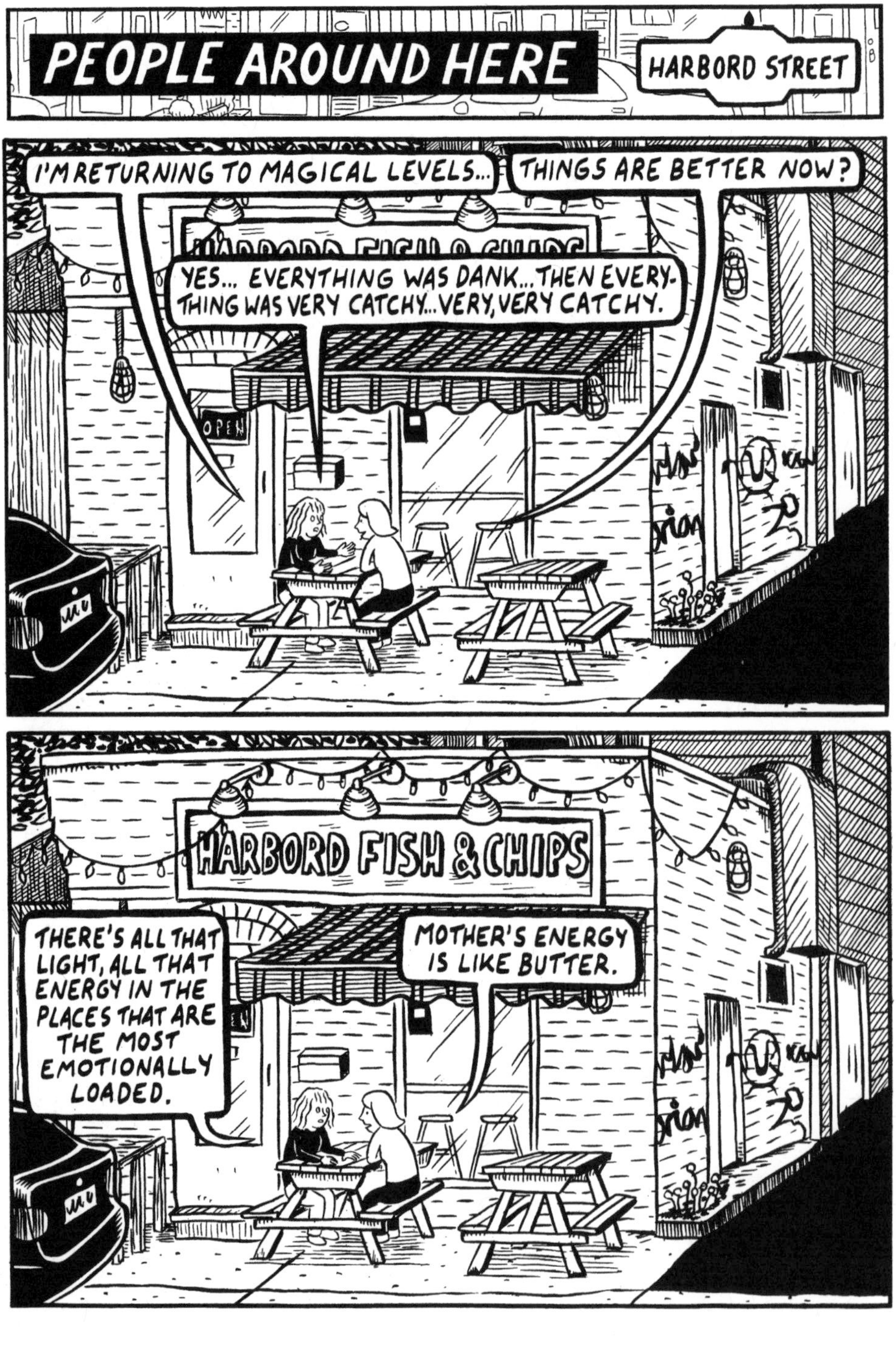
PEOPLE AROUND HERE
HARBORD STREET
I'M RETURNING TO MAGICAL LEVELS...
THINGS ARE BETTER NOW?
YES... EVERYTHING WAS DANK... THEN EVERYTHING WAS VERY CATCHY... VERY, VERY CATCHY.
OPEN
HARBORD FISH & CHIPS
THERE'S ALL THAT LIGHT, ALL THAT ENERGY IN THE PLACES THAT ARE THE MOST EMOTIONALLY LOADED.
MOTHER'S ENERGY IS LIKE BUTTER.

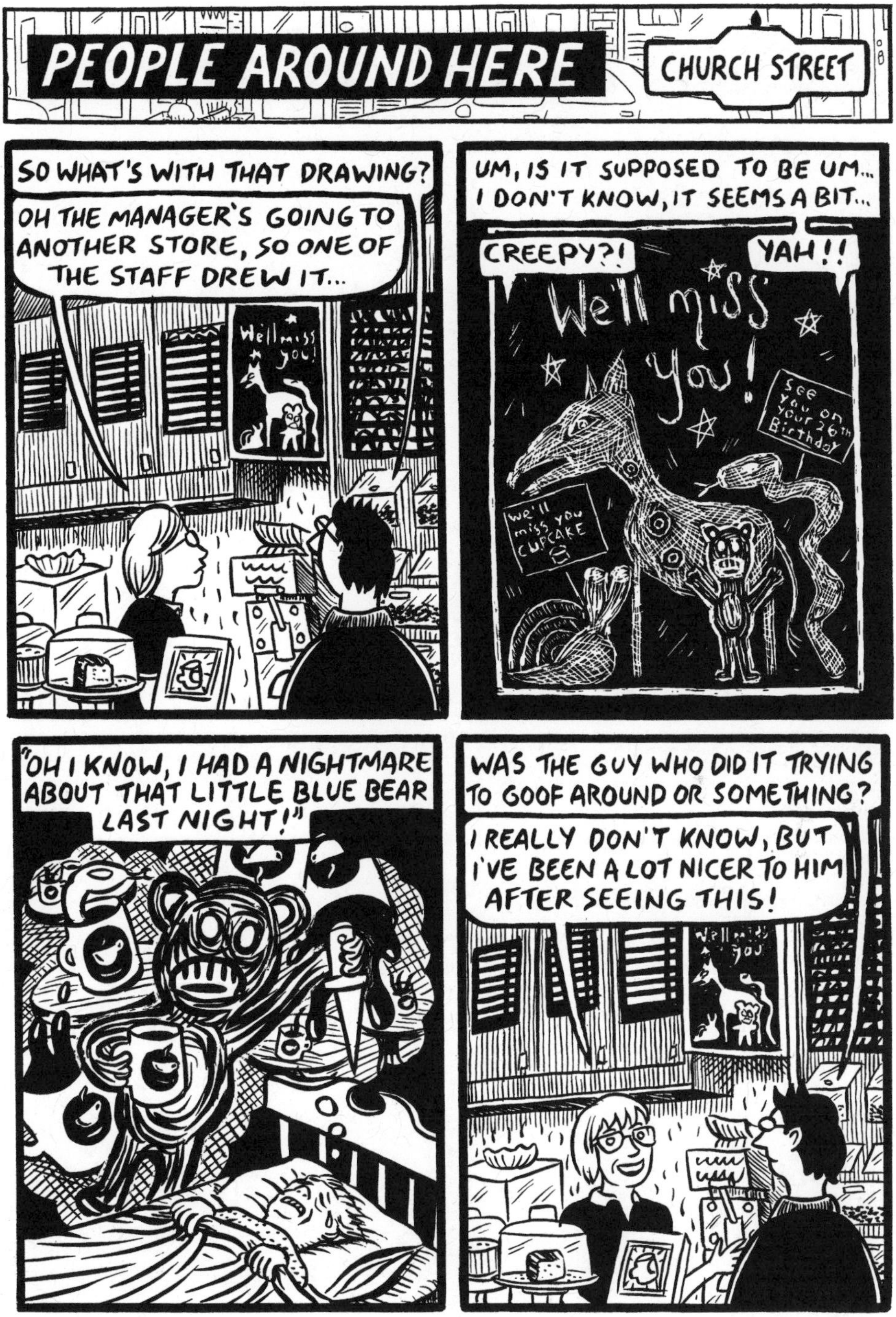
PEOPLE AROUND HERE
CHURCH STREET
SO WHAT'S WITH THAT DRAWING?
OH THE MANAGER'S GOING TO ANOTHER STORE, SO ONE OF THE STAFF DREW IT...
UM, IS IT SUPPOSED TO BE UM... I DON'T KNOW, IT SEEMS A BIT...
CREEPY?!
YAH!!
We'll miss you!
see you on your 26th Birthday
we'll miss you CUPCAKE
"OH I KNOW, I HAD A NIGHTMARE ABOUT THAT LITTLE BLUE BEAR LAST NIGHT!"
WAS THE GUY WHO DID IT TRYING TO GOOF AROUND OR SOMETHING?
I REALLY DON'T KNOW, BUT I'VE BEEN A LOT NICER TO HIM AFTER SEEING THIS!

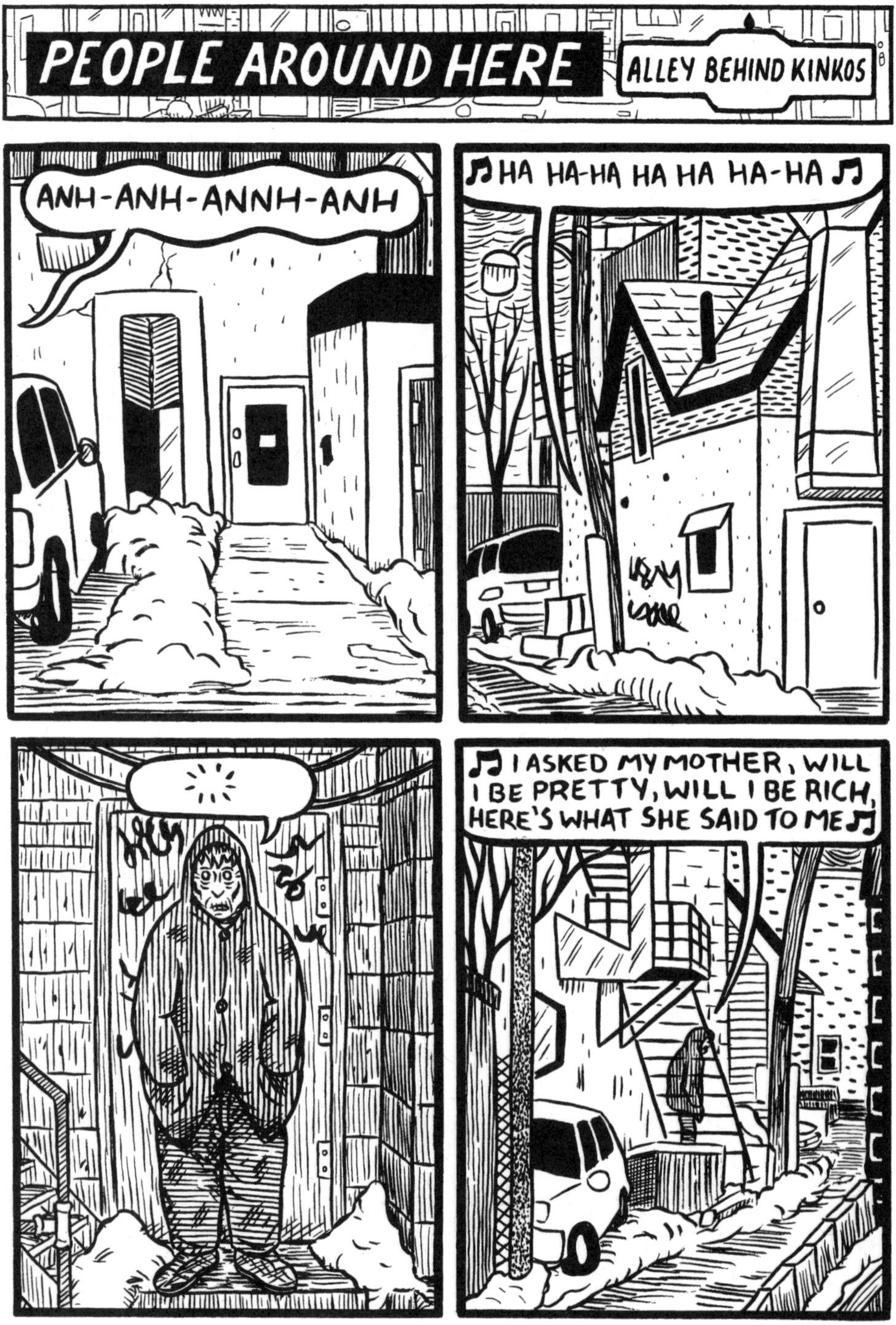
PEOPLE AROUND HERE
ALLEY BEHIND KINKOS
ANH-ANH-ANNH-ANH
♫ HA HA-HA HA HA HA-HA ♫
♫ I ASKED MY MOTHER, WILL I BE PRETTY, WILL I BE RICH, HERE'S WHAT SHE SAID TO ME ♫

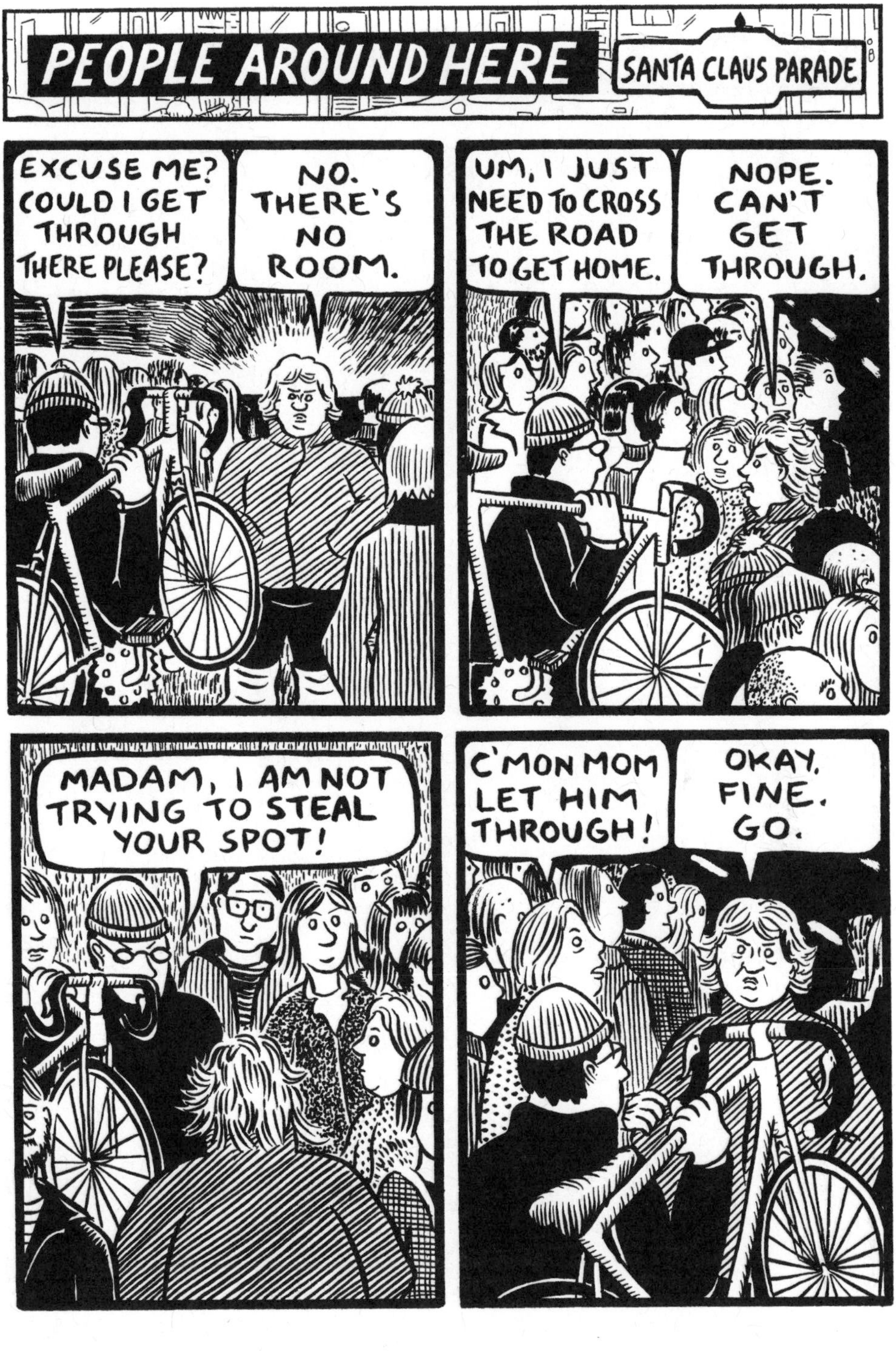
PEOPLE AROUND HERE
SANTA CLAUS PARADE
EXCUSE ME? COULD I GET THROUGH THERE PLEASE?
NO. THERE'S NO ROOM.
UM, I JUST NEED TO CROSS THE ROAD TO GET HOME.
NOPE. CAN'T GET THROUGH.
MADAM, I AM NOT TRYING TO STEAL YOUR SPOT!
C'MON MOM LET HIM THROUGH!
OKAY. FINE. GO.

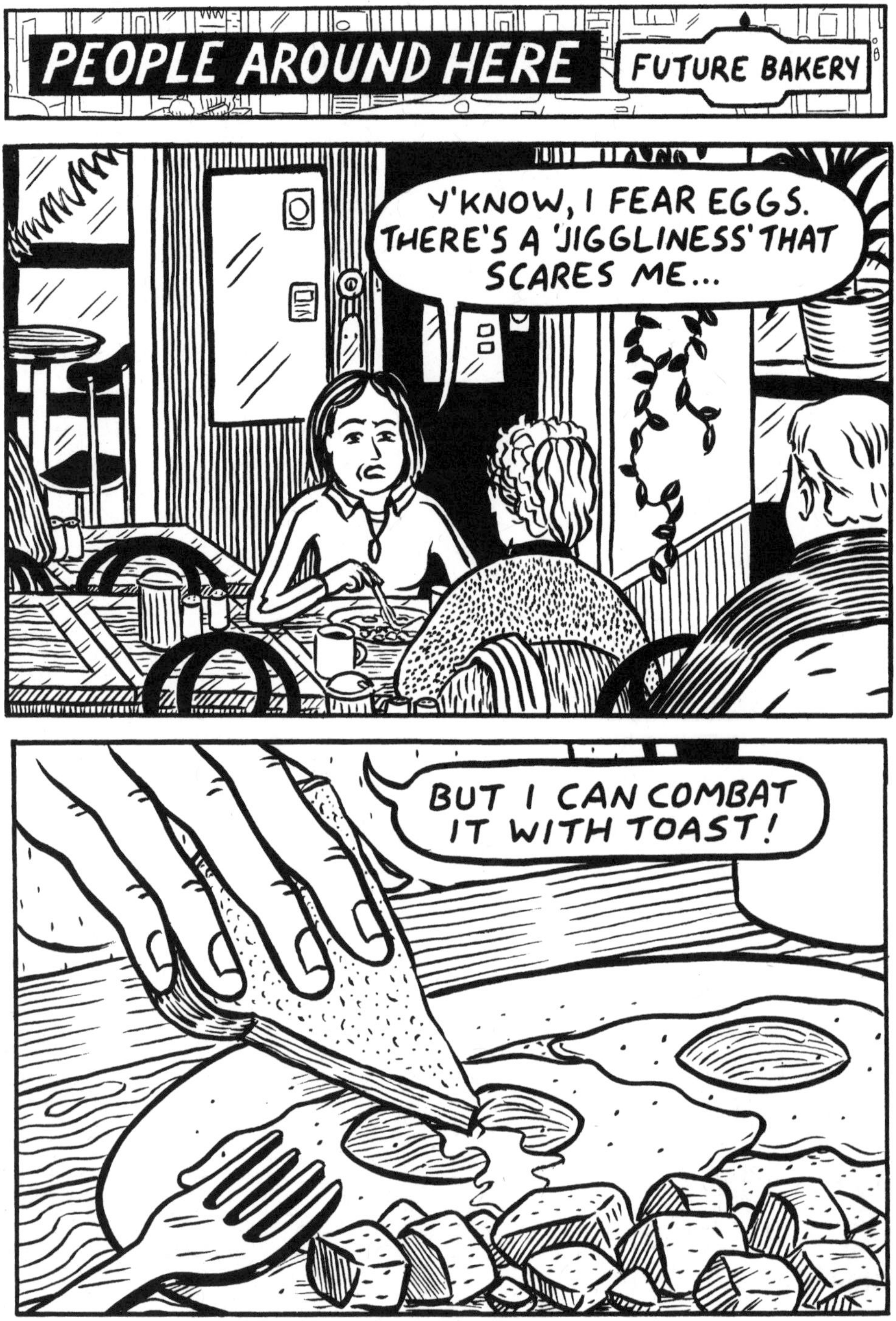
PEOPLE AROUND HERE
FUTURE BAKERY
Y'KNOW, I FEAR EGGS. THERE'S A 'JIGGLINESS' THAT SCARES ME...
BUT I CAN COMBAT IT WITH TOAST!

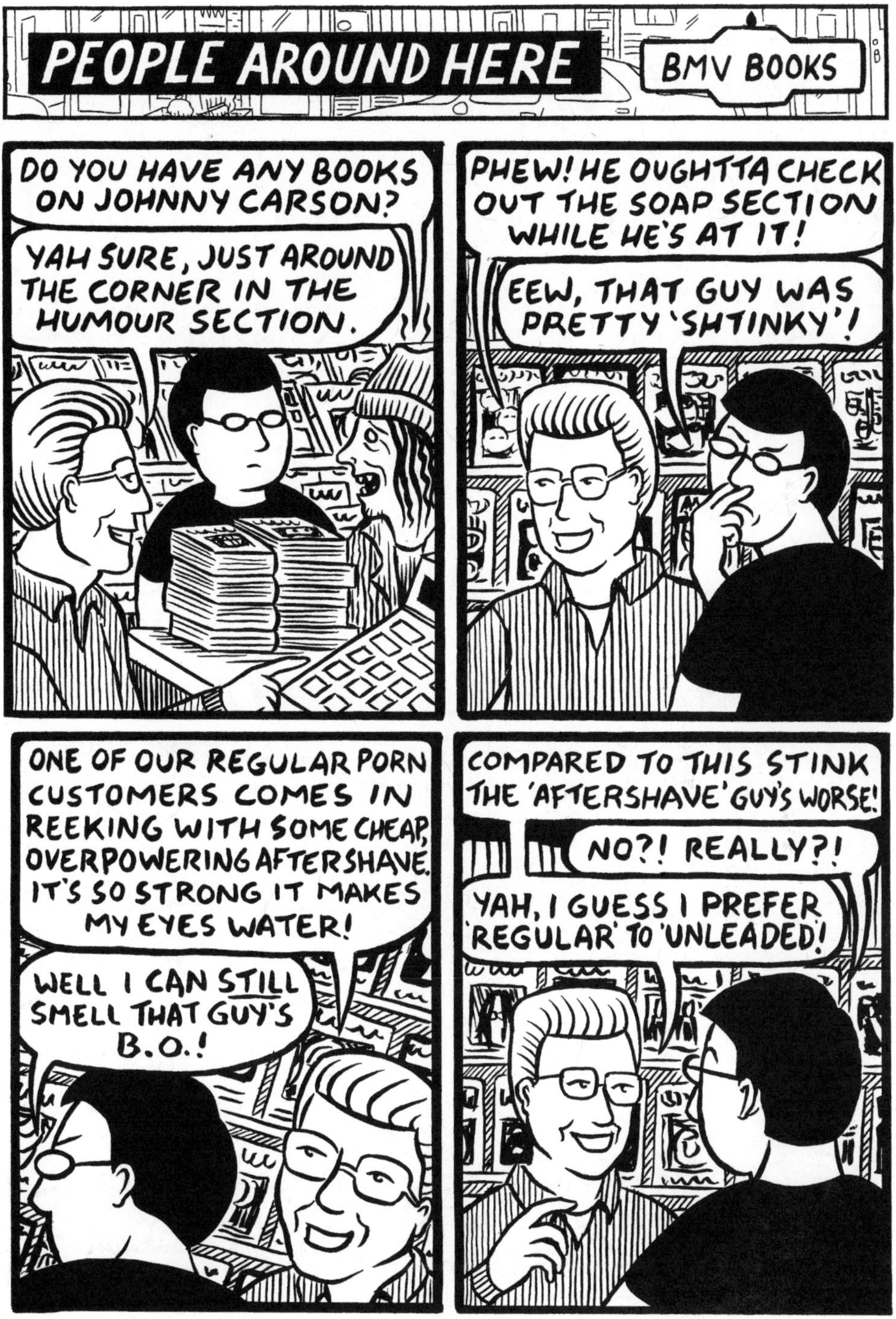
PEOPLE AROUND HERE
BMV BOOKS
DO YOU HAVE ANY BOOKS ON JOHNNY CARSON?
YAH SURE, JUST AROUND THE CORNER IN THE HUMOUR SECTION.
PHEW! HE OUGHTTA CHECK OUT THE SOAP SECTION WHILE HE'S AT IT!
EEW, THAT GUY WAS PRETTY 'SHTINKY'!
ONE OF OUR REGULAR PORN CUSTOMERS COMES IN REEKING WITH SOME CHEAP, OVERPOWERING AFTERSHAVE. IT'S SO STRONG IT MAKES MY EYES WATER!
WELL I CAN STILL SMELL THAT GUY'S B.O.!
COMPARED TO THIS STINK THE 'AFTERSHAVE' GUY'S WORSE!
NO?! REALLY?!
YAH, I GUESS I PREFER 'REGULAR' TO 'UNLEADED'!

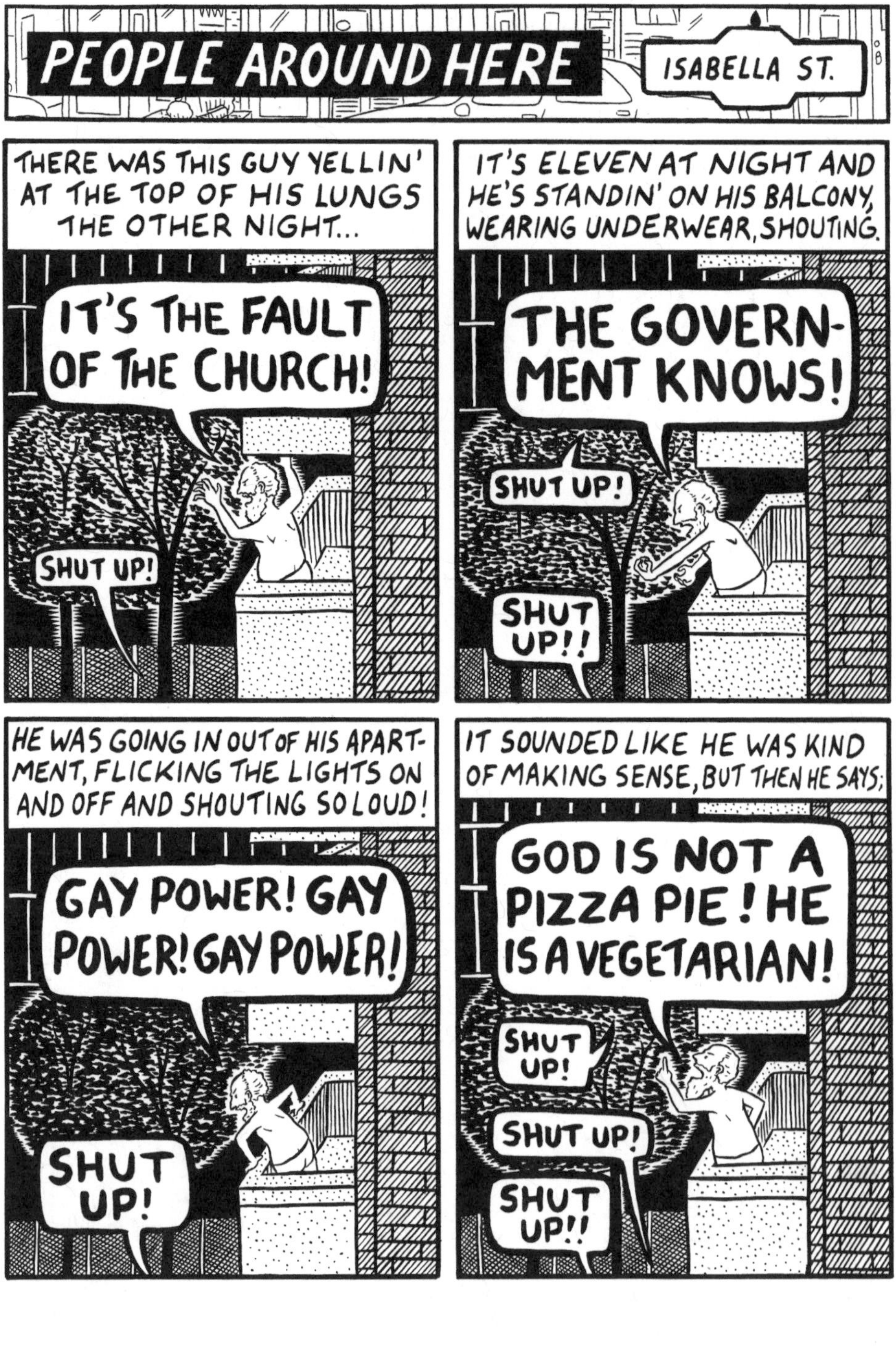
PEOPLE AROUND HERE
ISABELLA ST.
THERE WAS THIS GUY YELLIN' AT THE TOP OF HIS LUNGS THE OTHER NIGHT...
IT'S THE FAULT OF THE CHURCH!
SHUT UP!
IT'S ELEVEN AT NIGHT AND HE'S STANDIN' ON HIS BALCONY, WEARING UNDERWEAR, SHOUTING.
THE GOVERN-MENT KNOWS!
SHUT UP!
SHUT UP!!
HE WAS GOING IN OUT OF HIS APART-MENT, FLICKING THE LIGHTS ON AND OFF AND SHOUTING SO LOUD!
GAY POWER! GAY POWER! GAY POWER!
SHUT UP!
IT SOUNDED LIKE HE WAS KIND OF MAKING SENSE, BUT THEN HE SAYS;
GOD IS NOT A PIZZA PIE! HE IS A VEGETARIAN!
SHUT UP!
SHUT UP!
SHUT UP!!

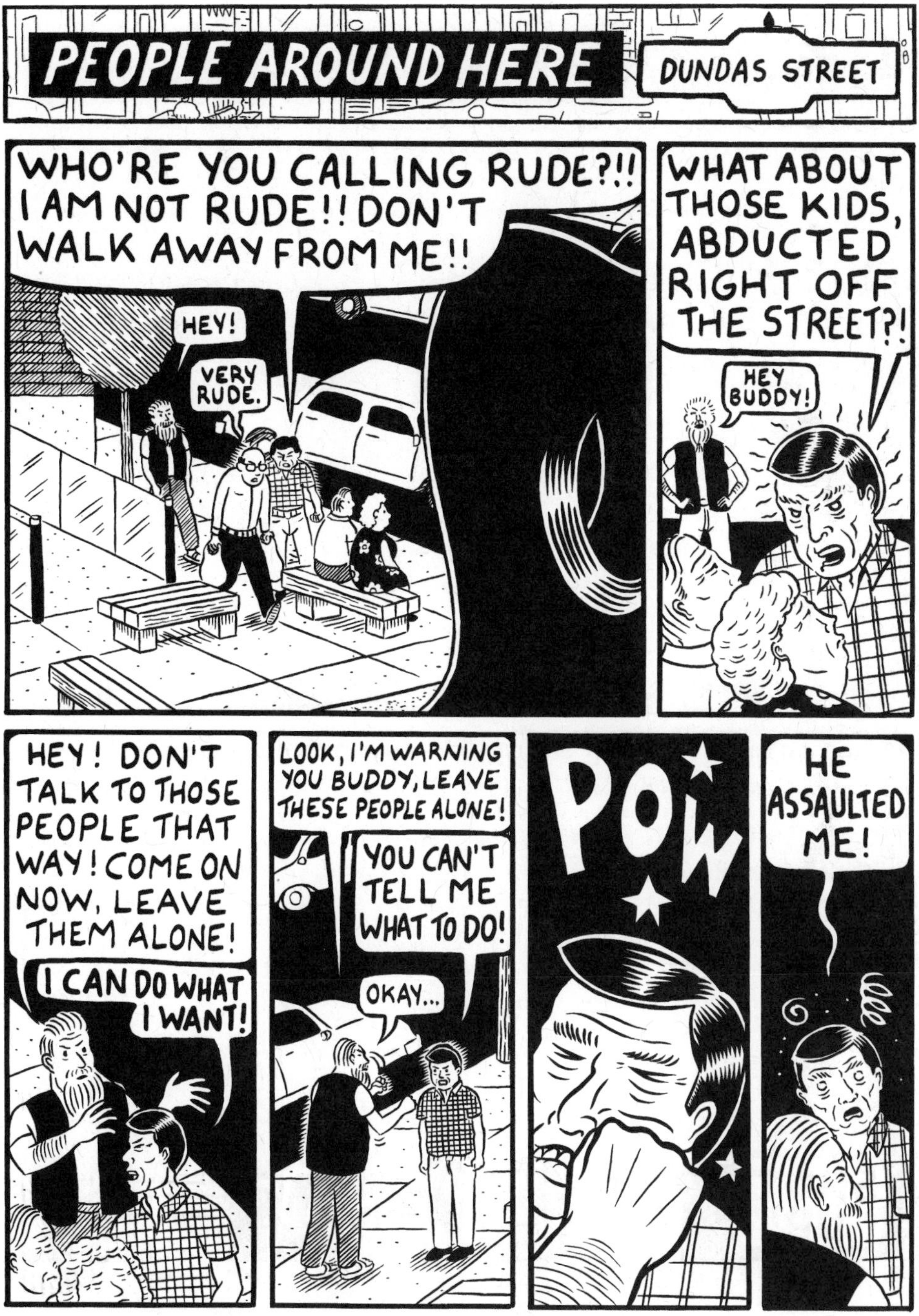
PEOPLE AROUND HERE
DUNDAS STREET
WHO'RE YOU CALLING RUDE?!! I AM NOT RUDE!! DON'T WALK AWAY FROM ME!!
HEY!
VERY RUDE.
WHAT ABOUT THOSE KIDS, ABDUCTED RIGHT OFF THE STREET?!
HEY BUDDY!
HEY! DON'T TALK TO THOSE PEOPLE THAT WAY! COME ON NOW, LEAVE THEM ALONE!
I CAN DO WHAT I WANT!
LOOK, I'M WARNING YOU BUDDY, LEAVE THESE PEOPLE ALONE!
YOU CAN'T TELL ME WHAT TO DO!
OKAY...
POW
HE ASSAULTED ME!

# PEOPLE AROUND HERE

BALMUTO ST.

EXCUSE ME, IS THIS YOUR REGULAR WORK AREA?

PARDON ME?

UH, DO YOU USUALLY WORK IN THIS AREA AROUND THIS TIME?

YES...

"I KNOW THIS SOUNDS STRANGE, BUT HAVE YOU EVER NOTICED THE LITTLE CLEAR PLASTIC BAGS OF DOG POO IN THE CURB OVER THERE?"

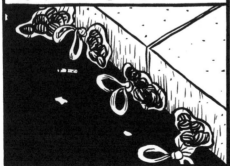

"HAVE YOU EVER SEEN THE PERSON WHO LEAVES THEM THERE?"

"YAH. SOME BLIND GUY DROPS IT THERE... BUT Y'KNOW IF HE'S SEEING ENOUGH TO BAG IT, IT'S ONLY A FEW MORE STEPS TO THE GARBAGE CAN."

HEH, YAH. ONE WEEK NOBODY CLEANED UP AND THERE WERE SEVEN BAGS SITTING THERE!

I KNOW THIS ISN'T VERY 'PC', BUT I MEAN HOW IS HE PICKING IT UP?... BY SMELLING IT?

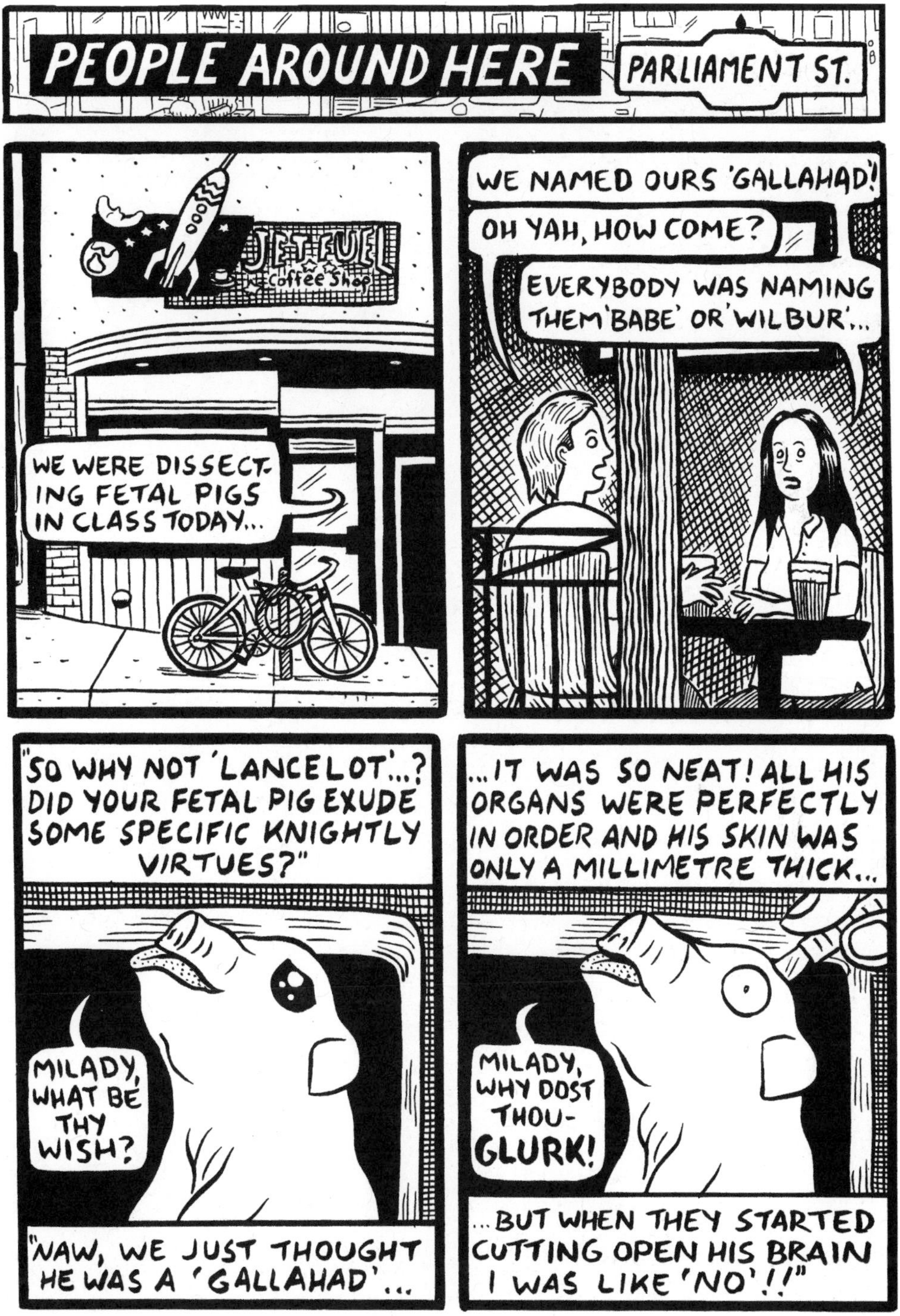
PEOPLE AROUND HERE
PARLIAMENT ST.
JET FUEL Coffee Shop
WE WERE DISSECTING FETAL PIGS IN CLASS TODAY...
WE NAMED OURS 'GALLAHAD'!
OH YAH, HOW COME?
EVERYBODY WAS NAMING THEM 'BABE' OR 'WILBUR'...
"SO WHY NOT 'LANCELOT'...? DID YOUR FETAL PIG EXUDE SOME SPECIFIC KNIGHTLY VIRTUES?"
MILADY, WHAT BE THY WISH?
"NAW, WE JUST THOUGHT HE WAS A 'GALLAHAD'...
...IT WAS SO NEAT! ALL HIS ORGANS WERE PERFECTLY IN ORDER AND HIS SKIN WAS ONLY A MILLIMETRE THICK...
MILADY, WHY DOST THOU- GLURK!
...BUT WHEN THEY STARTED CUTTING OPEN HIS BRAIN I WAS LIKE 'NO'!!"

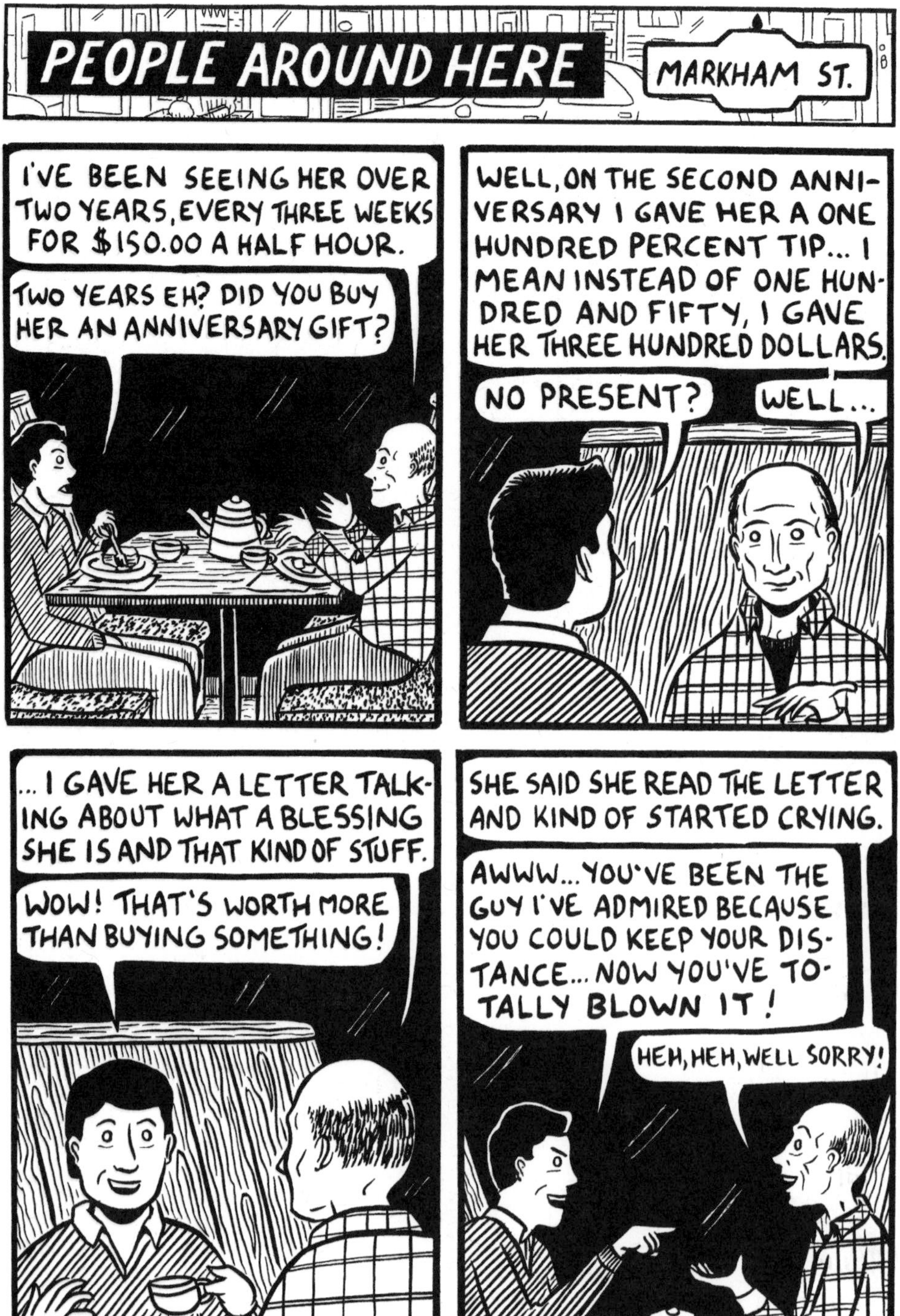
PEOPLE AROUND HERE
MARKHAM ST.
I'VE BEEN SEEING HER OVER TWO YEARS, EVERY THREE WEEKS FOR $150.00 A HALF HOUR.
TWO YEARS EH? DID YOU BUY HER AN ANNIVERSARY GIFT?
WELL, ON THE SECOND ANNIVERSARY I GAVE HER A ONE HUNDRED PERCENT TIP... I MEAN INSTEAD OF ONE HUNDRED AND FIFTY, I GAVE HER THREE HUNDRED DOLLARS.
NO PRESENT?
WELL...
... I GAVE HER A LETTER TALKING ABOUT WHAT A BLESSING SHE IS AND THAT KIND OF STUFF.
WOW! THAT'S WORTH MORE THAN BUYING SOMETHING!
SHE SAID SHE READ THE LETTER AND KIND OF STARTED CRYING.
AWWW... YOU'VE BEEN THE GUY I'VE ADMIRED BECAUSE YOU COULD KEEP YOUR DISTANCE... NOW YOU'VE TOTALLY BLOWN IT!
HEH, HEH, WELL SORRY!

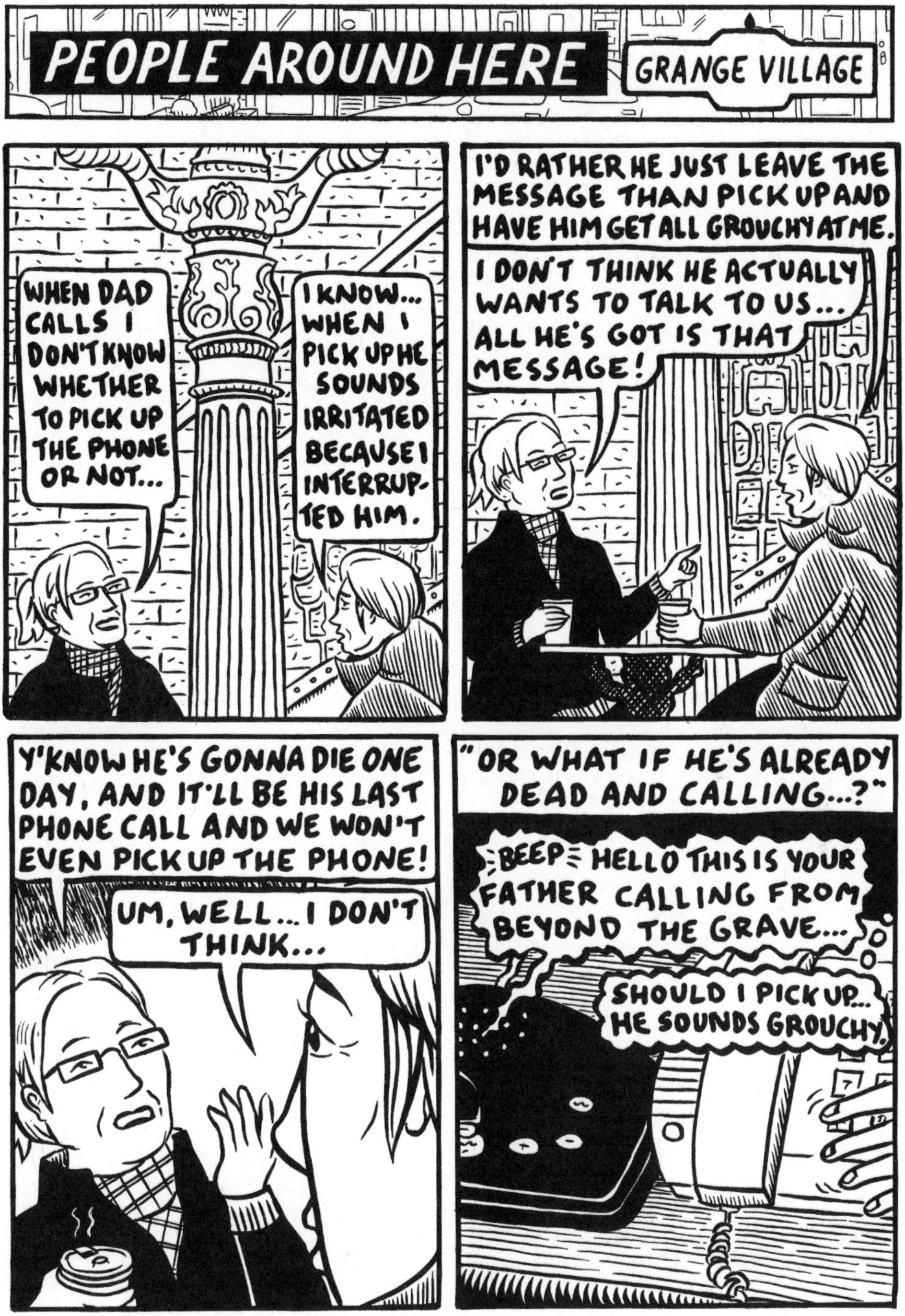
PEOPLE AROUND HERE
GRANGE VILLAGE
WHEN DAD CALLS I DON'T KNOW WHETHER TO PICK UP THE PHONE OR NOT...
I KNOW... WHEN I PICK UP HE SOUNDS IRRITATED BECAUSE I INTERRUPTED HIM.
I'D RATHER HE JUST LEAVE THE MESSAGE THAN PICK UP AND HAVE HIM GET ALL GROUCHY AT ME.
I DON'T THINK HE ACTUALLY WANTS TO TALK TO US... ALL HE'S GOT IS THAT MESSAGE!
Y'KNOW HE'S GONNA DIE ONE DAY, AND IT'LL BE HIS LAST PHONE CALL AND WE WON'T EVEN PICK UP THE PHONE!
UM, WELL... I DON'T THINK...
"OR WHAT IF HE'S ALREADY DEAD AND CALLING...?"
BEEP HELLO THIS IS YOUR FATHER CALLING FROM BEYOND THE GRAVE...
SHOULD I PICK UP... HE SOUNDS GROUCHY.

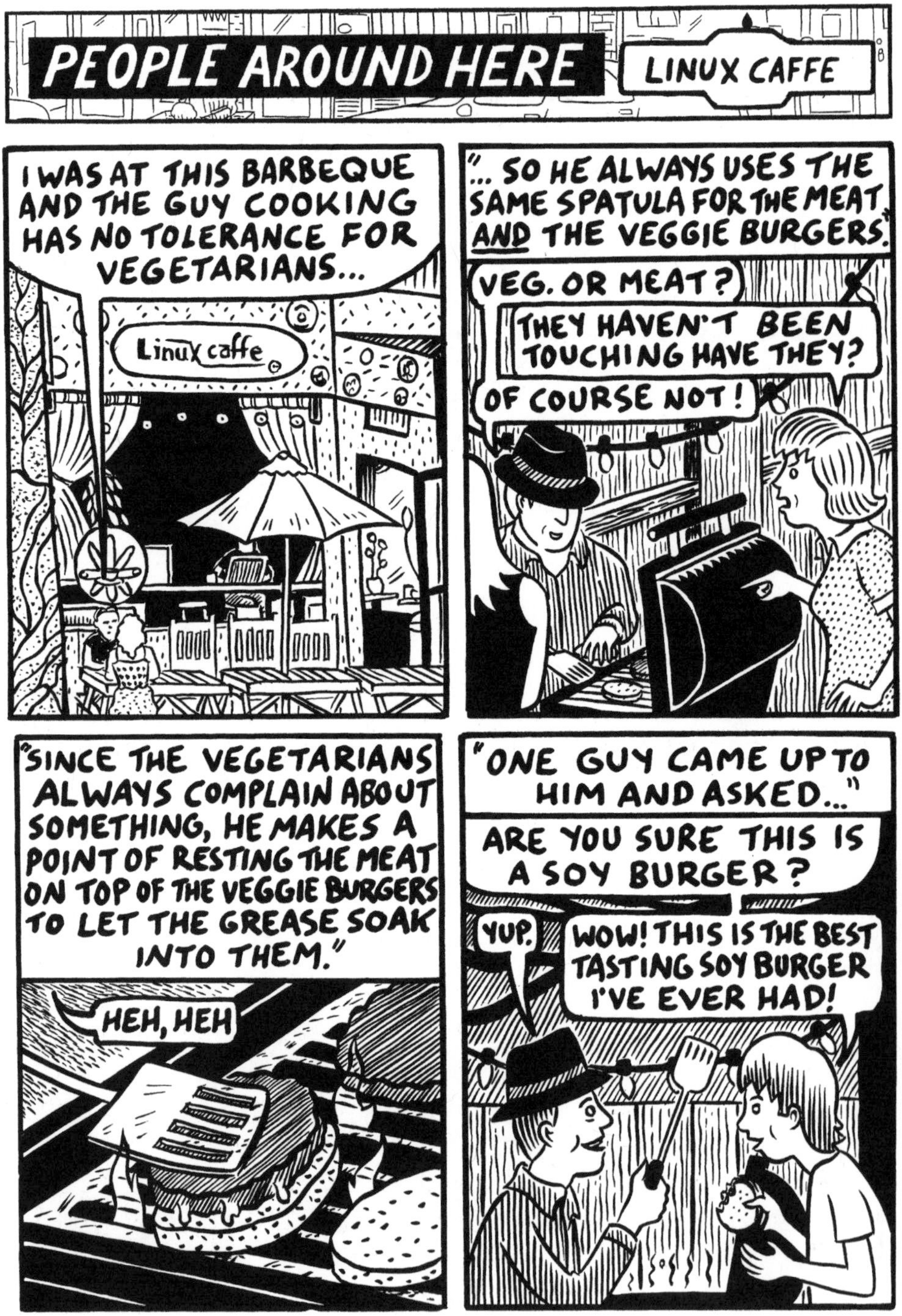
PEOPLE AROUND HERE
LINUX CAFFE
I WAS AT THIS BARBEQUE AND THE GUY COOKING HAS NO TOLERANCE FOR VEGETARIANS...
Linux caffe
"... SO HE ALWAYS USES THE SAME SPATULA FOR THE MEAT AND THE VEGGIE BURGERS."
VEG. OR MEAT?
THEY HAVEN'T BEEN TOUCHING HAVE THEY?
OF COURSE NOT!
"SINCE THE VEGETARIANS ALWAYS COMPLAIN ABOUT SOMETHING, HE MAKES A POINT OF RESTING THE MEAT ON TOP OF THE VEGGIE BURGERS TO LET THE GREASE SOAK INTO THEM."
HEH, HEH
"ONE GUY CAME UP TO HIM AND ASKED..."
ARE YOU SURE THIS IS A SOY BURGER?
YUP.
WOW! THIS IS THE BEST TASTING SOY BURGER I'VE EVER HAD!

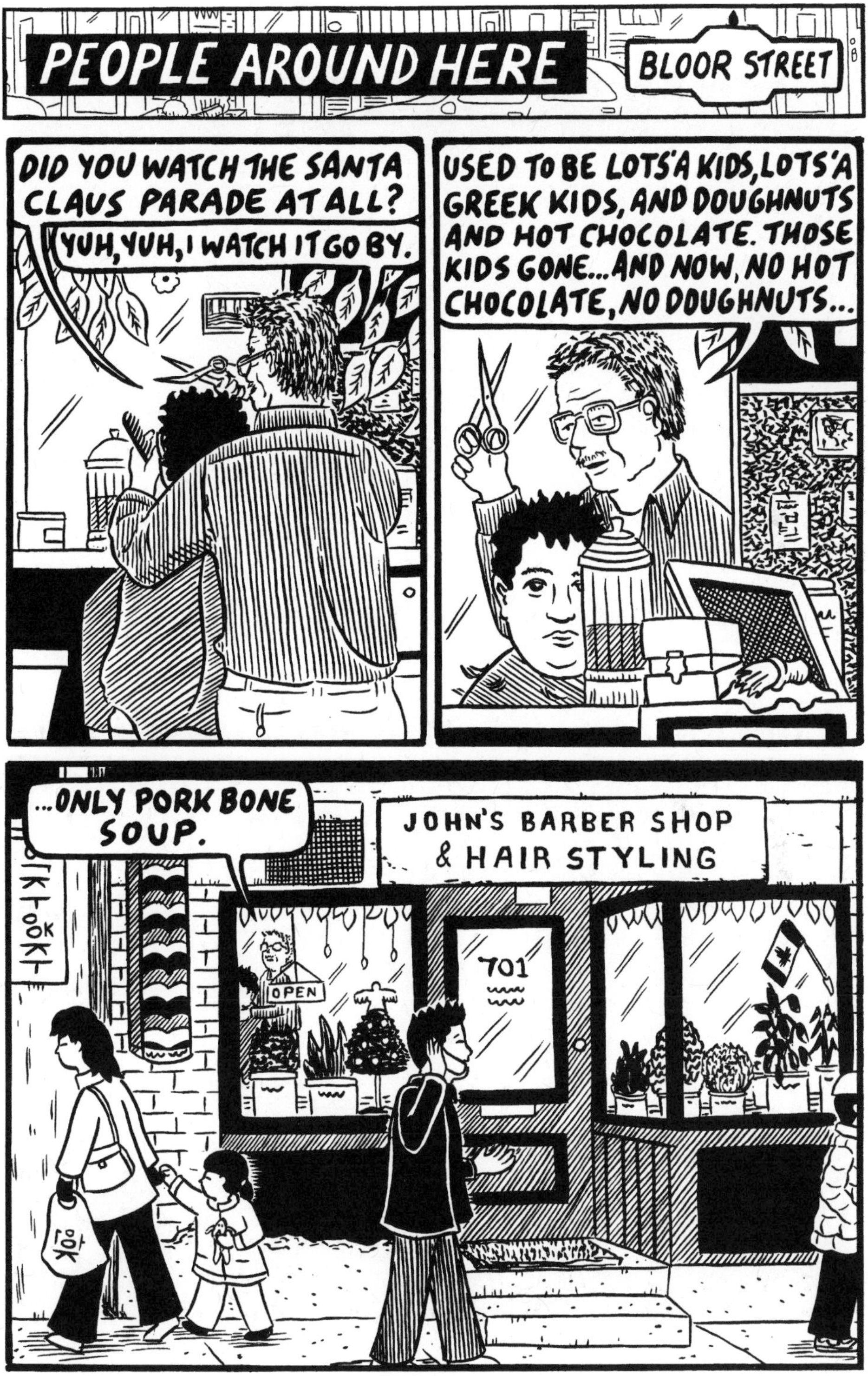
PEOPLE AROUND HERE
BLOOR STREET
DID YOU WATCH THE SANTA CLAUS PARADE AT ALL?
YUH, YUH, I WATCH IT GO BY.
USED TO BE LOTS'A KIDS, LOTS'A GREEK KIDS, AND DOUGHNUTS AND HOT CHOCOLATE. THOSE KIDS GONE... AND NOW, NO HOT CHOCOLATE, NO DOUGHNUTS...
...ONLY PORK BONE SOUP.
JOHN'S BARBER SHOP
& HAIR STYLING
OPEN
701

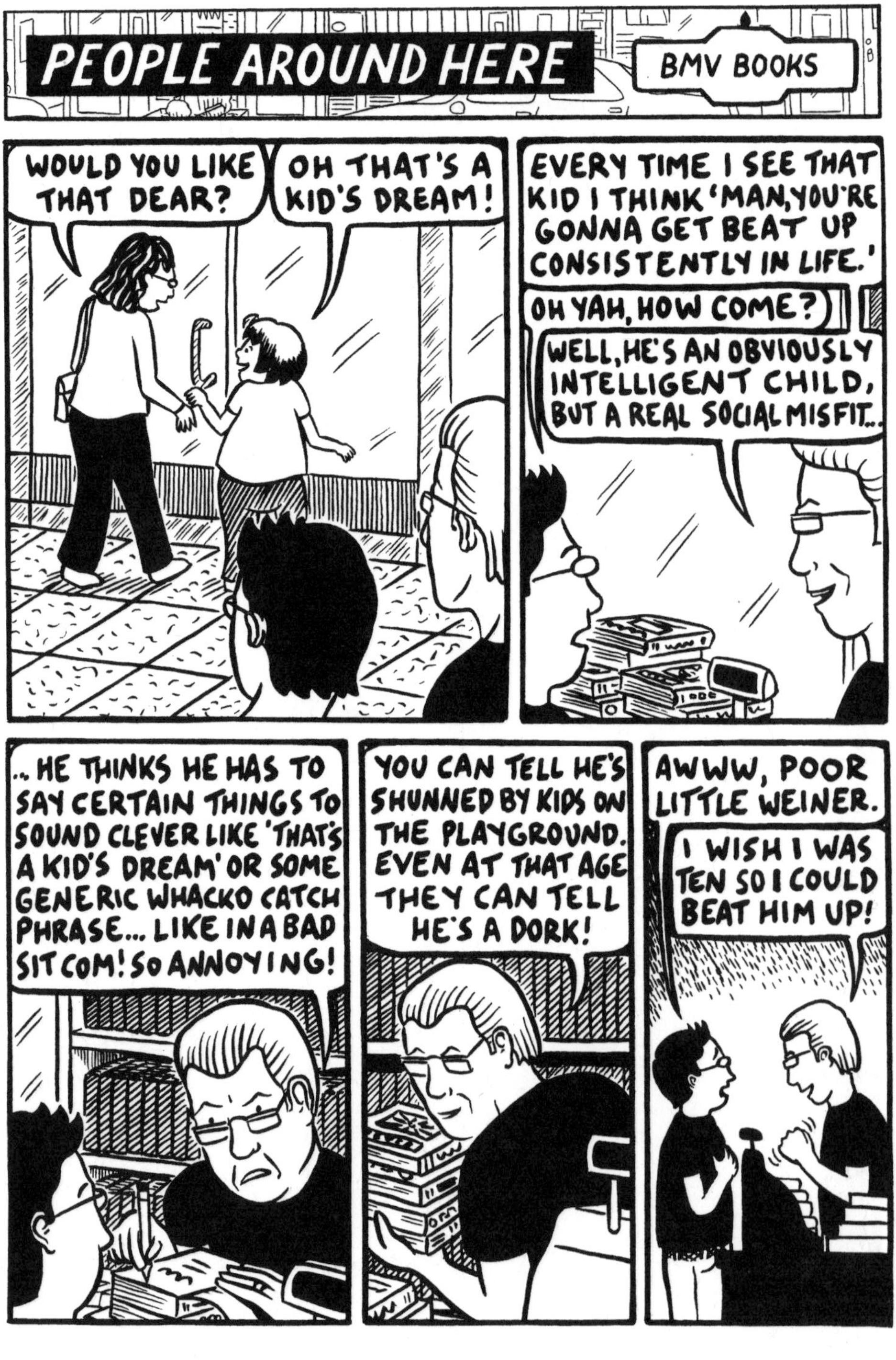
PEOPLE AROUND HERE
BMV BOOKS
WOULD YOU LIKE THAT DEAR?
OH THAT'S A KID'S DREAM!
EVERY TIME I SEE THAT KID I THINK 'MAN, YOU'RE GONNA GET BEAT UP CONSISTENTLY IN LIFE.'
OH YAH, HOW COME?
WELL, HE'S AN OBVIOUSLY INTELLIGENT CHILD, BUT A REAL SOCIAL MISFIT...
.. HE THINKS HE HAS TO SAY CERTAIN THINGS TO SOUND CLEVER LIKE 'THAT'S A KID'S DREAM' OR SOME GENERIC WHACKO CATCH PHRASE... LIKE IN A BAD SITCOM! SO ANNOYING!
YOU CAN TELL HE'S SHUNNED BY KIDS ON THE PLAYGROUND. EVEN AT THAT AGE THEY CAN TELL HE'S A DORK!
AWWW, POOR LITTLE WEINER.
I WISH I WAS TEN SO I COULD BEAT HIM UP!

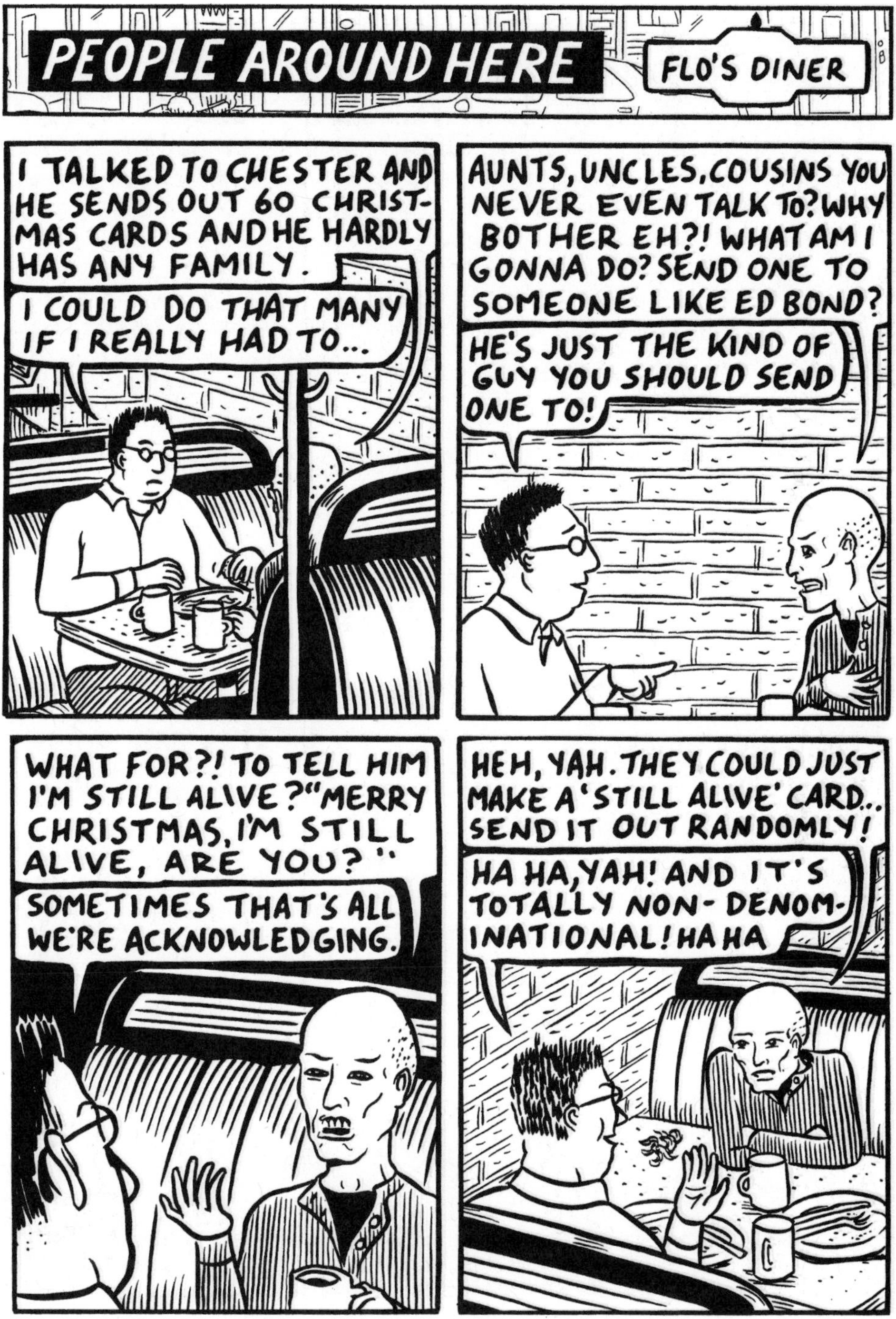
PEOPLE AROUND HERE
FLO'S DINER
I TALKED TO CHESTER AND HE SENDS OUT 60 CHRISTMAS CARDS AND HE HARDLY HAS ANY FAMILY.
I COULD DO THAT MANY IF I REALLY HAD TO...
AUNTS, UNCLES, COUSINS YOU NEVER EVEN TALK TO? WHY BOTHER EH?! WHAT AM I GONNA DO? SEND ONE TO SOMEONE LIKE ED BOND?
HE'S JUST THE KIND OF GUY YOU SHOULD SEND ONE TO!
WHAT FOR?! TO TELL HIM I'M STILL ALIVE? "MERRY CHRISTMAS, I'M STILL ALIVE, ARE YOU?"
SOMETIMES THAT'S ALL WE'RE ACKNOWLEDGING.
HEH, YAH. THEY COULD JUST MAKE A 'STILL ALIVE' CARD... SEND IT OUT RANDOMLY!
HA HA, YAH! AND IT'S TOTALLY NON-DENOMINATIONAL! HA HA

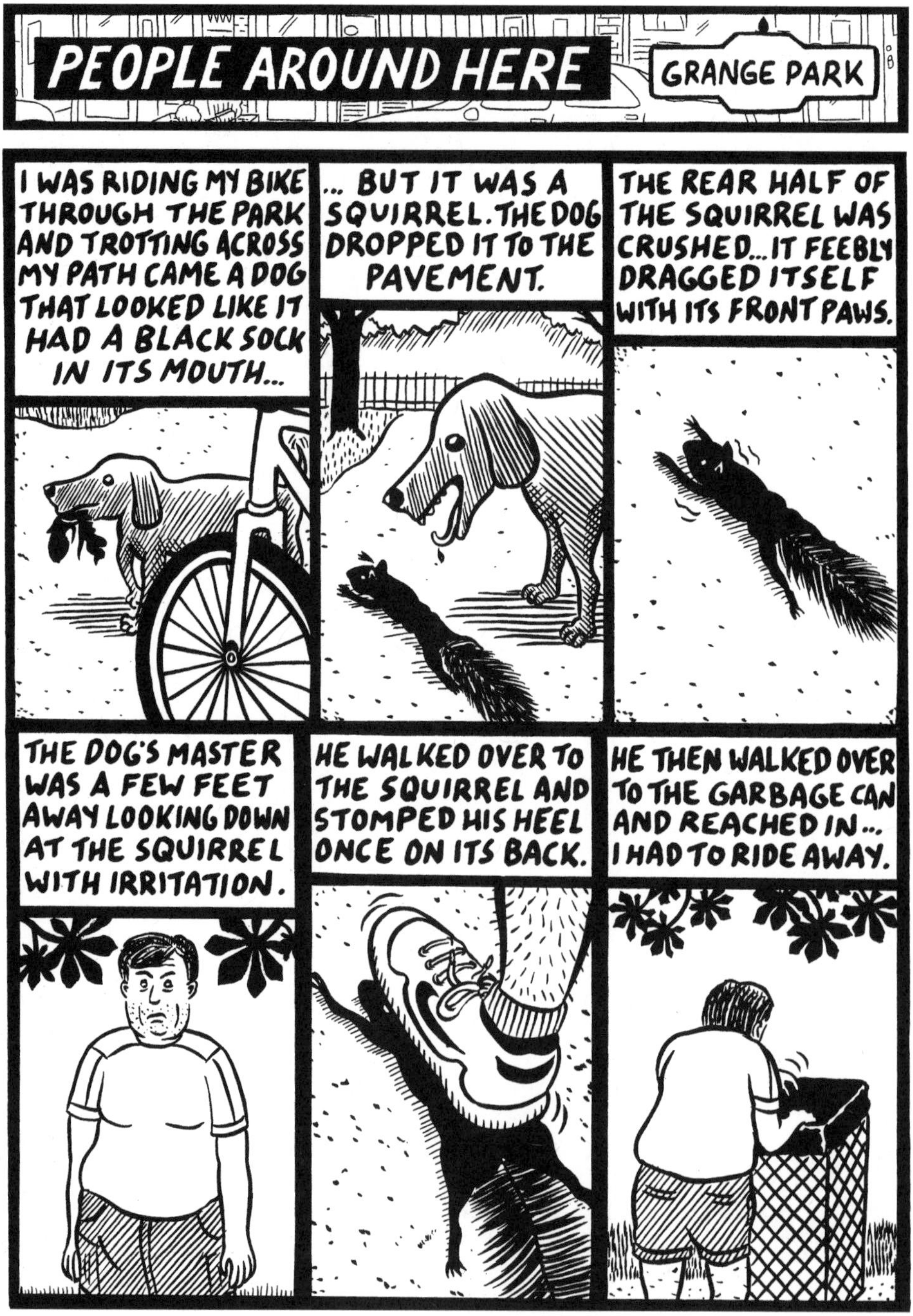
PEOPLE AROUND HERE
GRANGE PARK
I WAS RIDING MY BIKE THROUGH THE PARK AND TROTTING ACROSS MY PATH CAME A DOG THAT LOOKED LIKE IT HAD A BLACK SOCK IN ITS MOUTH...
... BUT IT WAS A SQUIRREL. THE DOG DROPPED IT TO THE PAVEMENT.
THE REAR HALF OF THE SQUIRREL WAS CRUSHED... IT FEEBLY DRAGGED ITSELF WITH ITS FRONT PAWS.
THE DOG'S MASTER WAS A FEW FEET AWAY LOOKING DOWN AT THE SQUIRREL WITH IRRITATION.
HE WALKED OVER TO THE SQUIRREL AND STOMPED HIS HEEL ONCE ON ITS BACK.
HE THEN WALKED OVER TO THE GARBAGE CAN AND REACHED IN... I HAD TO RIDE AWAY.

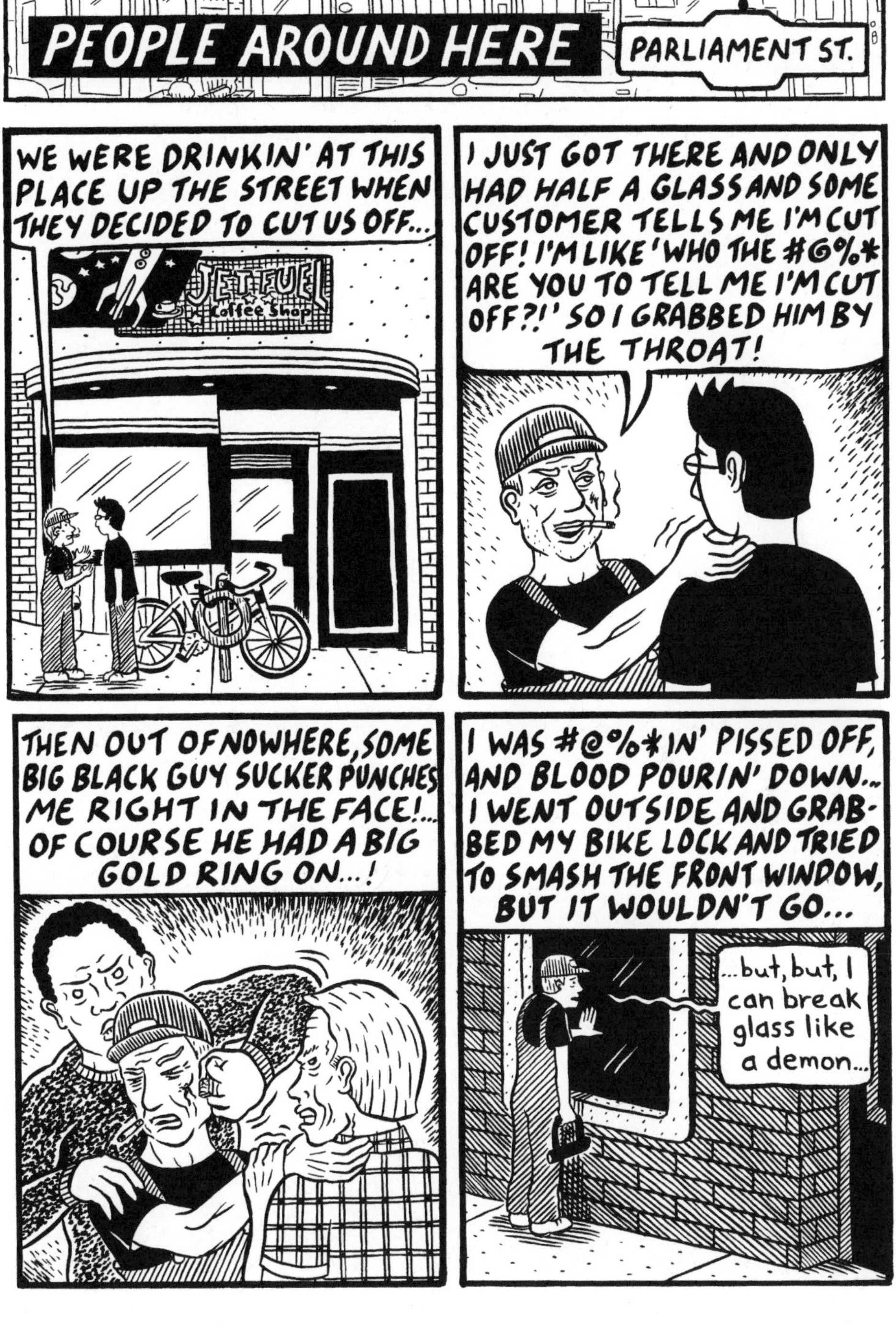
PEOPLE AROUND HERE
PARLIAMENT ST.
WE WERE DRINKIN' AT THIS PLACE UP THE STREET WHEN THEY DECIDED TO CUT US OFF...
JET FUEL Coffee Shop
I JUST GOT THERE AND ONLY HAD HALF A GLASS AND SOME CUSTOMER TELLS ME I'M CUT OFF! I'M LIKE 'WHO THE #@%* ARE YOU TO TELL ME I'M CUT OFF?!' SO I GRABBED HIM BY THE THROAT!
THEN OUT OF NOWHERE, SOME BIG BLACK GUY SUCKER PUNCHES ME RIGHT IN THE FACE!... OF COURSE HE HAD A BIG GOLD RING ON...!
I WAS #@%*IN' PISSED OFF, AND BLOOD POURIN' DOWN... I WENT OUTSIDE AND GRABBED MY BIKE LOCK AND TRIED TO SMASH THE FRONT WINDOW, BUT IT WOULDN'T GO...
...but, but, I can break glass like a demon...

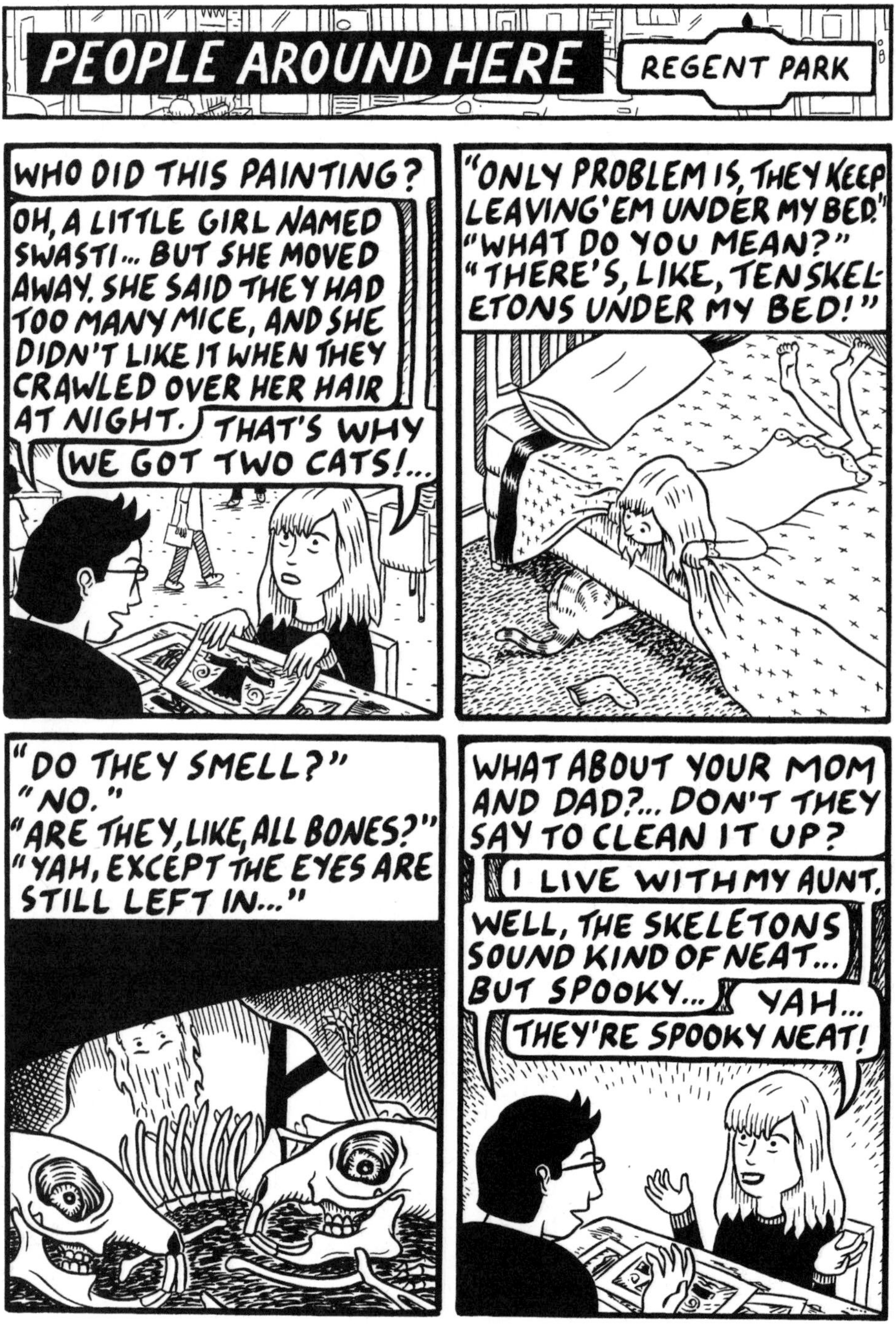
PEOPLE AROUND HERE
REGENT PARK
WHO DID THIS PAINTING?
OH, A LITTLE GIRL NAMED SWASTI... BUT SHE MOVED AWAY. SHE SAID THEY HAD TOO MANY MICE, AND SHE DIDN'T LIKE IT WHEN THEY CRAWLED OVER HER HAIR AT NIGHT.
THAT'S WHY WE GOT TWO CATS!...
"ONLY PROBLEM IS, THEY KEEP LEAVING 'EM UNDER MY BED."
"WHAT DO YOU MEAN?"
"THERE'S, LIKE, TEN SKELETONS UNDER MY BED!"
"DO THEY SMELL?"
"NO."
"ARE THEY, LIKE, ALL BONES?"
"YAH, EXCEPT THE EYES ARE STILL LEFT IN..."
WHAT ABOUT YOUR MOM AND DAD?... DON'T THEY SAY TO CLEAN IT UP?
I LIVE WITH MY AUNT.
WELL, THE SKELETONS SOUND KIND OF NEAT... BUT SPOOKY...
YAH... THEY'RE SPOOKY NEAT!

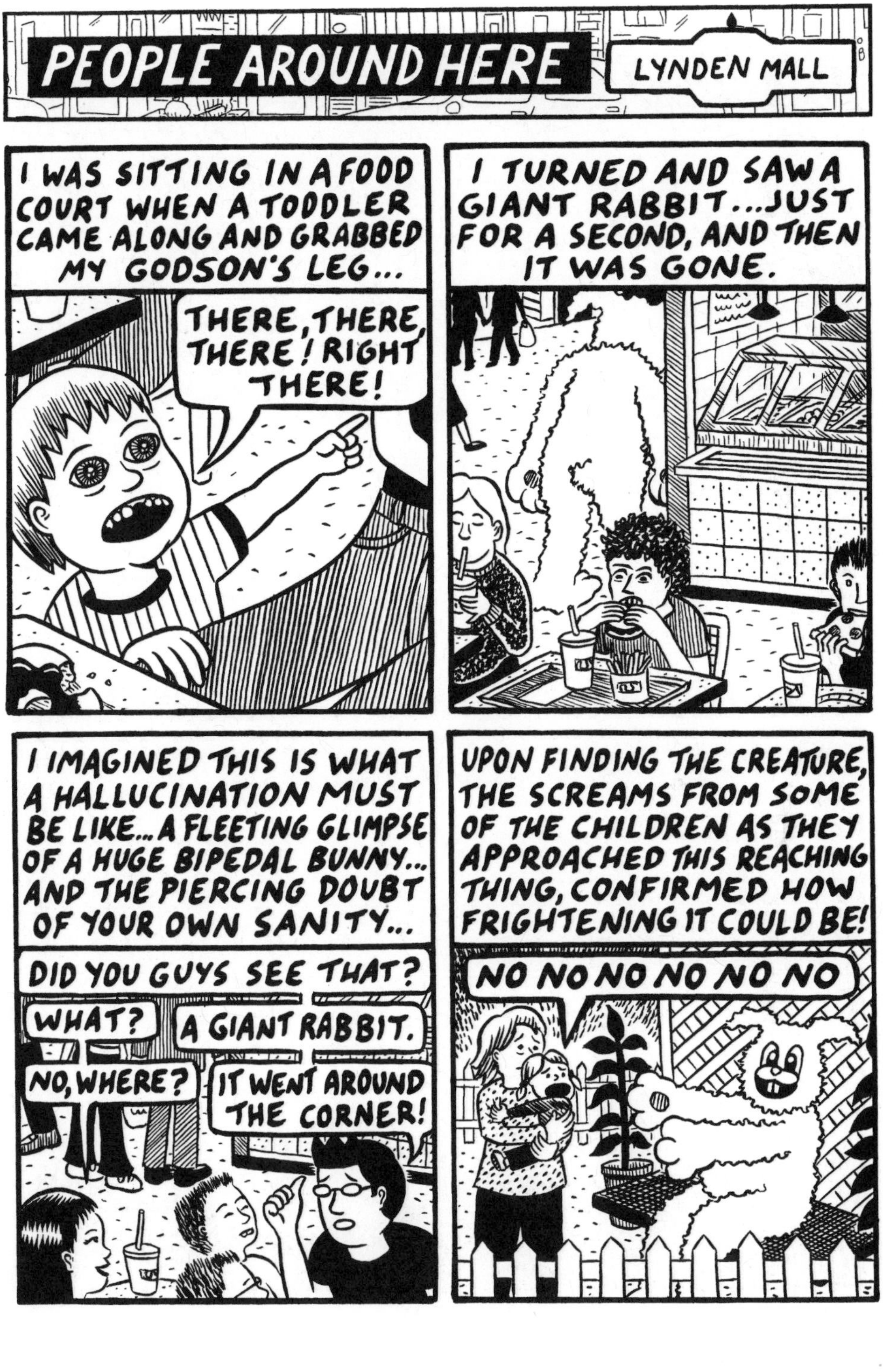
PEOPLE AROUND HERE
LYNDEN MALL
I WAS SITTING IN A FOOD COURT WHEN A TODDLER CAME ALONG AND GRABBED MY GODSON'S LEG...
THERE, THERE, THERE! RIGHT THERE!
I TURNED AND SAW A GIANT RABBIT...JUST FOR A SECOND, AND THEN IT WAS GONE.
I IMAGINED THIS IS WHAT A HALLUCINATION MUST BE LIKE... A FLEETING GLIMPSE OF A HUGE BIPEDAL BUNNY... AND THE PIERCING DOUBT OF YOUR OWN SANITY...
DID YOU GUYS SEE THAT?
WHAT?
A GIANT RABBIT.
NO, WHERE?
IT WENT AROUND THE CORNER!
UPON FINDING THE CREATURE, THE SCREAMS FROM SOME OF THE CHILDREN AS THEY APPROACHED THIS REACHING THING, CONFIRMED HOW FRIGHTENING IT COULD BE!
NO NO NO NO NO NO

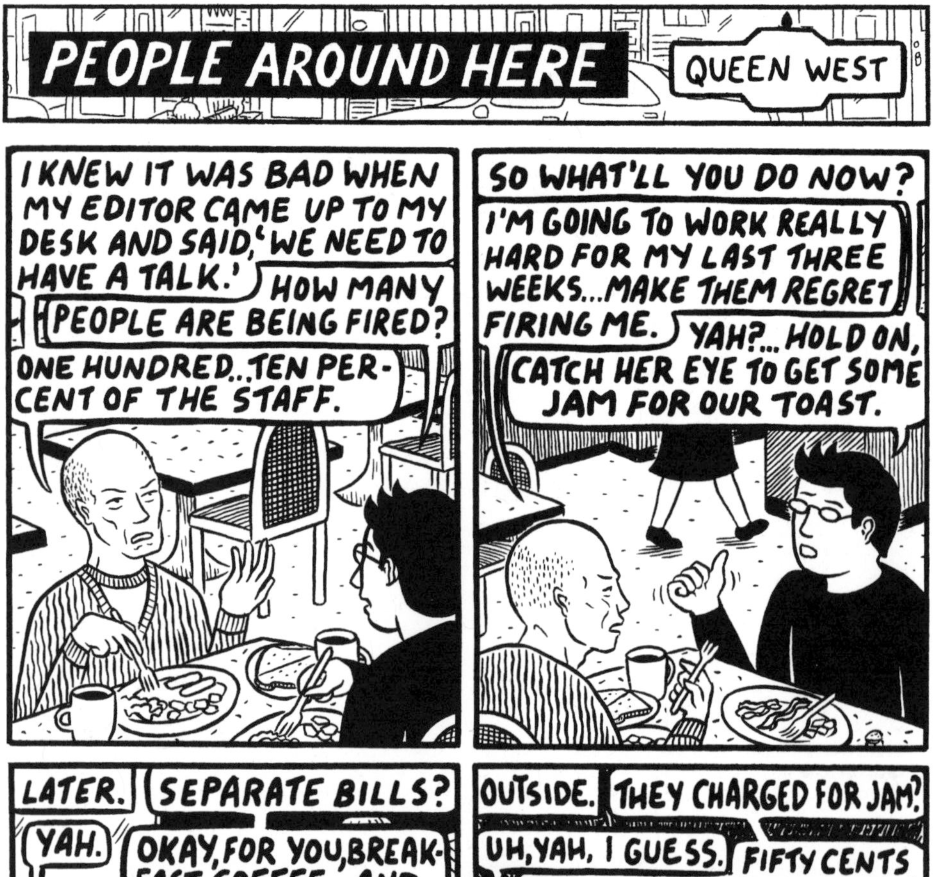

PEOPLE AROUND HERE
QUEEN WEST
I KNEW IT WAS BAD WHEN MY EDITOR CAME UP TO MY DESK AND SAID, 'WE NEED TO HAVE A TALK.'
HOW MANY PEOPLE ARE BEING FIRED?
ONE HUNDRED... TEN PER-CENT OF THE STAFF.
SO WHAT'LL YOU DO NOW?
I'M GOING TO WORK REALLY HARD FOR MY LAST THREE WEEKS... MAKE THEM REGRET FIRING ME.
YAH?... HOLD ON, CATCH HER EYE TO GET SOME JAM FOR OUR TOAST.
LATER.
SEPARATE BILLS?
YAH.
OKAY, FOR YOU, BREAK-FAST, COFFEE, AND TWO JAMS... $8.50...
...AND YOU HAD THE BREAK-FAST AND A COFFEE, $7.85.
OUTSIDE.
THEY CHARGED FOR JAM?
UH, YAH, I GUESS.
FIFTY CENTS FOR TWO JAMS?! AND HOW COME SHE DIDN'T CHARGE YOU? WHY'D I HAVE TO PAY FOR TWO?! THEY CAN'T EX-PECT PEOPLE TO PAY FOR THOSE LITTLE JAMS! THAT REALLY PISSES ME OFF!
YAH... NOT A GOOD SIGN...

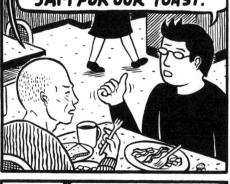

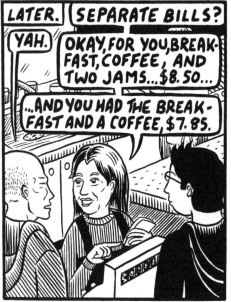

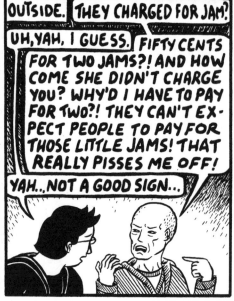

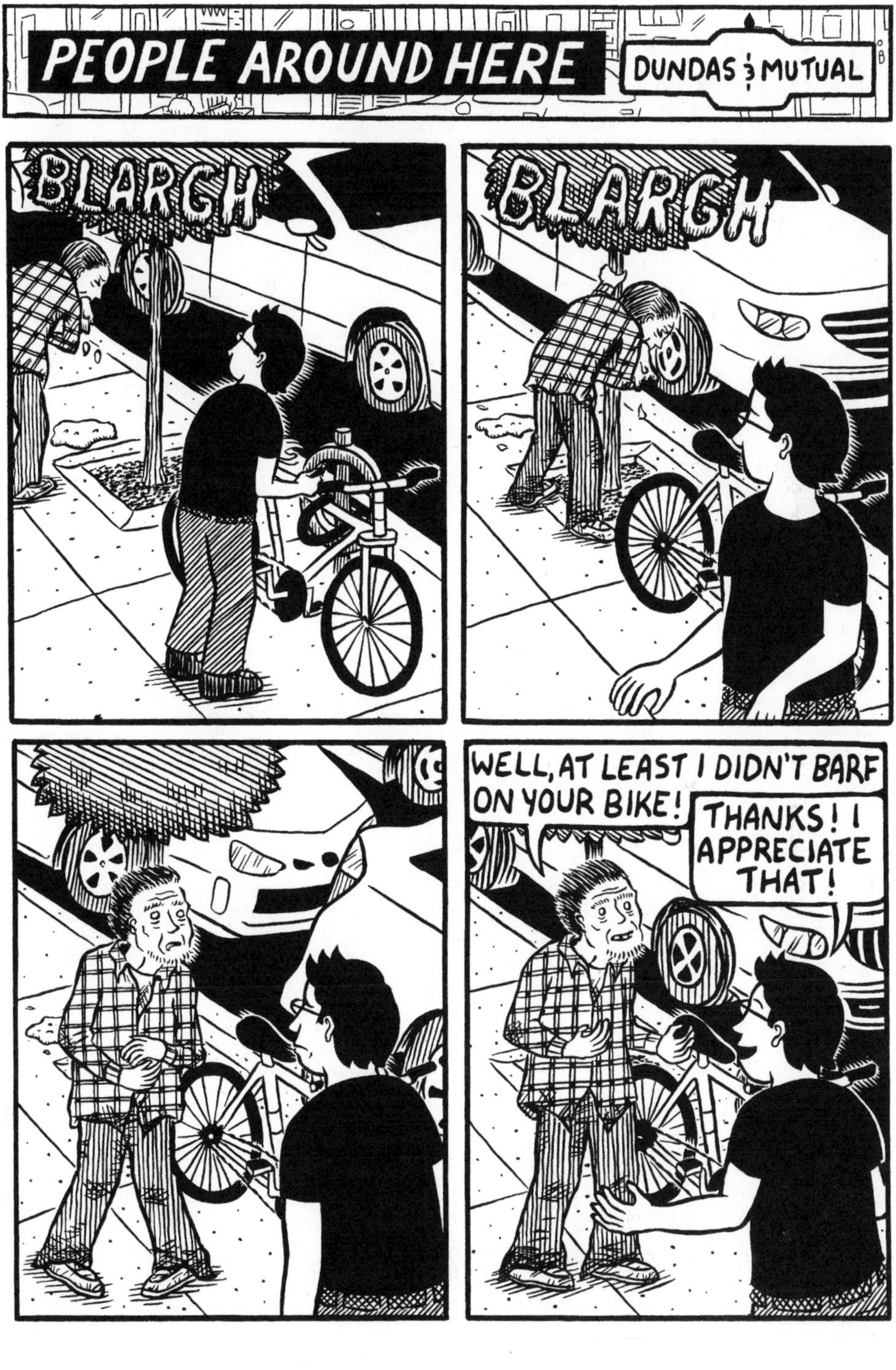
PEOPLE AROUND HERE
DUNDAS & MUTUAL
BLARGH
BLARGH
WELL, AT LEAST I DIDN'T BARF ON YOUR BIKE!
THANKS! I APPRECIATE THAT!

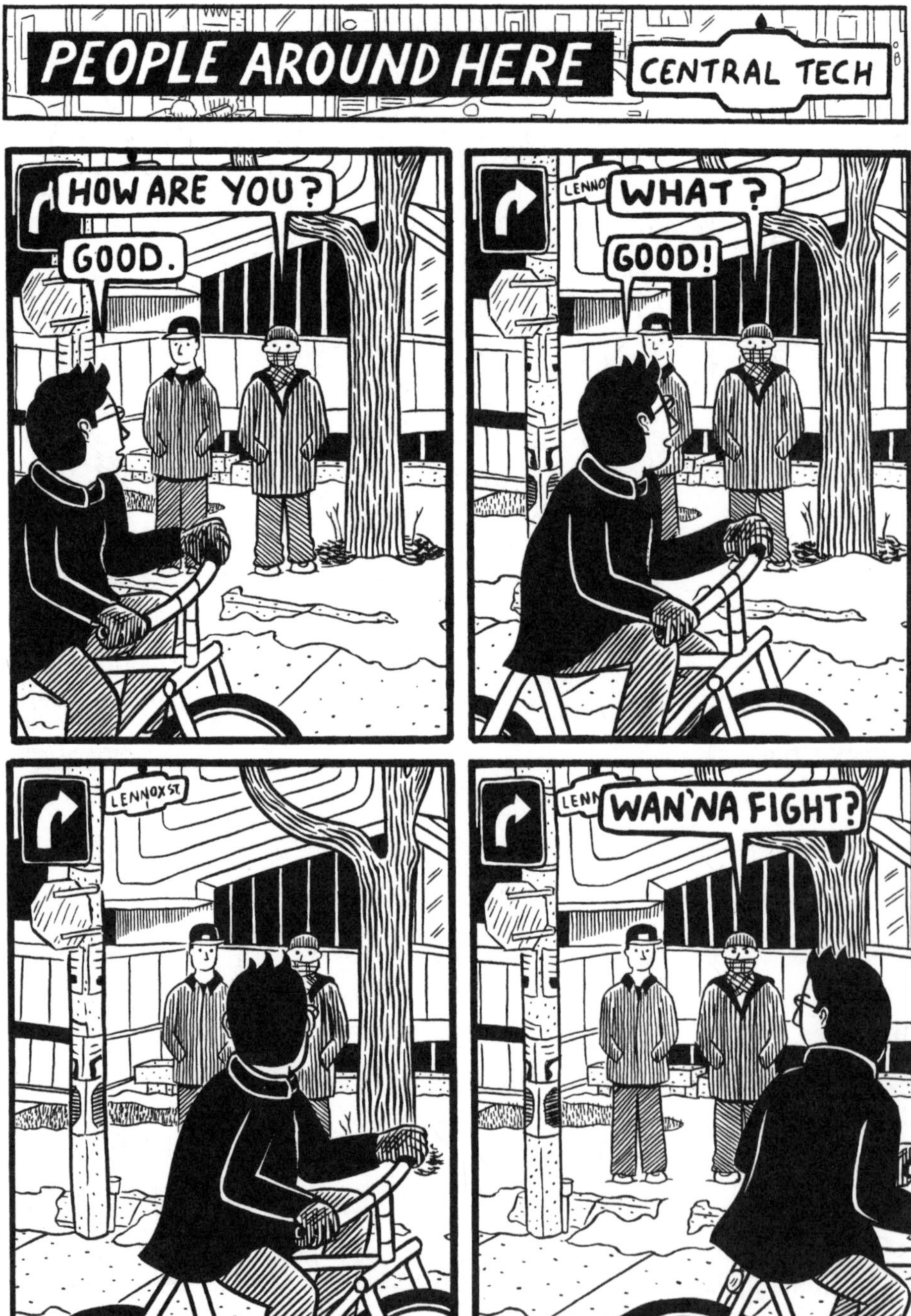
PEOPLE AROUND HERE
CENTRAL TECH
HOW ARE YOU?
GOOD.
WHAT?
GOOD!
LENNOX ST.
WAN'NA FIGHT?

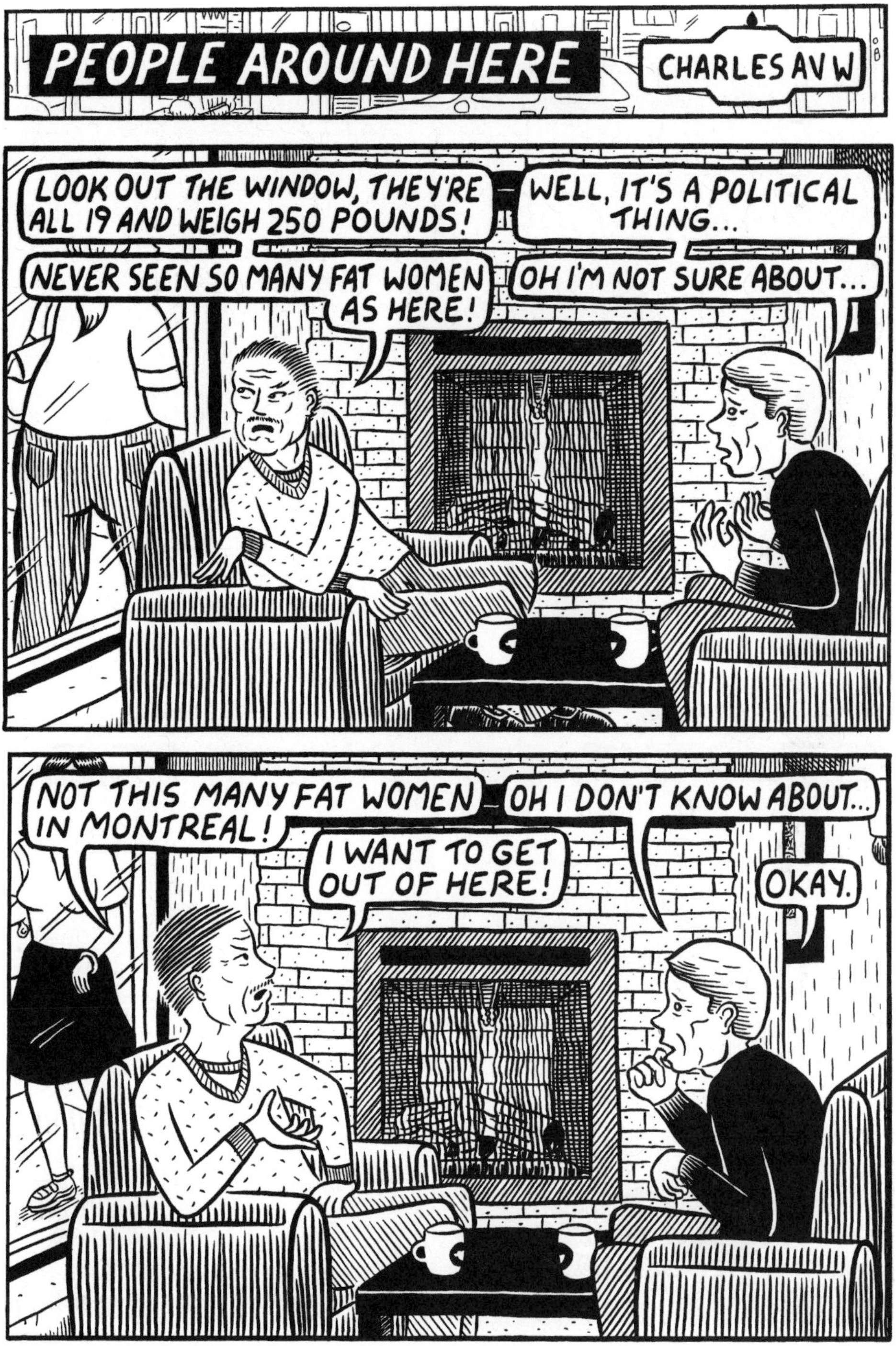
PEOPLE AROUND HERE
CHARLES AV W
LOOK OUT THE WINDOW, THEY'RE ALL 19 AND WEIGH 250 POUNDS!
NEVER SEEN SO MANY FAT WOMEN AS HERE!
WELL, IT'S A POLITICAL THING...
OH I'M NOT SURE ABOUT...
NOT THIS MANY FAT WOMEN IN MONTREAL!
I WANT TO GET OUT OF HERE!
OH I DON'T KNOW ABOUT...
OKAY.

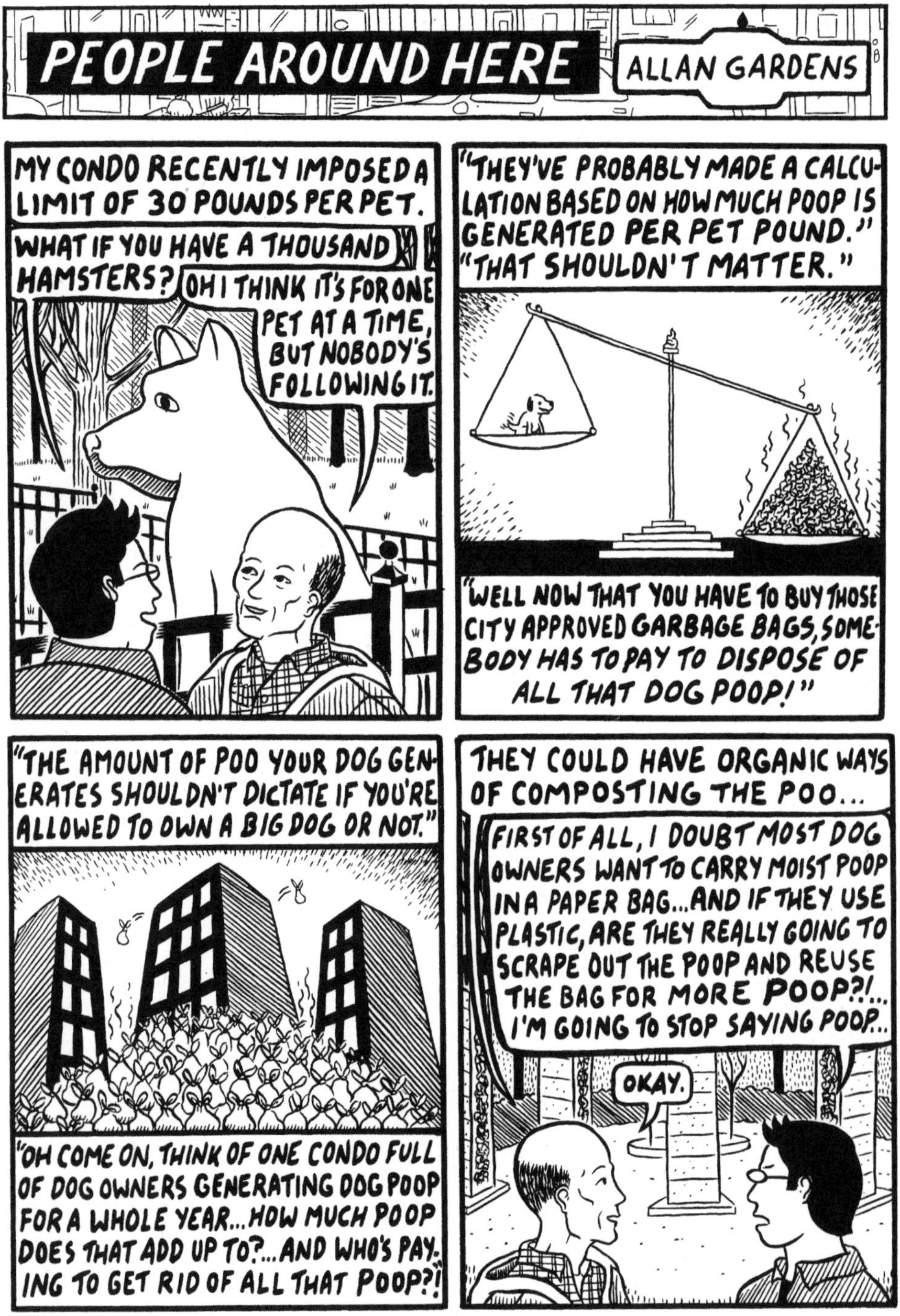
PEOPLE AROUND HERE
ALLAN GARDENS
MY CONDO RECENTLY IMPOSED A LIMIT OF 30 POUNDS PER PET.
WHAT IF YOU HAVE A THOUSAND HAMSTERS?
OH I THINK IT'S FOR ONE PET AT A TIME, BUT NOBODY'S FOLLOWING IT.
"THEY'VE PROBABLY MADE A CALCULATION BASED ON HOW MUCH POOP IS GENERATED PER PET POUND."
"THAT SHOULDN'T MATTER."
"WELL NOW THAT YOU HAVE TO BUY THOSE CITY APPROVED GARBAGE BAGS, SOMEBODY HAS TO PAY TO DISPOSE OF ALL THAT DOG POOP!"
"THE AMOUNT OF POO YOUR DOG GENERATES SHOULDN'T DICTATE IF YOU'RE ALLOWED TO OWN A BIG DOG OR NOT."
"OH COME ON, THINK OF ONE CONDO FULL OF DOG OWNERS GENERATING DOG POOP FOR A WHOLE YEAR... HOW MUCH POOP DOES THAT ADD UP TO?... AND WHO'S PAYING TO GET RID OF ALL THAT POOP?!
THEY COULD HAVE ORGANIC WAYS OF COMPOSTING THE POO...
FIRST OF ALL, I DOUBT MOST DOG OWNERS WANT TO CARRY MOIST POOP IN A PAPER BAG... AND IF THEY USE PLASTIC, ARE THEY REALLY GOING TO SCRAPE OUT THE POOP AND REUSE THE BAG FOR MORE POOP?!... I'M GOING TO STOP SAYING POOP...
OKAY.

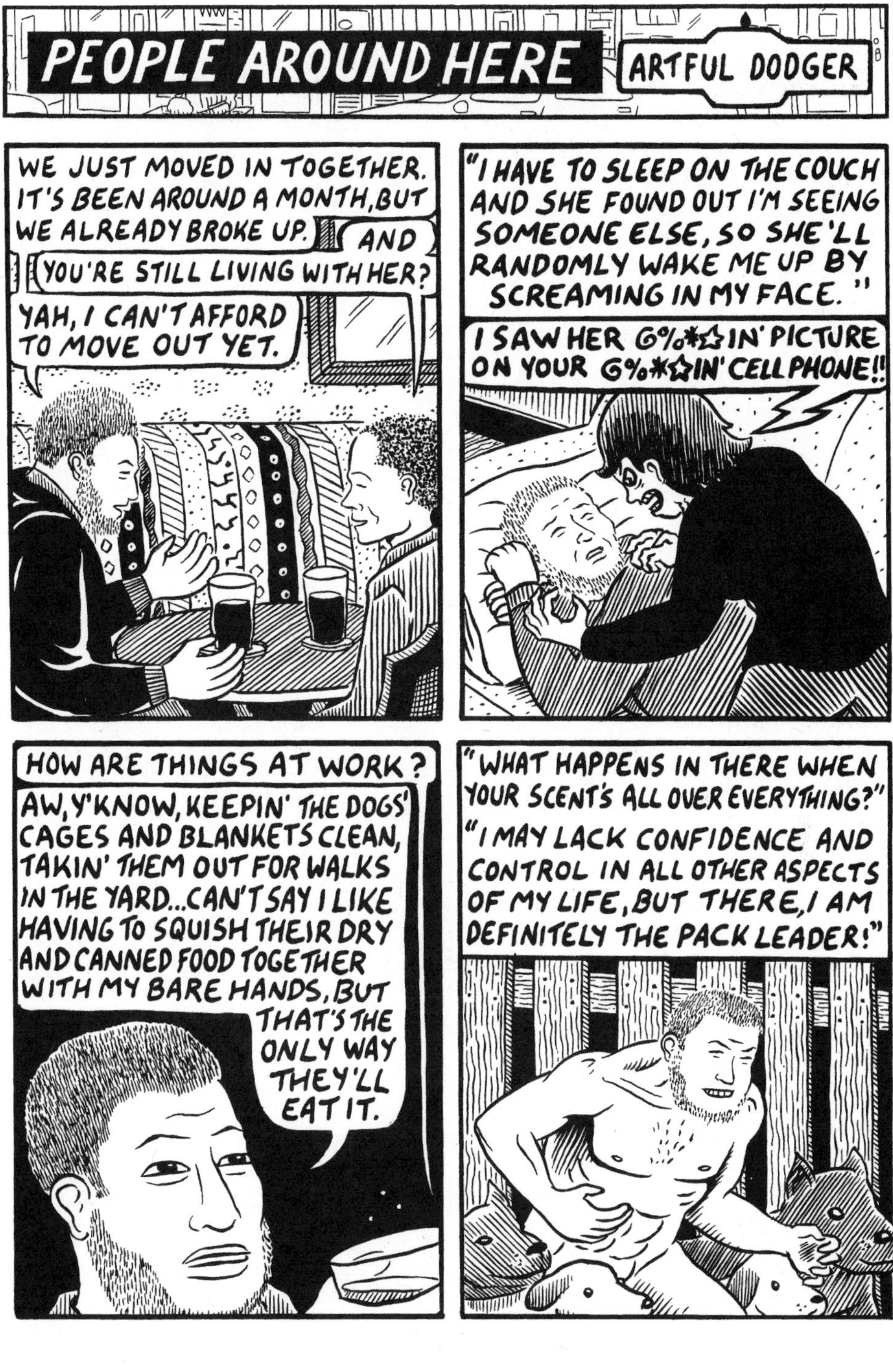
PEOPLE AROUND HERE
ARTFUL DODGER
WE JUST MOVED IN TOGETHER. IT'S BEEN AROUND A MONTH, BUT WE ALREADY BROKE UP.
AND YOU'RE STILL LIVING WITH HER?
YAH, I CAN'T AFFORD TO MOVE OUT YET.
"I HAVE TO SLEEP ON THE COUCH AND SHE FOUND OUT I'M SEEING SOMEONE ELSE, SO SHE'LL RANDOMLY WAKE ME UP BY SCREAMING IN MY FACE."
I SAW HER G%*✩IN' PICTURE ON YOUR G%*✩IN' CELL PHONE!!
HOW ARE THINGS AT WORK?
AW, Y'KNOW, KEEPIN' THE DOGS' CAGES AND BLANKETS CLEAN, TAKIN' THEM OUT FOR WALKS IN THE YARD...CAN'T SAY I LIKE HAVING TO SQUISH THEIR DRY AND CANNED FOOD TOGETHER WITH MY BARE HANDS, BUT THAT'S THE ONLY WAY THEY'LL EAT IT.
"WHAT HAPPENS IN THERE WHEN YOUR SCENT'S ALL OVER EVERYTHING?"
"I MAY LACK CONFIDENCE AND CONTROL IN ALL OTHER ASPECTS OF MY LIFE, BUT THERE, I AM DEFINITELY THE PACK LEADER!"

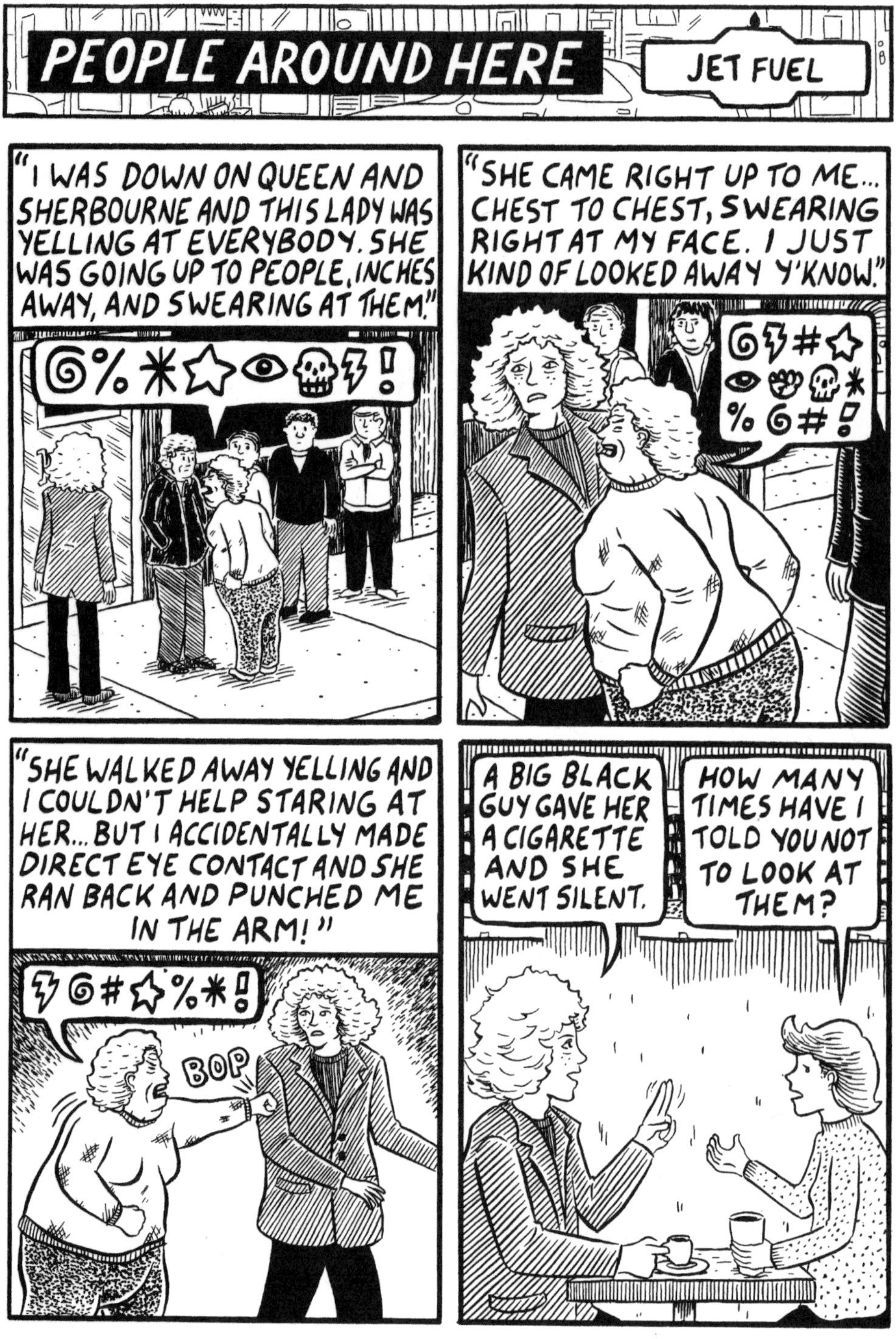
PEOPLE AROUND HERE
JET FUEL
"I WAS DOWN ON QUEEN AND SHERBOURNE AND THIS LADY WAS YELLING AT EVERYBODY. SHE WAS GOING UP TO PEOPLE, INCHES AWAY, AND SWEARING AT THEM."
"SHE CAME RIGHT UP TO ME... CHEST TO CHEST, SWEARING RIGHT AT MY FACE. I JUST KIND OF LOOKED AWAY Y'KNOW."
"SHE WALKED AWAY YELLING AND I COULDN'T HELP STARING AT HER... BUT I ACCIDENTALLY MADE DIRECT EYE CONTACT AND SHE RAN BACK AND PUNCHED ME IN THE ARM!"
BOP
A BIG BLACK GUY GAVE HER A CIGARETTE AND SHE WENT SILENT.
HOW MANY TIMES HAVE I TOLD YOU NOT TO LOOK AT THEM?

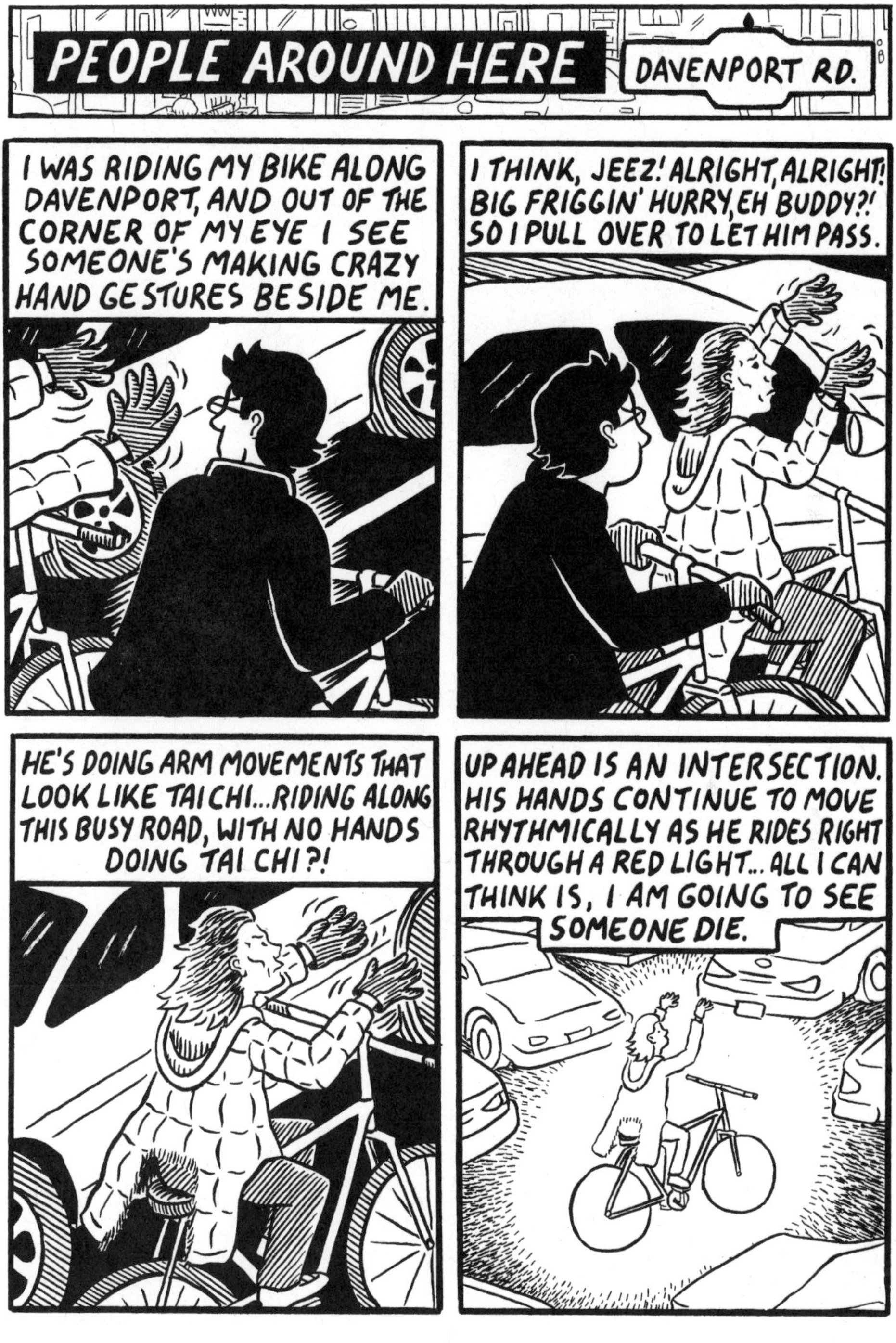
PEOPLE AROUND HERE
DAVENPORT RD.
I WAS RIDING MY BIKE ALONG DAVENPORT, AND OUT OF THE CORNER OF MY EYE I SEE SOMEONE'S MAKING CRAZY HAND GESTURES BESIDE ME.
I THINK, JEEZ! ALRIGHT, ALRIGHT! BIG FRIGGIN' HURRY, EH BUDDY?! SO I PULL OVER TO LET HIM PASS.
HE'S DOING ARM MOVEMENTS THAT LOOK LIKE TAI CHI... RIDING ALONG THIS BUSY ROAD, WITH NO HANDS DOING TAI CHI?!
UP AHEAD IS AN INTERSECTION. HIS HANDS CONTINUE TO MOVE RHYTHMICALLY AS HE RIDES RIGHT THROUGH A RED LIGHT... ALL I CAN THINK IS, I AM GOING TO SEE SOMEONE DIE.

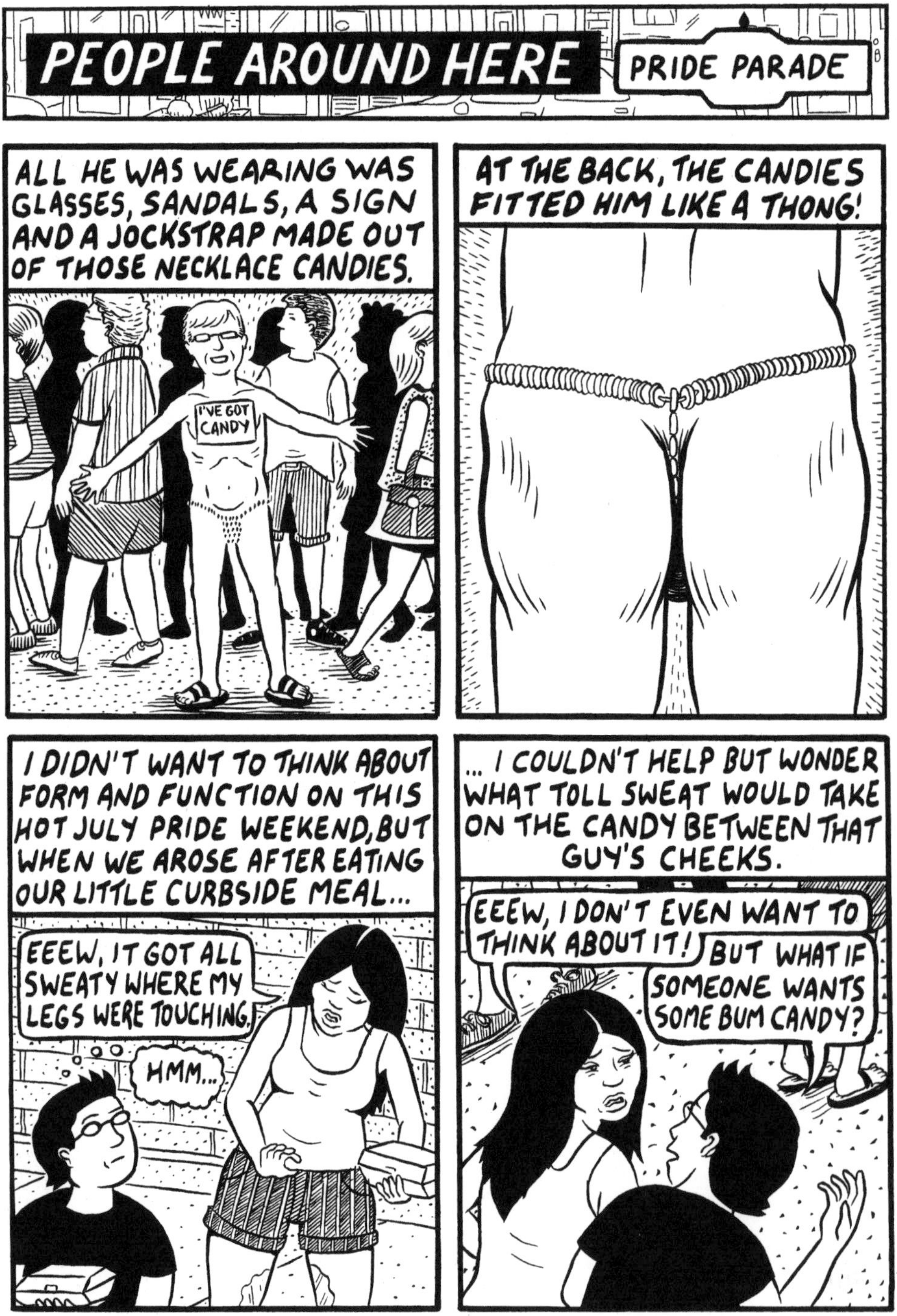
PEOPLE AROUND HERE
PRIDE PARADE
ALL HE WAS WEARING WAS GLASSES, SANDALS, A SIGN AND A JOCKSTRAP MADE OUT OF THOSE NECKLACE CANDIES.
I'VE GOT CANDY
AT THE BACK, THE CANDIES FITTED HIM LIKE A THONG!
I DIDN'T WANT TO THINK ABOUT FORM AND FUNCTION ON THIS HOT JULY PRIDE WEEKEND, BUT WHEN WE AROSE AFTER EATING OUR LITTLE CURBSIDE MEAL...
EEEW, IT GOT ALL SWEATY WHERE MY LEGS WERE TOUCHING.
HMM...
... I COULDN'T HELP BUT WONDER WHAT TOLL SWEAT WOULD TAKE ON THE CANDY BETWEEN THAT GUY'S CHEEKS.
EEEW, I DON'T EVEN WANT TO THINK ABOUT IT!
BUT WHAT IF SOMEONE WANTS SOME BUM CANDY?

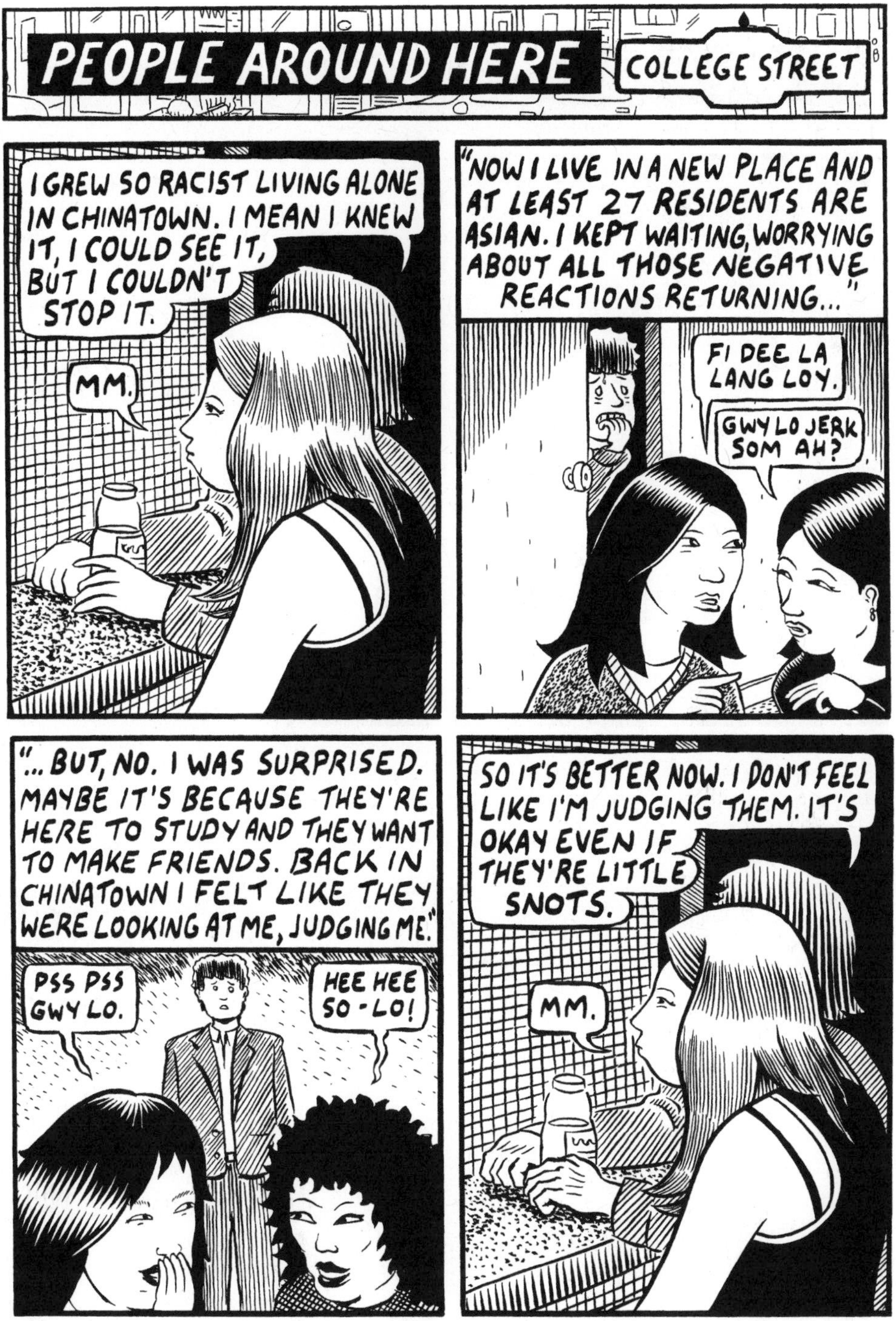
PEOPLE AROUND HERE
COLLEGE STREET
I GREW SO RACIST LIVING ALONE IN CHINATOWN. I MEAN I KNEW IT, I COULD SEE IT, BUT I COULDN'T STOP IT.
MM.
"NOW I LIVE IN A NEW PLACE AND AT LEAST 27 RESIDENTS ARE ASIAN. I KEPT WAITING, WORRYING ABOUT ALL THOSE NEGATIVE REACTIONS RETURNING..."
FI DEE LA LANG LOY.
GWY LO JERK SOM AH?
"...BUT, NO. I WAS SURPRISED. MAYBE IT'S BECAUSE THEY'RE HERE TO STUDY AND THEY WANT TO MAKE FRIENDS. BACK IN CHINATOWN I FELT LIKE THEY WERE LOOKING AT ME, JUDGING ME."
PSS PSS GWY LO.
HEE HEE SO-LO!
SO IT'S BETTER NOW. I DON'T FEEL LIKE I'M JUDGING THEM. IT'S OKAY EVEN IF THEY'RE LITTLE SNOTS.
MM.

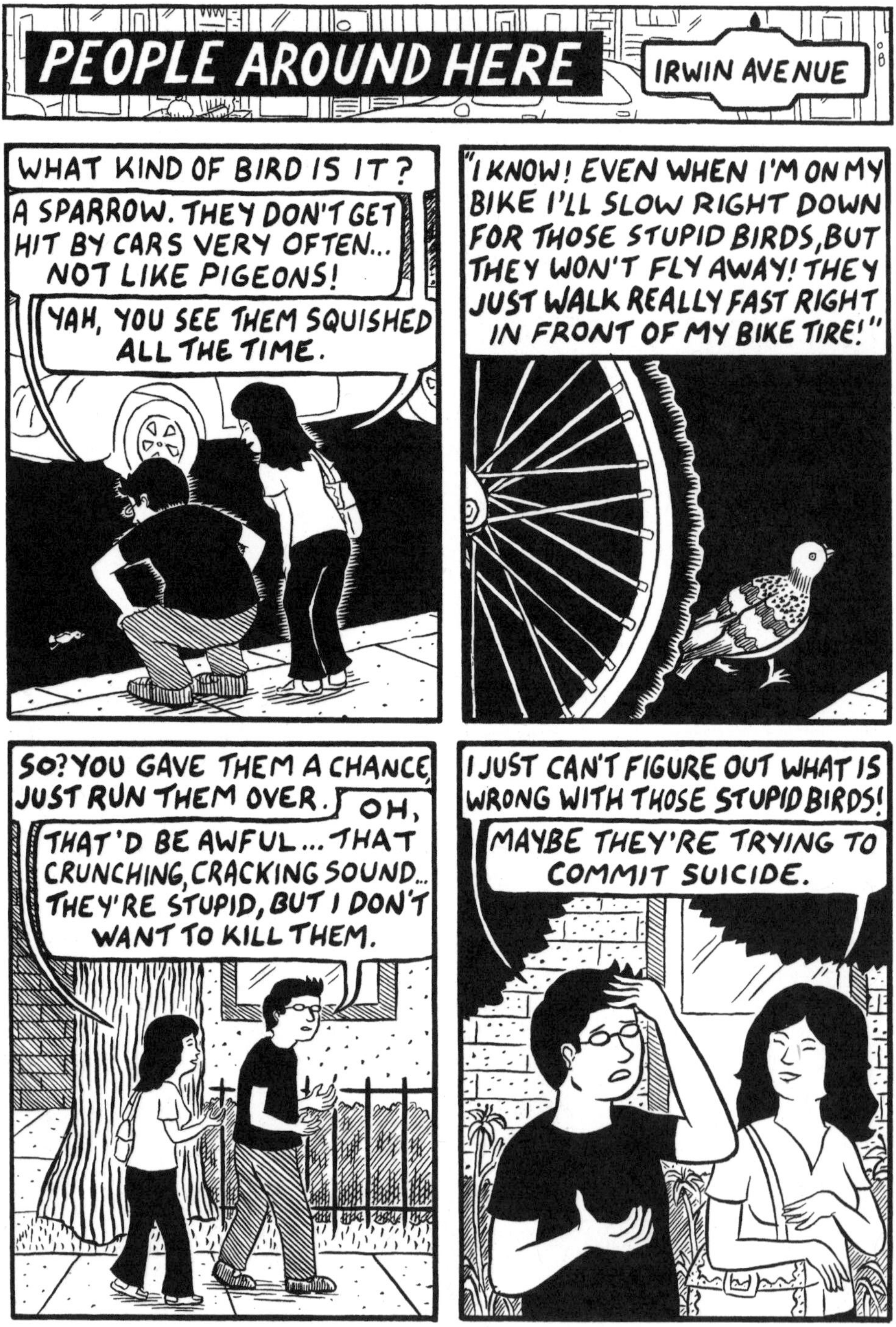
PEOPLE AROUND HERE
IRWIN AVENUE
WHAT KIND OF BIRD IS IT?
A SPARROW. THEY DON'T GET HIT BY CARS VERY OFTEN... NOT LIKE PIGEONS!
YAH, YOU SEE THEM SQUISHED ALL THE TIME.
"I KNOW! EVEN WHEN I'M ON MY BIKE I'LL SLOW RIGHT DOWN FOR THOSE STUPID BIRDS, BUT THEY WON'T FLY AWAY! THEY JUST WALK REALLY FAST RIGHT IN FRONT OF MY BIKE TIRE!"
SO? YOU GAVE THEM A CHANCE, JUST RUN THEM OVER.
OH, THAT'D BE AWFUL... THAT CRUNCHING, CRACKING SOUND... THEY'RE STUPID, BUT I DON'T WANT TO KILL THEM.
I JUST CAN'T FIGURE OUT WHAT IS WRONG WITH THOSE STUPID BIRDS!
MAYBE THEY'RE TRYING TO COMMIT SUICIDE.

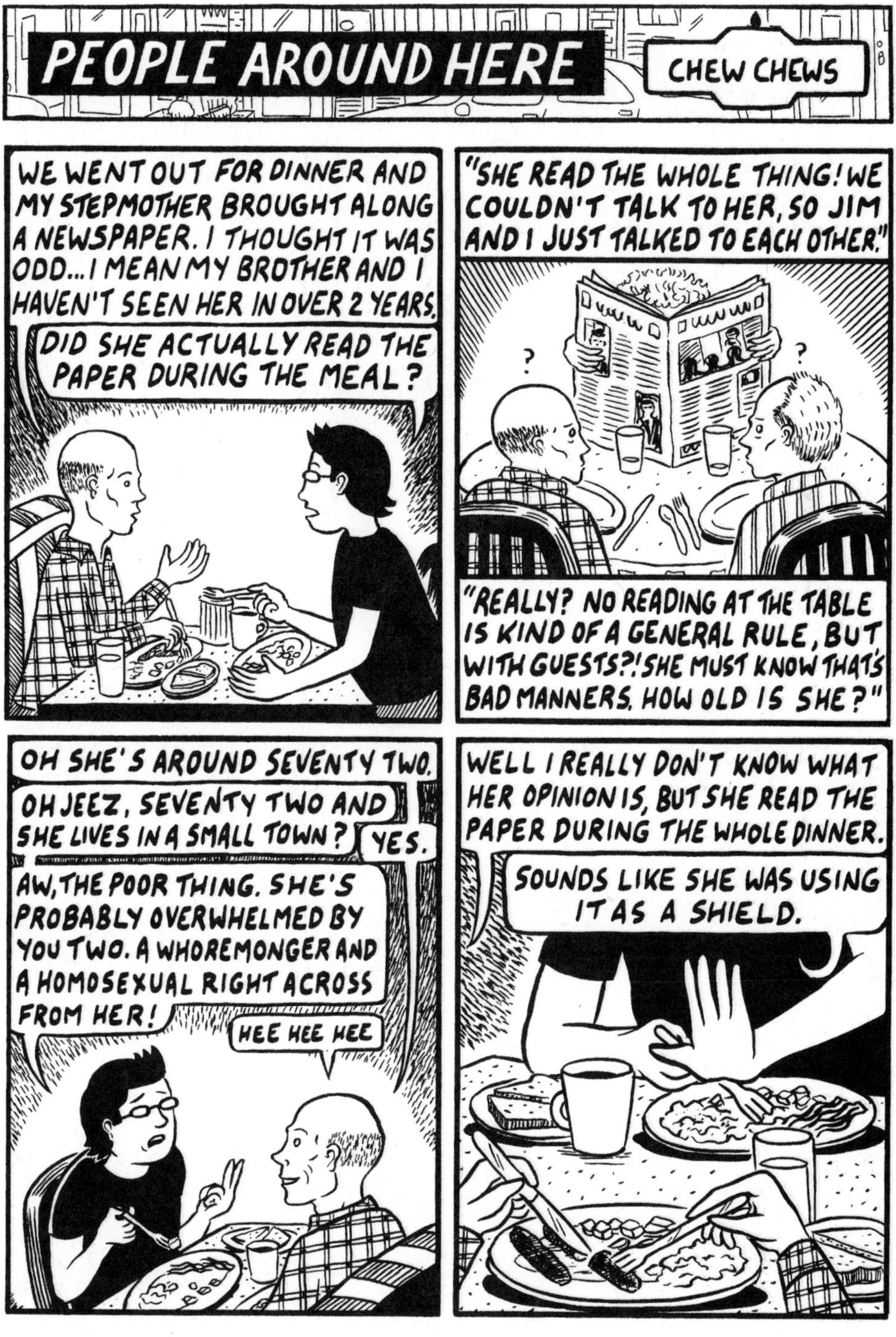
PEOPLE AROUND HERE
CHEW CHEWS
WE WENT OUT FOR DINNER AND MY STEPMOTHER BROUGHT ALONG A NEWSPAPER. I THOUGHT IT WAS ODD... I MEAN MY BROTHER AND I HAVEN'T SEEN HER IN OVER 2 YEARS.
DID SHE ACTUALLY READ THE PAPER DURING THE MEAL?
"SHE READ THE WHOLE THING! WE COULDN'T TALK TO HER, SO JIM AND I JUST TALKED TO EACH OTHER."
?
?
"REALLY? NO READING AT THE TABLE IS KIND OF A GENERAL RULE, BUT WITH GUESTS?! SHE MUST KNOW THAT'S BAD MANNERS. HOW OLD IS SHE?"
OH SHE'S AROUND SEVENTY TWO.
OH JEEZ, SEVENTY TWO AND SHE LIVES IN A SMALL TOWN?
YES.
AW, THE POOR THING. SHE'S PROBABLY OVERWHELMED BY YOU TWO. A WHOREMONGER AND A HOMOSEXUAL RIGHT ACROSS FROM HER!
HEE HEE HEE
WELL I REALLY DON'T KNOW WHAT HER OPINION IS, BUT SHE READ THE PAPER DURING THE WHOLE DINNER.
SOUNDS LIKE SHE WAS USING IT AS A SHIELD.

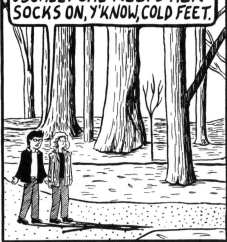

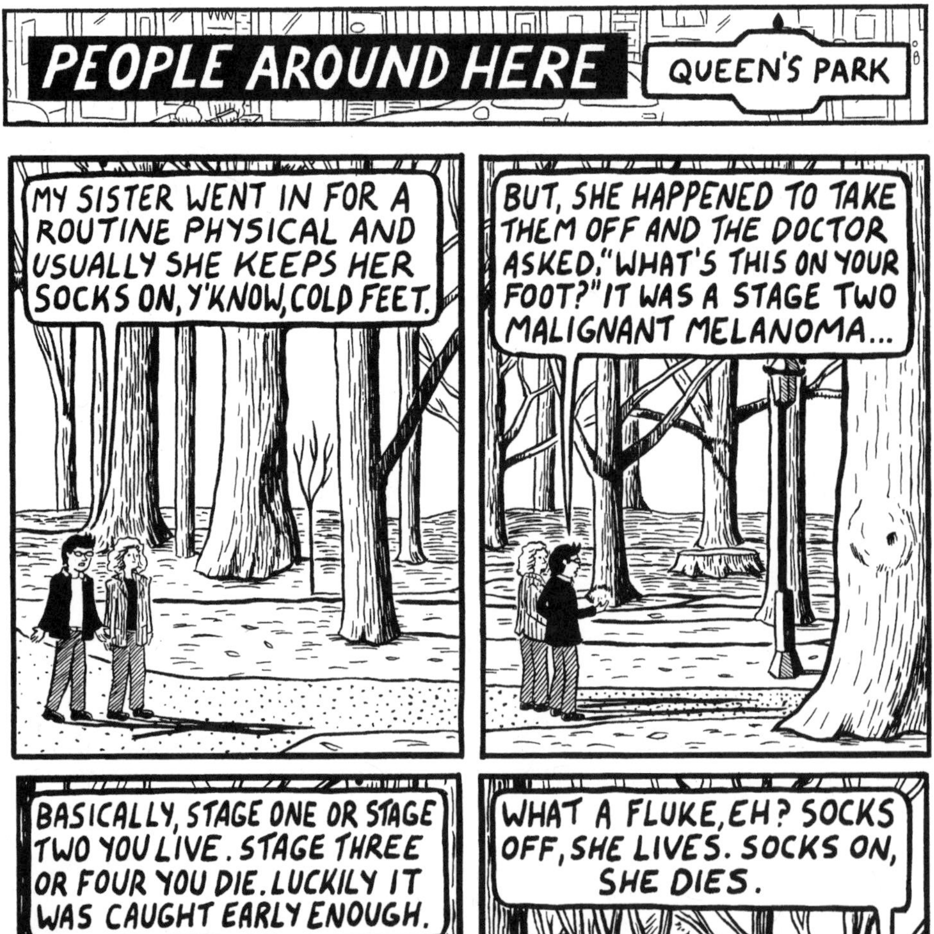

PEOPLE AROUND HERE
QUEEN'S PARK
MY SISTER WENT IN FOR A ROUTINE PHYSICAL AND USUALLY SHE KEEPS HER SOCKS ON, Y'KNOW, COLD FEET.
BUT, SHE HAPPENED TO TAKE THEM OFF AND THE DOCTOR ASKED, "WHAT'S THIS ON YOUR FOOT?" IT WAS A STAGE TWO MALIGNANT MELANOMA...
BASICALLY, STAGE ONE OR STAGE TWO YOU LIVE. STAGE THREE OR FOUR YOU DIE. LUCKILY IT WAS CAUGHT EARLY ENOUGH.
WHAT A FLUKE, EH? SOCKS OFF, SHE LIVES. SOCKS ON, SHE DIES.

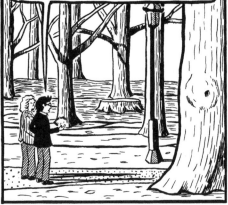

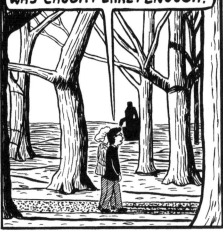

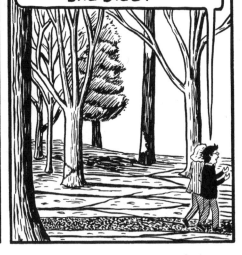

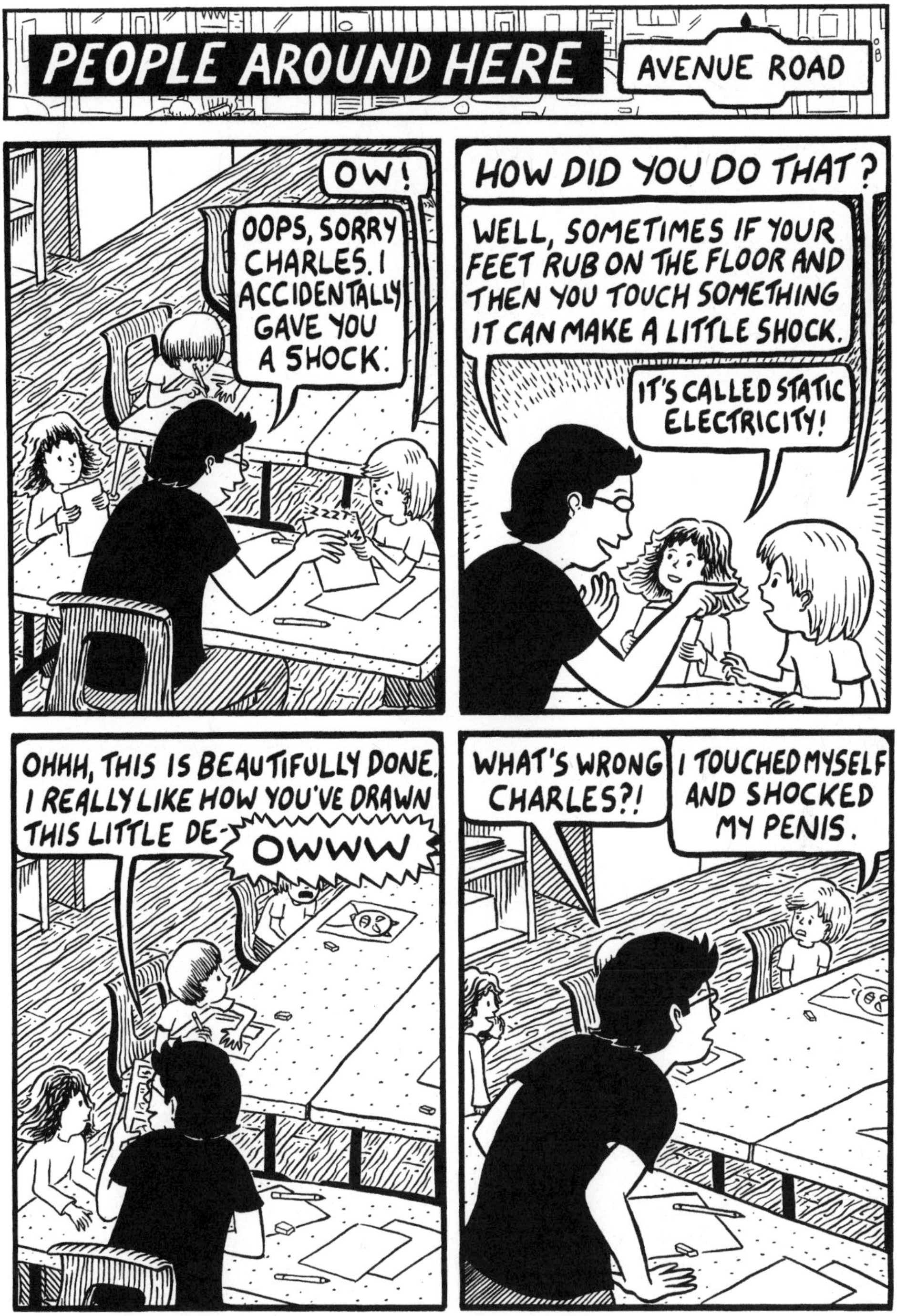
PEOPLE AROUND HERE
AVENUE ROAD
OW!
OOPS, SORRY CHARLES. I ACCIDENTALLY GAVE YOU A SHOCK.
HOW DID YOU DO THAT?
WELL, SOMETIMES IF YOUR FEET RUB ON THE FLOOR AND THEN YOU TOUCH SOMETHING IT CAN MAKE A LITTLE SHOCK.
IT'S CALLED STATIC ELECTRICITY!
OHHH, THIS IS BEAUTIFULLY DONE. I REALLY LIKE HOW YOU'VE DRAWN THIS LITTLE DE-
OWWW
WHAT'S WRONG CHARLES?!
I TOUCHED MYSELF AND SHOCKED MY PENIS.

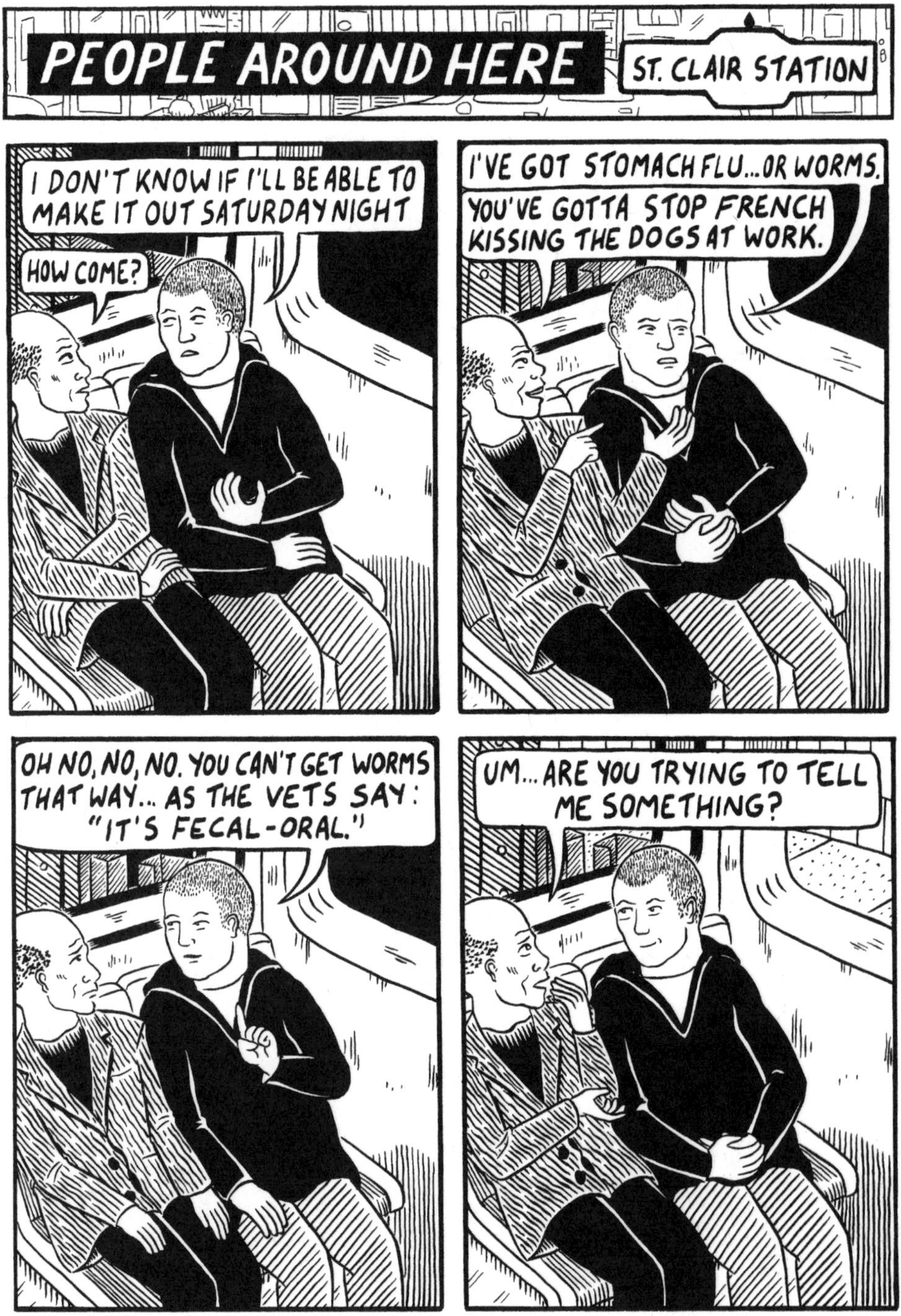
PEOPLE AROUND HERE
ST. CLAIR STATION
I DON'T KNOW IF I'LL BE ABLE TO MAKE IT OUT SATURDAY NIGHT
HOW COME?
I'VE GOT STOMACH FLU...OR WORMS.
YOU'VE GOTTA STOP FRENCH KISSING THE DOGS AT WORK.
OH NO, NO, NO. YOU CAN'T GET WORMS THAT WAY... AS THE VETS SAY: "IT'S FECAL-ORAL."
UM... ARE YOU TRYING TO TELL ME SOMETHING?

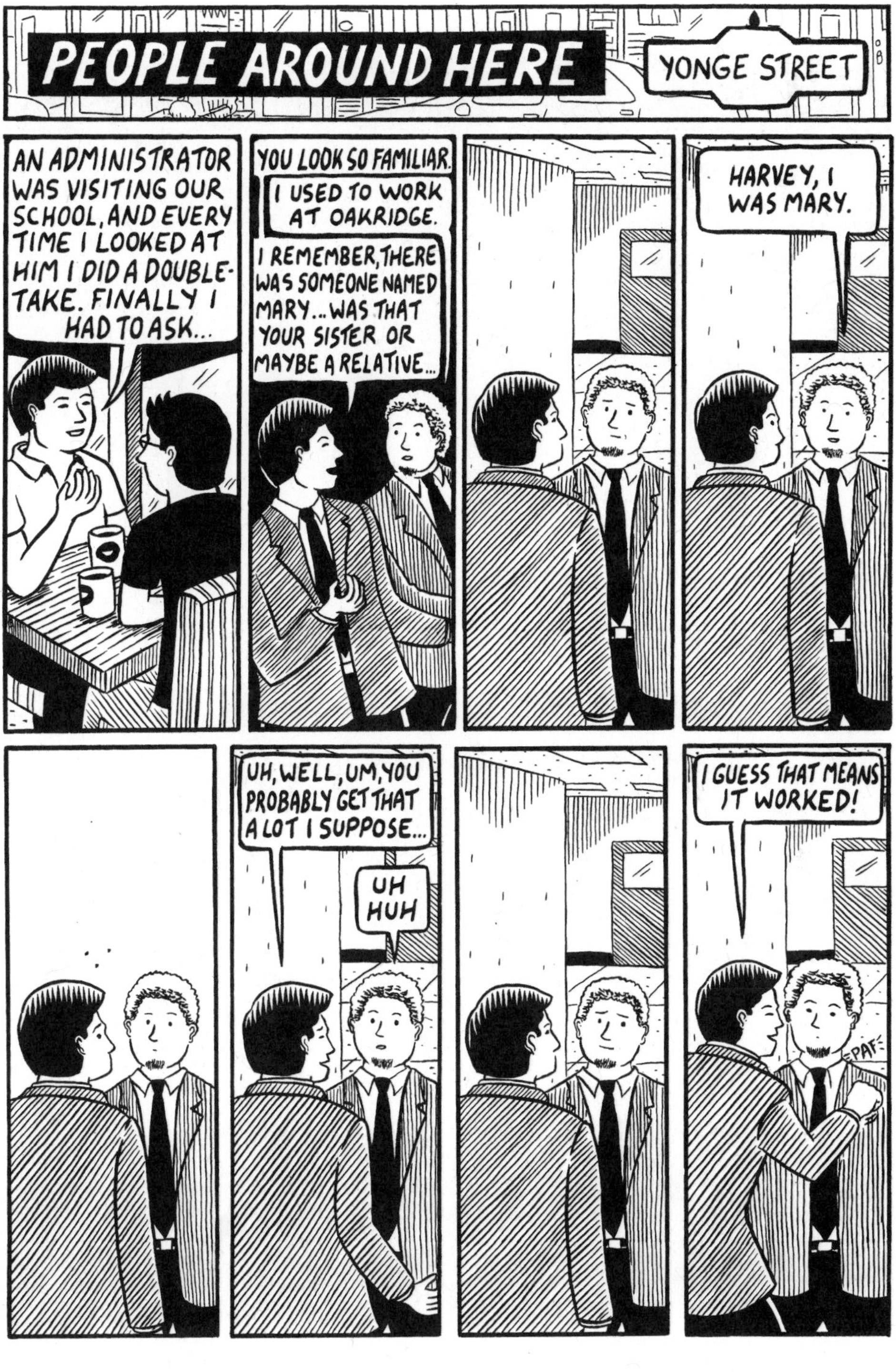
PEOPLE AROUND HERE
YONGE STREET
AN ADMINISTRATOR WAS VISITING OUR SCHOOL, AND EVERY TIME I LOOKED AT HIM I DID A DOUBLE-TAKE. FINALLY I HAD TO ASK...
YOU LOOK SO FAMILIAR.
I USED TO WORK AT OAKRIDGE.
I REMEMBER, THERE WAS SOMEONE NAMED MARY... WAS THAT YOUR SISTER OR MAYBE A RELATIVE...
HARVEY, I WAS MARY.
UH, WELL, UM, YOU PROBABLY GET THAT A LOT I SUPPOSE...
UH HUH
I GUESS THAT MEANS IT WORKED!
PAF

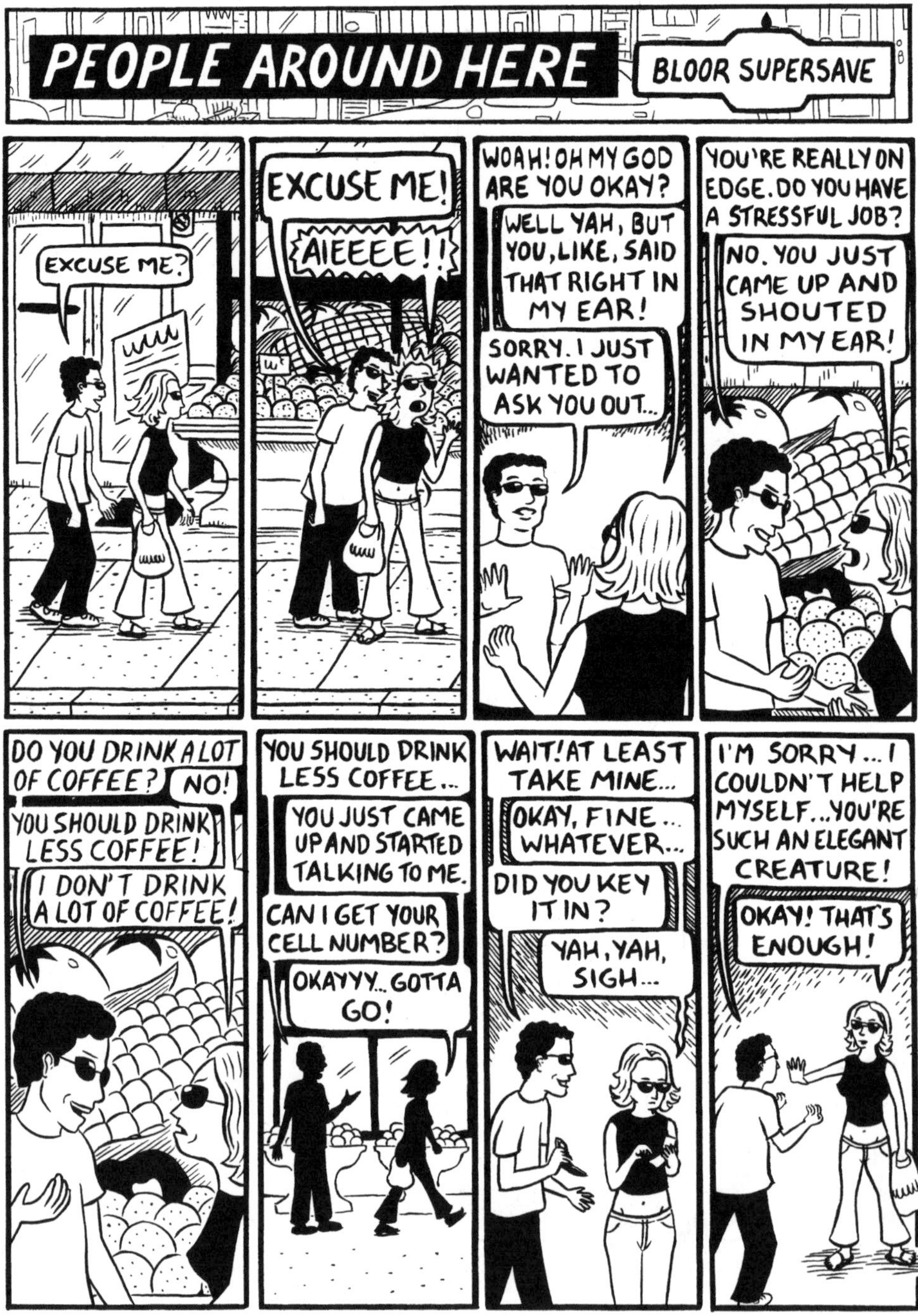
PEOPLE AROUND HERE
BLOOR SUPERSAVE
EXCUSE ME?
EXCUSE ME!
AIEEEE!!
WOAH! OH MY GOD ARE YOU OKAY?
WELL YAH, BUT YOU, LIKE, SAID THAT RIGHT IN MY EAR!
SORRY. I JUST WANTED TO ASK YOU OUT...
YOU'RE REALLY ON EDGE. DO YOU HAVE A STRESSFUL JOB?
NO. YOU JUST CAME UP AND SHOUTED IN MY EAR!
DO YOU DRINK A LOT OF COFFEE?
NO!
YOU SHOULD DRINK LESS COFFEE!
I DON'T DRINK A LOT OF COFFEE!
YOU SHOULD DRINK LESS COFFEE...
YOU JUST CAME UP AND STARTED TALKING TO ME.
CAN I GET YOUR CELL NUMBER?
OKAYYY... GOTTA GO!
WAIT! AT LEAST TAKE MINE...
OKAY, FINE... WHATEVER...
DID YOU KEY IT IN?
YAH, YAH, SIGH...
I'M SORRY... I COULDN'T HELP MYSELF... YOU'RE SUCH AN ELEGANT CREATURE!
OKAY! THAT'S ENOUGH!

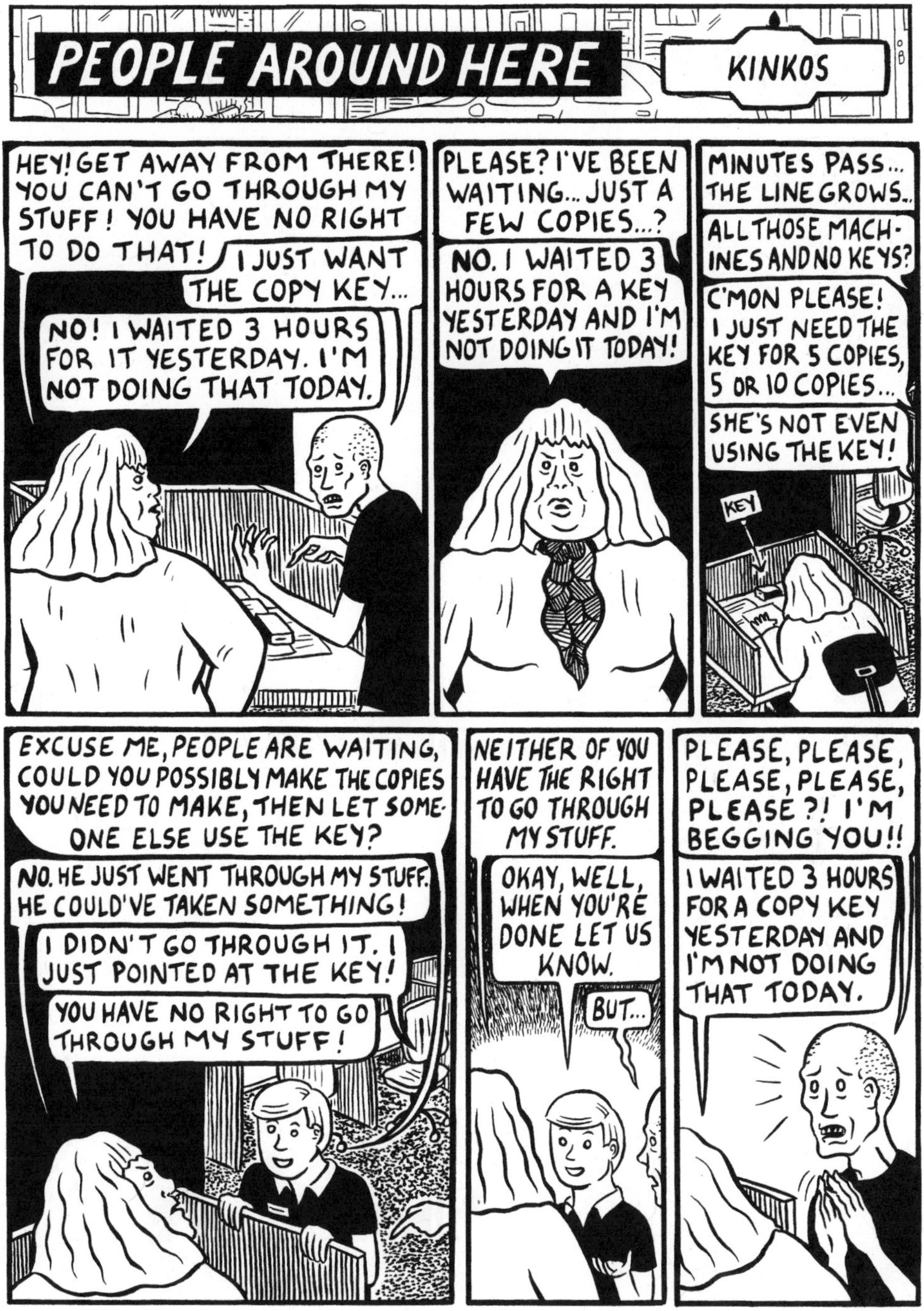
PEOPLE AROUND HERE
KINKOS
HEY! GET AWAY FROM THERE! YOU CAN'T GO THROUGH MY STUFF! YOU HAVE NO RIGHT TO DO THAT!
I JUST WANT THE COPY KEY...
NO! I WAITED 3 HOURS FOR IT YESTERDAY. I'M NOT DOING THAT TODAY.
PLEASE? I'VE BEEN WAITING... JUST A FEW COPIES...?
NO. I WAITED 3 HOURS FOR A KEY YESTERDAY AND I'M NOT DOING IT TODAY!
MINUTES PASS... THE LINE GROWS..
ALL THOSE MACH-INES AND NO KEYS?
C'MON PLEASE! I JUST NEED THE KEY FOR 5 COPIES, 5 OR 10 COPIES...
SHE'S NOT EVEN USING THE KEY!
KEY
EXCUSE ME, PEOPLE ARE WAITING, COULD YOU POSSIBLY MAKE THE COPIES YOU NEED TO MAKE, THEN LET SOME-ONE ELSE USE THE KEY?
NO. HE JUST WENT THROUGH MY STUFF. HE COULD'VE TAKEN SOMETHING!
I DIDN'T GO THROUGH IT. I JUST POINTED AT THE KEY!
YOU HAVE NO RIGHT TO GO THROUGH MY STUFF!
NEITHER OF YOU HAVE THE RIGHT TO GO THROUGH MY STUFF.
OKAY, WELL, WHEN YOU'RE DONE LET US KNOW.
BUT...
PLEASE, PLEASE, PLEASE, PLEASE, PLEASE?! I'M BEGGING YOU!!
I WAITED 3 HOURS FOR A COPY KEY YESTERDAY AND I'M NOT DOING THAT TODAY.

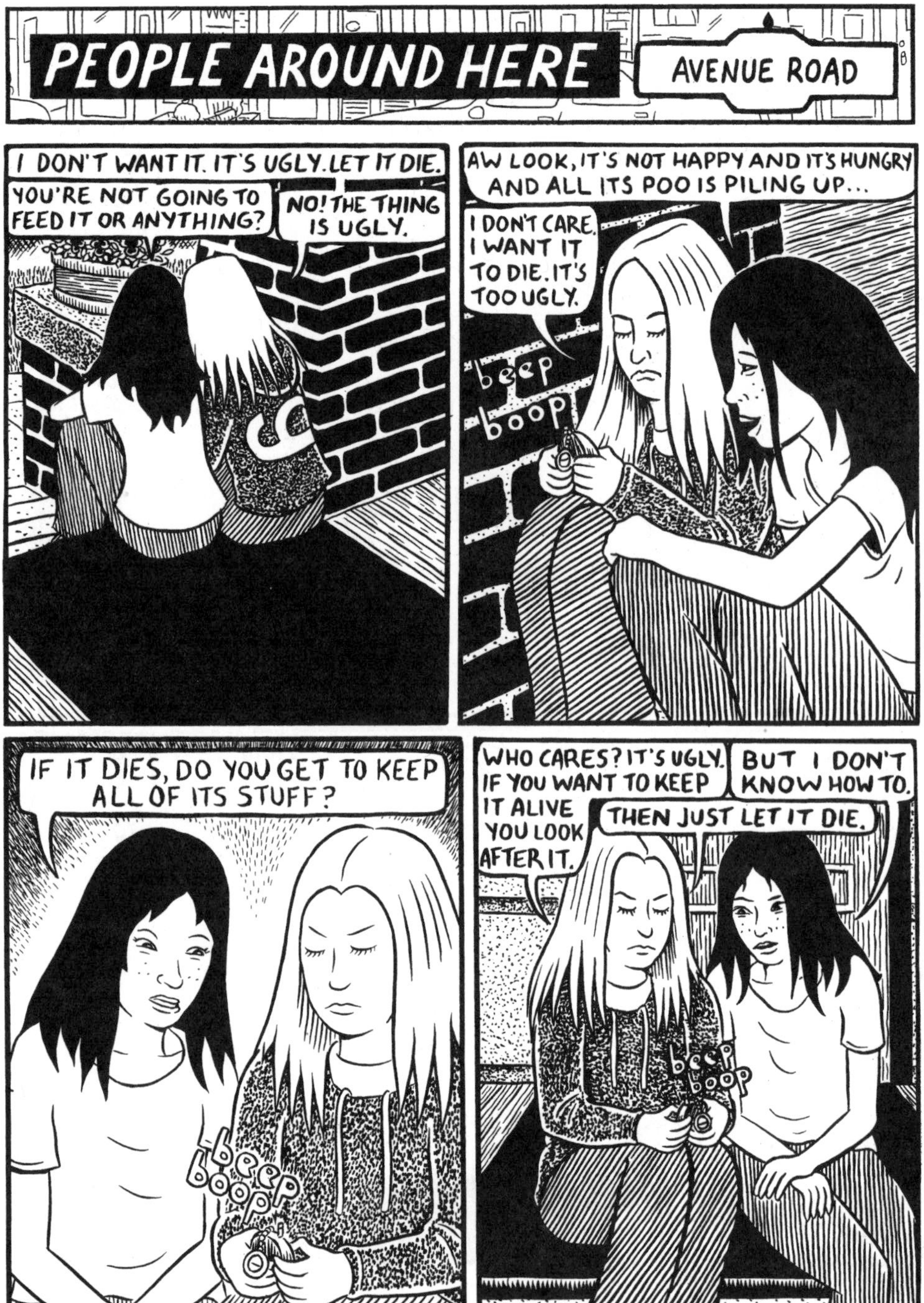

PEOPLE AROUND HERE
AVENUE ROAD
I DON'T WANT IT. IT'S UGLY. LET IT DIE.
YOU'RE NOT GOING TO FEED IT OR ANYTHING?
NO! THE THING IS UGLY.
AW LOOK, IT'S NOT HAPPY AND IT'S HUNGRY AND ALL ITS POO IS PILING UP...
I DON'T CARE. I WANT IT TO DIE. IT'S TOO UGLY.
beep
boop
IF IT DIES, DO YOU GET TO KEEP ALL OF ITS STUFF?
beep
boop
WHO CARES? IT'S UGLY. IF YOU WANT TO KEEP IT ALIVE YOU LOOK AFTER IT.
BUT I DON'T KNOW HOW TO.
THEN JUST LET IT DIE.
beep
boop

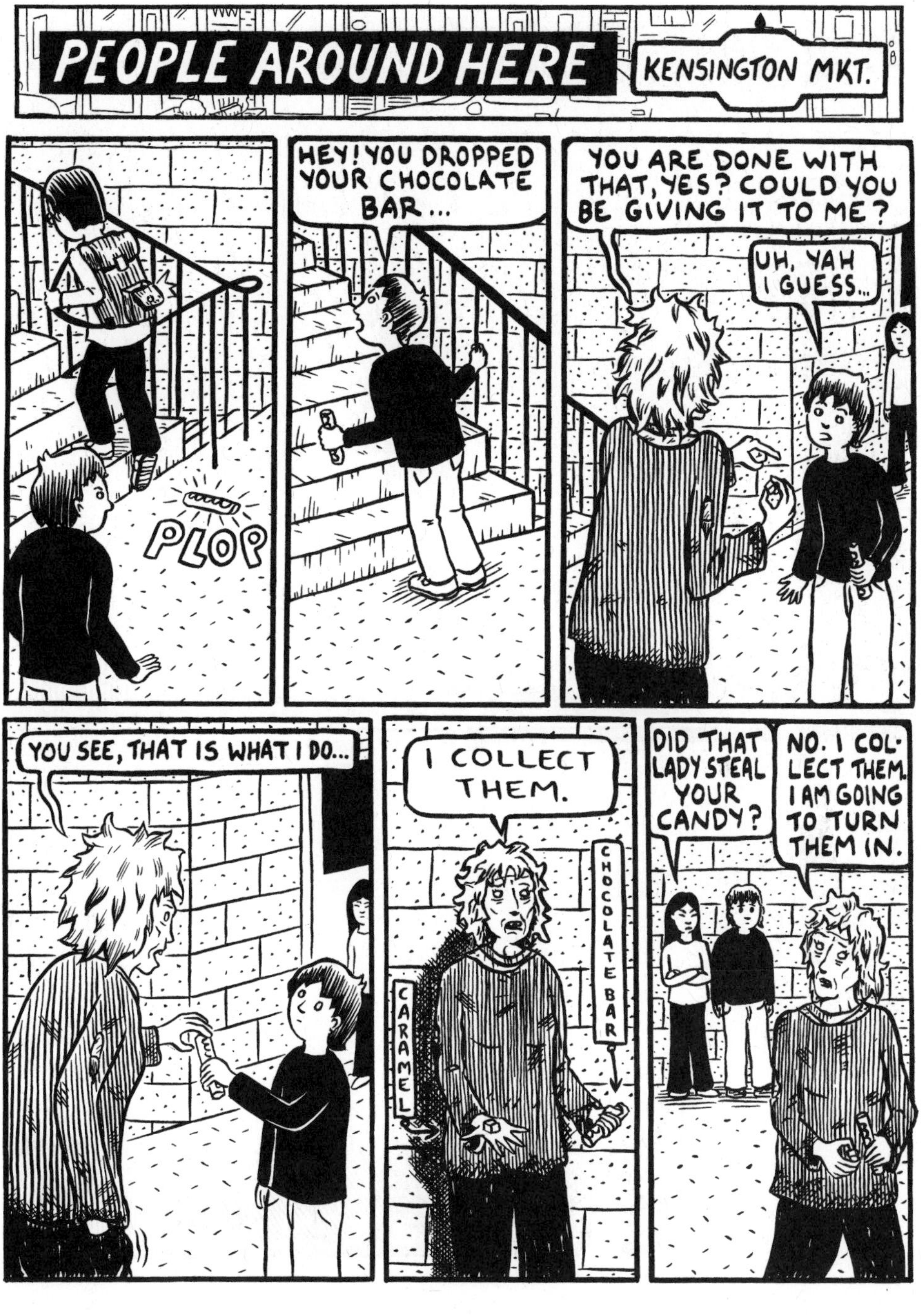
PEOPLE AROUND HERE
KENSINGTON MKT.
PLOP
HEY! YOU DROPPED YOUR CHOCOLATE BAR...
YOU ARE DONE WITH THAT, YES? COULD YOU BE GIVING IT TO ME?
UH, YAH I GUESS...
YOU SEE, THAT IS WHAT I DO...
I COLLECT THEM.
CARAMEL
CHOCOLATE BAR
DID THAT LADY STEAL YOUR CANDY?
NO. I COLLECT THEM. I AM GOING TO TURN THEM IN.

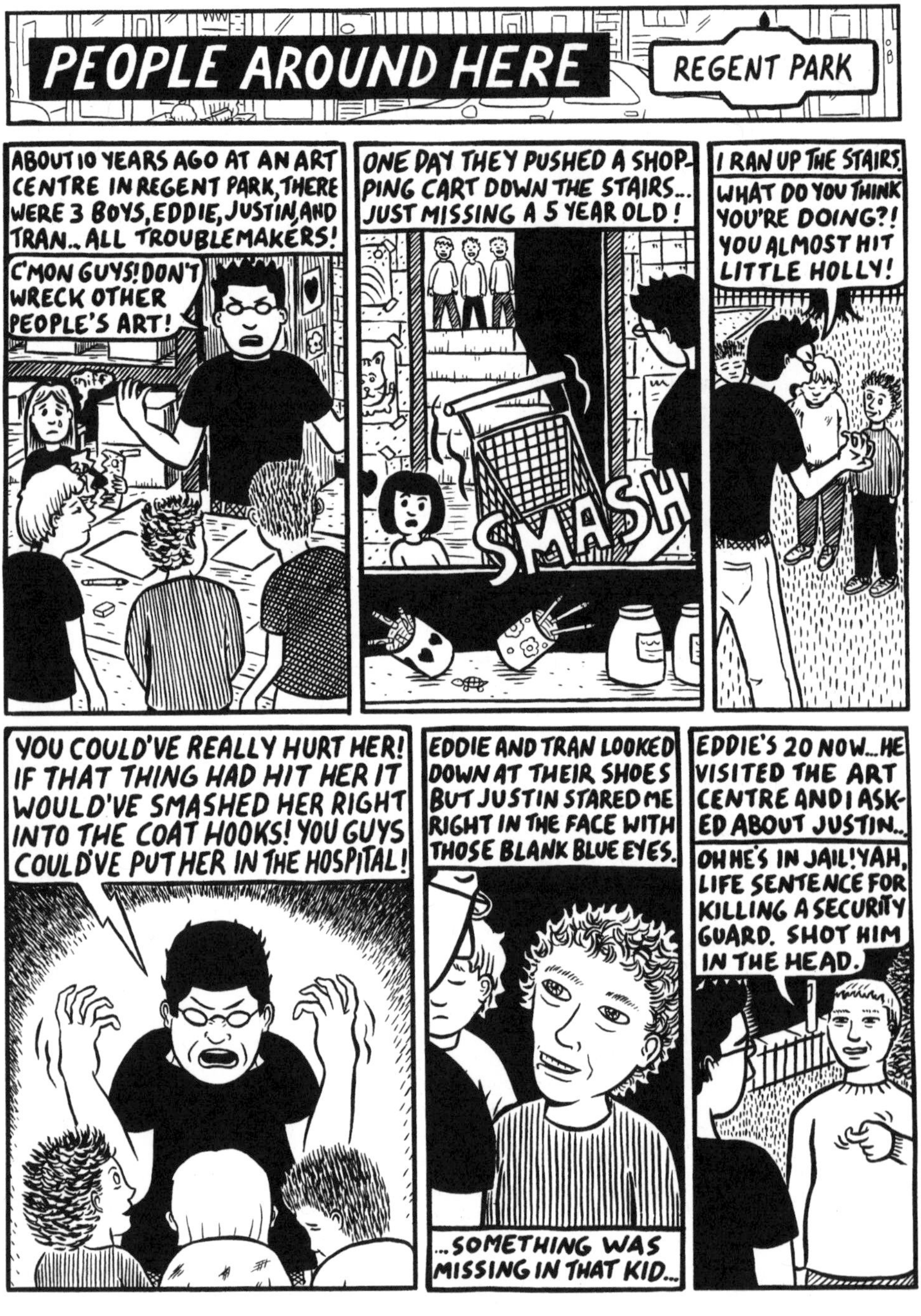
PEOPLE AROUND HERE
REGENT PARK
ABOUT 10 YEARS AGO AT AN ART CENTRE IN REGENT PARK, THERE WERE 3 BOYS, EDDIE, JUSTIN, AND TRAN.. ALL TROUBLEMAKERS!
C'MON GUYS! DON'T WRECK OTHER PEOPLE'S ART!
sniff
ONE DAY THEY PUSHED A SHOPPING CART DOWN THE STAIRS... JUST MISSING A 5 YEAR OLD!
SMASH
I RAN UP THE STAIRS.
WHAT DO YOU THINK YOU'RE DOING?! YOU ALMOST HIT LITTLE HOLLY!
YOU COULD'VE REALLY HURT HER! IF THAT THING HAD HIT HER IT WOULD'VE SMASHED HER RIGHT INTO THE COAT HOOKS! YOU GUYS COULD'VE PUT HER IN THE HOSPITAL!
EDDIE AND TRAN LOOKED DOWN AT THEIR SHOES BUT JUSTIN STARED ME RIGHT IN THE FACE WITH THOSE BLANK BLUE EYES.
...SOMETHING WAS MISSING IN THAT KID...
EDDIE'S 20 NOW... HE VISITED THE ART CENTRE AND I ASKED ABOUT JUSTIN...
OH HE'S IN JAIL! YAH, LIFE SENTENCE FOR KILLING A SECURITY GUARD. SHOT HIM IN THE HEAD.

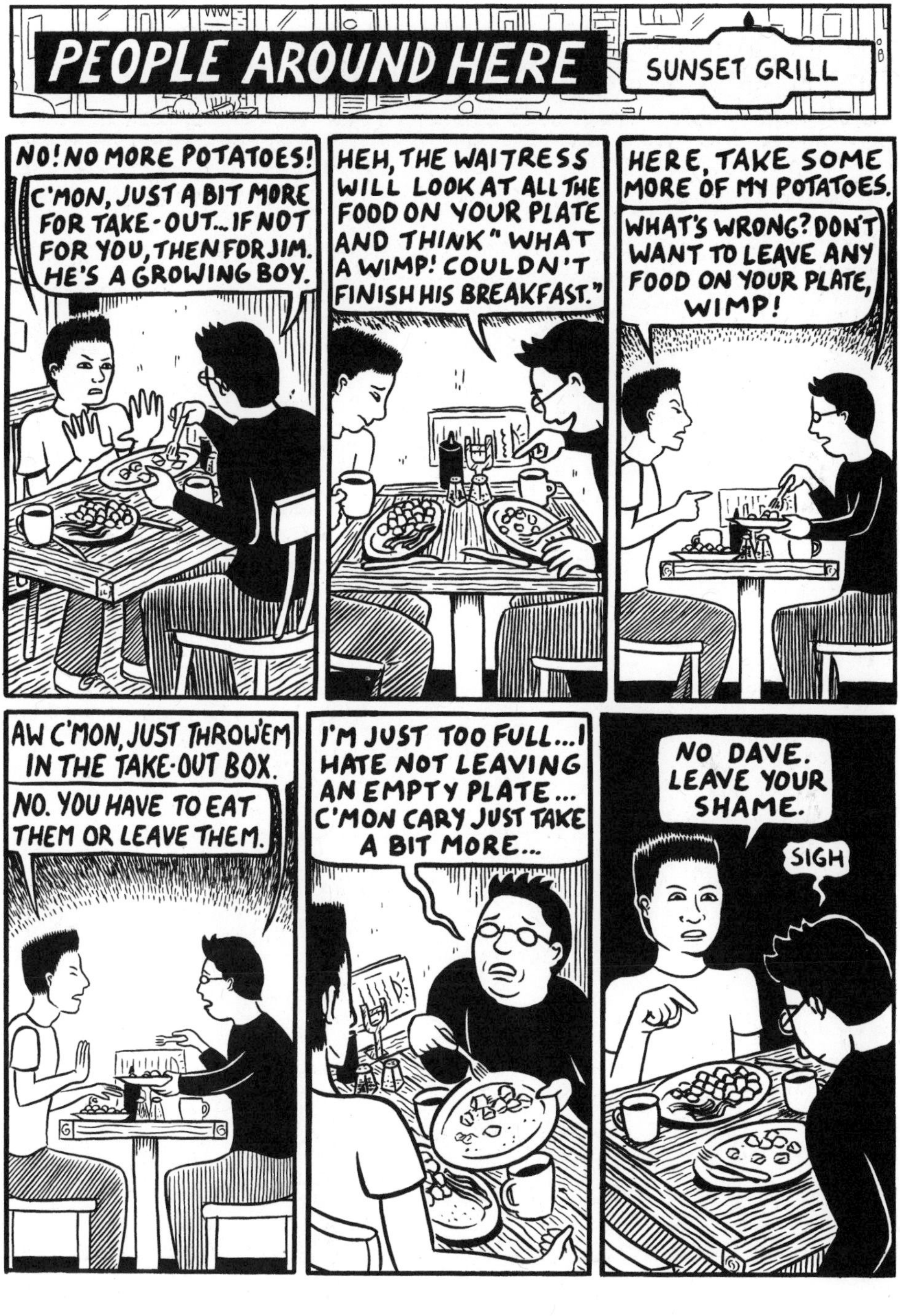

PEOPLE AROUND HERE
SUNSET GRILL
NO! NO MORE POTATOES!
C'MON, JUST A BIT MORE FOR TAKE-OUT... IF NOT FOR YOU, THEN FOR JIM. HE'S A GROWING BOY.
HEH, THE WAITRESS WILL LOOK AT ALL THE FOOD ON YOUR PLATE AND THINK "WHAT A WIMP! COULDN'T FINISH HIS BREAKFAST."
HERE, TAKE SOME MORE OF MY POTATOES.
WHAT'S WRONG? DON'T WANT TO LEAVE ANY FOOD ON YOUR PLATE, WIMP!
AW C'MON, JUST THROW 'EM IN THE TAKE-OUT BOX.
NO. YOU HAVE TO EAT THEM OR LEAVE THEM.
I'M JUST TOO FULL... I HATE NOT LEAVING AN EMPTY PLATE... C'MON CARY JUST TAKE A BIT MORE...
NO DAVE. LEAVE YOUR SHAME.
SIGH

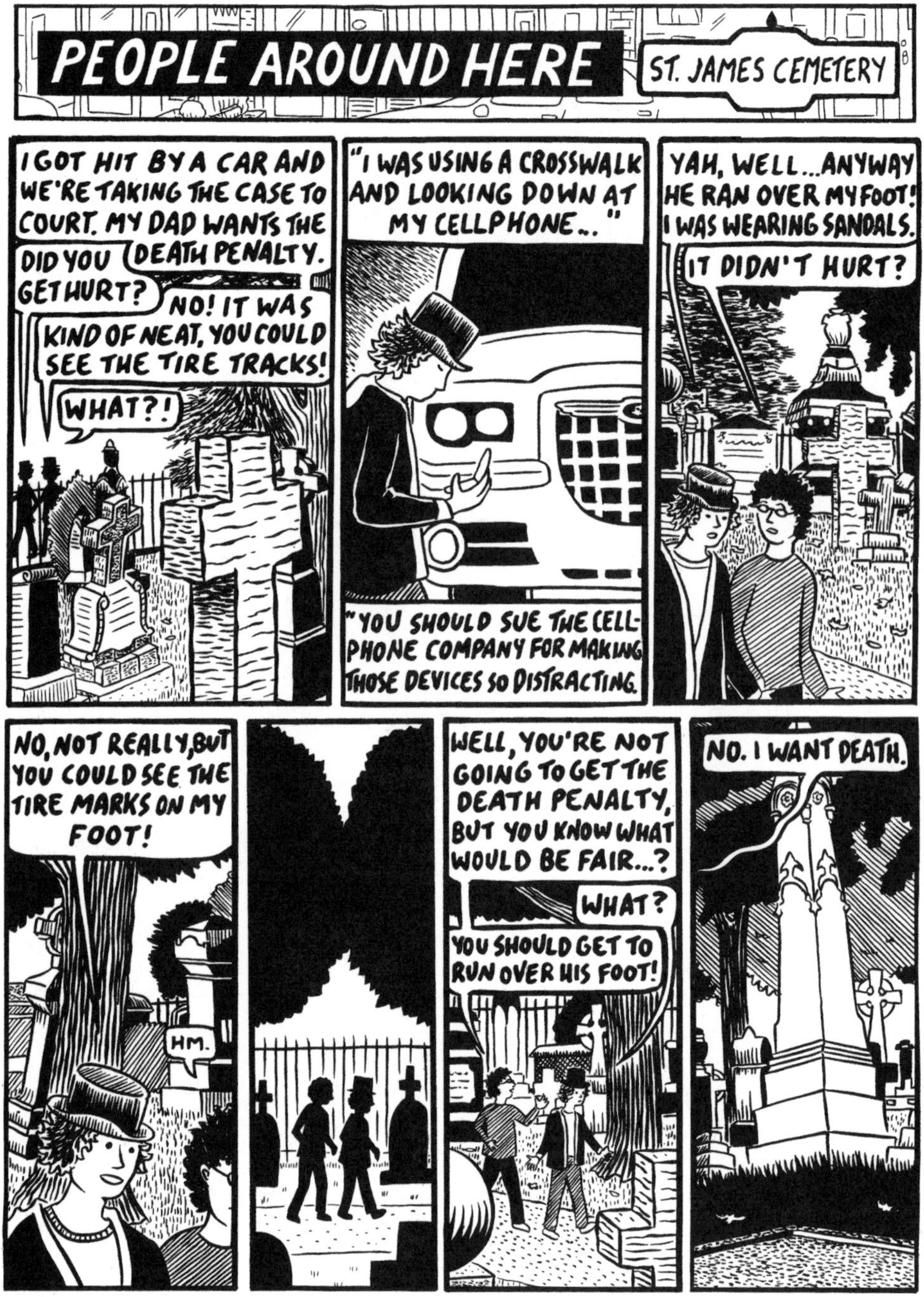
PEOPLE AROUND HERE
ST. JAMES CEMETERY
I GOT HIT BY A CAR AND WE'RE TAKING THE CASE TO COURT. MY DAD WANTS THE DEATH PENALTY.
DID YOU GET HURT?
NO! IT WAS KIND OF NEAT, YOU COULD SEE THE TIRE TRACKS!
WHAT?!
"I WAS USING A CROSSWALK AND LOOKING DOWN AT MY CELLPHONE..."
"YOU SHOULD SUE THE CELLPHONE COMPANY FOR MAKING THOSE DEVICES SO DISTRACTING.
YAH, WELL...ANYWAY HE RAN OVER MY FOOT! I WAS WEARING SANDALS.
IT DIDN'T HURT?
NO, NOT REALLY, BUT YOU COULD SEE THE TIRE MARKS ON MY FOOT!
HM.
WELL, YOU'RE NOT GOING TO GET THE DEATH PENALTY, BUT YOU KNOW WHAT WOULD BE FAIR...?
WHAT?
YOU SHOULD GET TO RUN OVER HIS FOOT!
NO. I WANT DEATH.

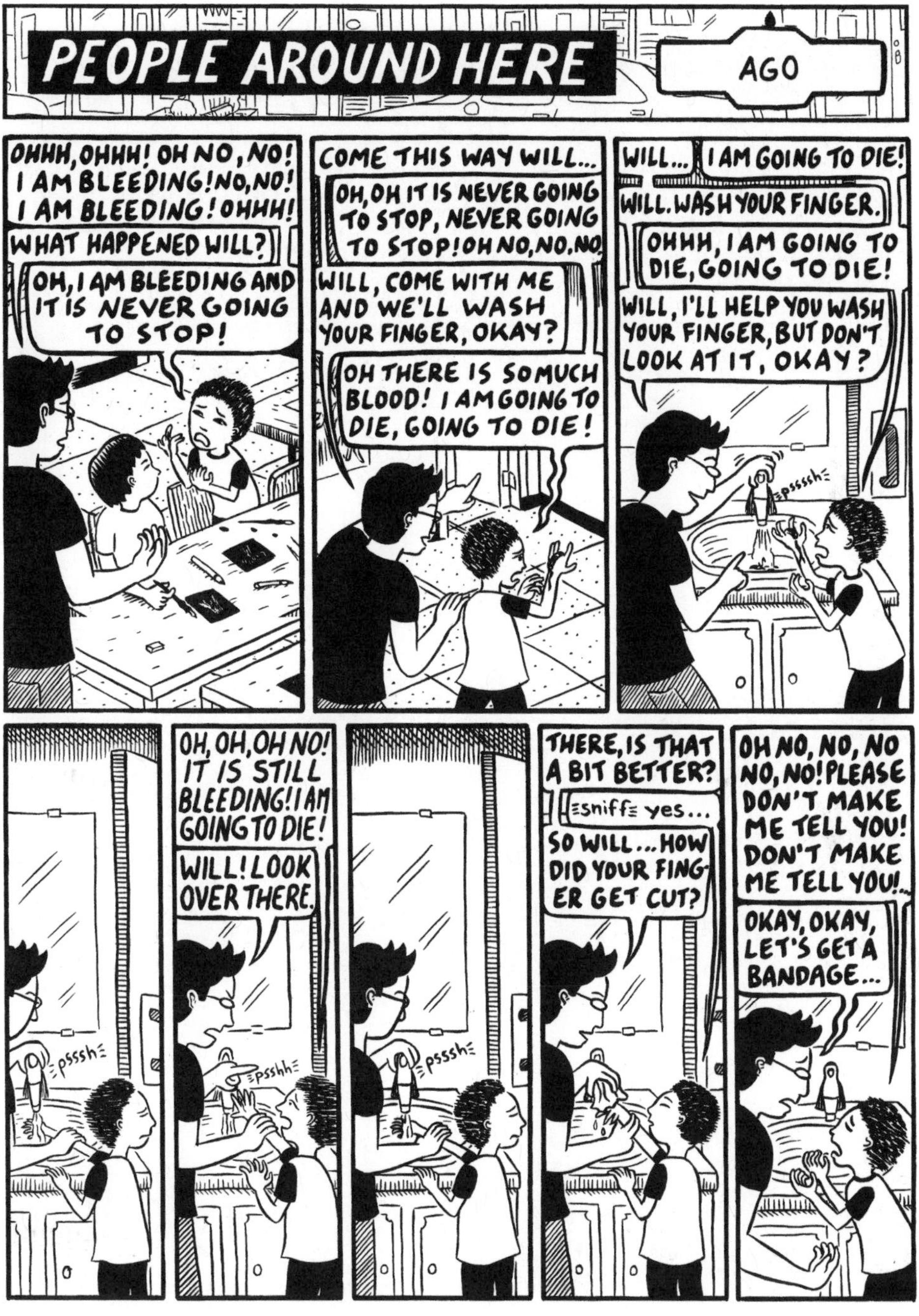
PEOPLE AROUND HERE
AGO
OHHH, OHHH! OH NO, NO! I AM BLEEDING! NO, NO! I AM BLEEDING! OHHH!
WHAT HAPPENED WILL?
OH, I AM BLEEDING AND IT IS NEVER GOING TO STOP!
COME THIS WAY WILL...
OH, OH IT IS NEVER GOING TO STOP, NEVER GOING TO STOP! OH NO, NO, NO
WILL, COME WITH ME AND WE'LL WASH YOUR FINGER, OKAY?
OH THERE IS SO MUCH BLOOD! I AM GOING TO DIE, GOING TO DIE!
WILL...
I AM GOING TO DIE!
WILL. WASH YOUR FINGER.
OHHH, I AM GOING TO DIE, GOING TO DIE!
WILL, I'LL HELP YOU WASH YOUR FINGER, BUT DON'T LOOK AT IT, OKAY?
pssssh
pssshh
OH, OH, OH NO! IT IS STILL BLEEDING! I AM GOING TO DIE!
WILL! LOOK OVER THERE.
psssh
psssh
THERE, IS THAT A BIT BETTER?
sniff yes...
SO WILL... HOW DID YOUR FINGER GET CUT?
OH NO, NO, NO NO, NO! PLEASE DON'T MAKE ME TELL YOU! DON'T MAKE ME TELL YOU!...
OKAY, OKAY, LET'S GET A BANDAGE...

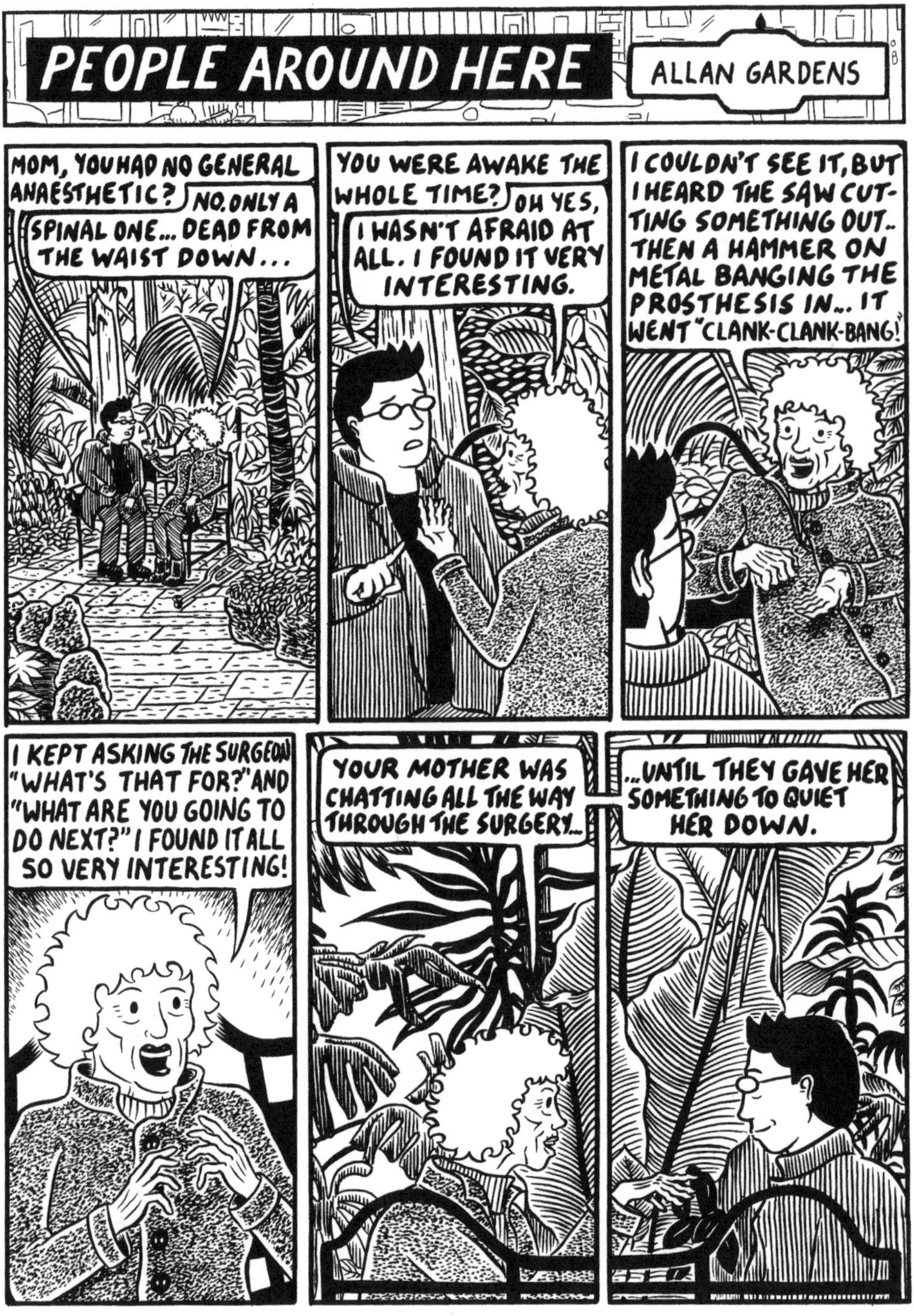
PEOPLE AROUND HERE
ALLAN GARDENS
MOM, YOU HAD NO GENERAL ANAESTHETIC?
NO. ONLY A SPINAL ONE... DEAD FROM THE WAIST DOWN...
YOU WERE AWAKE THE WHOLE TIME?
OH YES, I WASN'T AFRAID AT ALL. I FOUND IT VERY INTERESTING.
I COULDN'T SEE IT, BUT I HEARD THE SAW CUTTING SOMETHING OUT.. THEN A HAMMER ON METAL BANGING THE PROSTHESIS IN... IT WENT "CLANK-CLANK-BANG!"
I KEPT ASKING THE SURGEON "WHAT'S THAT FOR?" AND "WHAT ARE YOU GOING TO DO NEXT?" I FOUND IT ALL SO VERY INTERESTING!
YOUR MOTHER WAS CHATTING ALL THE WAY THROUGH THE SURGERY...
...UNTIL THEY GAVE HER SOMETHING TO QUIET HER DOWN.

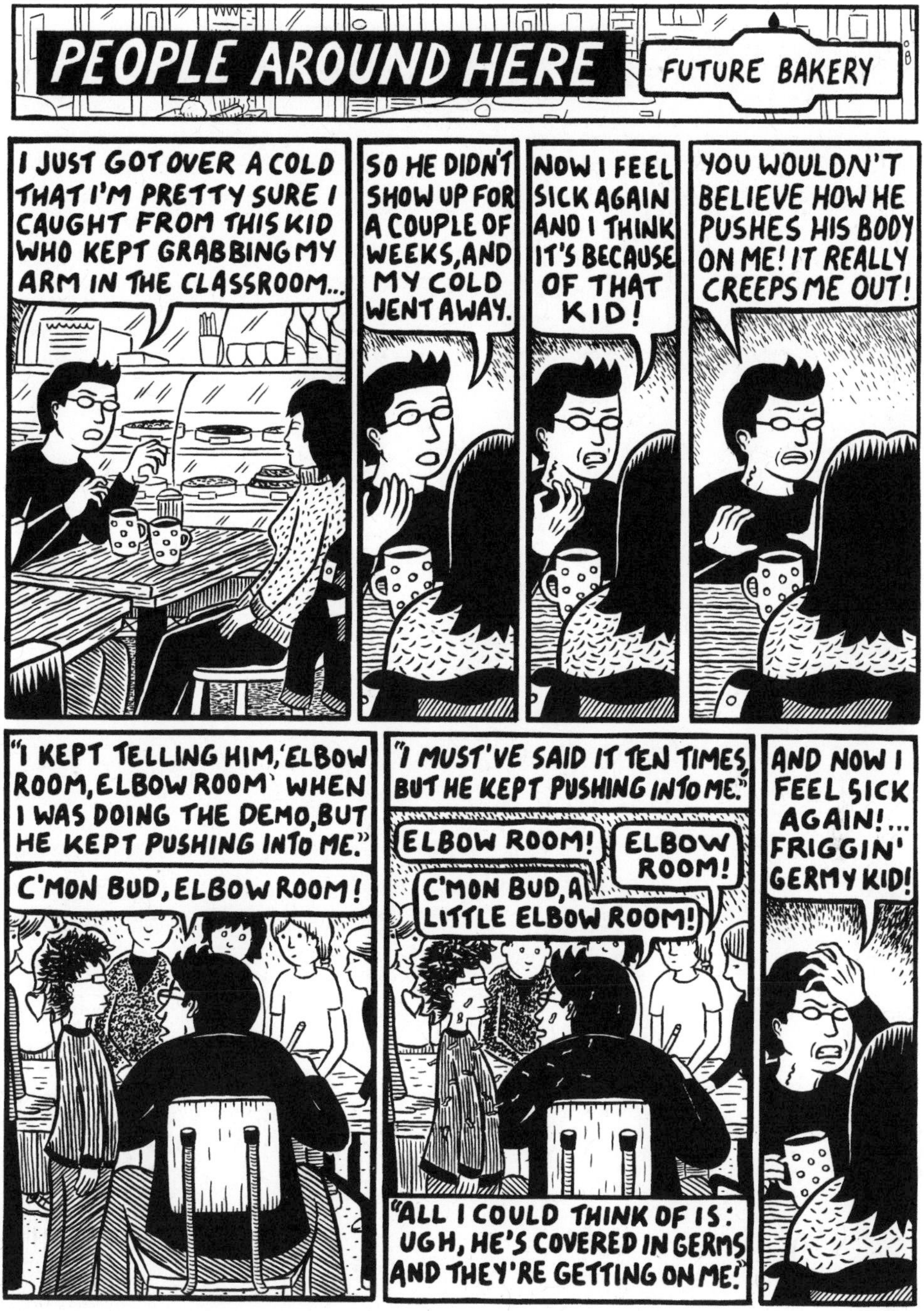
PEOPLE AROUND HERE
FUTURE BAKERY
I JUST GOT OVER A COLD THAT I'M PRETTY SURE I CAUGHT FROM THIS KID WHO KEPT GRABBING MY ARM IN THE CLASSROOM...
SO HE DIDN'T SHOW UP FOR A COUPLE OF WEEKS, AND MY COLD WENT AWAY.
NOW I FEEL SICK AGAIN AND I THINK IT'S BECAUSE OF THAT KID!
YOU WOULDN'T BELIEVE HOW HE PUSHES HIS BODY ON ME! IT REALLY CREEPS ME OUT!
"I KEPT TELLING HIM, 'ELBOW ROOM, ELBOW ROOM' WHEN I WAS DOING THE DEMO, BUT HE KEPT PUSHING INTO ME."
C'MON BUD, ELBOW ROOM!
"I MUST'VE SAID IT TEN TIMES, BUT HE KEPT PUSHING INTO ME."
ELBOW ROOM!
ELBOW ROOM!
C'MON BUD, A LITTLE ELBOW ROOM!
"ALL I COULD THINK OF IS: UGH, HE'S COVERED IN GERMS AND THEY'RE GETTING ON ME!"
AND NOW I FEEL SICK AGAIN!... FRIGGIN' GERMY KID!

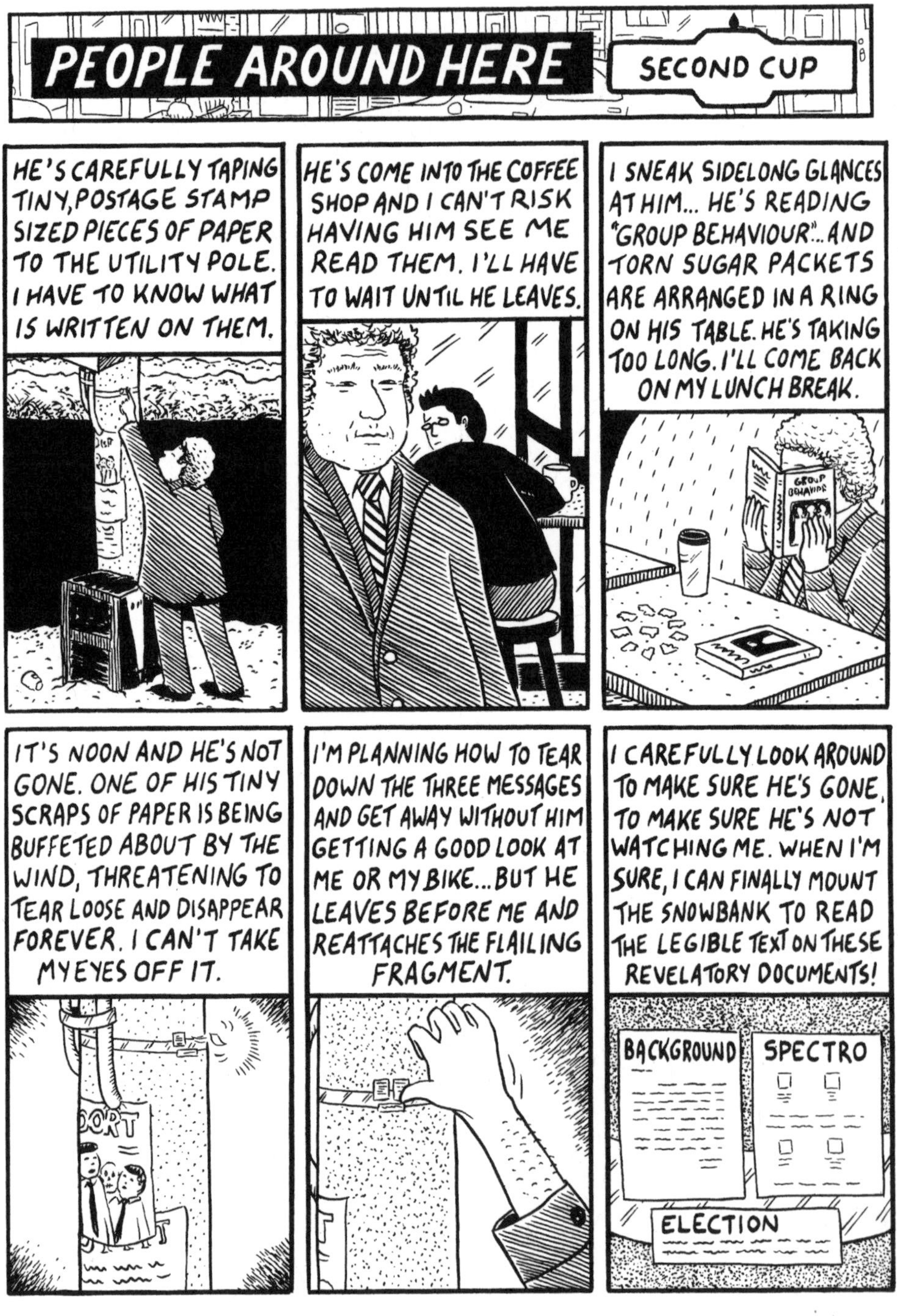
PEOPLE AROUND HERE
SECOND CUP
HE'S CAREFULLY TAPING TINY, POSTAGE STAMP SIZED PIECES OF PAPER TO THE UTILITY POLE. I HAVE TO KNOW WHAT IS WRITTEN ON THEM.
HE'S COME INTO THE COFFEE SHOP AND I CAN'T RISK HAVING HIM SEE ME READ THEM. I'LL HAVE TO WAIT UNTIL HE LEAVES.
I SNEAK SIDELONG GLANCES AT HIM... HE'S READING "GROUP BEHAVIOUR"... AND TORN SUGAR PACKETS ARE ARRANGED IN A RING ON HIS TABLE. HE'S TAKING TOO LONG. I'LL COME BACK ON MY LUNCH BREAK.
IT'S NOON AND HE'S NOT GONE. ONE OF HIS TINY SCRAPS OF PAPER IS BEING BUFFETED ABOUT BY THE WIND, THREATENING TO TEAR LOOSE AND DISAPPEAR FOREVER. I CAN'T TAKE MY EYES OFF IT.
I'M PLANNING HOW TO TEAR DOWN THE THREE MESSAGES AND GET AWAY WITHOUT HIM GETTING A GOOD LOOK AT ME OR MY BIKE... BUT HE LEAVES BEFORE ME AND REATTACHES THE FLAILING FRAGMENT.
I CAREFULLY LOOK AROUND TO MAKE SURE HE'S GONE, TO MAKE SURE HE'S NOT WATCHING ME. WHEN I'M SURE, I CAN FINALLY MOUNT THE SNOWBANK TO READ THE LEGIBLE TEXT ON THESE REVELATORY DOCUMENTS!
BACKGROUND
SPECTRO
ELECTION

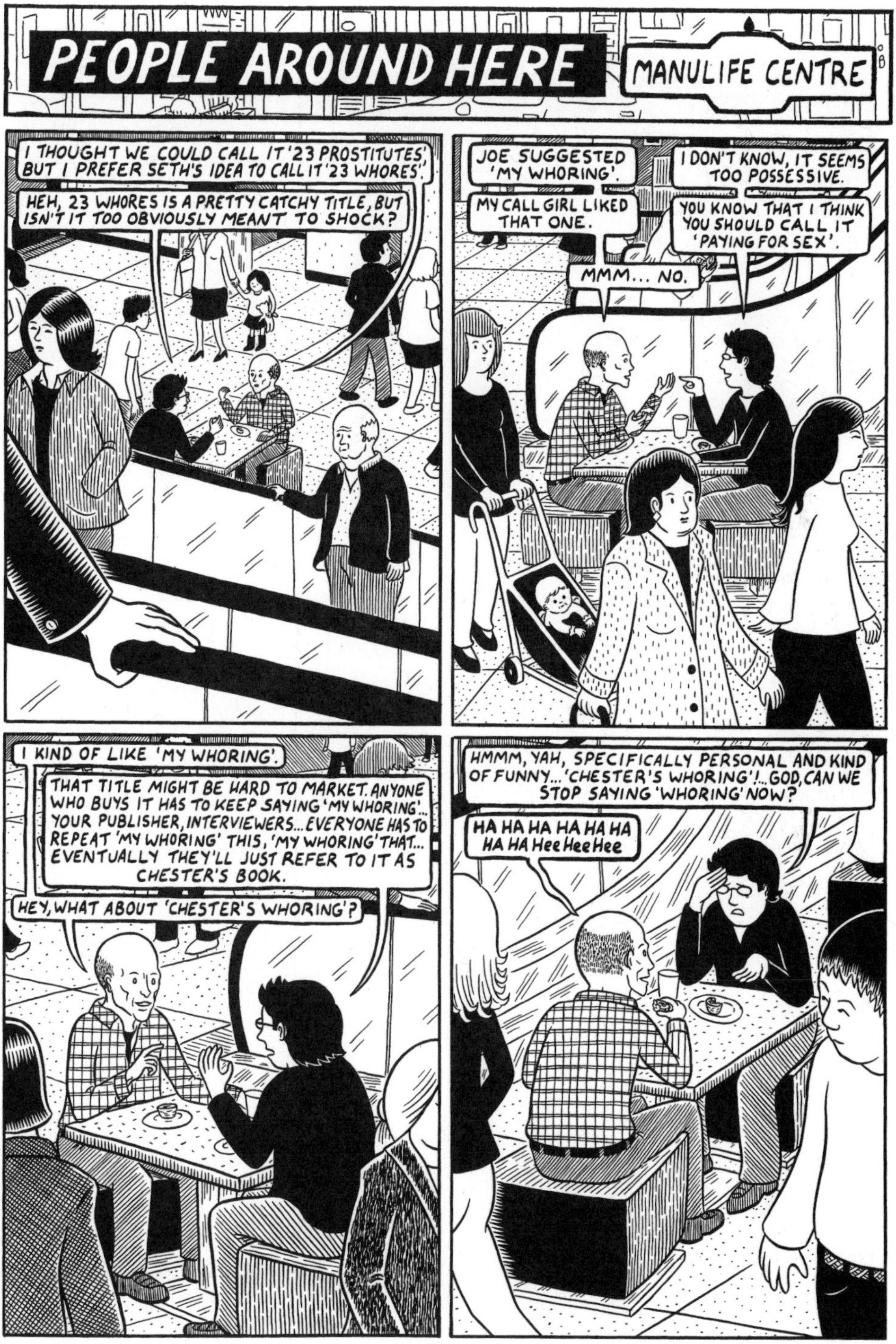
PEOPLE AROUND HERE
MANULIFE CENTRE
I THOUGHT WE COULD CALL IT '23 PROSTITUTES' BUT I PREFER SETH'S IDEA TO CALL IT '23 WHORES'.
HEH, 23 WHORES IS A PRETTY CATCHY TITLE, BUT ISN'T IT TOO OBVIOUSLY MEANT TO SHOCK?
JOE SUGGESTED 'MY WHORING'.
MY CALL GIRL LIKED THAT ONE.
MMM... NO.
I DON'T KNOW, IT SEEMS TOO POSSESSIVE.
YOU KNOW THAT I THINK YOU SHOULD CALL IT 'PAYING FOR SEX'.
I KIND OF LIKE 'MY WHORING'.
THAT TITLE MIGHT BE HARD TO MARKET. ANYONE WHO BUYS IT HAS TO KEEP SAYING 'MY WHORING'... YOUR PUBLISHER, INTERVIEWERS... EVERYONE HAS TO REPEAT 'MY WHORING' THIS, 'MY WHORING' THAT... EVENTUALLY THEY'LL JUST REFER TO IT AS CHESTER'S BOOK.
HEY, WHAT ABOUT 'CHESTER'S WHORING'?
HMMM, YAH, SPECIFICALLY PERSONAL AND KIND OF FUNNY... 'CHESTER'S WHORING'!.. GOD, CAN WE STOP SAYING 'WHORING' NOW?
HA HA HA HA HA HA HA HA Hee Hee Hee

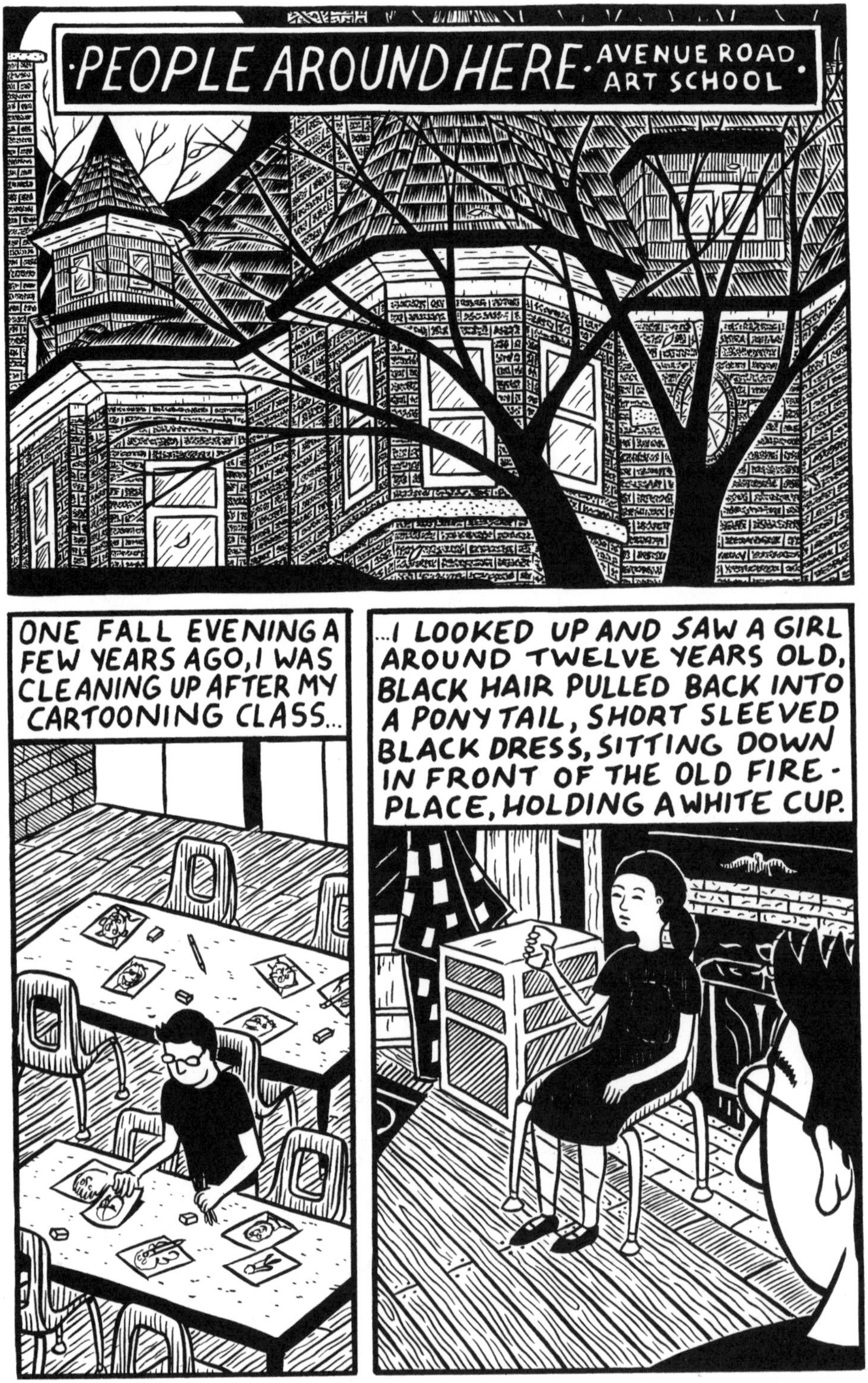
PEOPLE AROUND HERE
AVENUE ROAD ART SCHOOL
ONE FALL EVENING A FEW YEARS AGO, I WAS CLEANING UP AFTER MY CARTOONING CLASS...
...I LOOKED UP AND SAW A GIRL AROUND TWELVE YEARS OLD, BLACK HAIR PULLED BACK INTO A PONY TAIL, SHORT SLEEVED BLACK DRESS, SITTING DOWN IN FRONT OF THE OLD FIRE-PLACE, HOLDING A WHITE CUP.

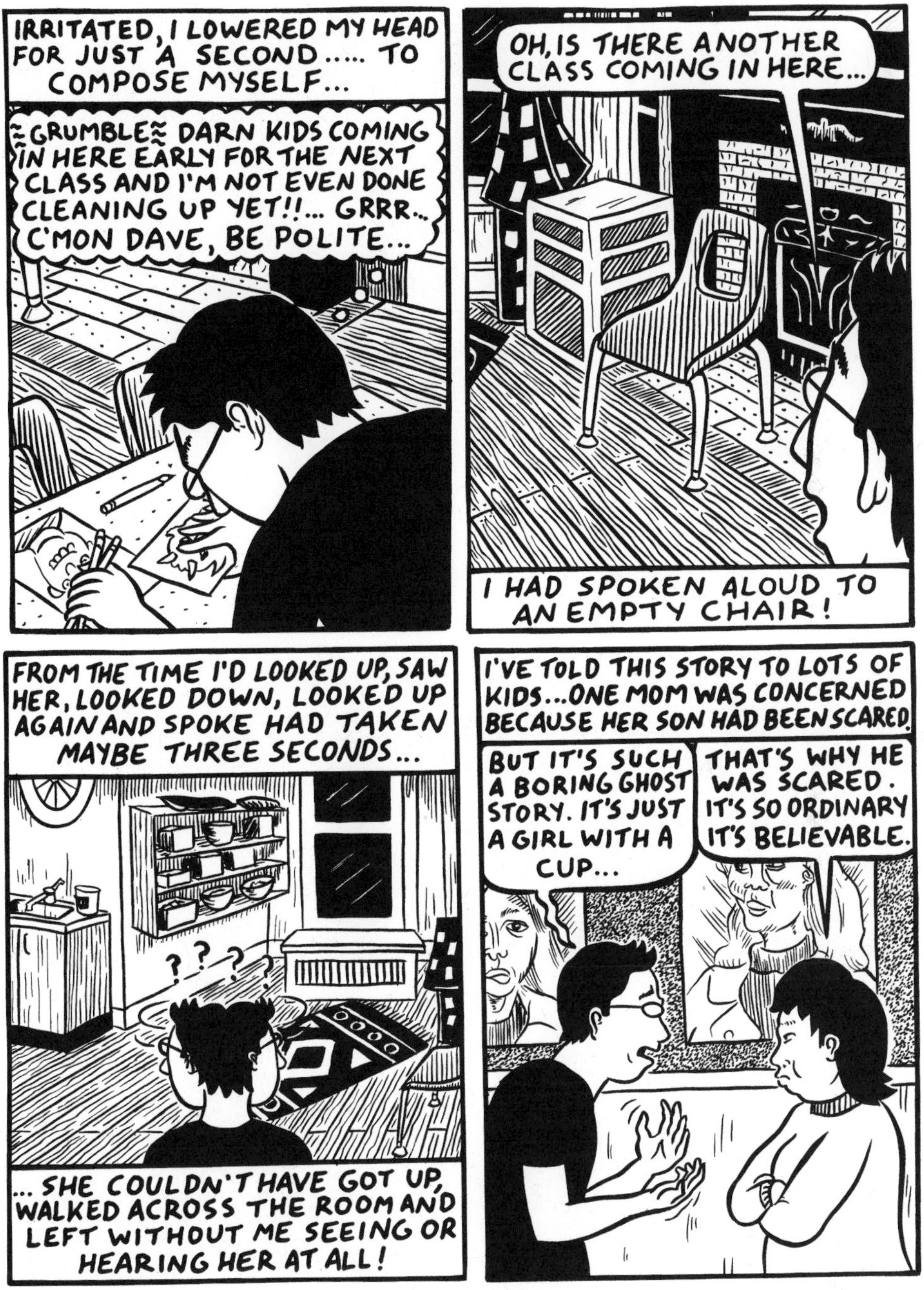
IRRITATED, I LOWERED MY HEAD FOR JUST A SECOND..... TO COMPOSE MYSELF...
~GRUMBLE~ DARN KIDS COMING IN HERE EARLY FOR THE NEXT CLASS AND I'M NOT EVEN DONE CLEANING UP YET!!... GRRR... C'MON DAVE, BE POLITE...
OH, IS THERE ANOTHER CLASS COMING IN HERE...
I HAD SPOKEN ALOUD TO AN EMPTY CHAIR!
FROM THE TIME I'D LOOKED UP, SAW HER, LOOKED DOWN, LOOKED UP AGAIN AND SPOKE HAD TAKEN MAYBE THREE SECONDS...
? ? ? ?
...SHE COULDN'T HAVE GOT UP, WALKED ACROSS THE ROOM AND LEFT WITHOUT ME SEEING OR HEARING HER AT ALL!
I'VE TOLD THIS STORY TO LOTS OF KIDS...ONE MOM WAS CONCERNED BECAUSE HER SON HAD BEEN SCARED.
BUT IT'S SUCH A BORING GHOST STORY. IT'S JUST A GIRL WITH A CUP...
THAT'S WHY HE WAS SCARED. IT'S SO ORDINARY IT'S BELIEVABLE.

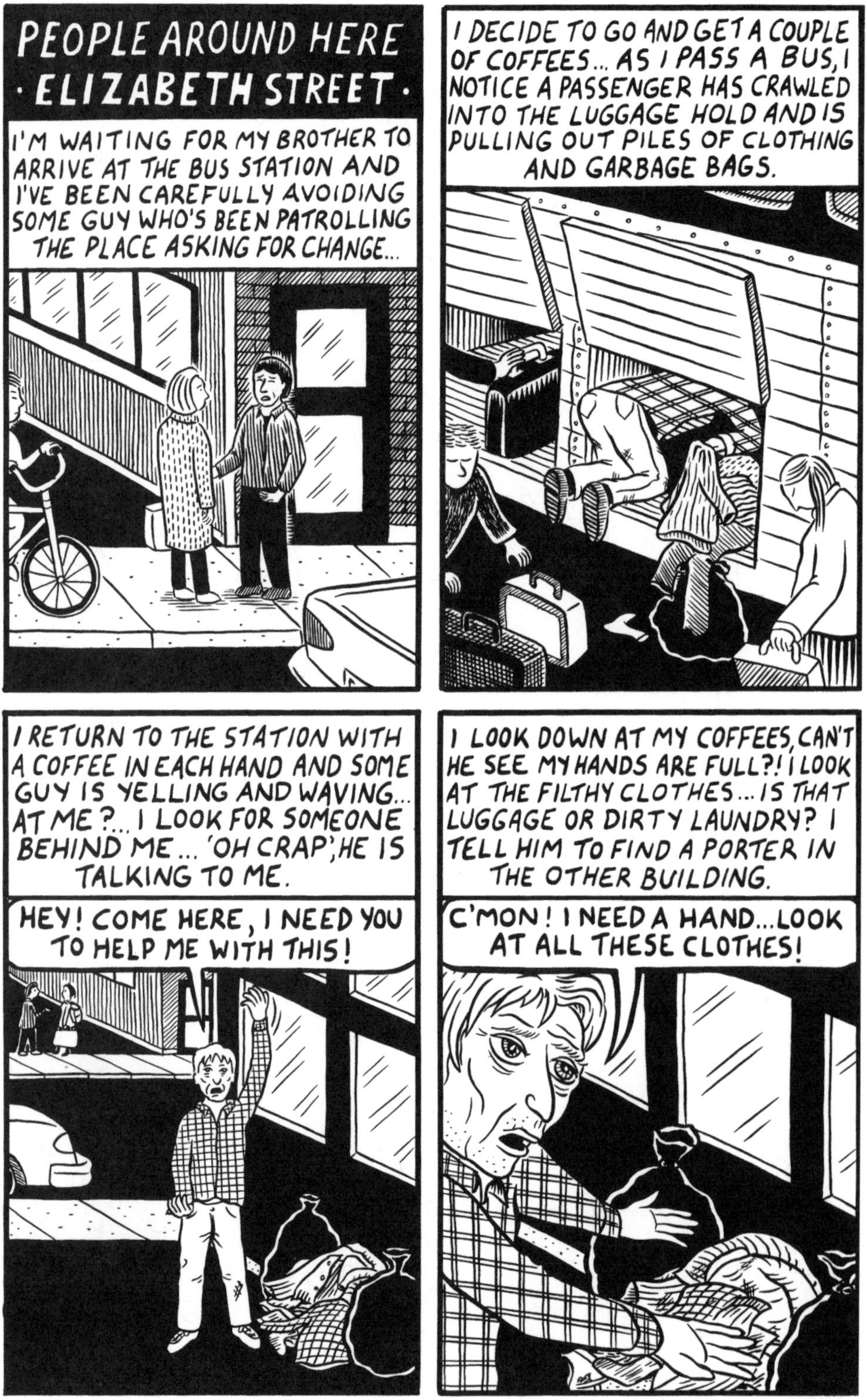
PEOPLE AROUND HERE
· ELIZABETH STREET ·
I'M WAITING FOR MY BROTHER TO ARRIVE AT THE BUS STATION AND I'VE BEEN CAREFULLY AVOIDING SOME GUY WHO'S BEEN PATROLLING THE PLACE ASKING FOR CHANGE...
I DECIDE TO GO AND GET A COUPLE OF COFFEES... AS I PASS A BUS, I NOTICE A PASSENGER HAS CRAWLED INTO THE LUGGAGE HOLD AND IS PULLING OUT PILES OF CLOTHING AND GARBAGE BAGS.
I RETURN TO THE STATION WITH A COFFEE IN EACH HAND AND SOME GUY IS YELLING AND WAVING... AT ME?... I LOOK FOR SOMEONE BEHIND ME... 'OH CRAP', HE IS TALKING TO ME.
HEY! COME HERE, I NEED YOU TO HELP ME WITH THIS!
I LOOK DOWN AT MY COFFEES, CAN'T HE SEE MY HANDS ARE FULL?! I LOOK AT THE FILTHY CLOTHES... IS THAT LUGGAGE OR DIRTY LAUNDRY? I TELL HIM TO FIND A PORTER IN THE OTHER BUILDING.
C'MON! I NEED A HAND...LOOK AT ALL THESE CLOTHES!

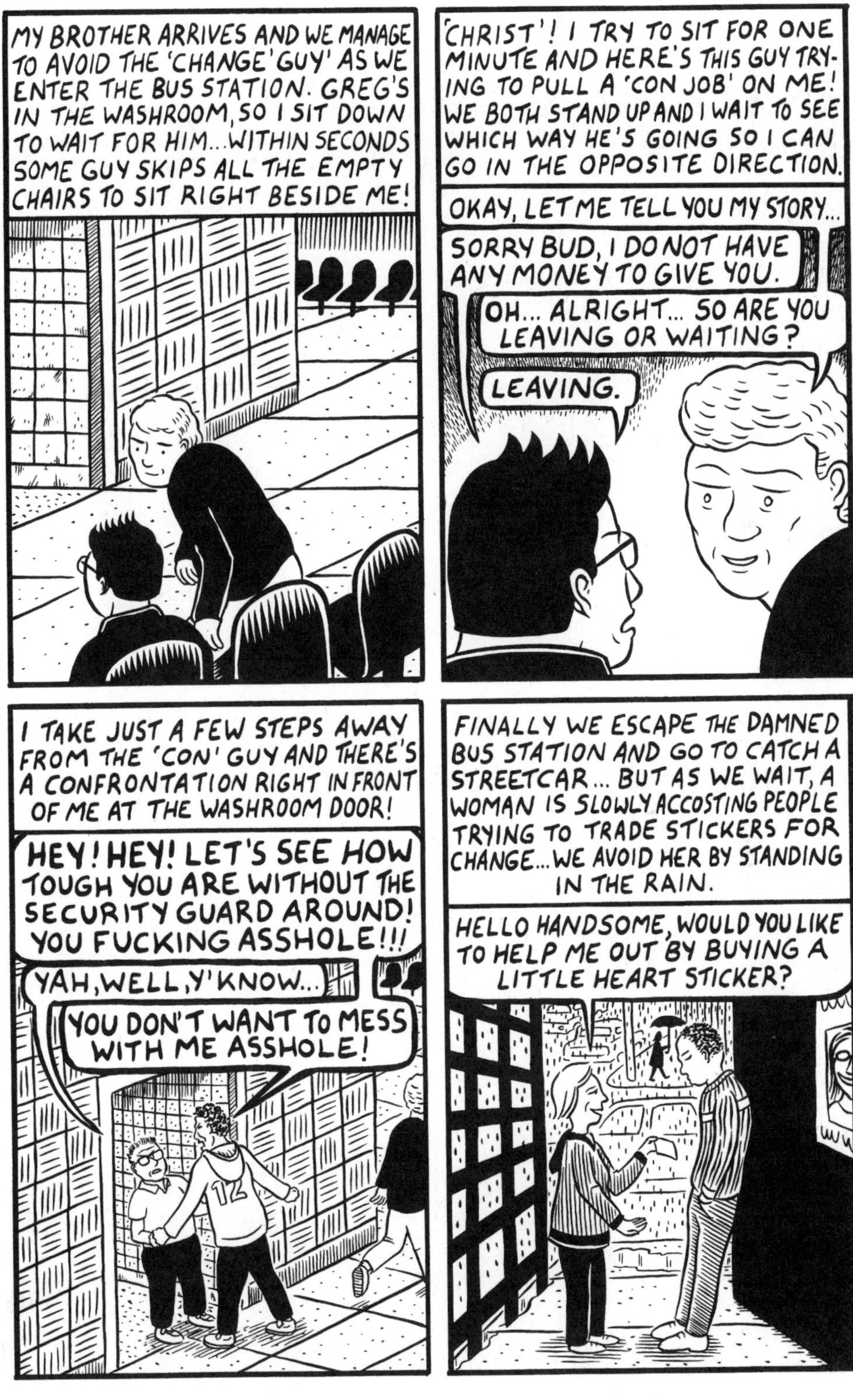
MY BROTHER ARRIVES AND WE MANAGE TO AVOID THE 'CHANGE' GUY' AS WE ENTER THE BUS STATION. GREG'S IN THE WASHROOM, SO I SIT DOWN TO WAIT FOR HIM... WITHIN SECONDS SOME GUY SKIPS ALL THE EMPTY CHAIRS TO SIT RIGHT BESIDE ME!
'CHRIST'! I TRY TO SIT FOR ONE MINUTE AND HERE'S THIS GUY TRYING TO PULL A 'CON JOB' ON ME! WE BOTH STAND UP AND I WAIT TO SEE WHICH WAY HE'S GOING SO I CAN GO IN THE OPPOSITE DIRECTION.
OKAY, LET ME TELL YOU MY STORY...
SORRY BUD, I DO NOT HAVE ANY MONEY TO GIVE YOU.
OH... ALRIGHT... SO ARE YOU LEAVING OR WAITING?
LEAVING.
I TAKE JUST A FEW STEPS AWAY FROM THE 'CON' GUY AND THERE'S A CONFRONTATION RIGHT IN FRONT OF ME AT THE WASHROOM DOOR!
HEY! HEY! LET'S SEE HOW TOUGH YOU ARE WITHOUT THE SECURITY GUARD AROUND! YOU FUCKING ASSHOLE!!!
YAH, WELL, Y'KNOW...
YOU DON'T WANT TO MESS WITH ME ASSHOLE!
12
FINALLY WE ESCAPE THE DAMNED BUS STATION AND GO TO CATCH A STREETCAR... BUT AS WE WAIT, A WOMAN IS SLOWLY ACCOSTING PEOPLE TRYING TO TRADE STICKERS FOR CHANGE... WE AVOID HER BY STANDING IN THE RAIN.
HELLO HANDSOME, WOULD YOU LIKE TO HELP ME OUT BY BUYING A LITTLE HEART STICKER?

# PEOPLE AROUND HERE

G20

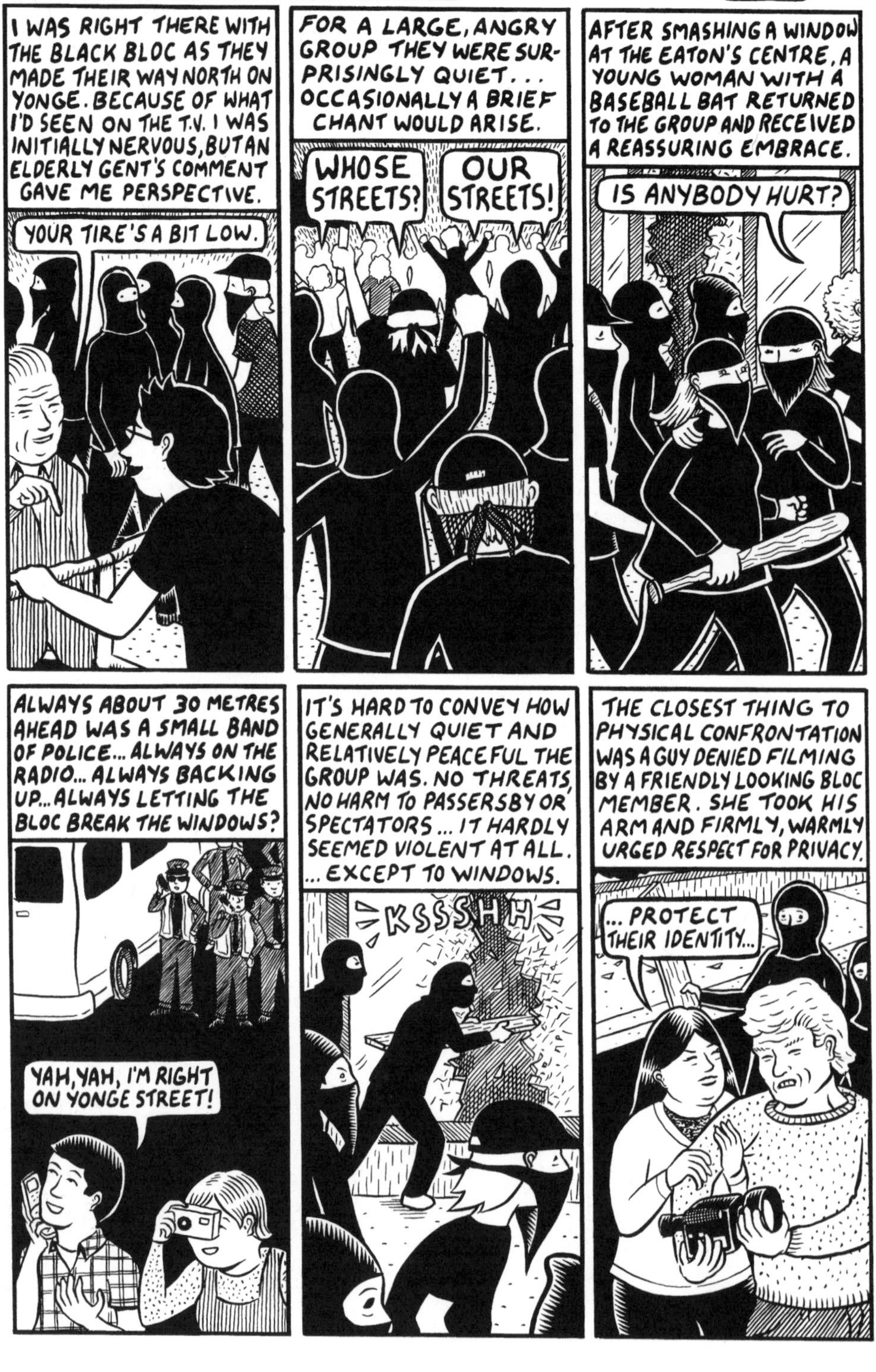
I WAS RIGHT THERE WITH THE BLACK BLOC AS THEY MADE THEIR WAY NORTH ON YONGE. BECAUSE OF WHAT I'D SEEN ON THE T.V. I WAS INITIALLY NERVOUS, BUT AN ELDERLY GENT'S COMMENT GAVE ME PERSPECTIVE.
YOUR TIRE'S A BIT LOW.
FOR A LARGE, ANGRY GROUP THEY WERE SURPRISINGLY QUIET... OCCASIONALLY A BRIEF CHANT WOULD ARISE.
WHOSE STREETS?
OUR STREETS!
AFTER SMASHING A WINDOW AT THE EATON'S CENTRE, A YOUNG WOMAN WITH A BASEBALL BAT RETURNED TO THE GROUP AND RECEIVED A REASSURING EMBRACE.
IS ANYBODY HURT?
ALWAYS ABOUT 30 METRES AHEAD WAS A SMALL BAND OF POLICE... ALWAYS ON THE RADIO... ALWAYS BACKING UP... ALWAYS LETTING THE BLOC BREAK THE WINDOWS?
YAH, YAH, I'M RIGHT ON YONGE STREET!
IT'S HARD TO CONVEY HOW GENERALLY QUIET AND RELATIVELY PEACEFUL THE GROUP WAS. NO THREATS, NO HARM TO PASSERSBY OR SPECTATORS... IT HARDLY SEEMED VIOLENT AT ALL. ... EXCEPT TO WINDOWS.
KSSSHH
THE CLOSEST THING TO PHYSICAL CONFRONTATION WAS A GUY DENIED FILMING BY A FRIENDLY LOOKING BLOC MEMBER. SHE TOOK HIS ARM AND FIRMLY, WARMLY URGED RESPECT FOR PRIVACY.
... PROTECT THEIR IDENTITY...

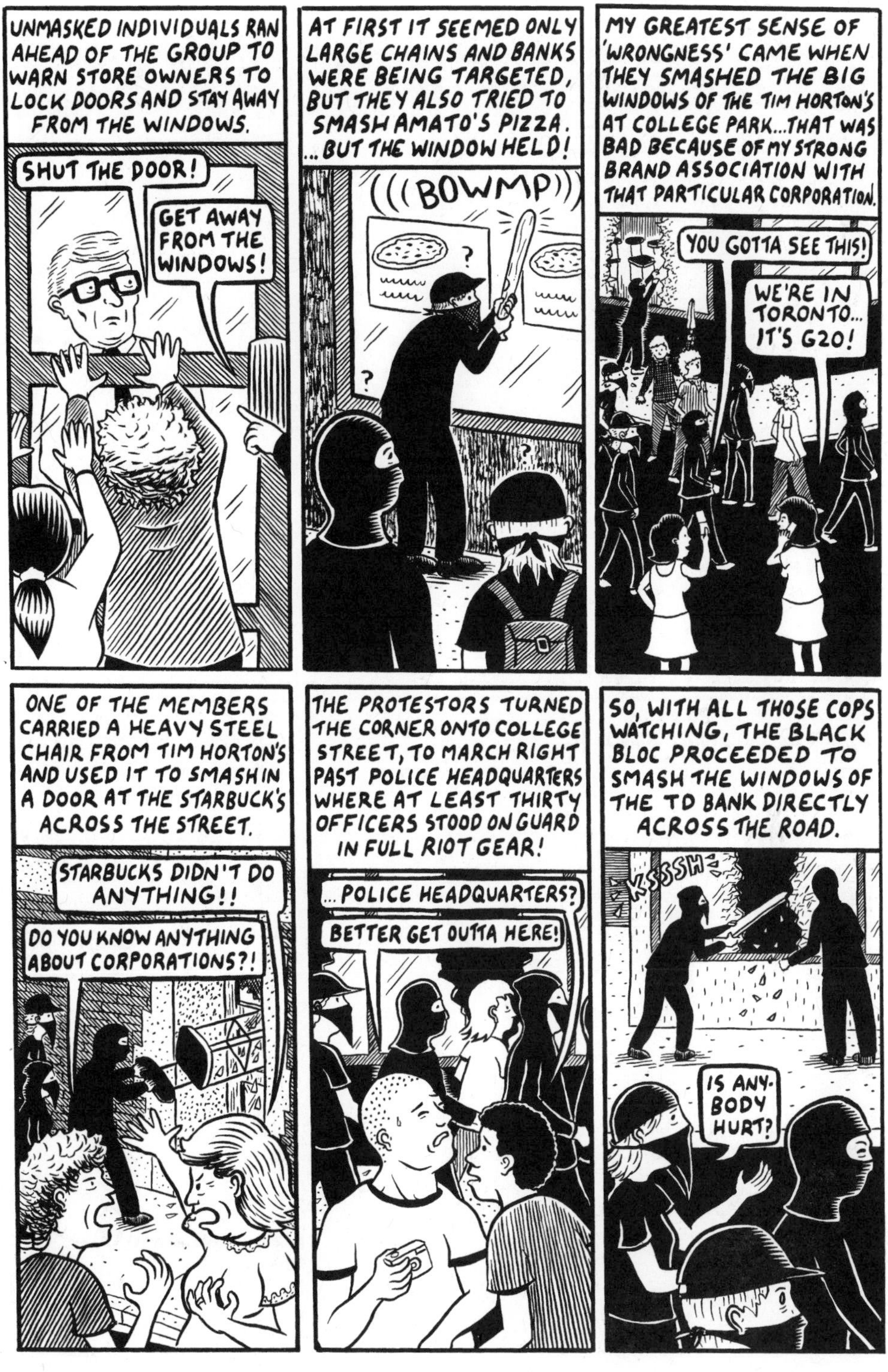
UNMASKED INDIVIDUALS RAN AHEAD OF THE GROUP TO WARN STORE OWNERS TO LOCK DOORS AND STAY AWAY FROM THE WINDOWS.
SHUT THE DOOR!
GET AWAY FROM THE WINDOWS!
AT FIRST IT SEEMED ONLY LARGE CHAINS AND BANKS WERE BEING TARGETED, BUT THEY ALSO TRIED TO SMASH AMATO'S PIZZA. ...BUT THE WINDOW HELD!
BOWMP
MY GREATEST SENSE OF 'WRONGNESS' CAME WHEN THEY SMASHED THE BIG WINDOWS OF THE TIM HORTON'S AT COLLEGE PARK...THAT WAS BAD BECAUSE OF MY STRONG BRAND ASSOCIATION WITH THAT PARTICULAR CORPORATION.
YOU GOTTA SEE THIS!
WE'RE IN TORONTO... IT'S G20!
ONE OF THE MEMBERS CARRIED A HEAVY STEEL CHAIR FROM TIM HORTON'S AND USED IT TO SMASH IN A DOOR AT THE STARBUCK'S ACROSS THE STREET.
STARBUCKS DIDN'T DO ANYTHING!!
DO YOU KNOW ANYTHING ABOUT CORPORATIONS?!
THE PROTESTORS TURNED THE CORNER ONTO COLLEGE STREET, TO MARCH RIGHT PAST POLICE HEADQUARTERS WHERE AT LEAST THIRTY OFFICERS STOOD ON GUARD IN FULL RIOT GEAR!
...POLICE HEADQUARTERS?
BETTER GET OUTTA HERE!
SO, WITH ALL THOSE COPS WATCHING, THE BLACK BLOC PROCEEDED TO SMASH THE WINDOWS OF THE TD BANK DIRECTLY ACROSS THE ROAD.
KSSSH
IS ANYBODY HURT?

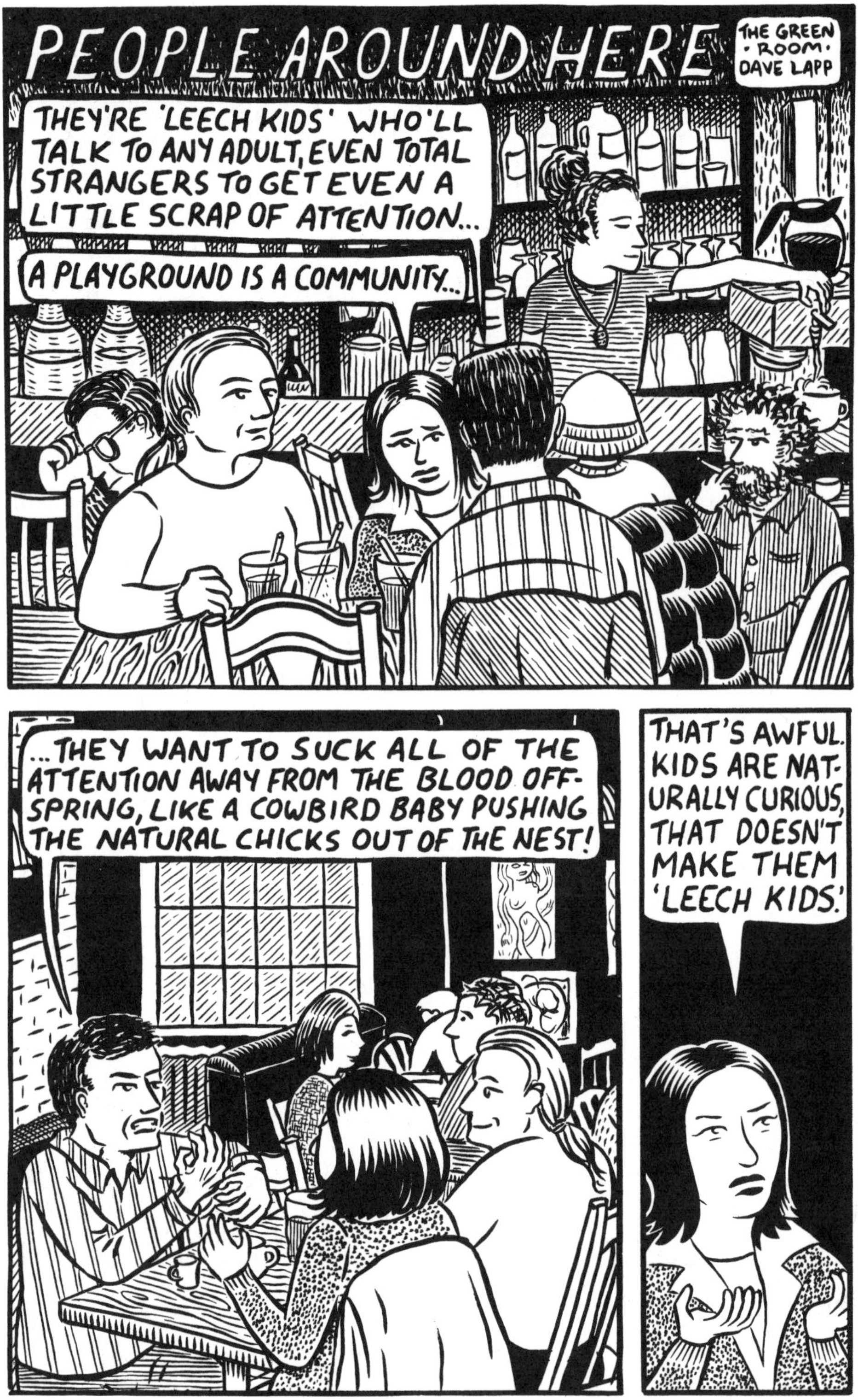
PEOPLE AROUND HERE
THE GREEN • ROOM • DAVE LAPP
THEY'RE 'LEECH KIDS' WHO'LL TALK TO ANY ADULT, EVEN TOTAL STRANGERS TO GET EVEN A LITTLE SCRAP OF ATTENTION...
A PLAYGROUND IS A COMMUNITY...
...THEY WANT TO SUCK ALL OF THE ATTENTION AWAY FROM THE BLOOD OFF-SPRING, LIKE A COWBIRD BABY PUSHING THE NATURAL CHICKS OUT OF THE NEST!
THAT'S AWFUL. KIDS ARE NAT-URALLY CURIOUS, THAT DOESN'T MAKE THEM 'LEECH KIDS.'

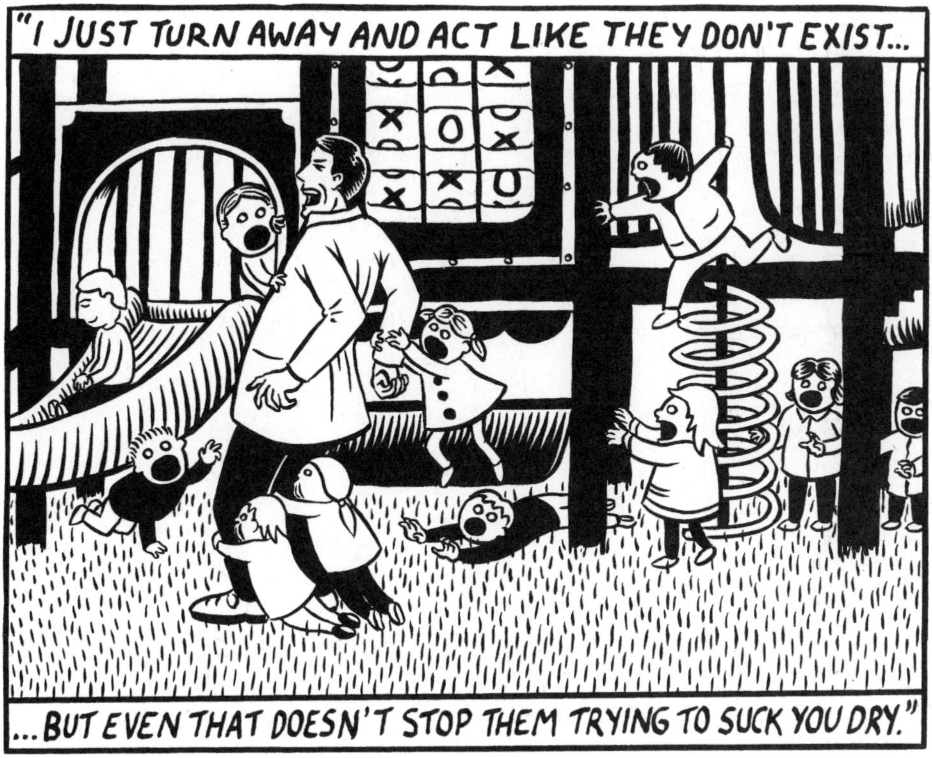
"I JUST TURN AWAY AND ACT LIKE THEY DON'T EXIST...
...BUT EVEN THAT DOESN'T STOP THEM TRYING TO SUCK YOU DRY."

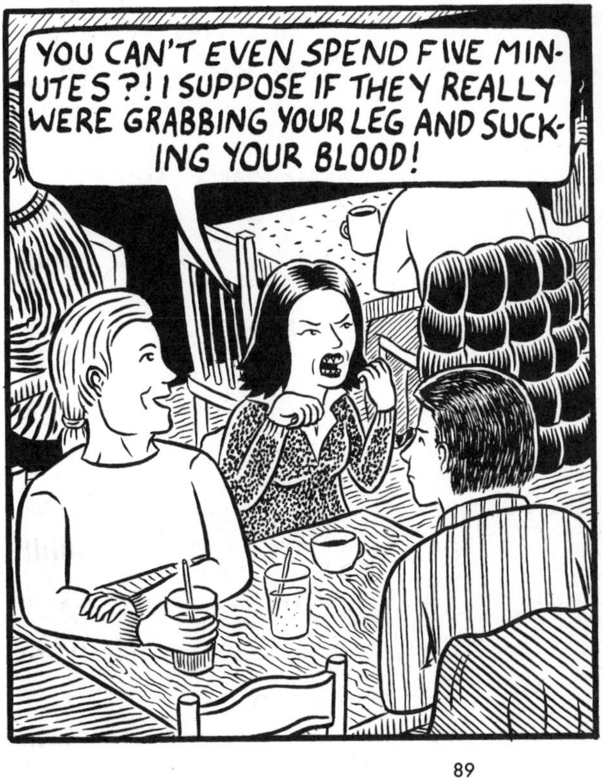
YOU CAN'T EVEN SPEND FIVE MINUTES?! I SUPPOSE IF THEY REALLY WERE GRABBING YOUR LEG AND SUCKING YOUR BLOOD!

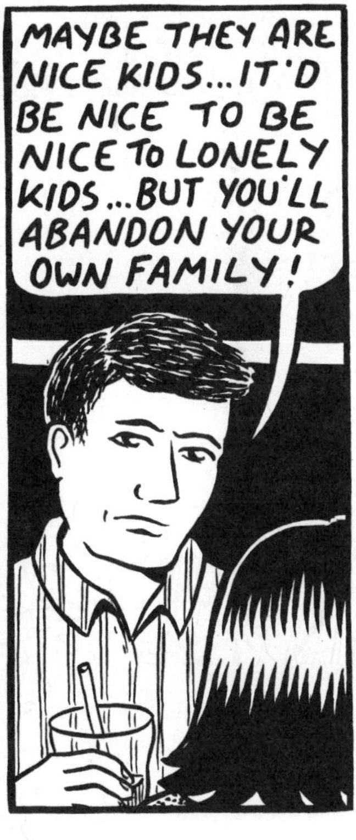
MAYBE THEY ARE NICE KIDS...IT'D BE NICE TO BE NICE TO LONELY KIDS...BUT YOU'LL ABANDON YOUR OWN FAMILY!

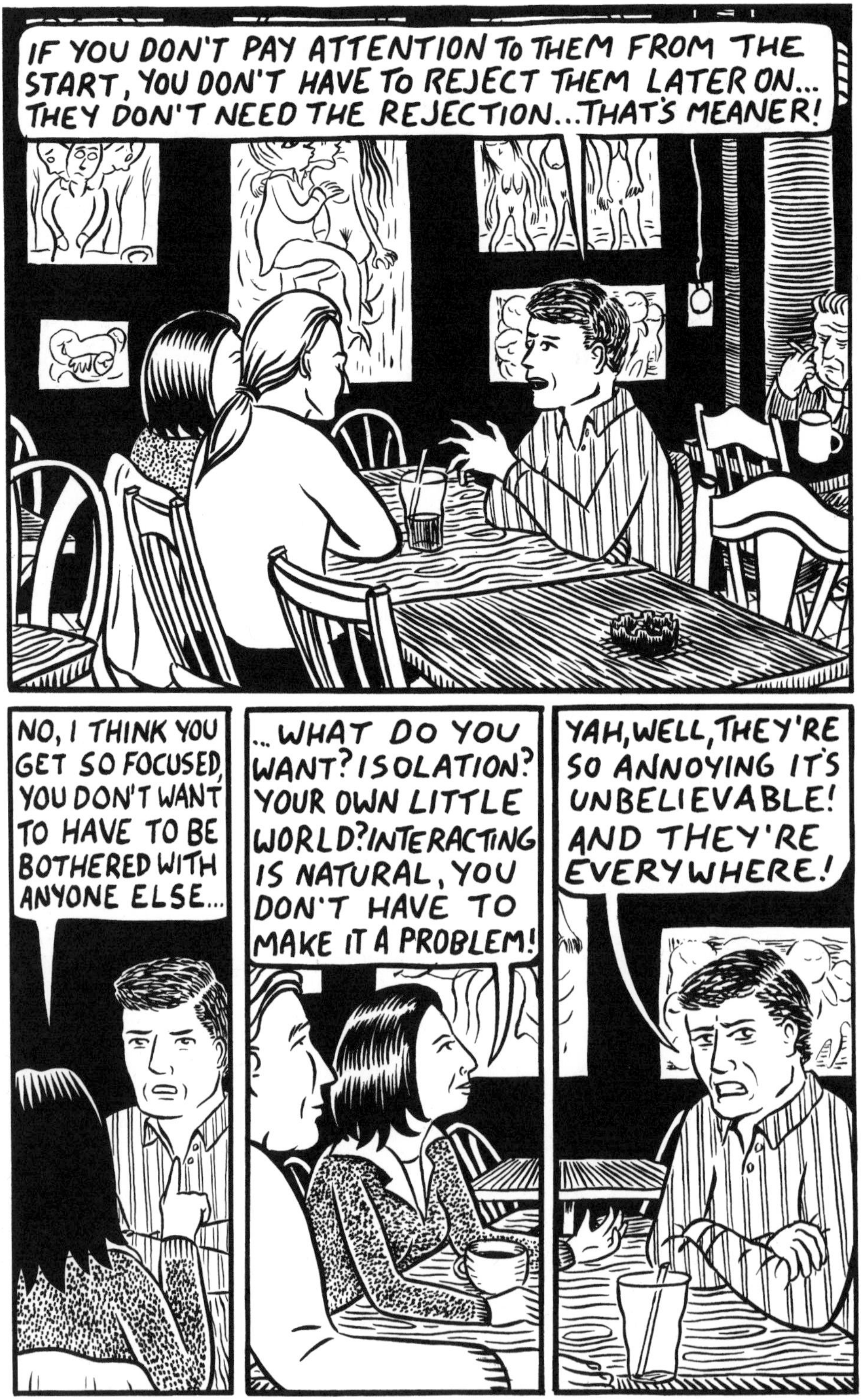
IF YOU DON'T PAY ATTENTION TO THEM FROM THE START, YOU DON'T HAVE TO REJECT THEM LATER ON... THEY DON'T NEED THE REJECTION...THAT'S MEANER!
NO, I THINK YOU GET SO FOCUSED, YOU DON'T WANT TO HAVE TO BE BOTHERED WITH ANYONE ELSE...
...WHAT DO YOU WANT? ISOLATION? YOUR OWN LITTLE WORLD? INTERACTING IS NATURAL, YOU DON'T HAVE TO MAKE IT A PROBLEM!
YAH, WELL, THEY'RE SO ANNOYING IT'S UNBELIEVABLE! AND THEY'RE EVERYWHERE!

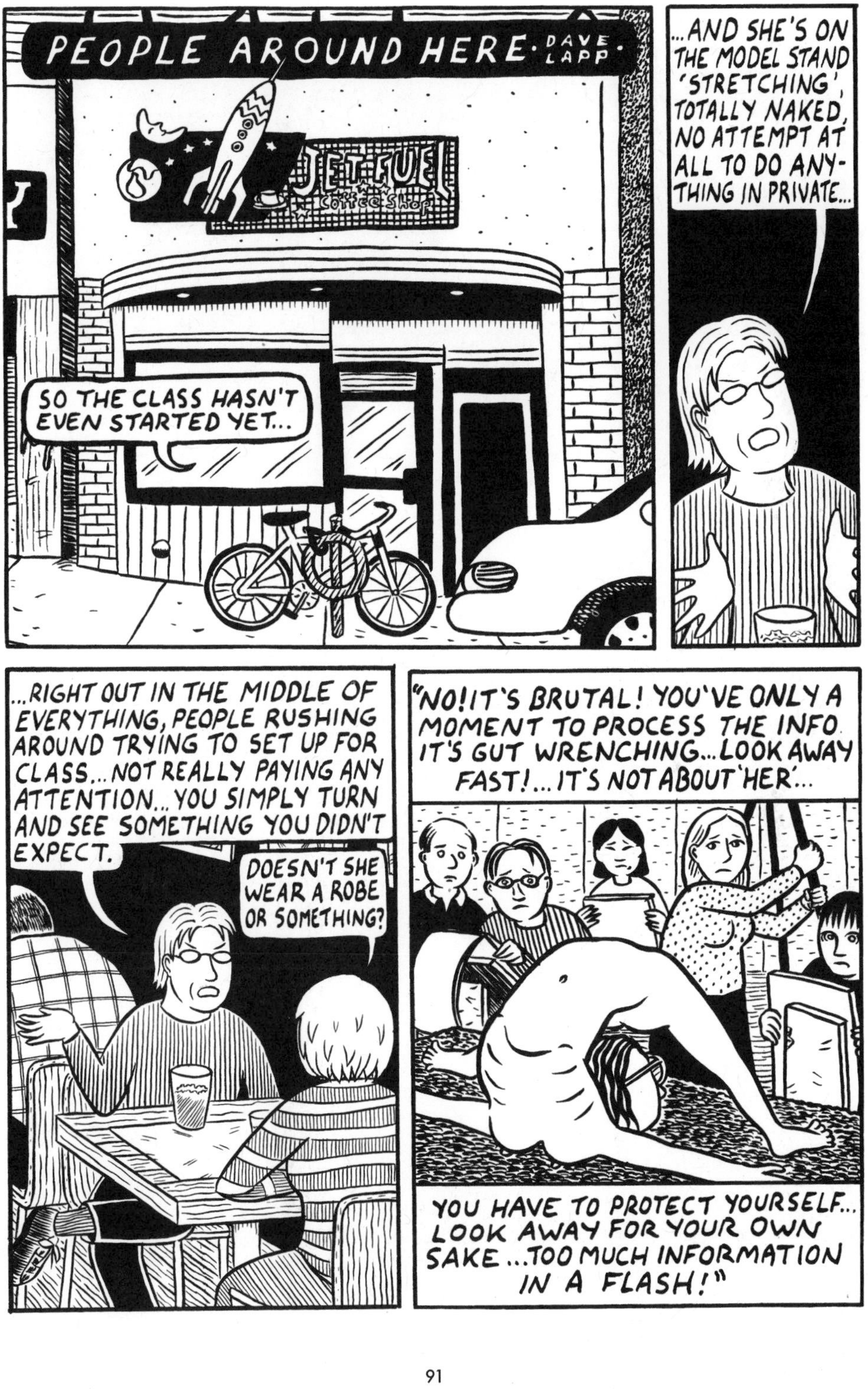
PEOPLE AROUND HERE · DAVE LAPP ·
JET FUEL Coffee Shop
SO THE CLASS HASN'T EVEN STARTED YET...
...AND SHE'S ON THE MODEL STAND 'STRETCHING', TOTALLY NAKED, NO ATTEMPT AT ALL TO DO ANYTHING IN PRIVATE...
...RIGHT OUT IN THE MIDDLE OF EVERYTHING, PEOPLE RUSHING AROUND TRYING TO SET UP FOR CLASS... NOT REALLY PAYING ANY ATTENTION... YOU SIMPLY TURN AND SEE SOMETHING YOU DIDN'T EXPECT.
DOESN'T SHE WEAR A ROBE OR SOMETHING?
"NO! IT'S BRUTAL! YOU'VE ONLY A MOMENT TO PROCESS THE INFO. IT'S GUT WRENCHING... LOOK AWAY FAST!... IT'S NOT ABOUT 'HER'...
YOU HAVE TO PROTECT YOURSELF... LOOK AWAY FOR YOUR OWN SAKE... TOO MUCH INFORMATION IN A FLASH!"

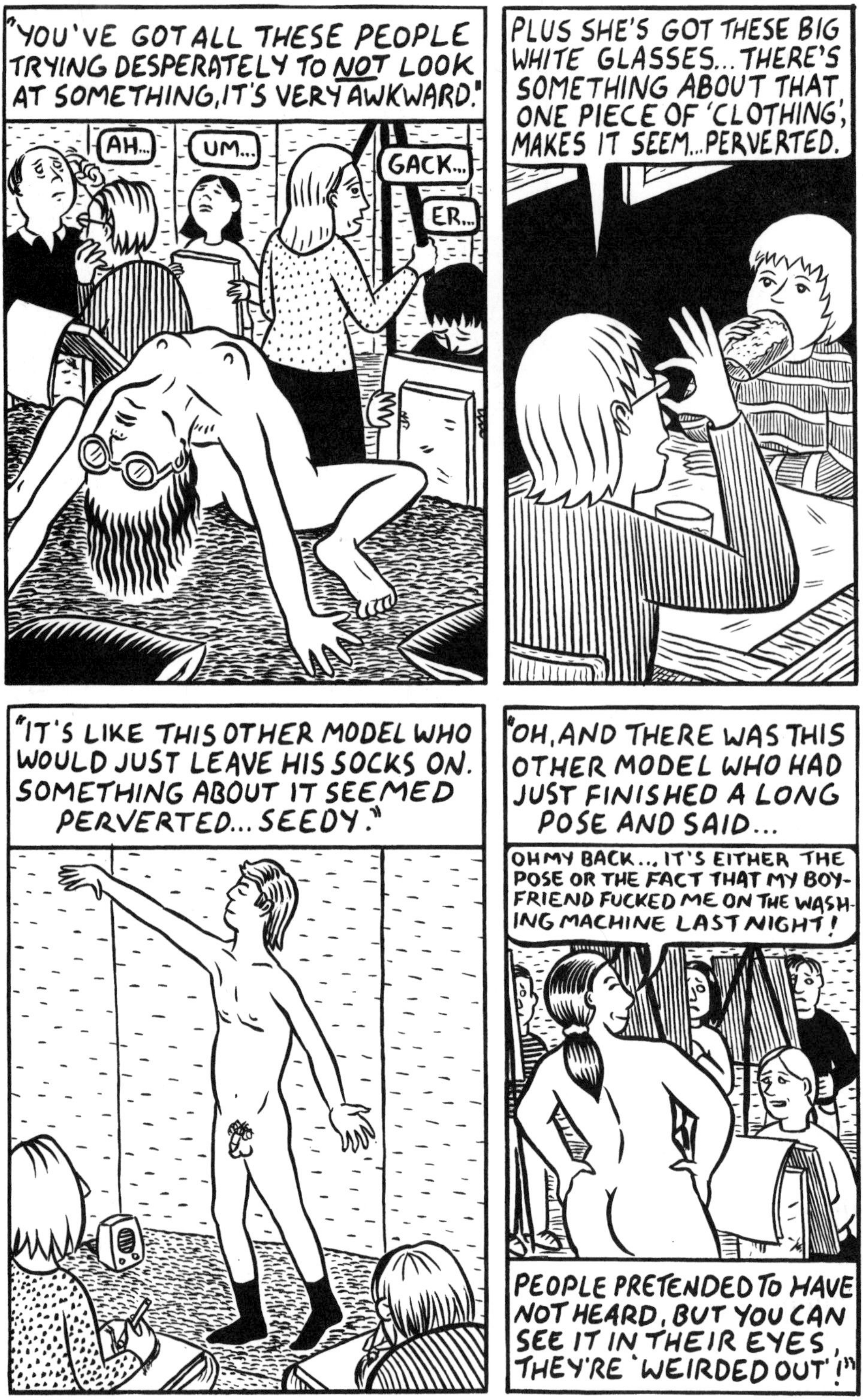
"YOU'VE GOT ALL THESE PEOPLE TRYING DESPERATELY TO NOT LOOK AT SOMETHING, IT'S VERY AWKWARD."
AH...
UM...
GACK...
ER...
PLUS SHE'S GOT THESE BIG WHITE GLASSES... THERE'S SOMETHING ABOUT THAT ONE PIECE OF 'CLOTHING', MAKES IT SEEM...PERVERTED.
"IT'S LIKE THIS OTHER MODEL WHO WOULD JUST LEAVE HIS SOCKS ON. SOMETHING ABOUT IT SEEMED PERVERTED... SEEDY."
"OH, AND THERE WAS THIS OTHER MODEL WHO HAD JUST FINISHED A LONG POSE AND SAID...
OH MY BACK..., IT'S EITHER THE POSE OR THE FACT THAT MY BOY-FRIEND FUCKED ME ON THE WASHING MACHINE LAST NIGHT!
PEOPLE PRETENDED TO HAVE NOT HEARD, BUT YOU CAN SEE IT IN THEIR EYES, THEY'RE 'WEIRDED OUT'!"

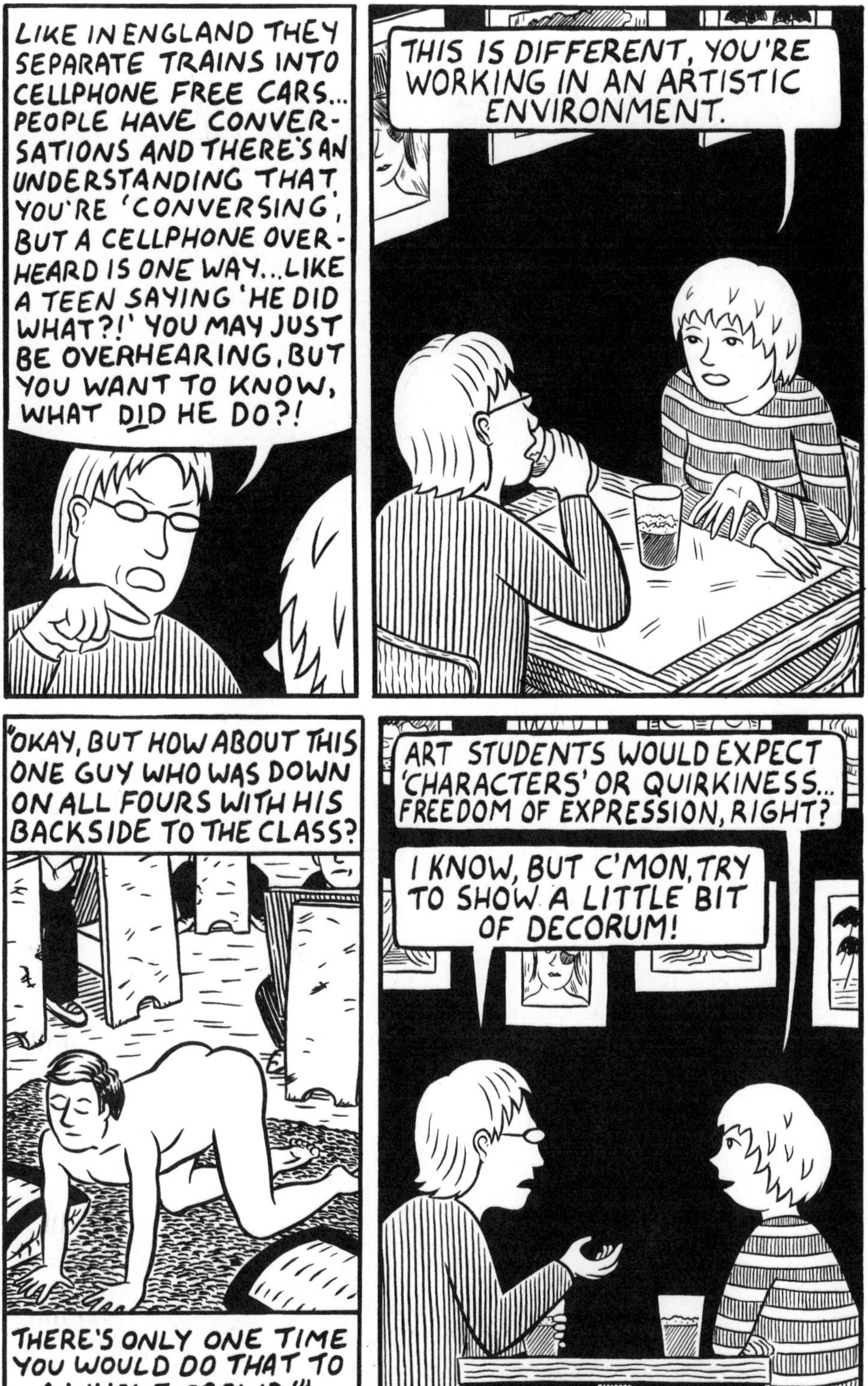
LIKE IN ENGLAND THEY SEPARATE TRAINS INTO CELLPHONE FREE CARS... PEOPLE HAVE CONVERSATIONS AND THERE'S AN UNDERSTANDING THAT YOU'RE 'CONVERSING', BUT A CELLPHONE OVERHEARD IS ONE WAY... LIKE A TEEN SAYING 'HE DID WHAT?!' YOU MAY JUST BE OVERHEARING, BUT YOU WANT TO KNOW, WHAT DID HE DO?!
THIS IS DIFFERENT, YOU'RE WORKING IN AN ARTISTIC ENVIRONMENT.
"OKAY, BUT HOW ABOUT THIS ONE GUY WHO WAS DOWN ON ALL FOURS WITH HIS BACKSIDE TO THE CLASS?
THERE'S ONLY ONE TIME YOU WOULD DO THAT TO A WHOLE CROWD!"
ART STUDENTS WOULD EXPECT 'CHARACTERS' OR QUIRKINESS... FREEDOM OF EXPRESSION, RIGHT?
I KNOW, BUT C'MON, TRY TO SHOW A LITTLE BIT OF DECORUM!

PEOPLE AROUND HERE

THE CAMERON HOUSE
· DAVE LAPP ·

HE'S BEEN GOING TO THE PARK EVERY DAY AND COUNTING CONDOMS!

PARK

"YAH! THE ONE DAY WE COUNTED 15 RUBBERS AND 14 WRAPPERS...

11, 12,... HEY THIS ONE'S GOT STUFF IN IT!

EEEW! DON'T TOUCH IT!

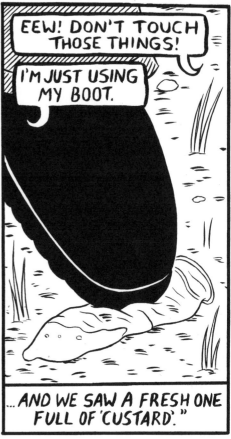

EEW! DON'T TOUCH THOSE THINGS!

I'M JUST USING MY BOOT.

...AND WE SAW A FRESH ONE FULL OF 'CUSTARD'."

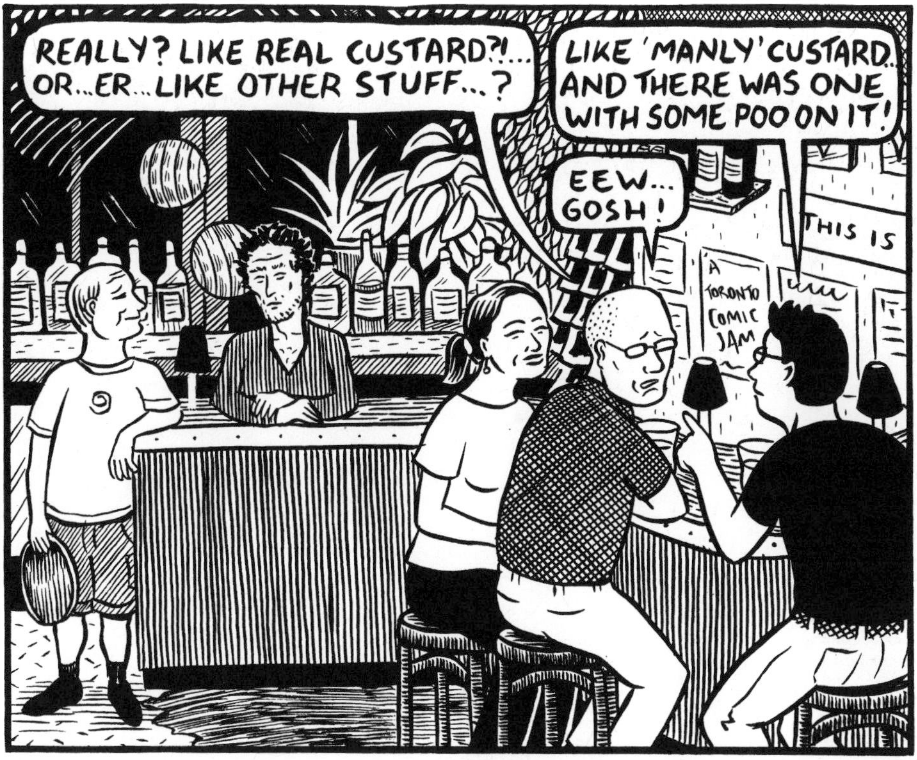
REALLY? LIKE REAL CUSTARD?!... OR...ER...LIKE OTHER STUFF...?
LIKE 'MANLY' CUSTARD.. AND THERE WAS ONE WITH SOME POO ON IT!
EEW... GOSH!
THIS IS
A TORONTO COMIC JAM

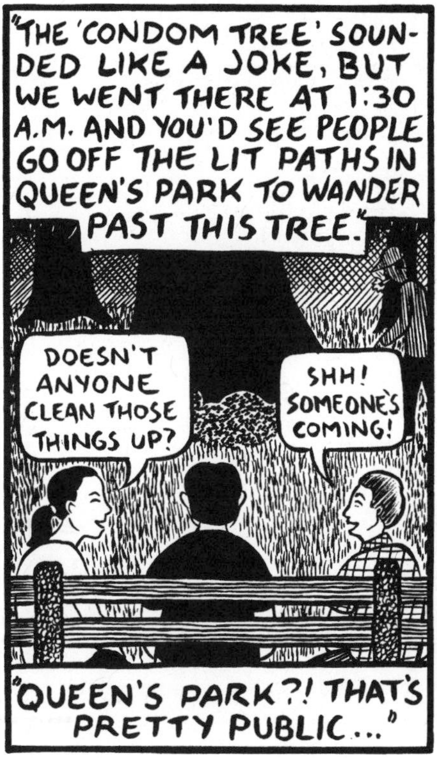
"THE 'CONDOM TREE' SOUNDED LIKE A JOKE, BUT WE WENT THERE AT 1:30 A.M. AND YOU'D SEE PEOPLE GO OFF THE LIT PATHS IN QUEEN'S PARK TO WANDER PAST THIS TREE."
DOESN'T ANYONE CLEAN THOSE THINGS UP?
SHH! SOMEONE'S COMING!
"QUEEN'S PARK?! THAT'S PRETTY PUBLIC..."

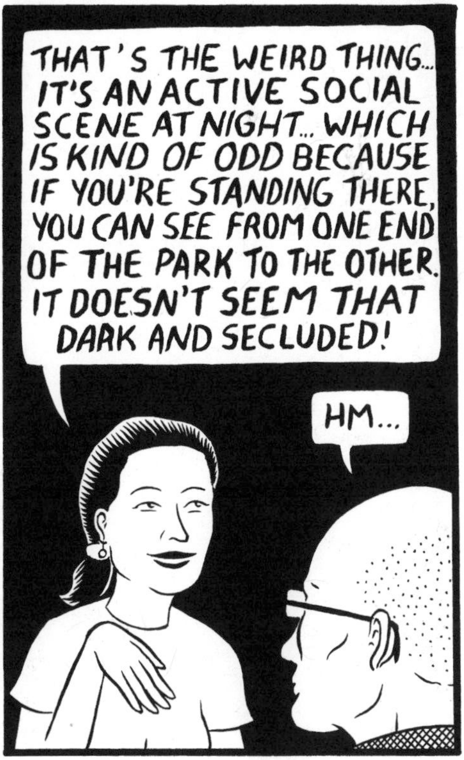
THAT'S THE WEIRD THING... IT'S AN ACTIVE SOCIAL SCENE AT NIGHT... WHICH IS KIND OF ODD BECAUSE IF YOU'RE STANDING THERE, YOU CAN SEE FROM ONE END OF THE PARK TO THE OTHER. IT DOESN'T SEEM THAT DARK AND SECLUDED!
HM...

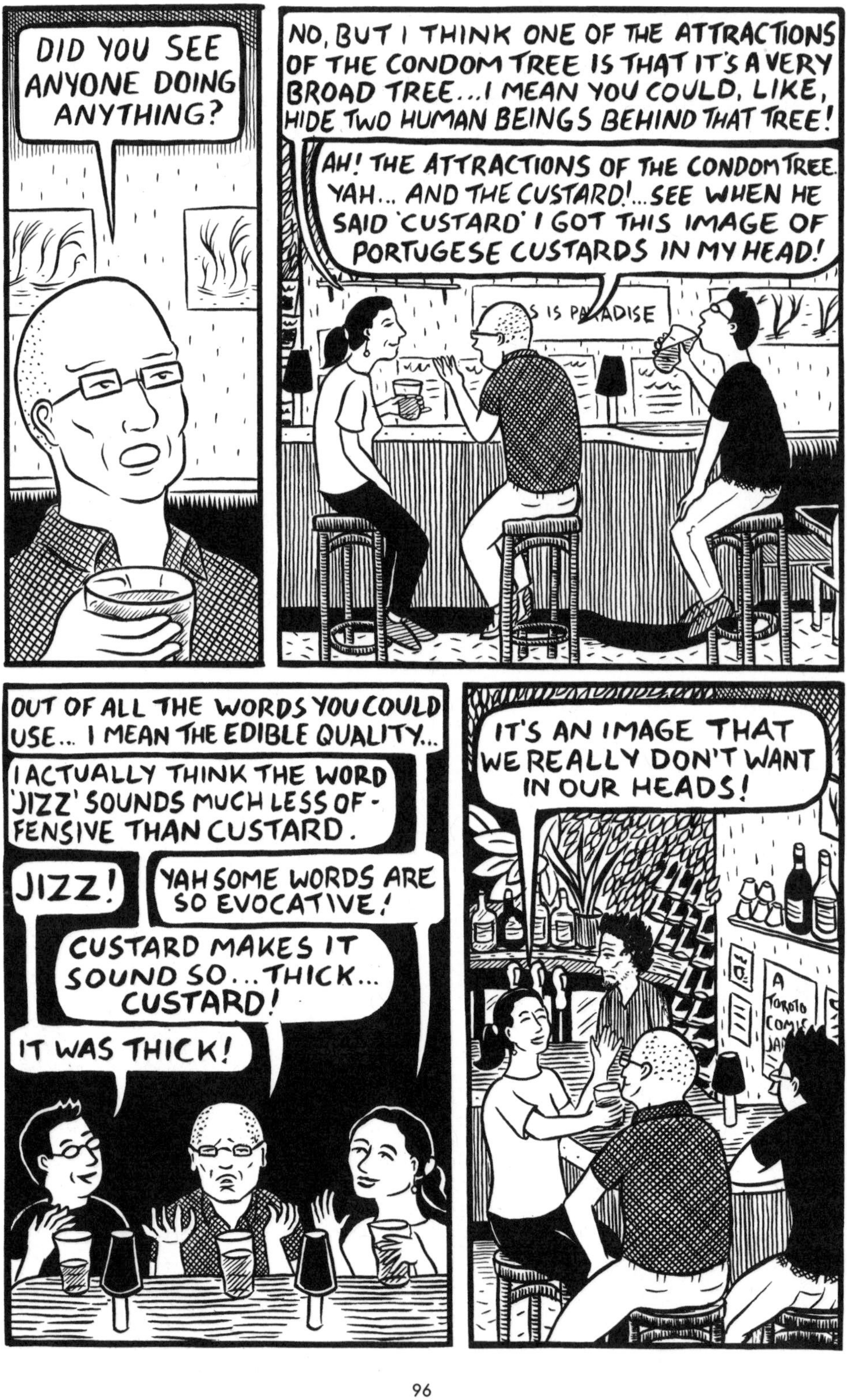
DID YOU SEE ANYONE DOING ANYTHING?
NO, BUT I THINK ONE OF THE ATTRACTIONS OF THE CONDOM TREE IS THAT IT'S A VERY BROAD TREE...I MEAN YOU COULD, LIKE, HIDE TWO HUMAN BEINGS BEHIND THAT TREE!
AH! THE ATTRACTIONS OF THE CONDOM TREE. YAH... AND THE CUSTARD!...SEE WHEN HE SAID 'CUSTARD' I GOT THIS IMAGE OF PORTUGESE CUSTARDS IN MY HEAD!
S IS PARADISE
OUT OF ALL THE WORDS YOU COULD USE... I MEAN THE EDIBLE QUALITY...
I ACTUALLY THINK THE WORD 'JIZZ' SOUNDS MUCH LESS OF-FENSIVE THAN CUSTARD.
JIZZ!
YAH SOME WORDS ARE SO EVOCATIVE!
CUSTARD MAKES IT SOUND SO...THICK... CUSTARD!
IT WAS THICK!
IT'S AN IMAGE THAT WE REALLY DON'T WANT IN OUR HEADS!

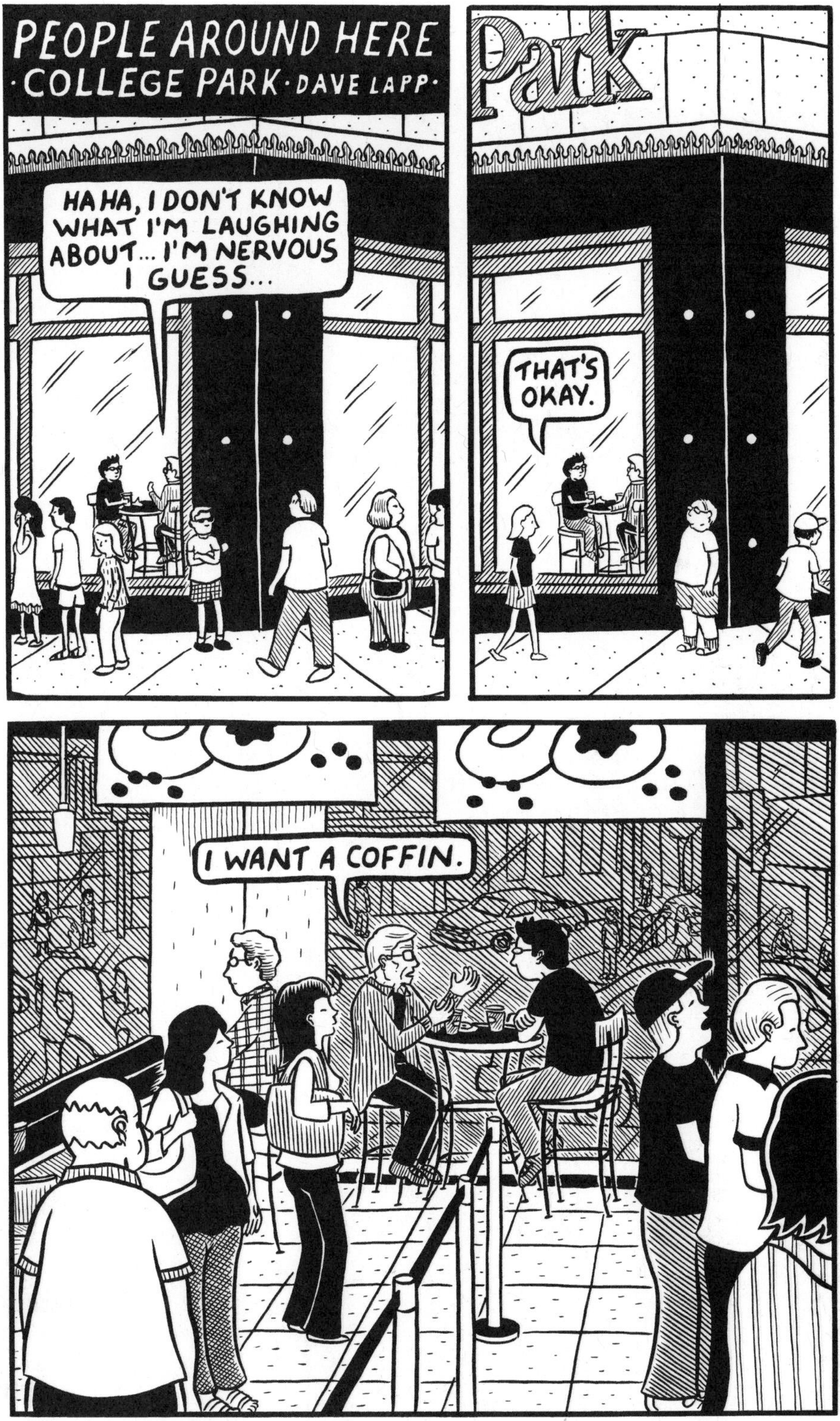
PEOPLE AROUND HERE
·COLLEGE PARK·DAVE LAPP·
HA HA, I DON'T KNOW WHAT I'M LAUGHING ABOUT... I'M NERVOUS I GUESS...
Park
THAT'S OKAY.
I WANT A COFFIN.

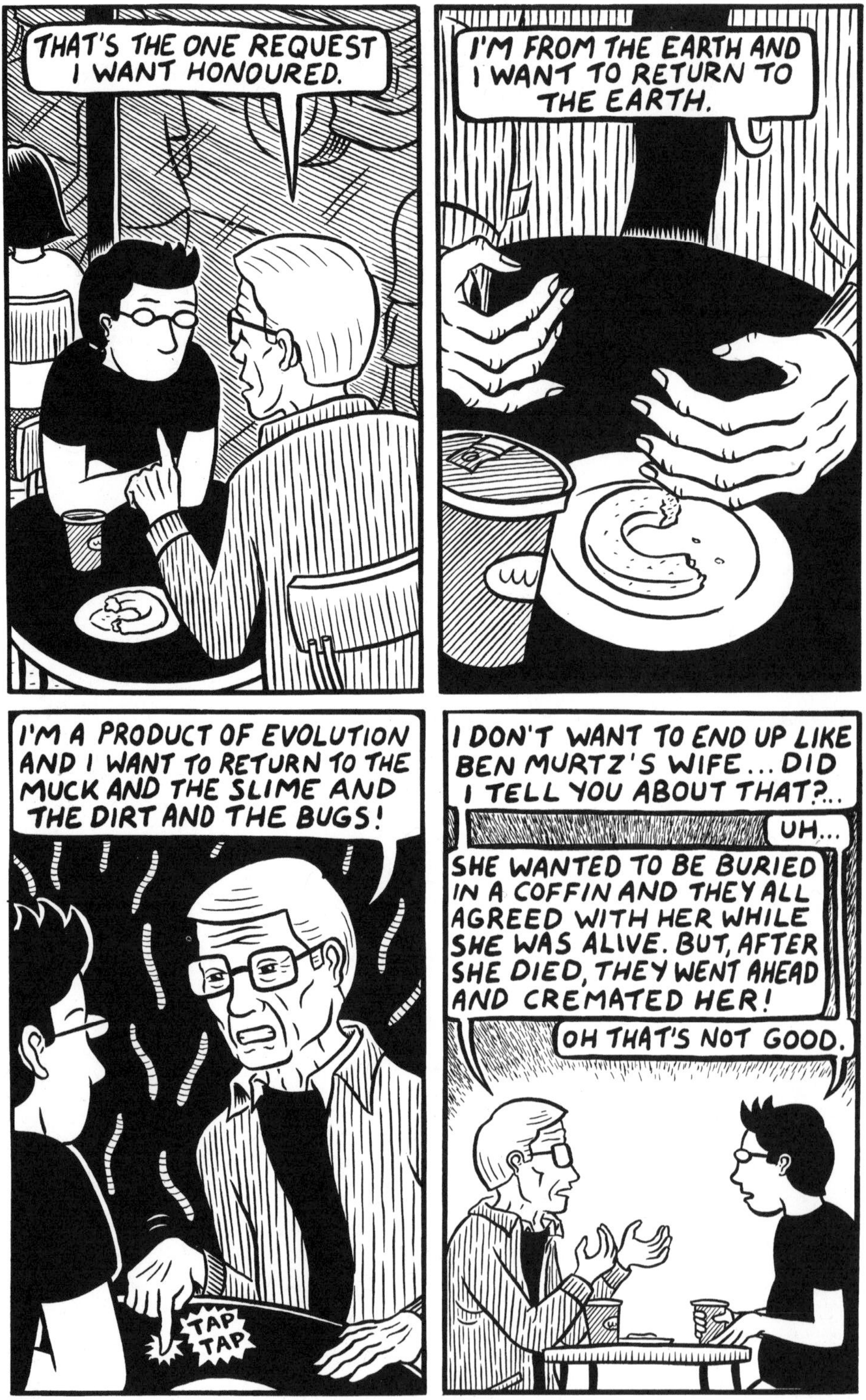
THAT'S THE ONE REQUEST I WANT HONOURED.
I'M FROM THE EARTH AND I WANT TO RETURN TO THE EARTH.
I'M A PRODUCT OF EVOLUTION AND I WANT TO RETURN TO THE MUCK AND THE SLIME AND THE DIRT AND THE BUGS!
TAP TAP
I DON'T WANT TO END UP LIKE BEN MURTZ'S WIFE... DID I TELL YOU ABOUT THAT?...
UH...
SHE WANTED TO BE BURIED IN A COFFIN AND THEY ALL AGREED WITH HER WHILE SHE WAS ALIVE. BUT, AFTER SHE DIED, THEY WENT AHEAD AND CREMATED HER!
OH THAT'S NOT GOOD.

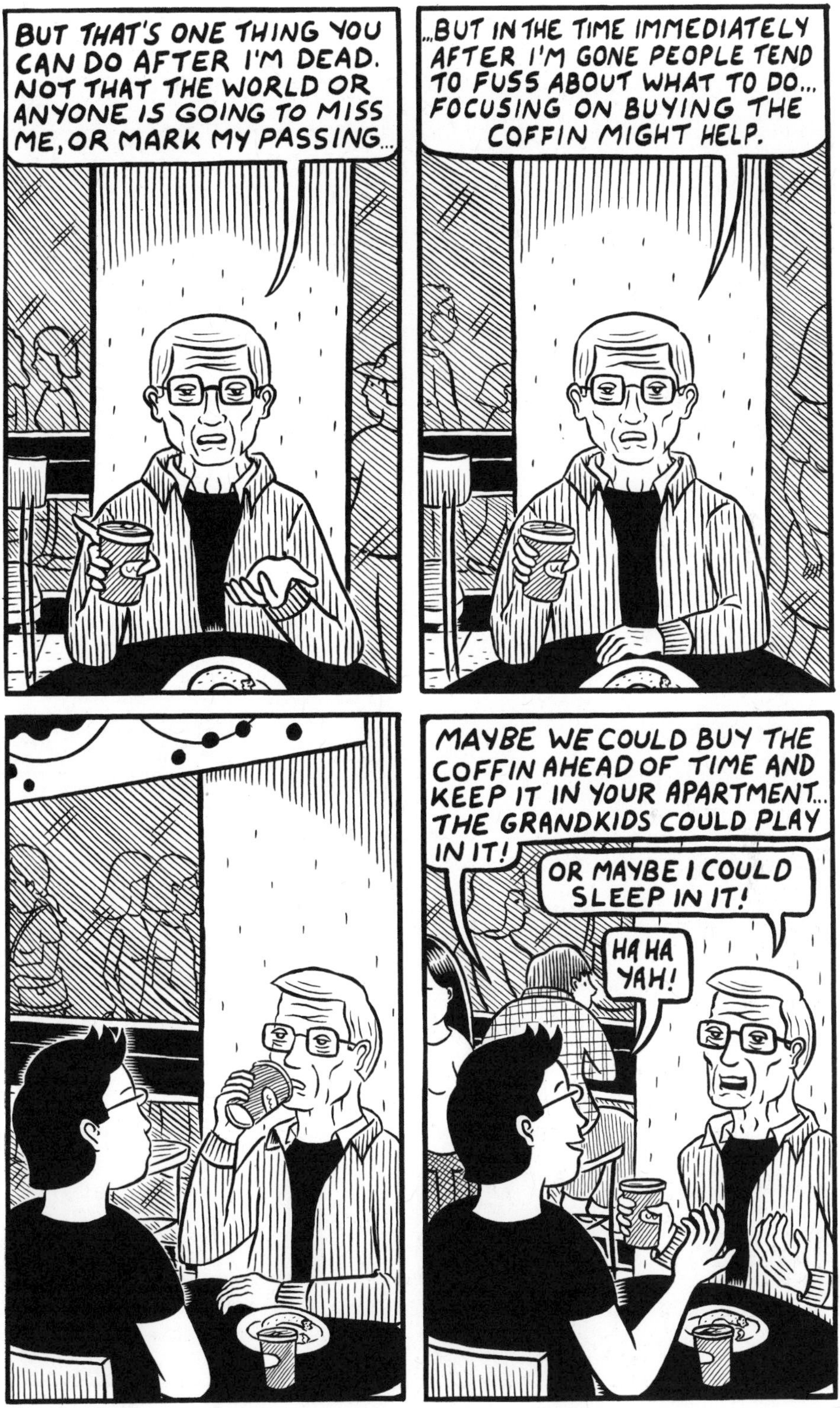
BUT THAT'S ONE THING YOU CAN DO AFTER I'M DEAD. NOT THAT THE WORLD OR ANYONE IS GOING TO MISS ME, OR MARK MY PASSING...
...BUT IN THE TIME IMMEDIATELY AFTER I'M GONE PEOPLE TEND TO FUSS ABOUT WHAT TO DO... FOCUSING ON BUYING THE COFFIN MIGHT HELP.
MAYBE WE COULD BUY THE COFFIN AHEAD OF TIME AND KEEP IT IN YOUR APARTMENT... THE GRANDKIDS COULD PLAY IN IT!
OR MAYBE I COULD SLEEP IN IT!
HA HA YAH!

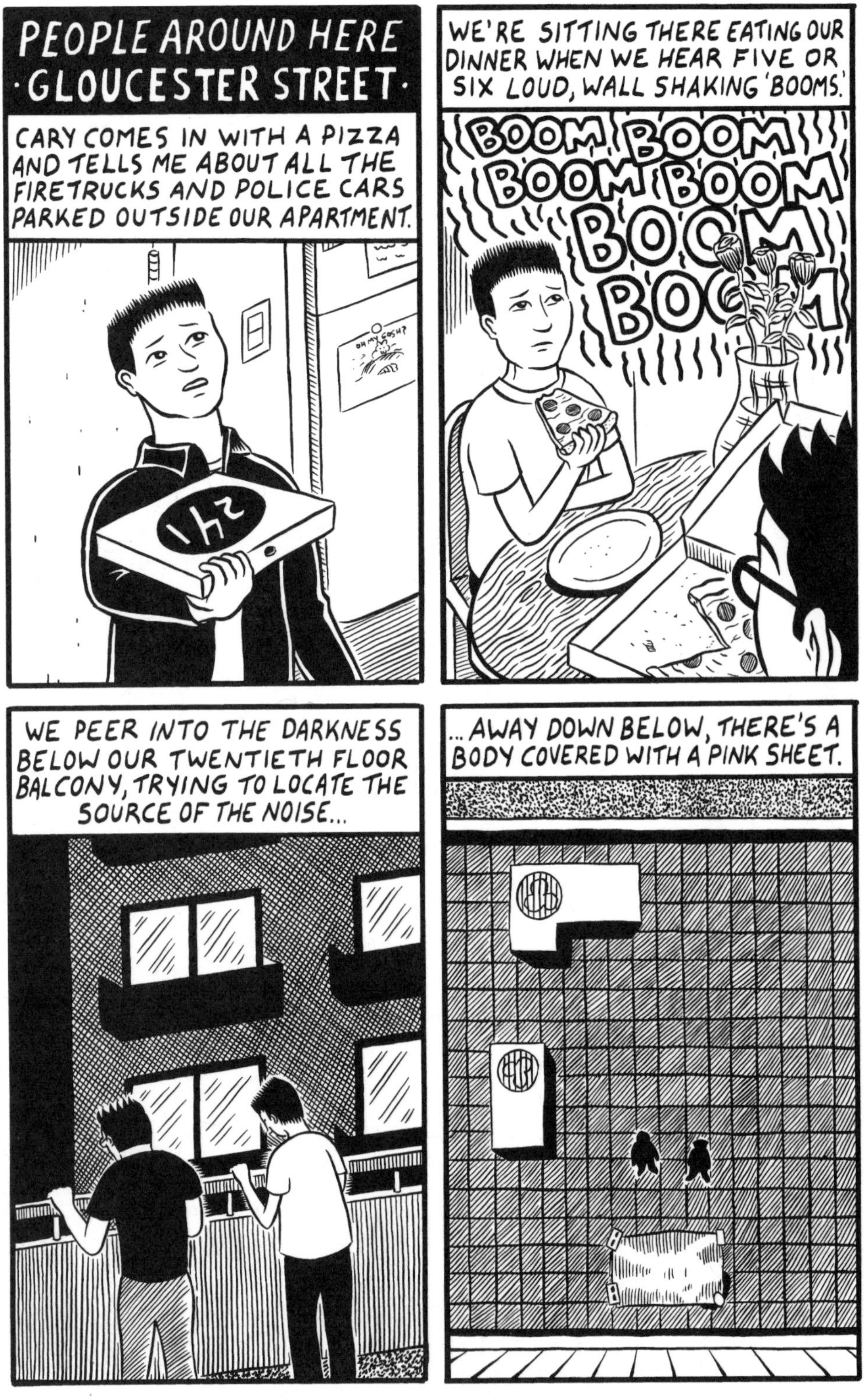
PEOPLE AROUND HERE
·GLOUCESTER STREET·
CARY COMES IN WITH A PIZZA AND TELLS ME ABOUT ALL THE FIRETRUCKS AND POLICE CARS PARKED OUTSIDE OUR APARTMENT.
OH MY GOSH?
WE'RE SITTING THERE EATING OUR DINNER WHEN WE HEAR FIVE OR SIX LOUD, WALL SHAKING 'BOOMS.'
BOOM BOOM
BOOM BOOM
BOOM
BOOM
WE PEER INTO THE DARKNESS BELOW OUR TWENTIETH FLOOR BALCONY, TRYING TO LOCATE THE SOURCE OF THE NOISE...
...AWAY DOWN BELOW, THERE'S A BODY COVERED WITH A PINK SHEET.

THE COLD WIND WHIPS THE SHEET SO HARD, YOU'D SWEAR SOMEONE WAS THRASHING BENEATH IT.

POLICE OFFICIALS WANDER ABOUT SHINING THEIR FLASHLIGHTS ACROSS THE FIGURE... CARY WONDERS IF THE DARK AREAS AT THE CORNERS OF THE SHEET ARE HAIR...OR BLOOD.

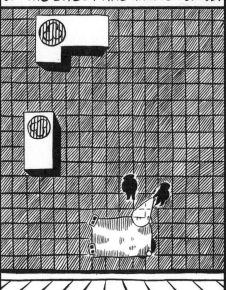

IN THE APARTMENT ACROSS FROM US A FEW HEADS POKE OUT FROM THEIR BALCONIES... SOMEONE IS SHINING A LASER POINTER... A FLASHLIGHT...ONE COUPLE HAS A PAIR OF BINOCULARS...

TURN THAT OFF!

IT'S FREEZING OUTSIDE, SO WE GO INSIDE AND WATCH 'THE ADDAMS FAMILY' ON TV ... THEN GO BACK OUT TO CHECK THE BODY...THEN TV...THEN BODY...THEN TV...

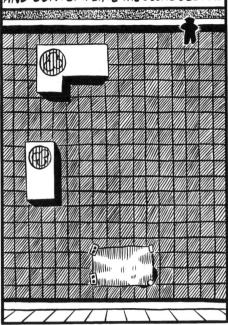

...THE BODY WINS OUT... SO WE PUT ON OUR WINTER COATS AND GLOVES AND CONTEMPLATE THE SCENE BELOW.

EVENTUALLY WE DECIDE TO TAKE THE ELEVATOR DOWN TO FIND OUT WHAT HAPPENED. ON THE SIXTEENTH FLOOR A POLICEMAN AND A CITY OFFICIAL COME IN...

THEY LAUGH AND JOKE ABOUT "THE FUCKIN' JOB THE FIRE GUYS DID TRYIN' TO GET IN THAT DOOR! WHAT A FUCKIN' MESS!" THEY KEEP LOOKING AT US LIKE WE'RE IN ON THE JOKE... OR SUSPECTS.

HAR HAR! FUCKIN' FIRE GUYS EH?!

BEHIND OUR BUILDING WE SEE THE ELEVATOR GUYS WITH SEVERAL OTHERS MOUNTING THE STAIRS TO WHERE THE BODY LIES... WE HURRY BACK TO OUR APARTMENT TO GET A BETTER VIEW FROM ABOVE.

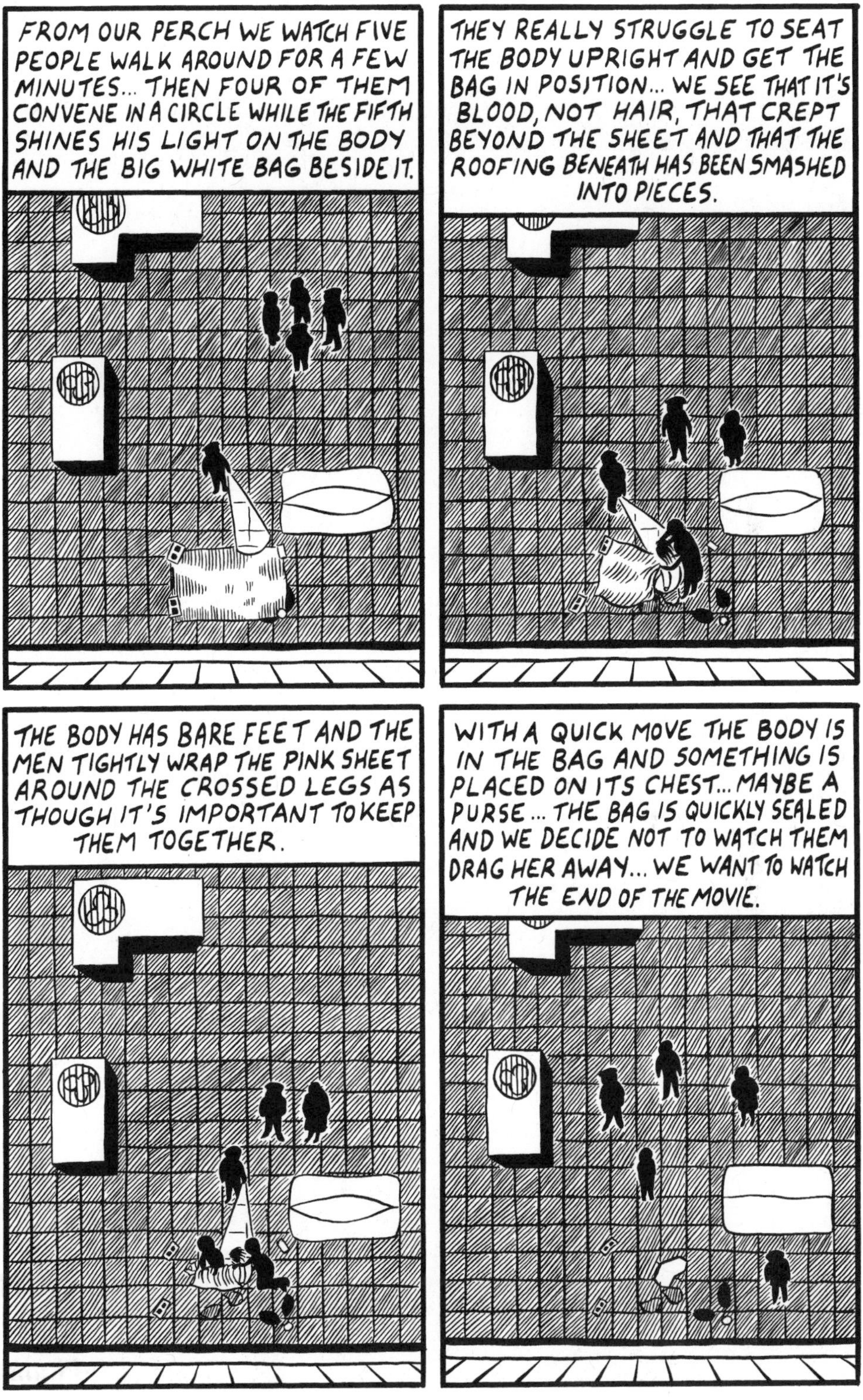
FROM OUR PERCH WE WATCH FIVE PEOPLE WALK AROUND FOR A FEW MINUTES... THEN FOUR OF THEM CONVENE IN A CIRCLE WHILE THE FIFTH SHINES HIS LIGHT ON THE BODY AND THE BIG WHITE BAG BESIDE IT.
THEY REALLY STRUGGLE TO SEAT THE BODY UPRIGHT AND GET THE BAG IN POSITION... WE SEE THAT IT'S BLOOD, NOT HAIR, THAT CREPT BEYOND THE SHEET AND THAT THE ROOFING BENEATH HAS BEEN SMASHED INTO PIECES.
THE BODY HAS BARE FEET AND THE MEN TIGHTLY WRAP THE PINK SHEET AROUND THE CROSSED LEGS AS THOUGH IT'S IMPORTANT TO KEEP THEM TOGETHER.
WITH A QUICK MOVE THE BODY IS IN THE BAG AND SOMETHING IS PLACED ON ITS CHEST... MAYBE A PURSE... THE BAG IS QUICKLY SEALED AND WE DECIDE NOT TO WATCH THEM DRAG HER AWAY... WE WANT TO WATCH THE END OF THE MOVIE.

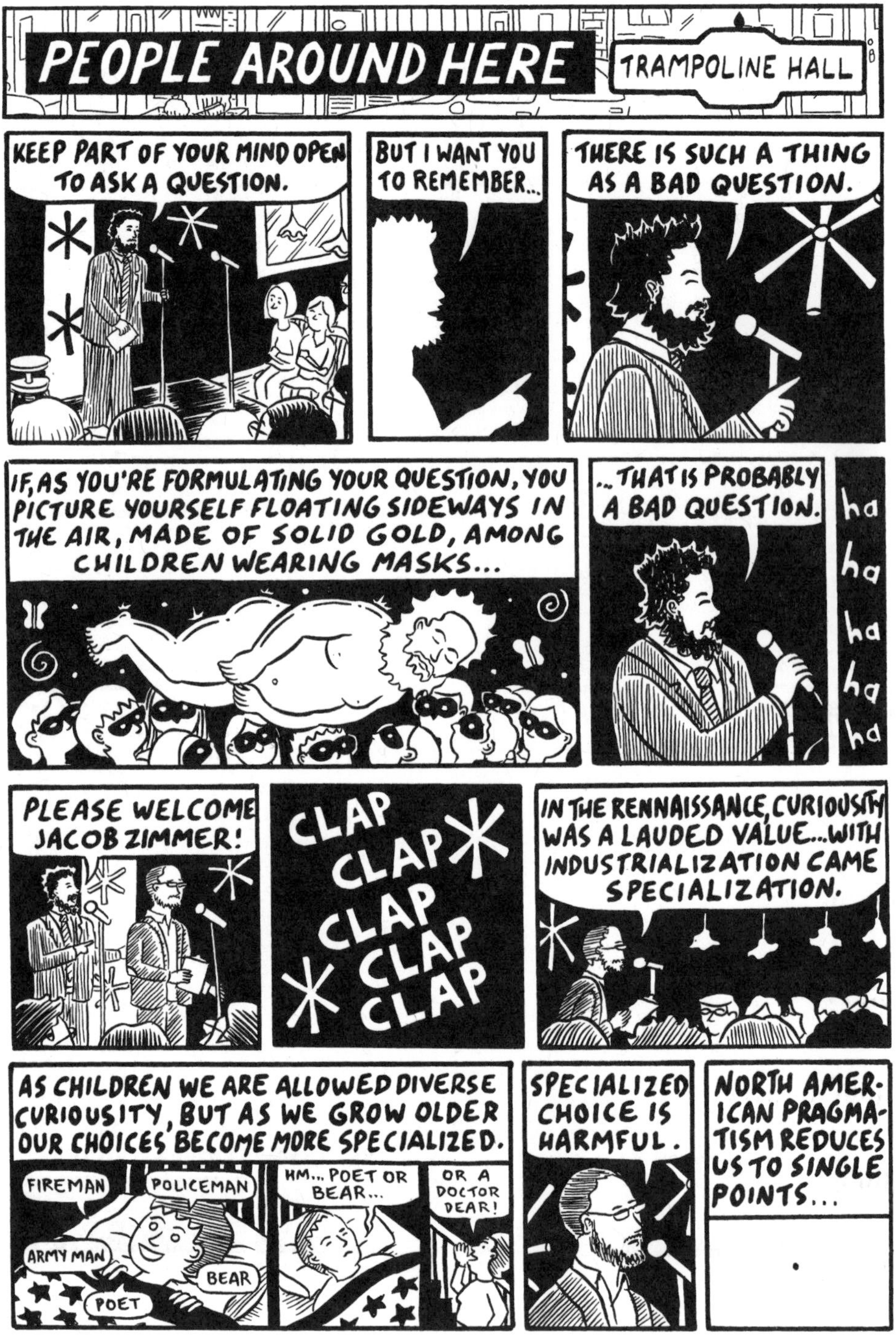
PEOPLE AROUND HERE
TRAMPOLINE HALL
KEEP PART OF YOUR MIND OPEN TO ASK A QUESTION.
BUT I WANT YOU TO REMEMBER...
THERE IS SUCH A THING AS A BAD QUESTION.
IF, AS YOU'RE FORMULATING YOUR QUESTION, YOU PICTURE YOURSELF FLOATING SIDEWAYS IN THE AIR, MADE OF SOLID GOLD, AMONG CHILDREN WEARING MASKS...
...THAT IS PROBABLY A BAD QUESTION.
ha ha ha ha ha
PLEASE WELCOME JACOB ZIMMER!
CLAP CLAP CLAP CLAP CLAP CLAP
IN THE RENNAISSANCE, CURIOUSITY WAS A LAUDED VALUE...WITH INDUSTRIALIZATION CAME SPECIALIZATION.
AS CHILDREN WE ARE ALLOWED DIVERSE CURIOUSITY, BUT AS WE GROW OLDER OUR CHOICES BECOME MORE SPECIALIZED.
FIREMAN
POLICEMAN
ARMY MAN
BEAR
POET
HM... POET OR BEAR...
OR A DOCTOR DEAR!
SPECIALIZED CHOICE IS HARMFUL.
NORTH AMERICAN PRAGMATISM REDUCES US TO SINGLE POINTS...

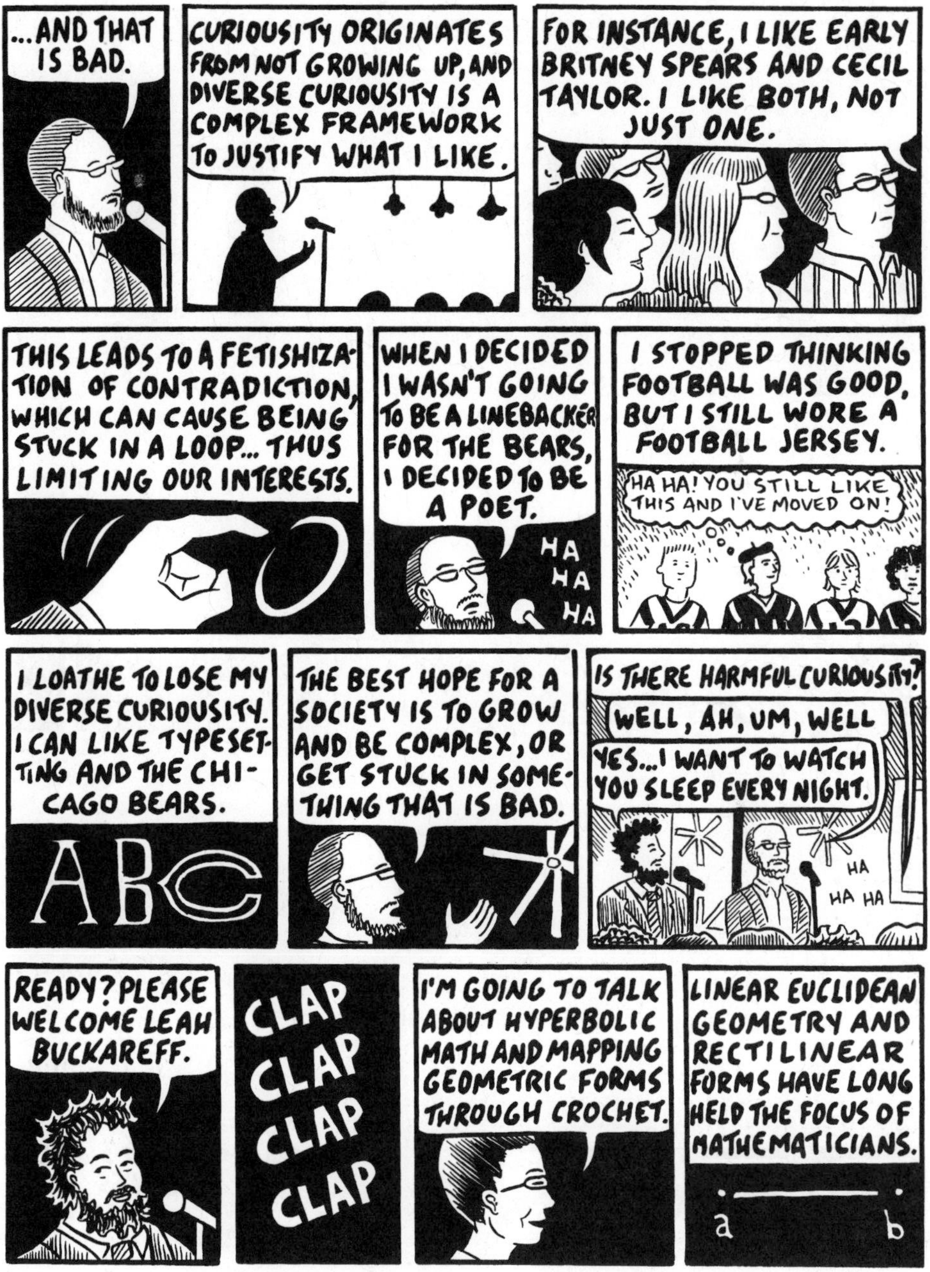

...AND THAT IS BAD.
CURIOUSITY ORIGINATES FROM NOT GROWING UP, AND DIVERSE CURIOUSITY IS A COMPLEX FRAMEWORK TO JUSTIFY WHAT I LIKE.
FOR INSTANCE, I LIKE EARLY BRITNEY SPEARS AND CECIL TAYLOR. I LIKE BOTH, NOT JUST ONE.
THIS LEADS TO A FETISHIZATION OF CONTRADICTION, WHICH CAN CAUSE BEING STUCK IN A LOOP... THUS LIMITING OUR INTERESTS.
WHEN I DECIDED I WASN'T GOING TO BE A LINEBACKER FOR THE BEARS, I DECIDED TO BE A POET.
HA HA HA
I STOPPED THINKING FOOTBALL WAS GOOD, BUT I STILL WORE A FOOTBALL JERSEY.
HA HA! YOU STILL LIKE THIS AND I'VE MOVED ON!
I LOATHE TO LOSE MY DIVERSE CURIOUSITY. I CAN LIKE TYPESETTING AND THE CHICAGO BEARS.
ABC
THE BEST HOPE FOR A SOCIETY IS TO GROW AND BE COMPLEX, OR GET STUCK IN SOMETHING THAT IS BAD.
IS THERE HARMFUL CURIOUSITY?
WELL, AH, UM, WELL
YES...I WANT TO WATCH YOU SLEEP EVERY NIGHT.
HA HA HA
READY? PLEASE WELCOME LEAH BUCKAREFF.
CLAP CLAP CLAP CLAP
I'M GOING TO TALK ABOUT HYPERBOLIC MATH AND MAPPING GEOMETRIC FORMS THROUGH CROCHET.
LINEAR EUCLIDEAN GEOMETRY AND RECTILINEAR FORMS HAVE LONG HELD THE FOCUS OF MATHEMATICIANS.
a b

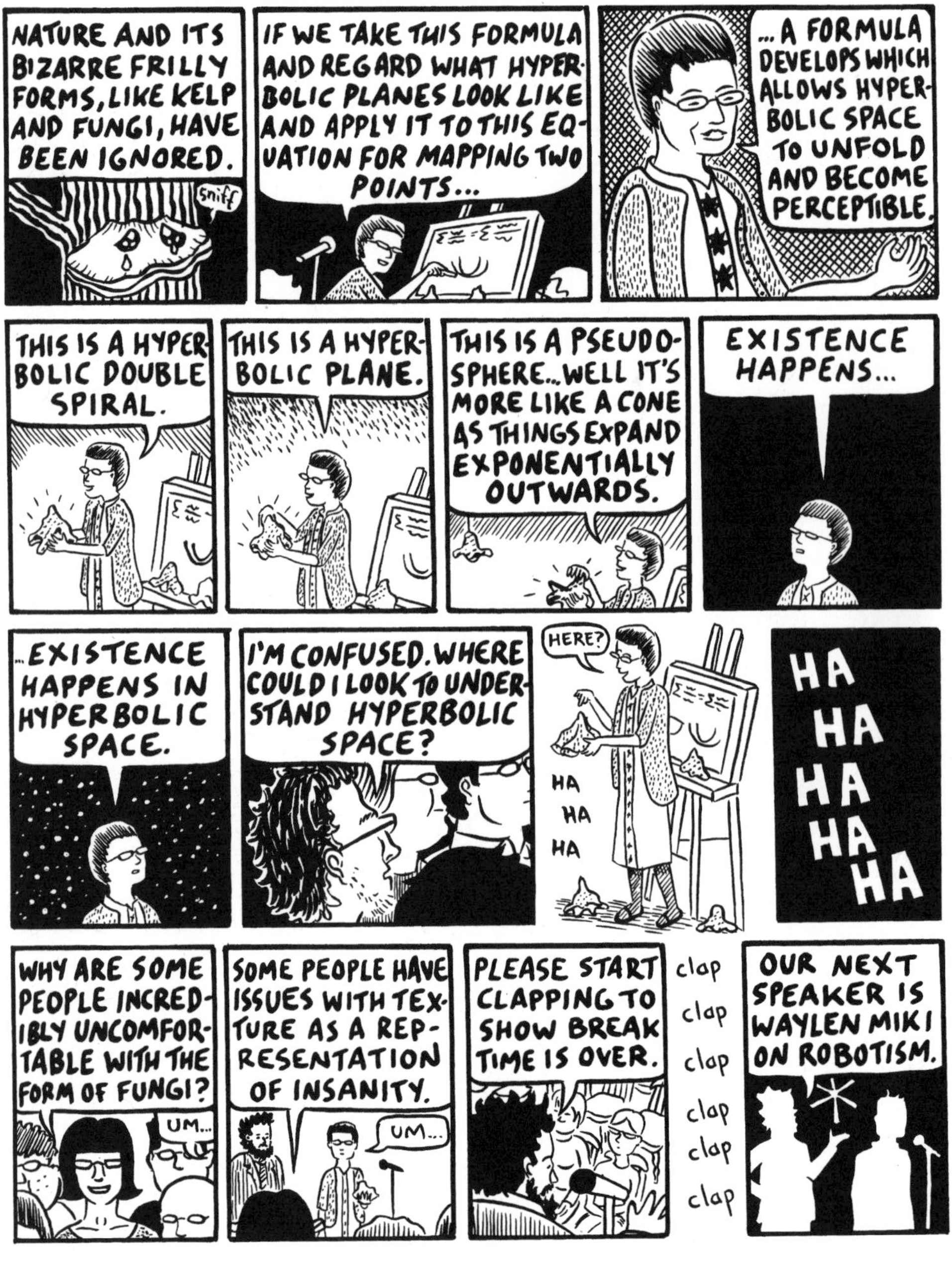

NATURE AND ITS BIZARRE FRILLY FORMS, LIKE KELP AND FUNGI, HAVE BEEN IGNORED.
sniff
IF WE TAKE THIS FORMULA AND REGARD WHAT HYPERBOLIC PLANES LOOK LIKE AND APPLY IT TO THIS EQUATION FOR MAPPING TWO POINTS...
...A FORMULA DEVELOPS WHICH ALLOWS HYPERBOLIC SPACE TO UNFOLD AND BECOME PERCEPTIBLE.
THIS IS A HYPERBOLIC DOUBLE SPIRAL.
THIS IS A HYPERBOLIC PLANE.
THIS IS A PSEUDOSPHERE...WELL IT'S MORE LIKE A CONE AS THINGS EXPAND EXPONENTIALLY OUTWARDS.
EXISTENCE HAPPENS...
...EXISTENCE HAPPENS IN HYPERBOLIC SPACE.
I'M CONFUSED. WHERE COULD I LOOK TO UNDERSTAND HYPERBOLIC SPACE?
HERE?
HA HA HA
HA HA HA HA HA
WHY ARE SOME PEOPLE INCREDIBLY UNCOMFORTABLE WITH THE FORM OF FUNGI?
UM...
SOME PEOPLE HAVE ISSUES WITH TEXTURE AS A REPRESENTATION OF INSANITY.
UM...
PLEASE START CLAPPING TO SHOW BREAK TIME IS OVER.
clap clap clap clap clap clap
OUR NEXT SPEAKER IS WAYLEN MIKI ON ROBOTISM.

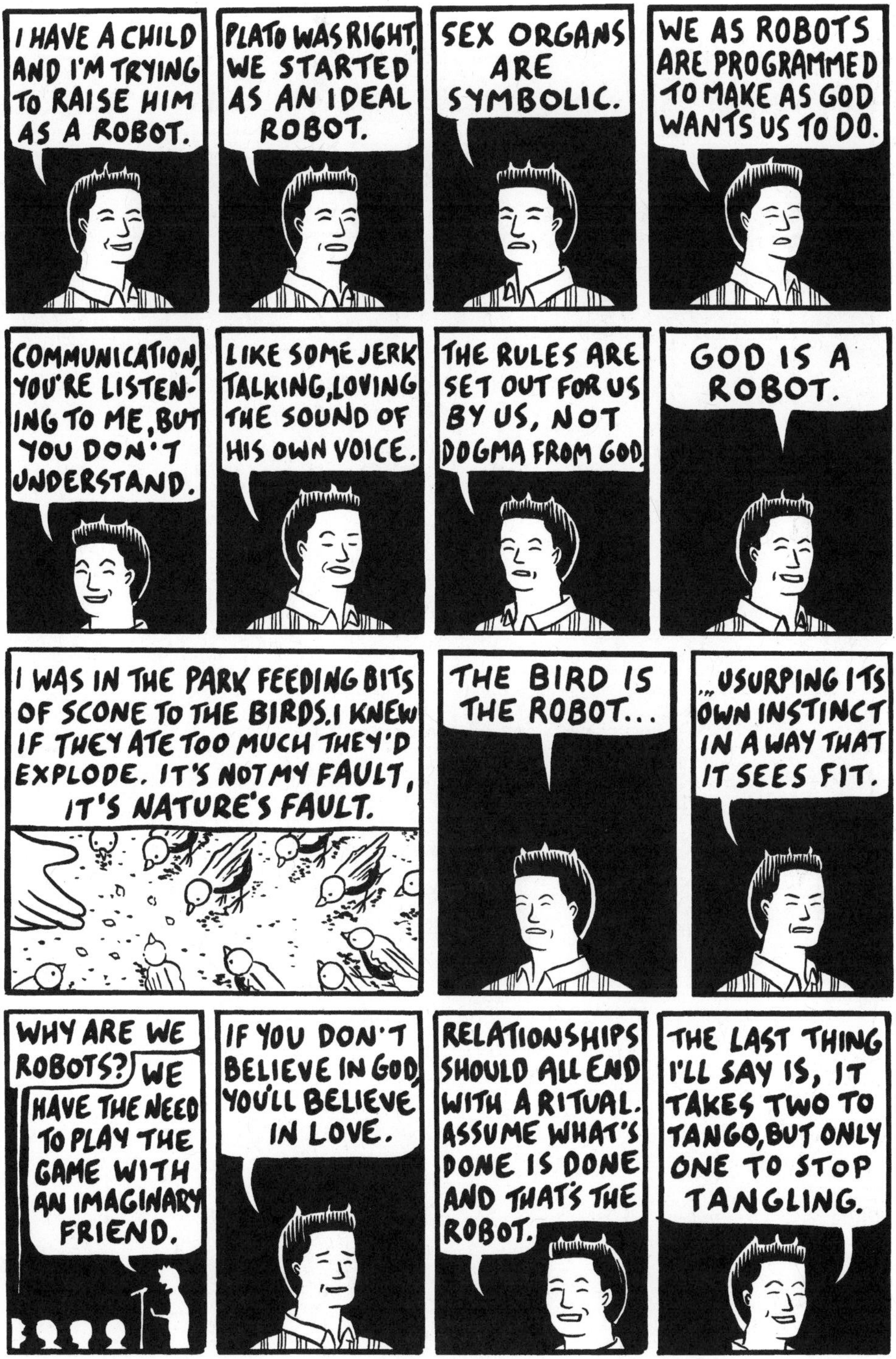
I HAVE A CHILD AND I'M TRYING TO RAISE HIM AS A ROBOT.
PLATO WAS RIGHT, WE STARTED AS AN IDEAL ROBOT.
SEX ORGANS ARE SYMBOLIC.
WE AS ROBOTS ARE PROGRAMMED TO MAKE AS GOD WANTS US TO DO.
COMMUNICATION, YOU'RE LISTENING TO ME, BUT YOU DON'T UNDERSTAND.
LIKE SOME JERK TALKING, LOVING THE SOUND OF HIS OWN VOICE.
THE RULES ARE SET OUT FOR US BY US, NOT DOGMA FROM GOD.
GOD IS A ROBOT.
I WAS IN THE PARK FEEDING BITS OF SCONE TO THE BIRDS. I KNEW IF THEY ATE TOO MUCH THEY'D EXPLODE. IT'S NOT MY FAULT, IT'S NATURE'S FAULT.
THE BIRD IS THE ROBOT...
...USURPING ITS OWN INSTINCT IN A WAY THAT IT SEES FIT.
WHY ARE WE ROBOTS?
WE HAVE THE NEED TO PLAY THE GAME WITH AN IMAGINARY FRIEND.
IF YOU DON'T BELIEVE IN GOD, YOU'LL BELIEVE IN LOVE.
RELATIONSHIPS SHOULD ALL END WITH A RITUAL. ASSUME WHAT'S DONE IS DONE AND THAT'S THE ROBOT.
THE LAST THING I'LL SAY IS, IT TAKES TWO TO TANGO, BUT ONLY ONE TO STOP TANGLING.

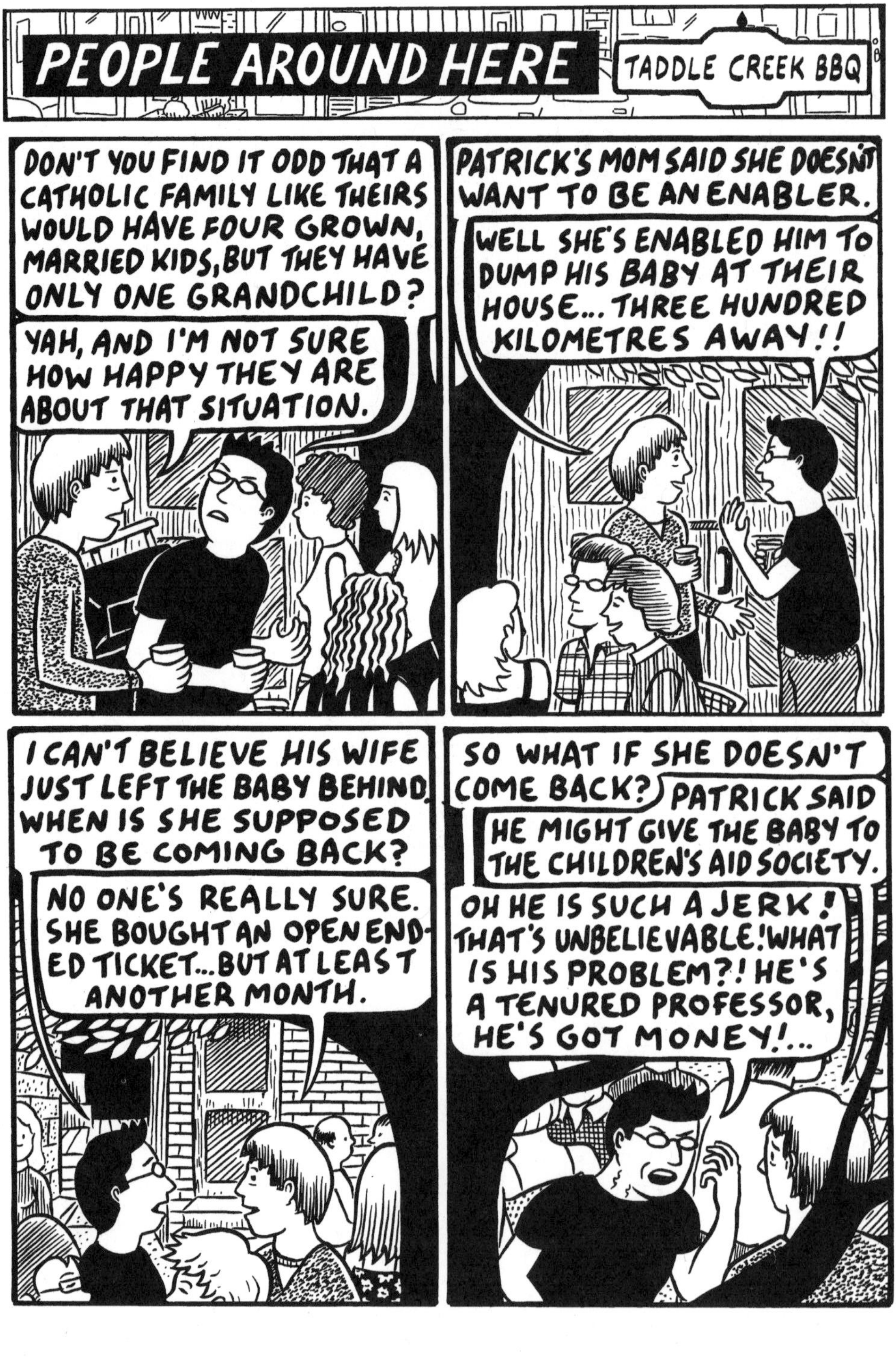
PEOPLE AROUND HERE
TADDLE CREEK BBQ
DON'T YOU FIND IT ODD THAT A CATHOLIC FAMILY LIKE THEIRS WOULD HAVE FOUR GROWN, MARRIED KIDS, BUT THEY HAVE ONLY ONE GRANDCHILD?
YAH, AND I'M NOT SURE HOW HAPPY THEY ARE ABOUT THAT SITUATION.
PATRICK'S MOM SAID SHE DOESN'T WANT TO BE AN ENABLER.
WELL SHE'S ENABLED HIM TO DUMP HIS BABY AT THEIR HOUSE... THREE HUNDRED KILOMETRES AWAY!!
I CAN'T BELIEVE HIS WIFE JUST LEFT THE BABY BEHIND. WHEN IS SHE SUPPOSED TO BE COMING BACK?
NO ONE'S REALLY SURE. SHE BOUGHT AN OPEN ENDED TICKET... BUT AT LEAST ANOTHER MONTH.
SO WHAT IF SHE DOESN'T COME BACK?
PATRICK SAID HE MIGHT GIVE THE BABY TO THE CHILDREN'S AID SOCIETY.
OH HE IS SUCH A JERK! THAT'S UNBELIEVABLE! WHAT IS HIS PROBLEM?! HE'S A TENURED PROFESSOR, HE'S GOT MONEY!...

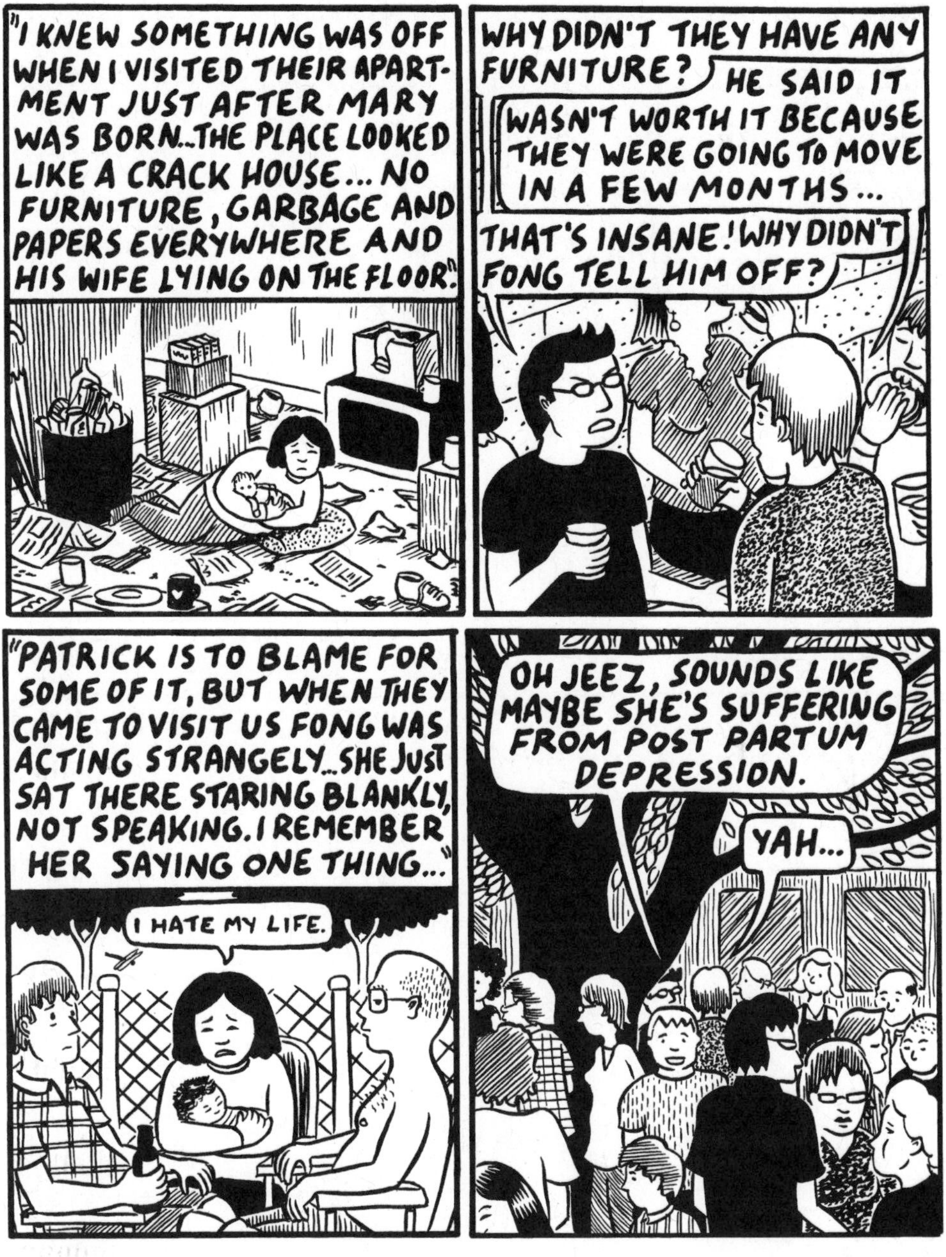

"I KNEW SOMETHING WAS OFF WHEN I VISITED THEIR APARTMENT JUST AFTER MARY WAS BORN...THE PLACE LOOKED LIKE A CRACK HOUSE... NO FURNITURE, GARBAGE AND PAPERS EVERYWHERE AND HIS WIFE LYING ON THE FLOOR."
WHY DIDN'T THEY HAVE ANY FURNITURE?
HE SAID IT WASN'T WORTH IT BECAUSE THEY WERE GOING TO MOVE IN A FEW MONTHS...
THAT'S INSANE! WHY DIDN'T FONG TELL HIM OFF?
"PATRICK IS TO BLAME FOR SOME OF IT, BUT WHEN THEY CAME TO VISIT US FONG WAS ACTING STRANGELY...SHE JUST SAT THERE STARING BLANKLY, NOT SPEAKING. I REMEMBER HER SAYING ONE THING..."
I HATE MY LIFE.
OH JEEZ, SOUNDS LIKE MAYBE SHE'S SUFFERING FROM POST PARTUM DEPRESSION.
YAH...

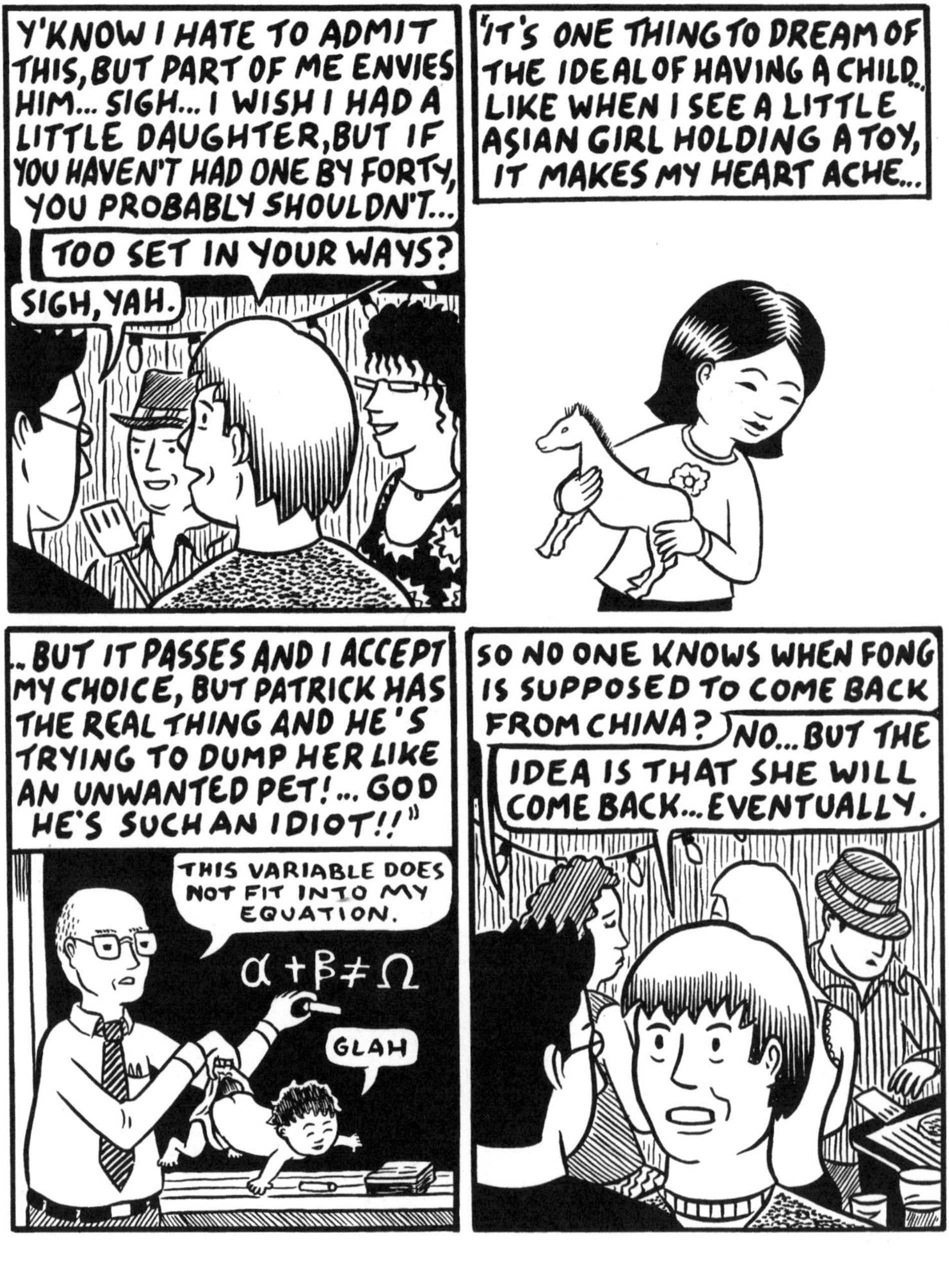

Y'KNOW I HATE TO ADMIT THIS, BUT PART OF ME ENVIES HIM... SIGH... I WISH I HAD A LITTLE DAUGHTER, BUT IF YOU HAVEN'T HAD ONE BY FORTY, YOU PROBABLY SHOULDN'T...
TOO SET IN YOUR WAYS?
SIGH, YAH.
"IT'S ONE THING TO DREAM OF THE IDEAL OF HAVING A CHILD... LIKE WHEN I SEE A LITTLE ASIAN GIRL HOLDING A TOY, IT MAKES MY HEART ACHE...
.. BUT IT PASSES AND I ACCEPT MY CHOICE, BUT PATRICK HAS THE REAL THING AND HE'S TRYING TO DUMP HER LIKE AN UNWANTED PET!... GOD HE'S SUCH AN IDIOT!!"
THIS VARIABLE DOES NOT FIT INTO MY EQUATION.
α + β ≠ Ω
GLAH
SO NO ONE KNOWS WHEN FONG IS SUPPOSED TO COME BACK FROM CHINA?
NO... BUT THE IDEA IS THAT SHE WILL COME BACK... EVENTUALLY.

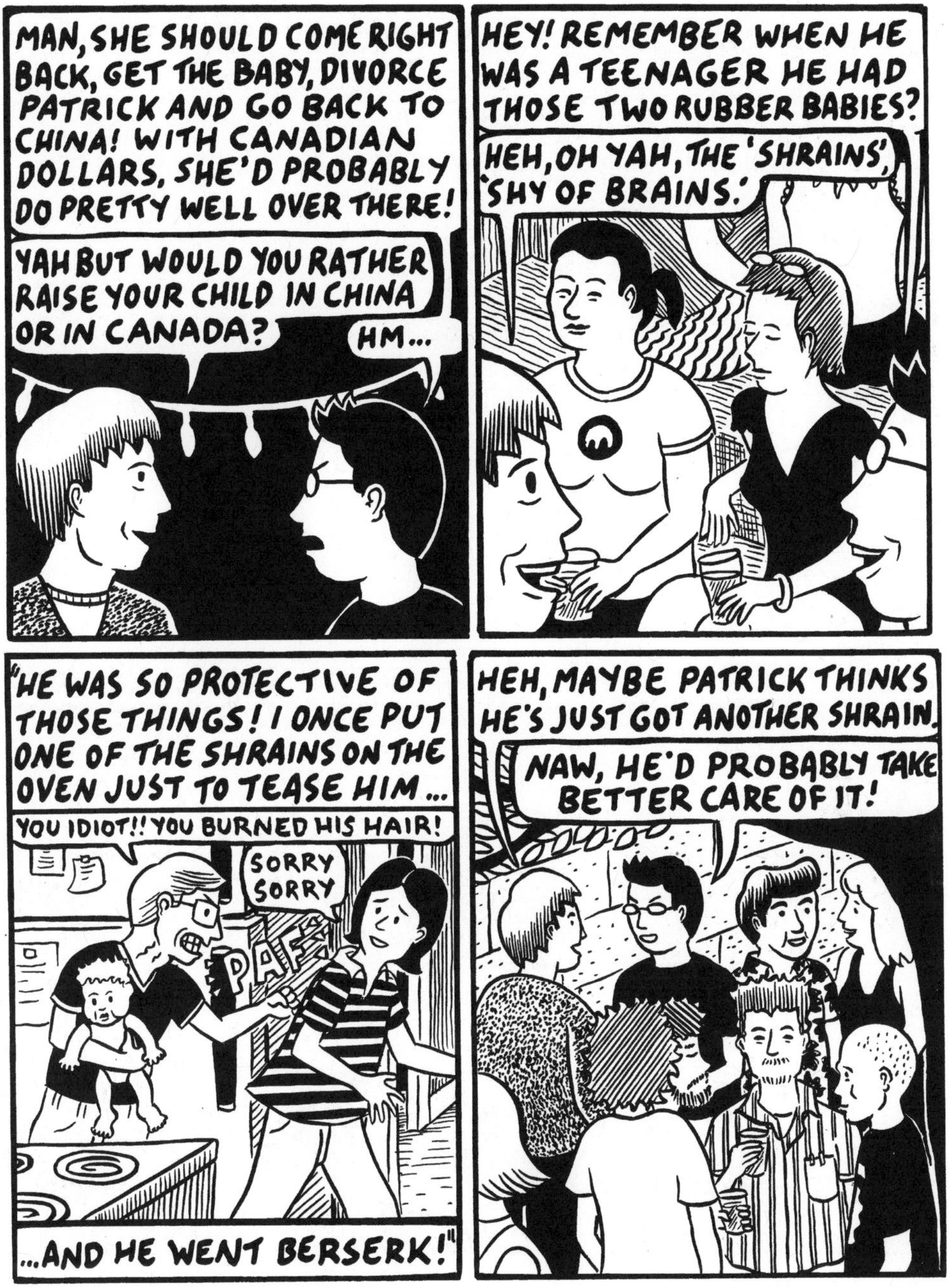
MAN, SHE SHOULD COME RIGHT BACK, GET THE BABY, DIVORCE PATRICK AND GO BACK TO CHINA! WITH CANADIAN DOLLARS, SHE'D PROBABLY DO PRETTY WELL OVER THERE!
YAH BUT WOULD YOU RATHER RAISE YOUR CHILD IN CHINA OR IN CANADA?
HM...
HEY! REMEMBER WHEN HE WAS A TEENAGER HE HAD THOSE TWO RUBBER BABIES?
HEH, OH YAH, THE 'SHRAINS', 'SHY OF BRAINS.'
"HE WAS SO PROTECTIVE OF THOSE THINGS! I ONCE PUT ONE OF THE SHRAINS ON THE OVEN JUST TO TEASE HIM...
YOU IDIOT!! YOU BURNED HIS HAIR!
SORRY SORRY
PAF
...AND HE WENT BERSERK!"
HEH, MAYBE PATRICK THINKS HE'S JUST GOT ANOTHER SHRAIN.
NAW, HE'D PROBABLY TAKE BETTER CARE OF IT!

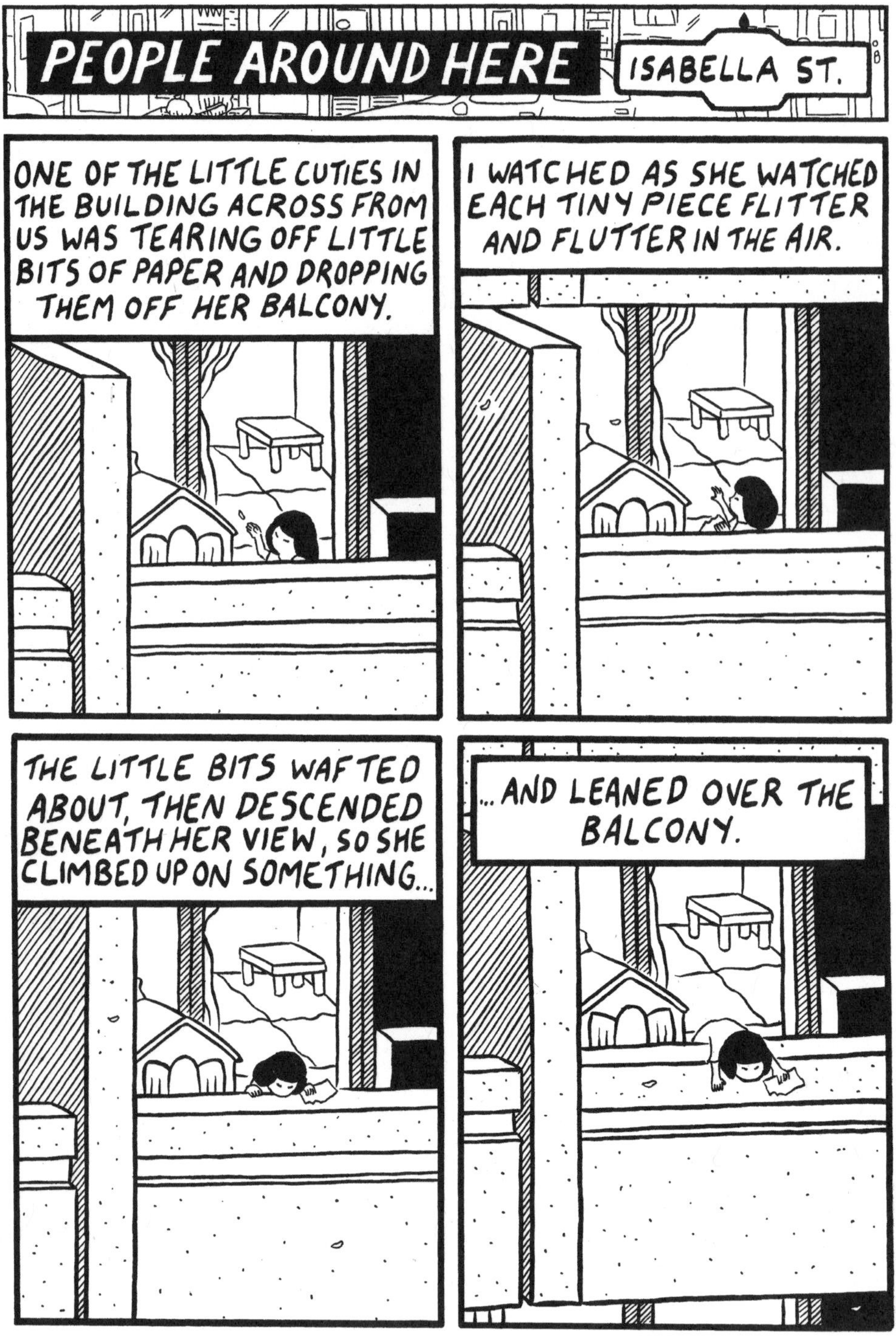
PEOPLE AROUND HERE
ISABELLA ST.
ONE OF THE LITTLE CUTIES IN THE BUILDING ACROSS FROM US WAS TEARING OFF LITTLE BITS OF PAPER AND DROPPING THEM OFF HER BALCONY.
I WATCHED AS SHE WATCHED EACH TINY PIECE FLITTER AND FLUTTER IN THE AIR.
THE LITTLE BITS WAFTED ABOUT, THEN DESCENDED BENEATH HER VIEW, SO SHE CLIMBED UP ON SOMETHING...
...AND LEANED OVER THE BALCONY.

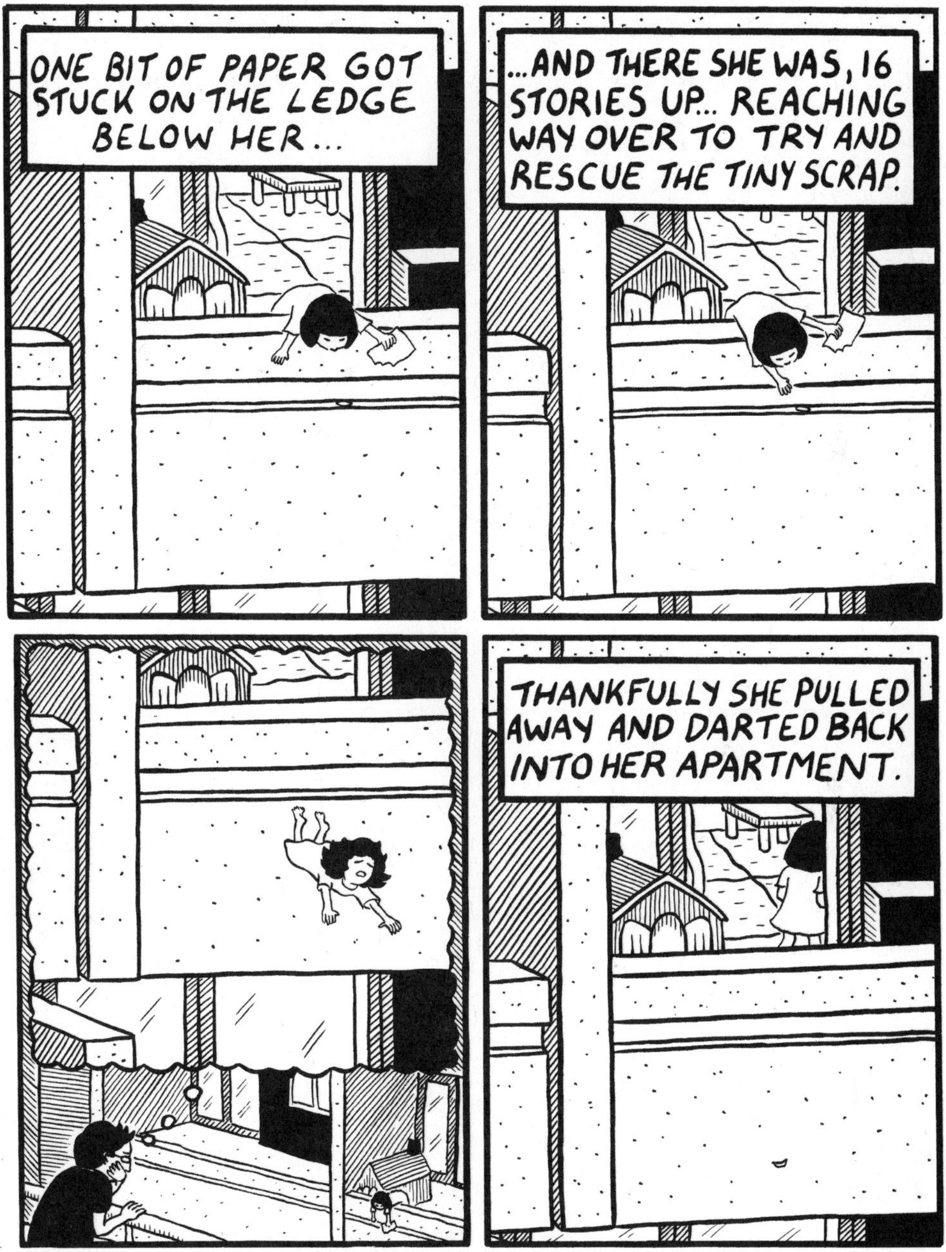
ONE BIT OF PAPER GOT STUCK ON THE LEDGE BELOW HER...
...AND THERE SHE WAS, 16 STORIES UP... REACHING WAY OVER TO TRY AND RESCUE THE TINY SCRAP.
THANKFULLY SHE PULLED AWAY AND DARTED BACK INTO HER APARTMENT.

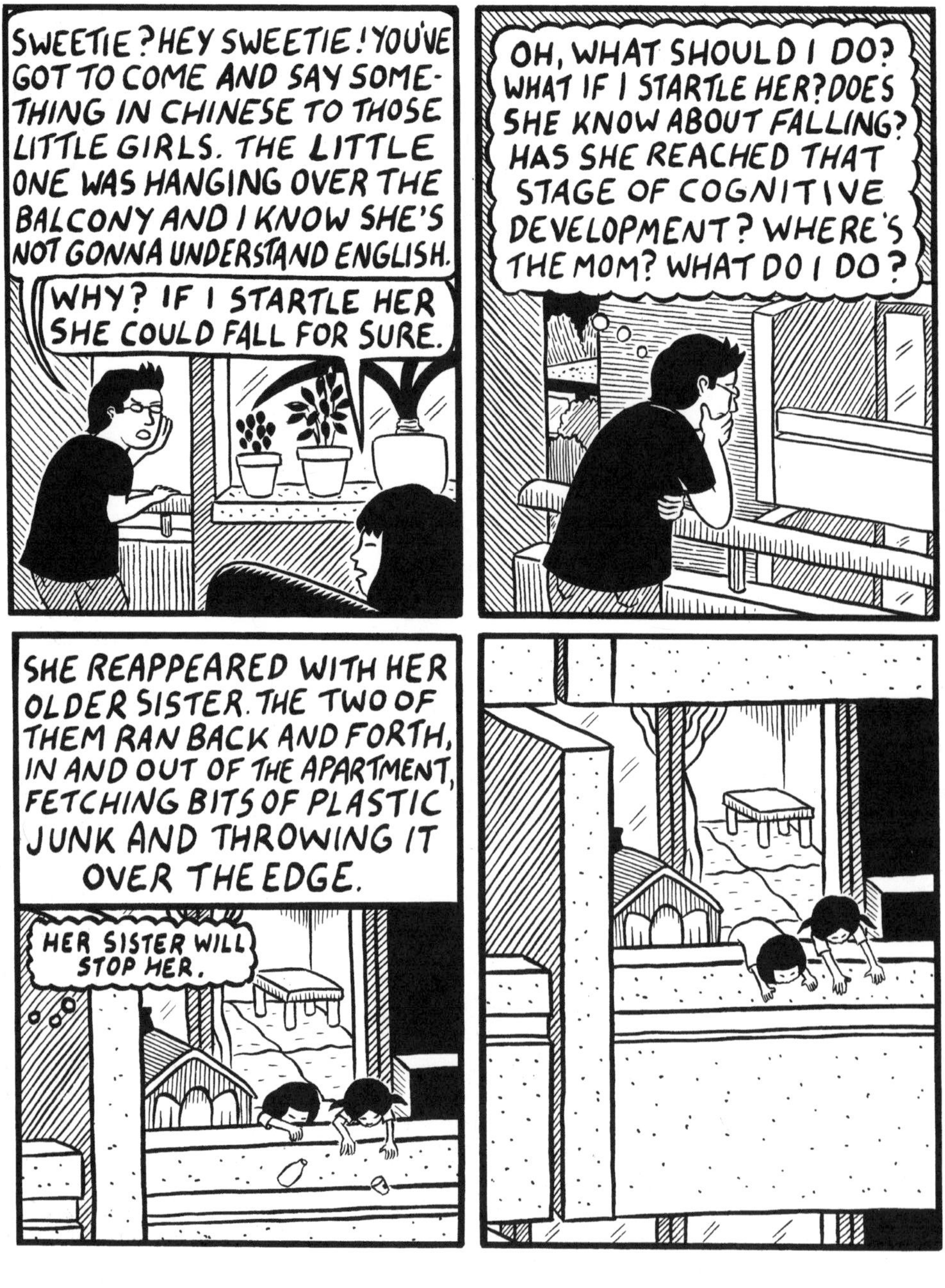
SWEETIE? HEY SWEETIE! YOU'VE GOT TO COME AND SAY SOMETHING IN CHINESE TO THOSE LITTLE GIRLS. THE LITTLE ONE WAS HANGING OVER THE BALCONY AND I KNOW SHE'S NOT GONNA UNDERSTAND ENGLISH.
WHY? IF I STARTLE HER SHE COULD FALL FOR SURE.
OH, WHAT SHOULD I DO? WHAT IF I STARTLE HER? DOES SHE KNOW ABOUT FALLING? HAS SHE REACHED THAT STAGE OF COGNITIVE DEVELOPMENT? WHERE'S THE MOM? WHAT DO I DO?
SHE REAPPEARED WITH HER OLDER SISTER. THE TWO OF THEM RAN BACK AND FORTH, IN AND OUT OF THE APARTMENT, FETCHING BITS OF PLASTIC JUNK AND THROWING IT OVER THE EDGE.
HER SISTER WILL STOP HER.

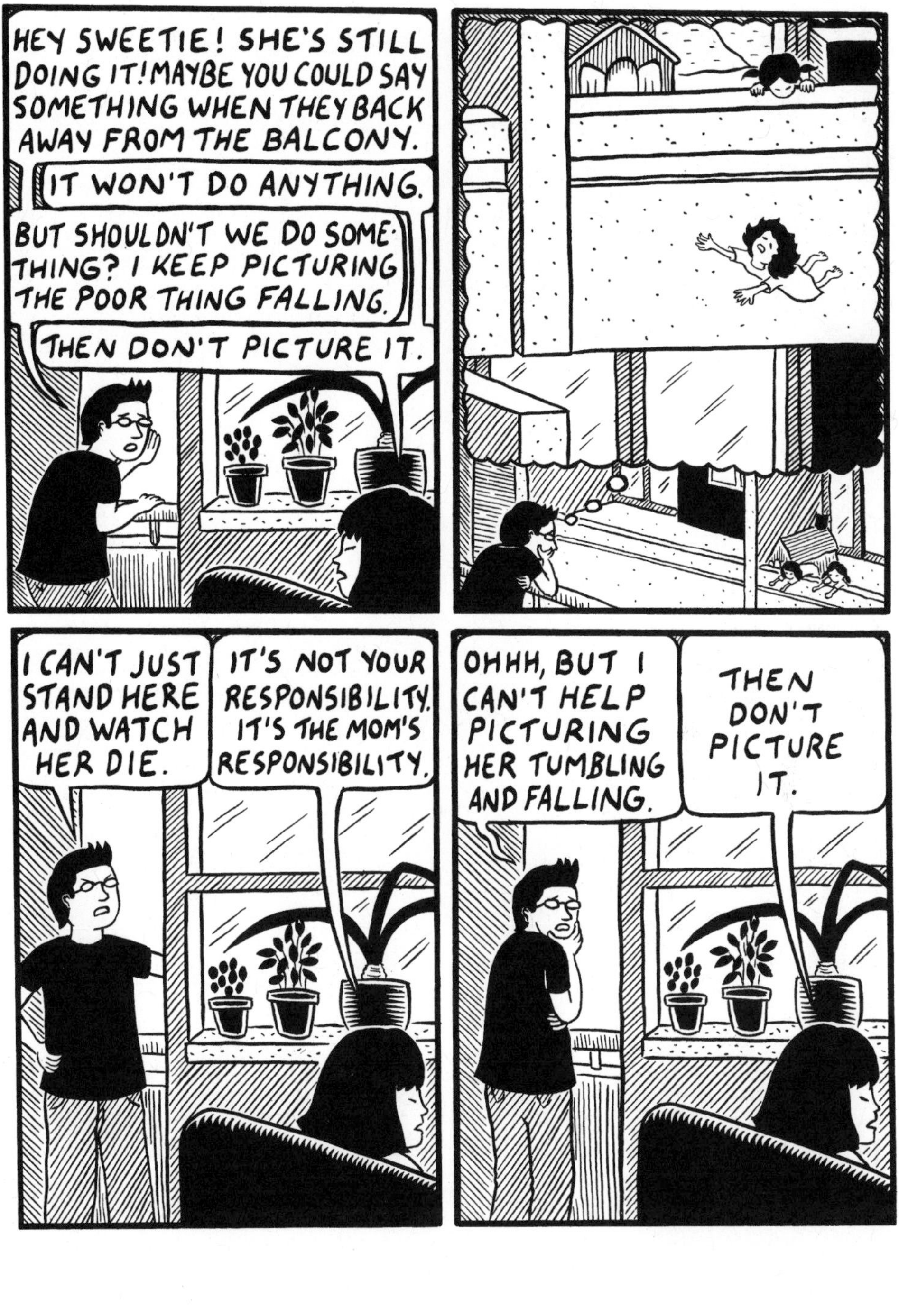
HEY SWEETIE! SHE'S STILL DOING IT! MAYBE YOU COULD SAY SOMETHING WHEN THEY BACK AWAY FROM THE BALCONY.
IT WON'T DO ANYTHING.
BUT SHOULDN'T WE DO SOMETHING? I KEEP PICTURING THE POOR THING FALLING.
THEN DON'T PICTURE IT.
I CAN'T JUST STAND HERE AND WATCH HER DIE.
IT'S NOT YOUR RESPONSIBILITY. IT'S THE MOM'S RESPONSIBILITY.
OHHH, BUT I CAN'T HELP PICTURING HER TUMBLING AND FALLING.
THEN DON'T PICTURE IT.

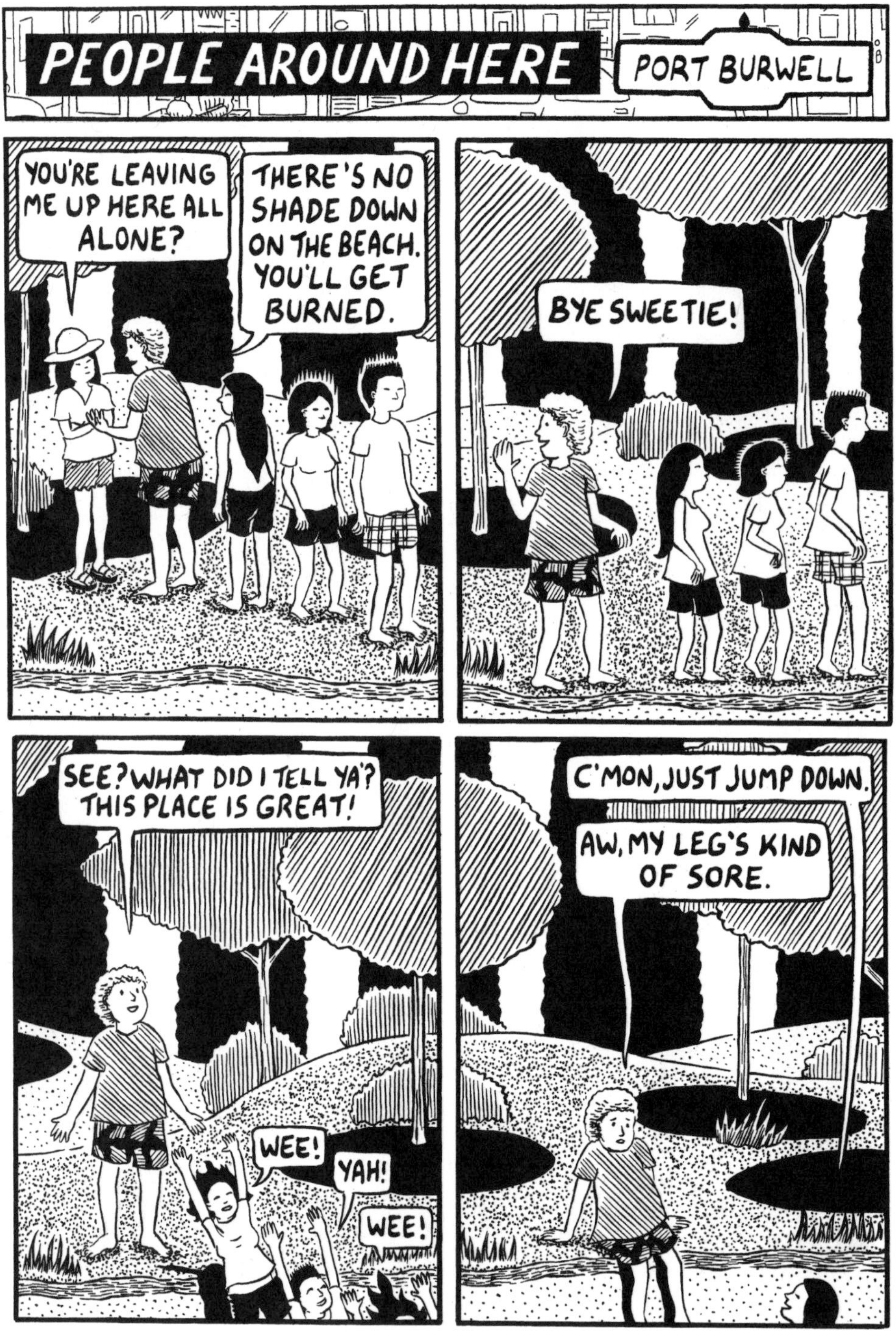
PEOPLE AROUND HERE
PORT BURWELL
YOU'RE LEAVING ME UP HERE ALL ALONE?
THERE'S NO SHADE DOWN ON THE BEACH. YOU'LL GET BURNED.
BYE SWEETIE!
SEE? WHAT DID I TELL YA? THIS PLACE IS GREAT!
WEE!
YAH!
WEE!
C'MON, JUST JUMP DOWN.
AW, MY LEG'S KIND OF SORE.

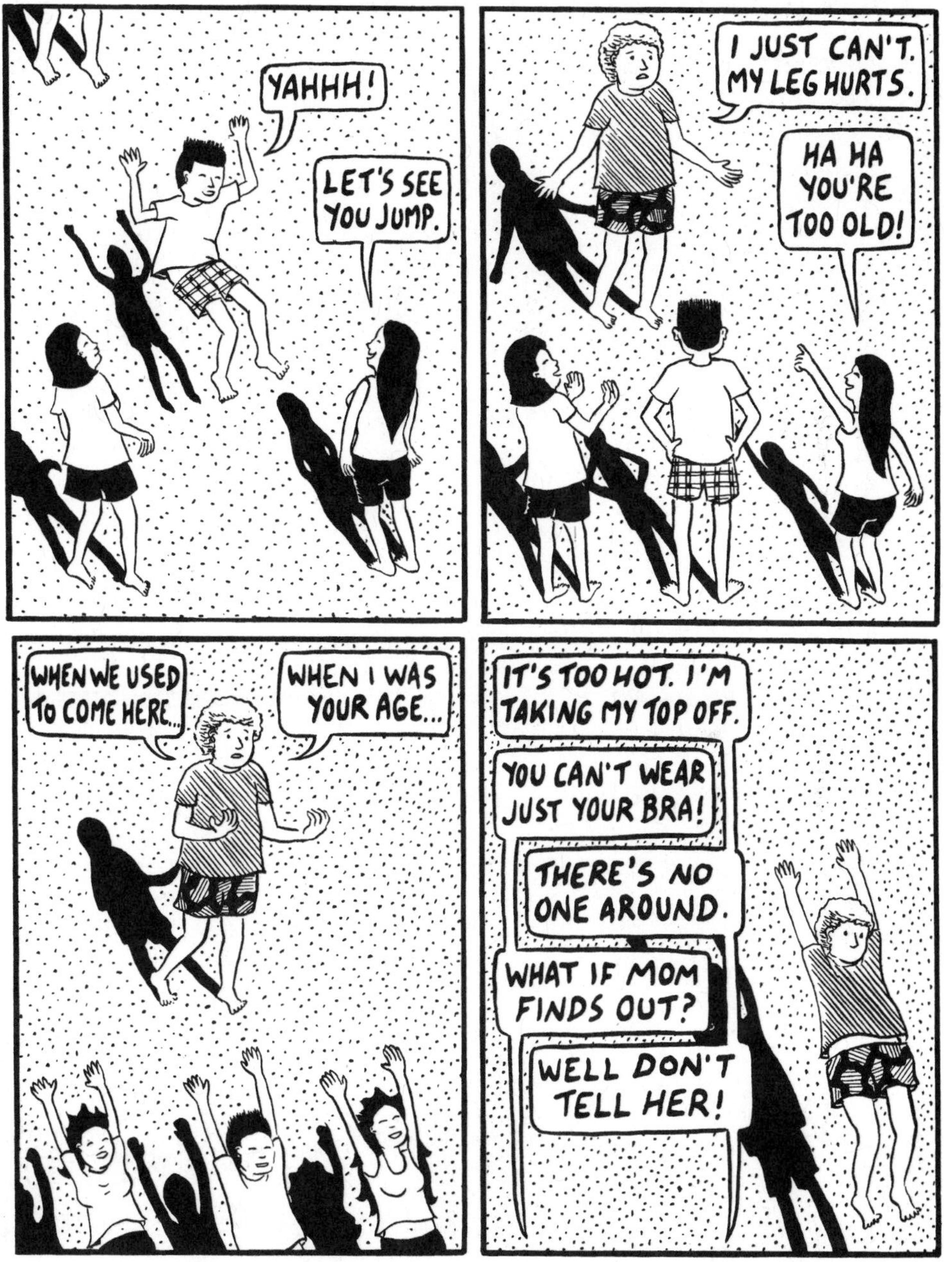
YAHHH!
LET'S SEE YOU JUMP.
I JUST CAN'T. MY LEG HURTS.
HA HA YOU'RE TOO OLD!
WHEN WE USED TO COME HERE...
WHEN I WAS YOUR AGE...
IT'S TOO HOT. I'M TAKING MY TOP OFF.
YOU CAN'T WEAR JUST YOUR BRA!
THERE'S NO ONE AROUND.
WHAT IF MOM FINDS OUT?
WELL DON'T TELL HER!

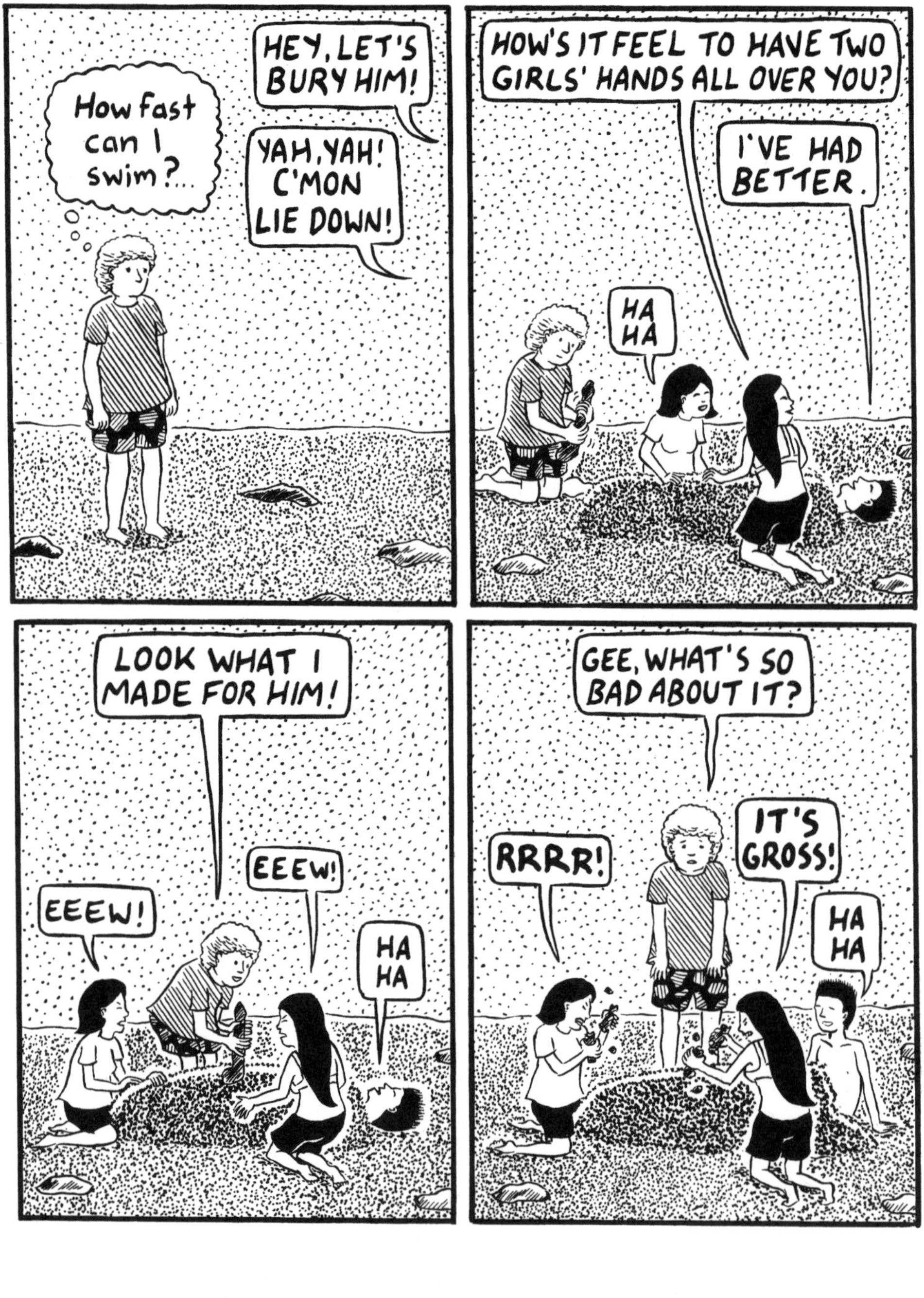
How fast can I swim?...
HEY, LET'S BURY HIM!
YAH, YAH! C'MON LIE DOWN!
HOW'S IT FEEL TO HAVE TWO GIRLS' HANDS ALL OVER YOU?
I'VE HAD BETTER.
HA HA
LOOK WHAT I MADE FOR HIM!
EEEW!
EEEW!
HA HA
GEE, WHAT'S SO BAD ABOUT IT?
RRRR!
IT'S GROSS!
HA HA

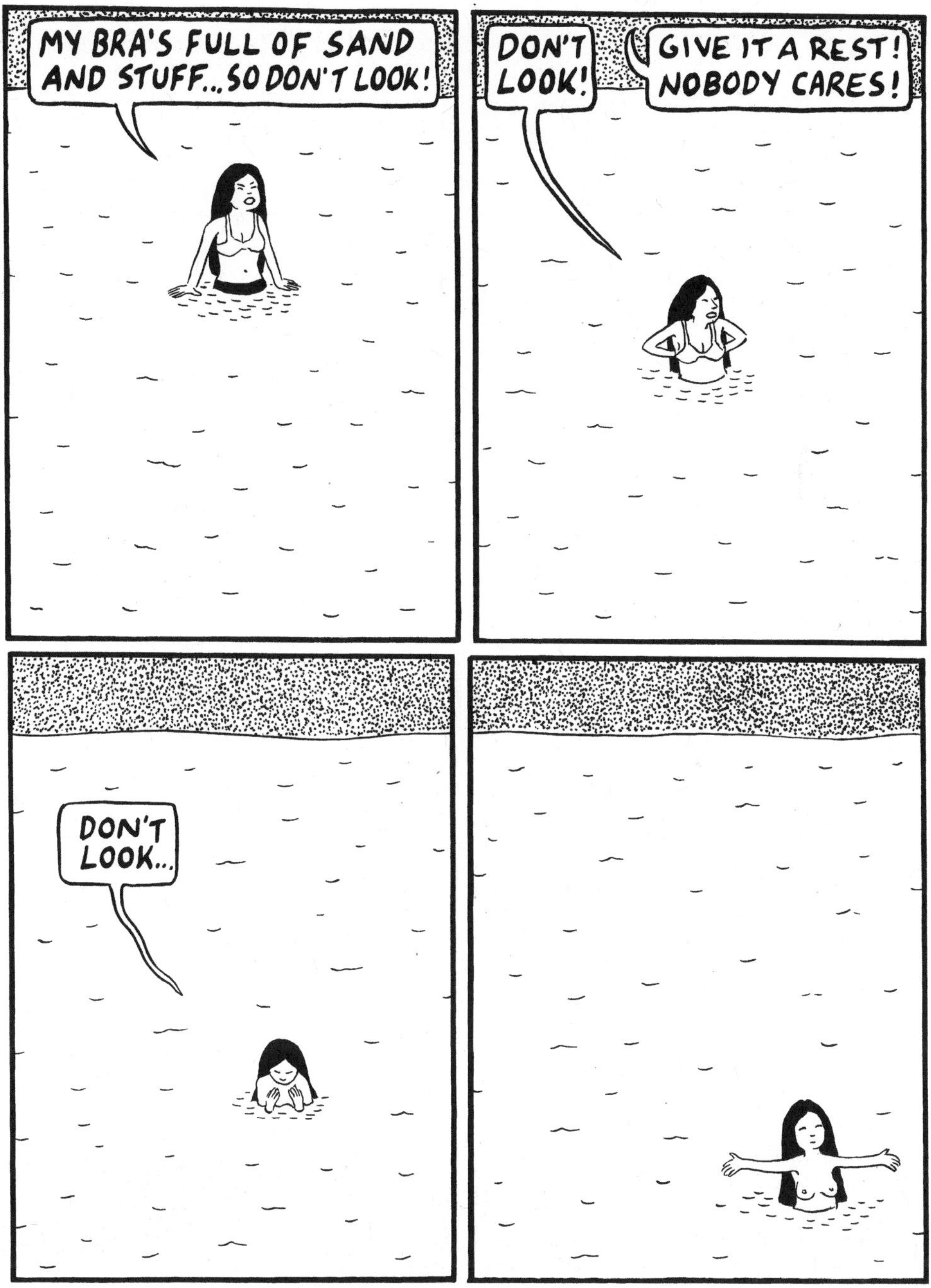
MY BRA'S FULL OF SAND
AND STUFF... SO DON'T LOOK!
DON'T
LOOK!
GIVE IT A REST!
NOBODY CARES!
DON'T
LOOK...

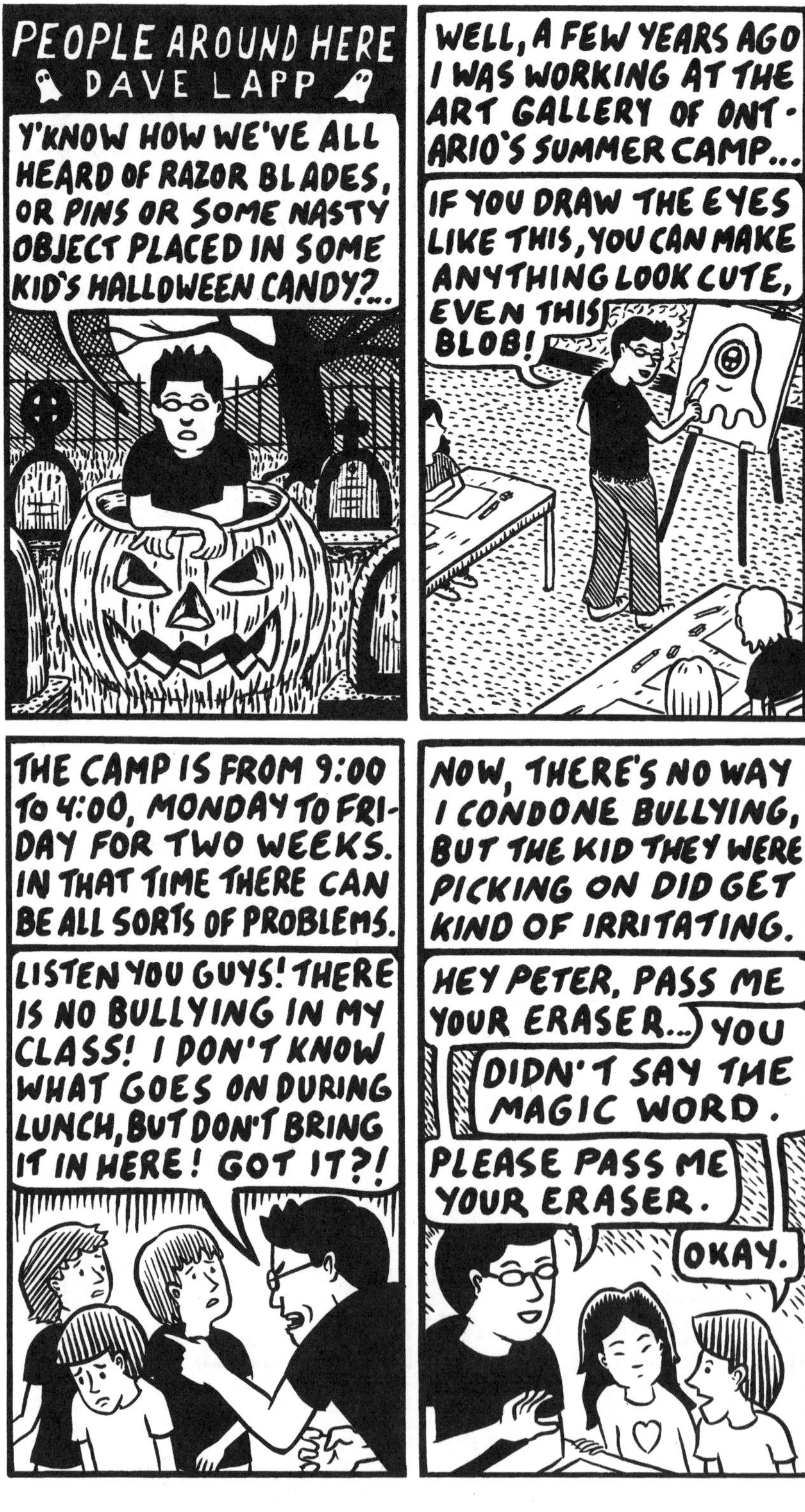
PEOPLE AROUND HERE
DAVE LAPP
Y'KNOW HOW WE'VE ALL HEARD OF RAZOR BLADES, OR PINS OR SOME NASTY OBJECT PLACED IN SOME KID'S HALLOWEEN CANDY?...
WELL, A FEW YEARS AGO I WAS WORKING AT THE ART GALLERY OF ONTARIO'S SUMMER CAMP...
IF YOU DRAW THE EYES LIKE THIS, YOU CAN MAKE ANYTHING LOOK CUTE, EVEN THIS BLOB!
THE CAMP IS FROM 9:00 TO 4:00, MONDAY TO FRIDAY FOR TWO WEEKS. IN THAT TIME THERE CAN BE ALL SORTS OF PROBLEMS.
LISTEN YOU GUYS! THERE IS NO BULLYING IN MY CLASS! I DON'T KNOW WHAT GOES ON DURING LUNCH, BUT DON'T BRING IT IN HERE! GOT IT?!
NOW, THERE'S NO WAY I CONDONE BULLYING, BUT THE KID THEY WERE PICKING ON DID GET KIND OF IRRITATING.
HEY PETER, PASS ME YOUR ERASER...
YOU DIDN'T SAY THE MAGIC WORD.
PLEASE PASS ME YOUR ERASER.
OKAY.

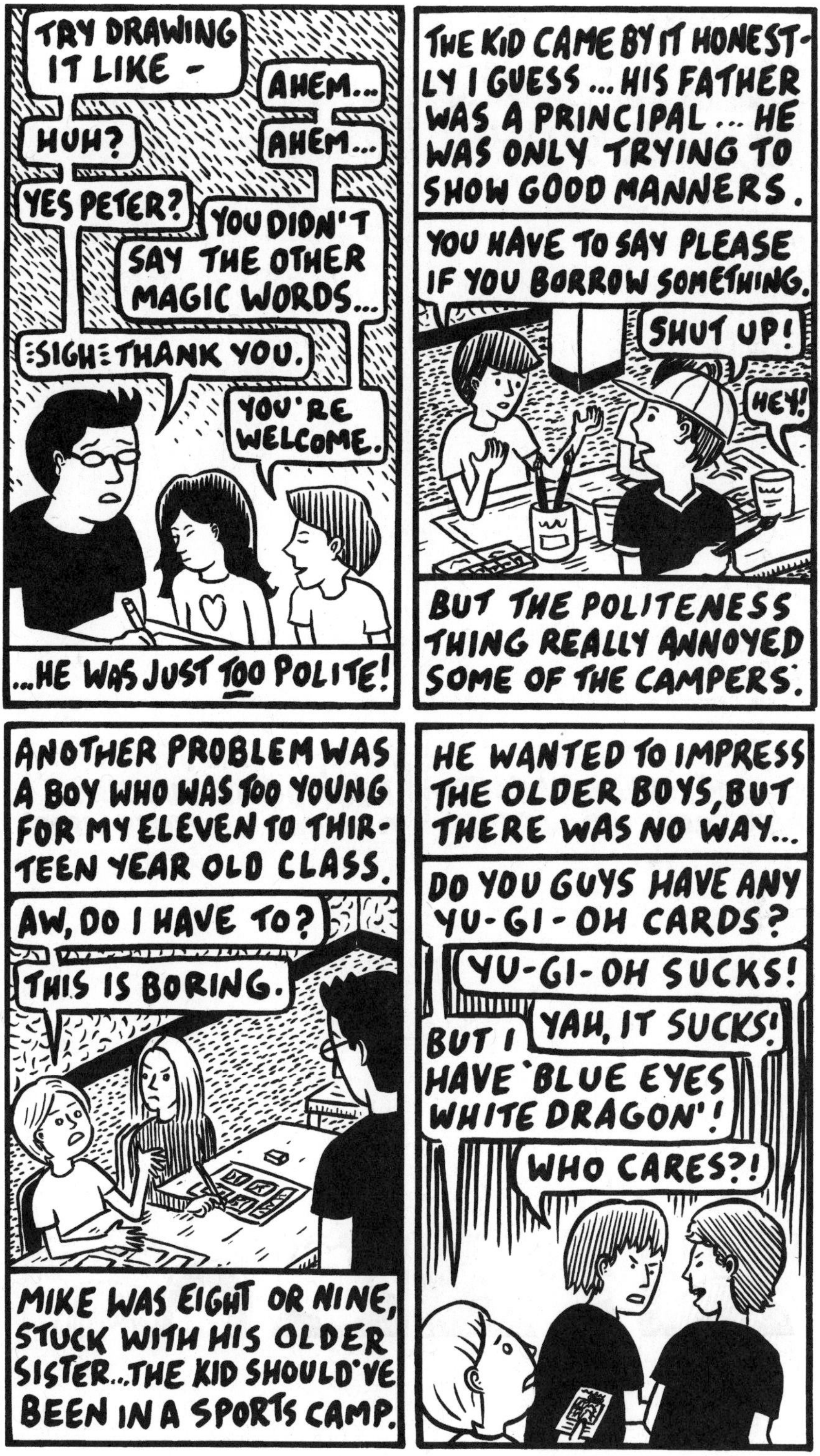
TRY DRAWING IT LIKE -
AHEM...
HUH?
AHEM...
YES PETER?
YOU DIDN'T SAY THE OTHER MAGIC WORDS...
:SIGH: THANK YOU.
YOU'RE WELCOME.
...HE WAS JUST TOO POLITE!
THE KID CAME BY IT HONESTLY I GUESS... HIS FATHER WAS A PRINCIPAL... HE WAS ONLY TRYING TO SHOW GOOD MANNERS.
YOU HAVE TO SAY PLEASE IF YOU BORROW SOMETHING.
SHUT UP!
HEY!
BUT THE POLITENESS THING REALLY ANNOYED SOME OF THE CAMPERS.
ANOTHER PROBLEM WAS A BOY WHO WAS TOO YOUNG FOR MY ELEVEN TO THIRTEEN YEAR OLD CLASS.
AW, DO I HAVE TO?
THIS IS BORING.
MIKE WAS EIGHT OR NINE, STUCK WITH HIS OLDER SISTER... THE KID SHOULD'VE BEEN IN A SPORTS CAMP.
HE WANTED TO IMPRESS THE OLDER BOYS, BUT THERE WAS NO WAY...
DO YOU GUYS HAVE ANY YU-GI-OH CARDS?
YU-GI-OH SUCKS!
YAH, IT SUCKS!
BUT I HAVE 'BLUE EYES WHITE DRAGON'!
WHO CARES?!

SO... WE COME TO THE LAST DAY OF CAMP AND EVERYONE IS GETTING READY FOR OUR BIG ART SHOW...

WHILE I WAS CHECKING ARTWORK, MIKE CAME UP WITH A PACKAGE OF CHERRY NIBS* AND OFFERED SOME TO PETER.

IS MINE DONE?

IS IT GOOD?

OH YAH!

HEY KID! THAT'S NOT A GOOD IDEA.

DON'T BUG ME.

PETER, WOULD YOU LIKE SOME NIBS?

OH YES PLEASE!

*CANDY LIKE LICORICE BUT SOLID

AWWW, HE'S SHARING...

THANK YOU!

THAT'S SO NICE...

MMM...

=chew=

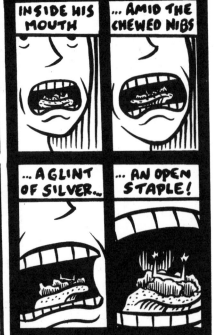

INSIDE HIS MOUTH

... AMID THE CHEWED NIBS

... A GLINT OF SILVER...

... AN OPEN STAPLE!

...BUT WAIT...

OH ... OH

...WAIT...

OW

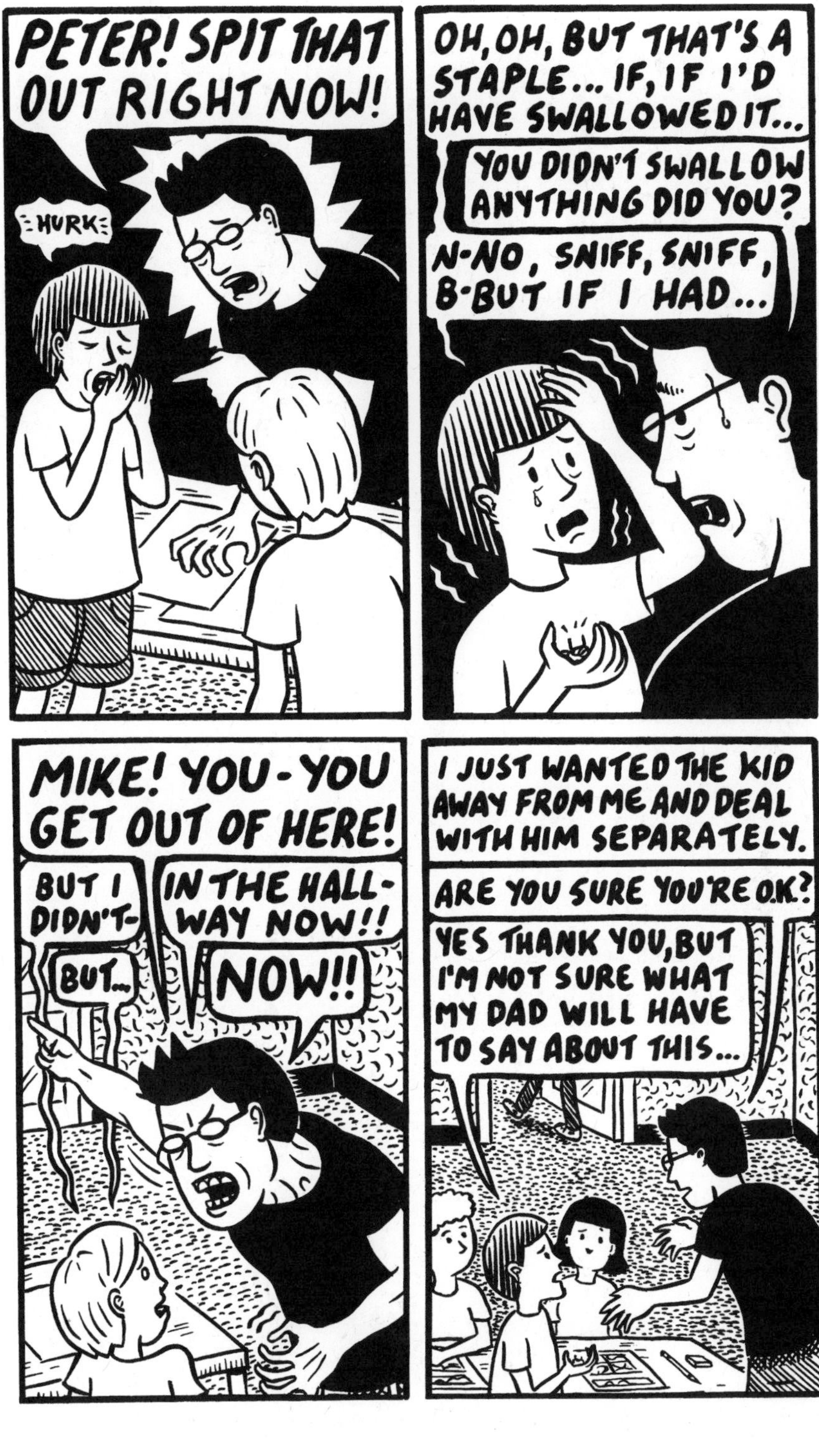
PETER! SPIT THAT OUT RIGHT NOW!
HURK
OH, OH, BUT THAT'S A STAPLE... IF, IF I'D HAVE SWALLOWED IT...
YOU DIDN'T SWALLOW ANYTHING DID YOU?
N-NO, SNIFF, SNIFF, B-BUT IF I HAD...
MIKE! YOU-YOU GET OUT OF HERE!
BUT I DIDN'T-
IN THE HALL-WAY NOW!!
BUT...
NOW!!
I JUST WANTED THE KID AWAY FROM ME AND DEAL WITH HIM SEPARATELY.
ARE YOU SURE YOU'RE O.K.?
YES THANK YOU, BUT I'M NOT SURE WHAT MY DAD WILL HAVE TO SAY ABOUT THIS...

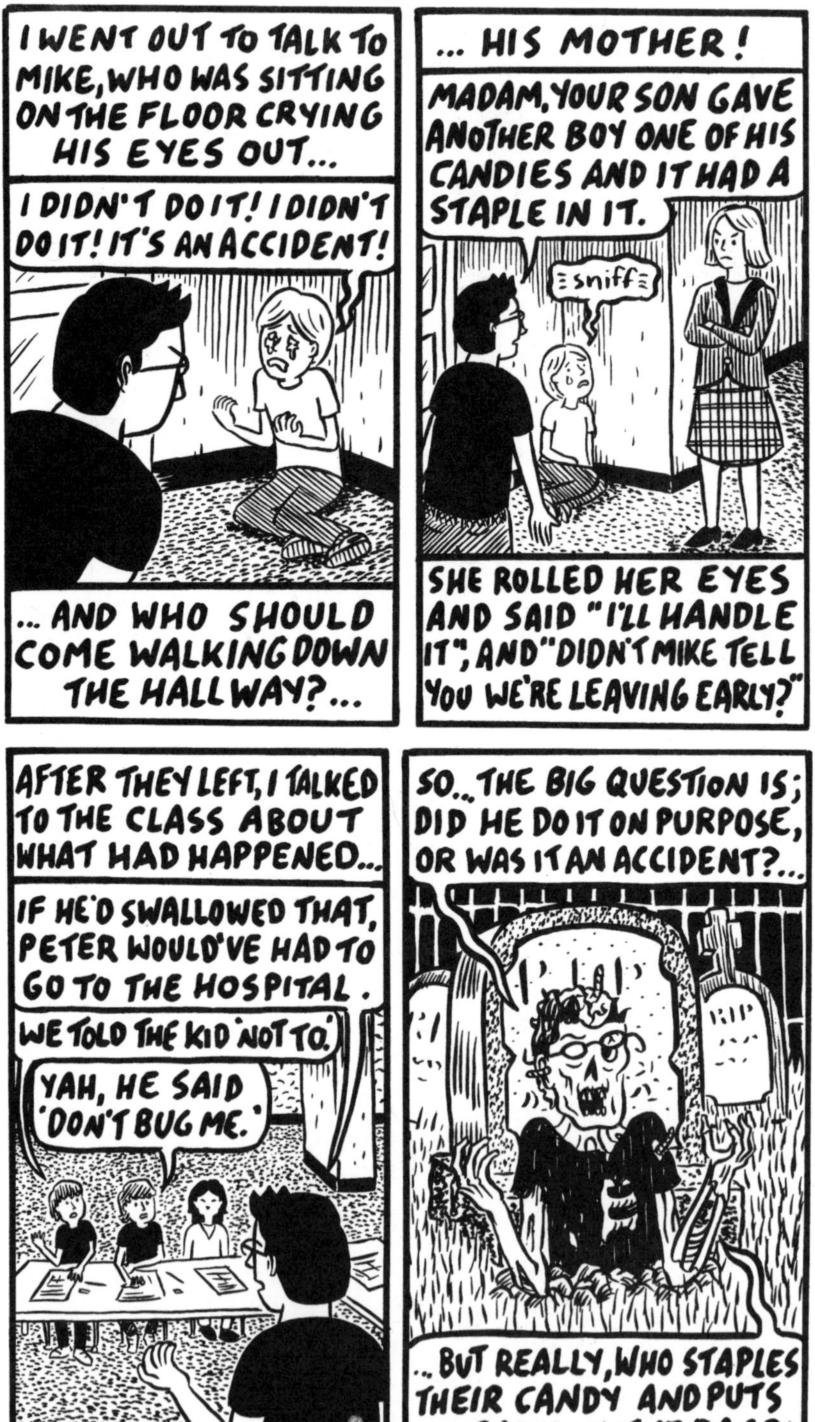
I WENT OUT TO TALK TO MIKE, WHO WAS SITTING ON THE FLOOR CRYING HIS EYES OUT...
I DIDN'T DO IT! I DIDN'T DO IT! IT'S AN ACCIDENT!
... AND WHO SHOULD COME WALKING DOWN THE HALLWAY?...
... HIS MOTHER!
MADAM, YOUR SON GAVE ANOTHER BOY ONE OF HIS CANDIES AND IT HAD A STAPLE IN IT.
sniff
SHE ROLLED HER EYES AND SAID "I'LL HANDLE IT", AND "DIDN'T MIKE TELL YOU WE'RE LEAVING EARLY?"
AFTER THEY LEFT, I TALKED TO THE CLASS ABOUT WHAT HAD HAPPENED...
IF HE'D SWALLOWED THAT, PETER WOULD'VE HAD TO GO TO THE HOSPITAL.
WE TOLD THE KID 'NOT TO.'
YAH, HE SAID 'DON'T BUG ME.'
SO... THE BIG QUESTION IS; DID HE DO IT ON PURPOSE, OR WAS IT AN ACCIDENT?...
RIP
... BUT REALLY, WHO STAPLES THEIR CANDY AND PUTS IT BACK IN THE BAG?!

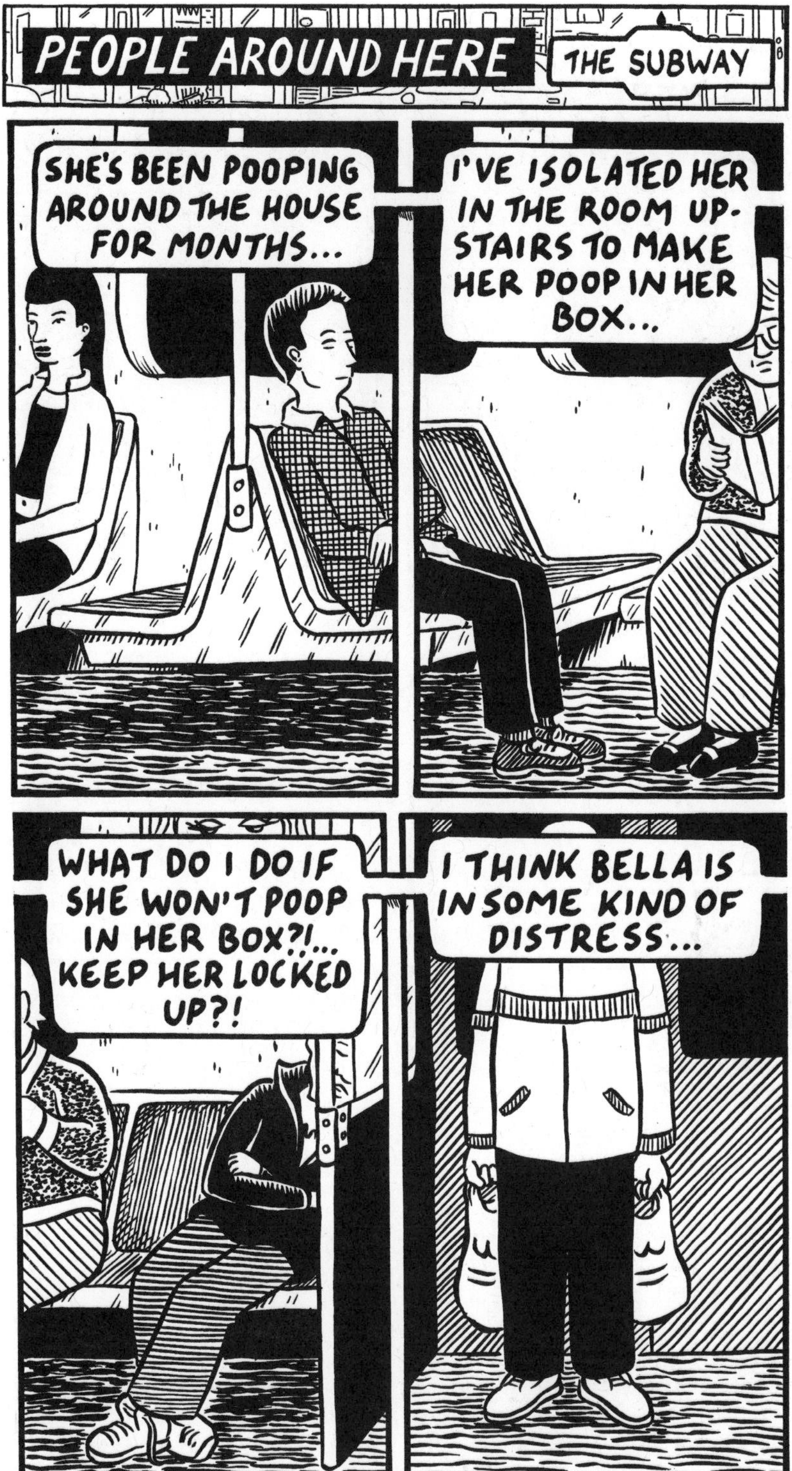
PEOPLE AROUND HERE
THE SUBWAY
SHE'S BEEN POOPING AROUND THE HOUSE FOR MONTHS...
I'VE ISOLATED HER IN THE ROOM UP-STAIRS TO MAKE HER POOP IN HER BOX...
WHAT DO I DO IF SHE WON'T POOP IN HER BOX?!... KEEP HER LOCKED UP?!
I THINK BELLA IS IN SOME KIND OF DISTRESS...

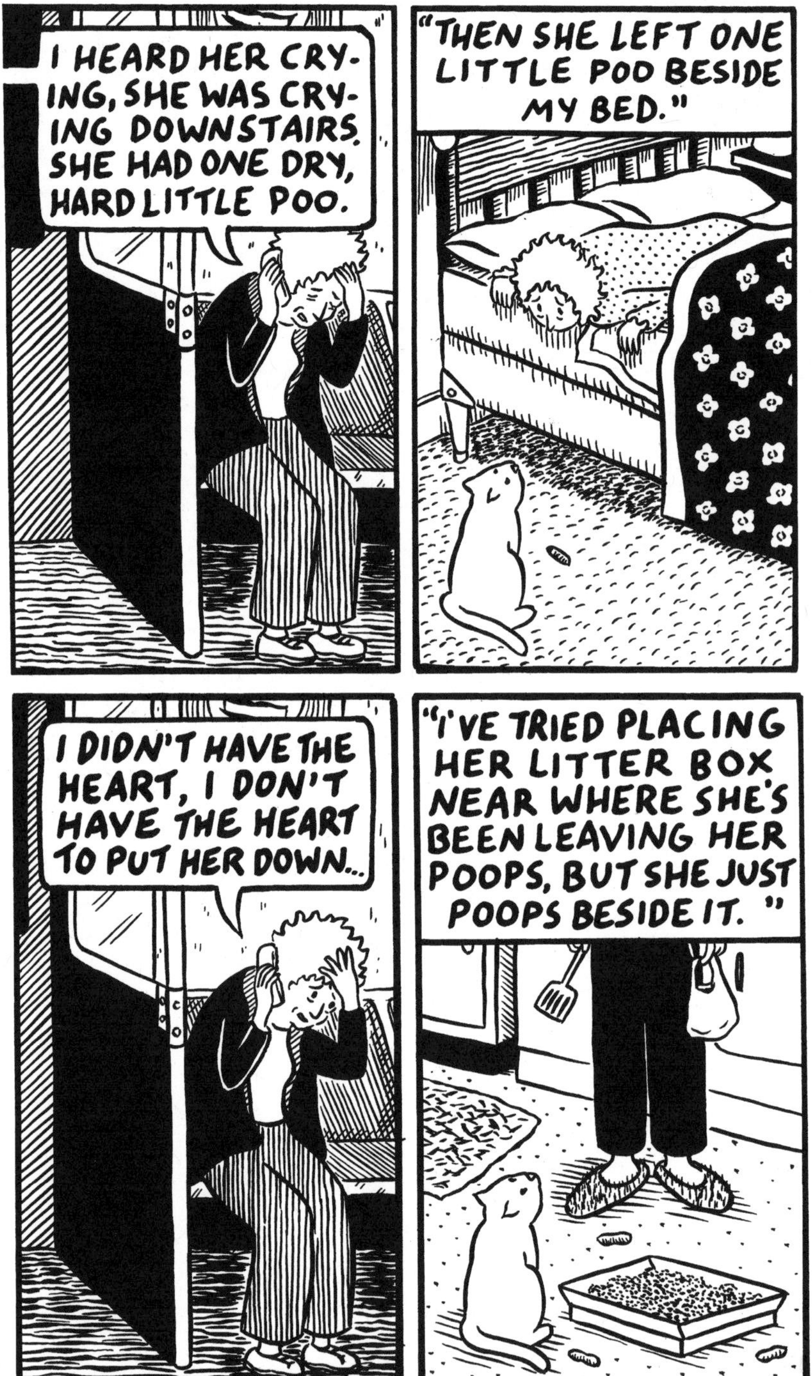
I HEARD HER CRYING, SHE WAS CRYING DOWNSTAIRS. SHE HAD ONE DRY, HARD LITTLE POO.
"THEN SHE LEFT ONE LITTLE POO BESIDE MY BED."
I DIDN'T HAVE THE HEART, I DON'T HAVE THE HEART TO PUT HER DOWN...
"I'VE TRIED PLACING HER LITTER BOX NEAR WHERE SHE'S BEEN LEAVING HER POOPS, BUT SHE JUST POOPS BESIDE IT."

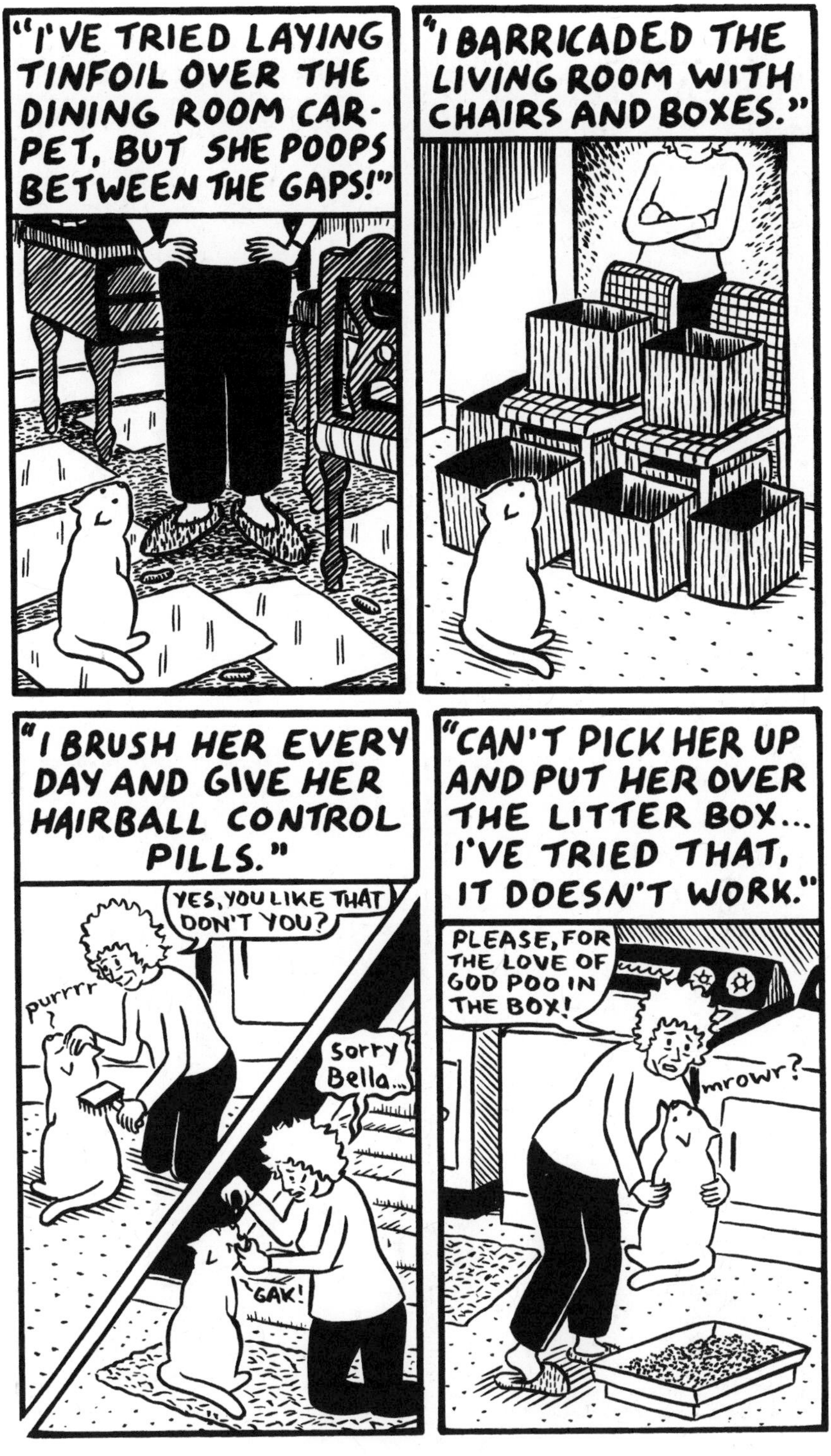
"I'VE TRIED LAYING TINFOIL OVER THE DINING ROOM CARPET, BUT SHE POOPS BETWEEN THE GAPS!"
"I BARRICADED THE LIVING ROOM WITH CHAIRS AND BOXES."
"I BRUSH HER EVERY DAY AND GIVE HER HAIRBALL CONTROL PILLS."
YES, YOU LIKE THAT DON'T YOU?
purrrr
Sorry Bella...
GAK!
"CAN'T PICK HER UP AND PUT HER OVER THE LITTER BOX... I'VE TRIED THAT, IT DOESN'T WORK."
PLEASE, FOR THE LOVE OF GOD POO IN THE BOX!
mrowr?

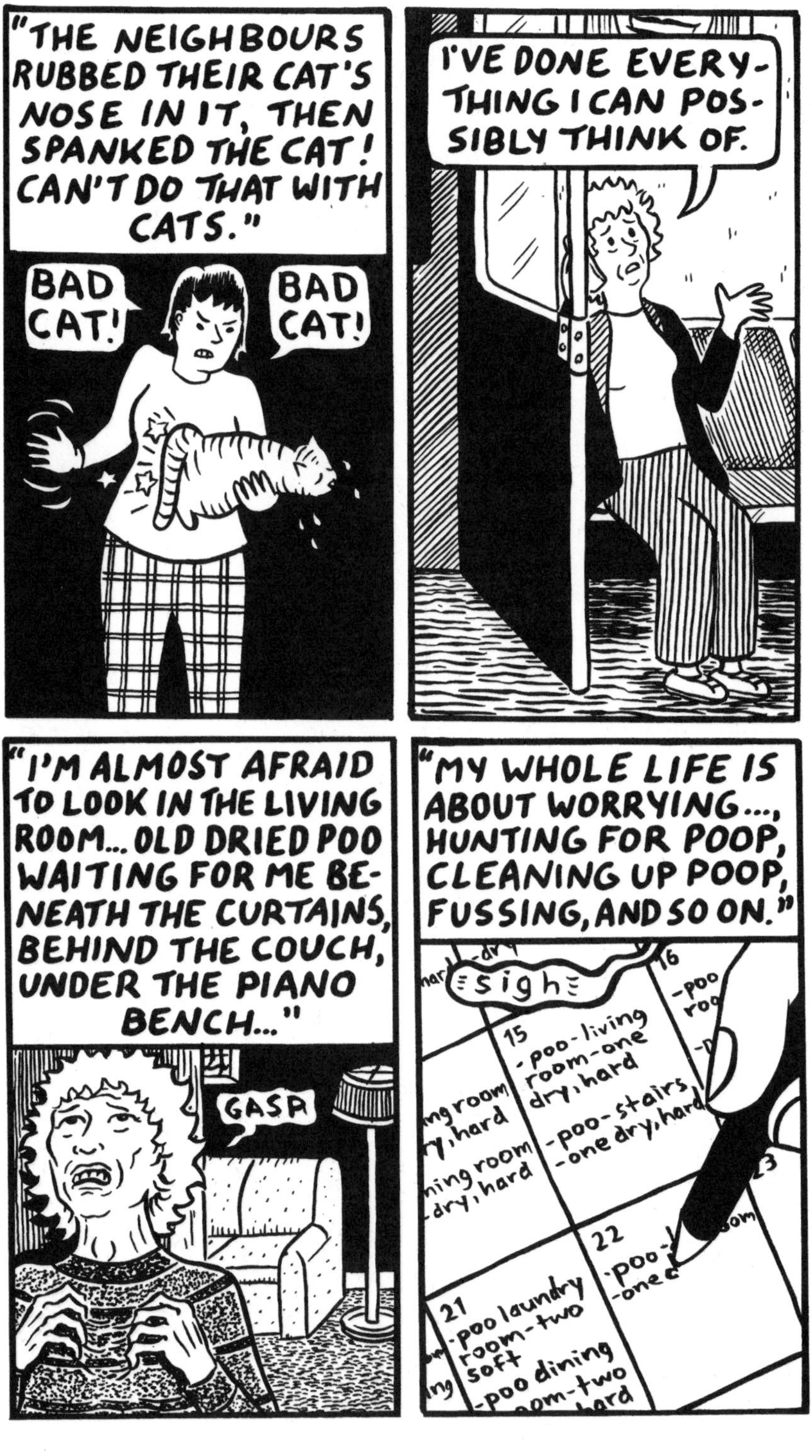
"THE NEIGHBOURS RUBBED THEIR CAT'S NOSE IN IT, THEN SPANKED THE CAT! CAN'T DO THAT WITH CATS."
BAD CAT!
BAD CAT!
I'VE DONE EVERY-THING I CAN POS-SIBLY THINK OF.
"I'M ALMOST AFRAID TO LOOK IN THE LIVING ROOM... OLD DRIED POO WAITING FOR ME BE-NEATH THE CURTAINS, BEHIND THE COUCH, UNDER THE PIANO BENCH..."
GASP
"MY WHOLE LIFE IS ABOUT WORRYING..., HUNTING FOR POOP, CLEANING UP POOP, FUSSING, AND SO ON."
sigh
15
-poo-living room-one dry, hard
-poo-stairs -one dry, hard
16
22
21
-poo laundry room-two soft
-poo dining

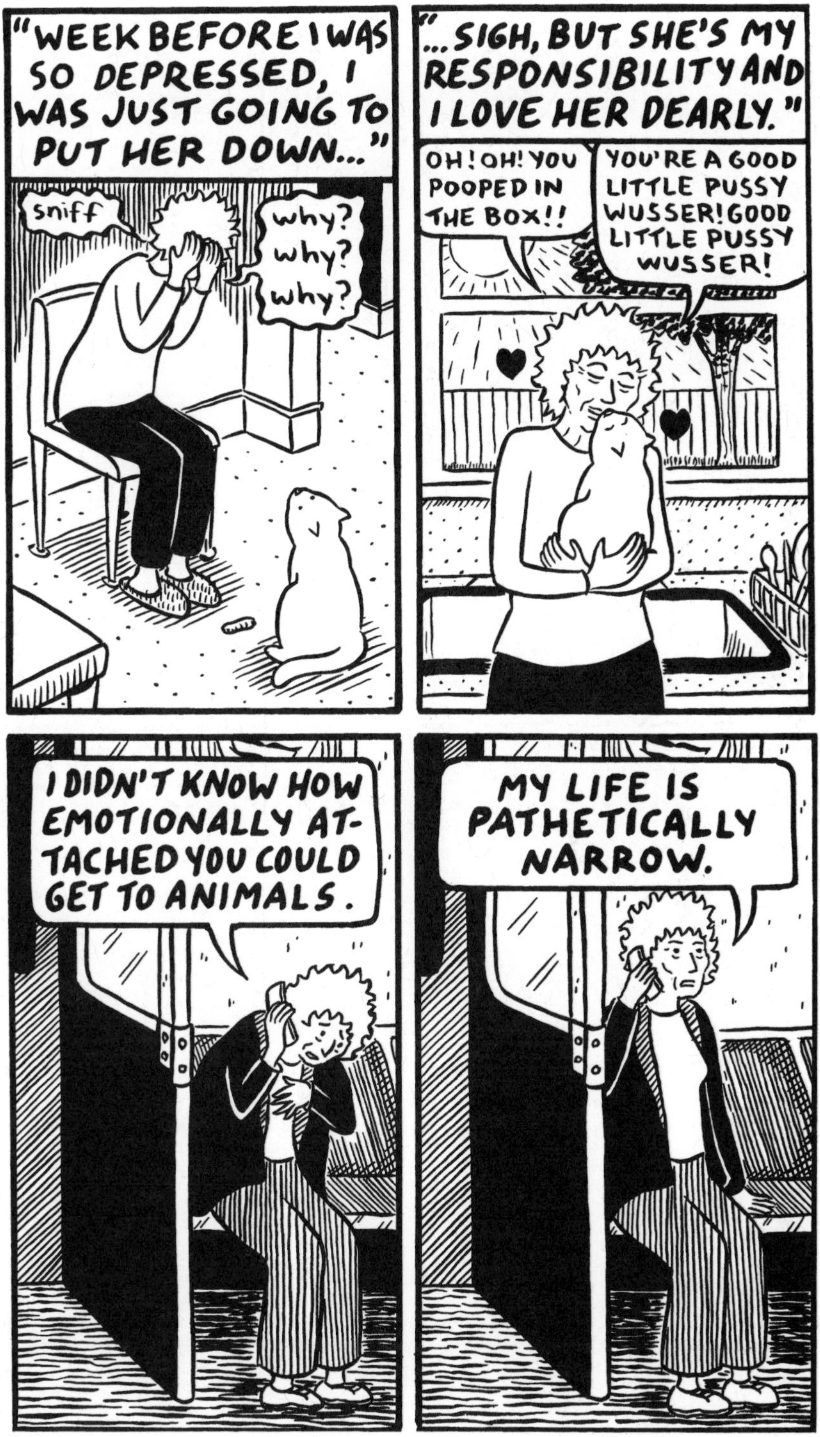
"WEEK BEFORE I WAS SO DEPRESSED, I WAS JUST GOING TO PUT HER DOWN..."
sniff
why? why? why?
"...SIGH, BUT SHE'S MY RESPONSIBILITY AND I LOVE HER DEARLY."
OH! OH! YOU POOPED IN THE BOX!!
YOU'RE A GOOD LITTLE PUSSY WUSSER! GOOD LITTLE PUSSY WUSSER!
I DIDN'T KNOW HOW EMOTIONALLY ATTACHED YOU COULD GET TO ANIMALS.
MY LIFE IS PATHETICALLY NARROW.

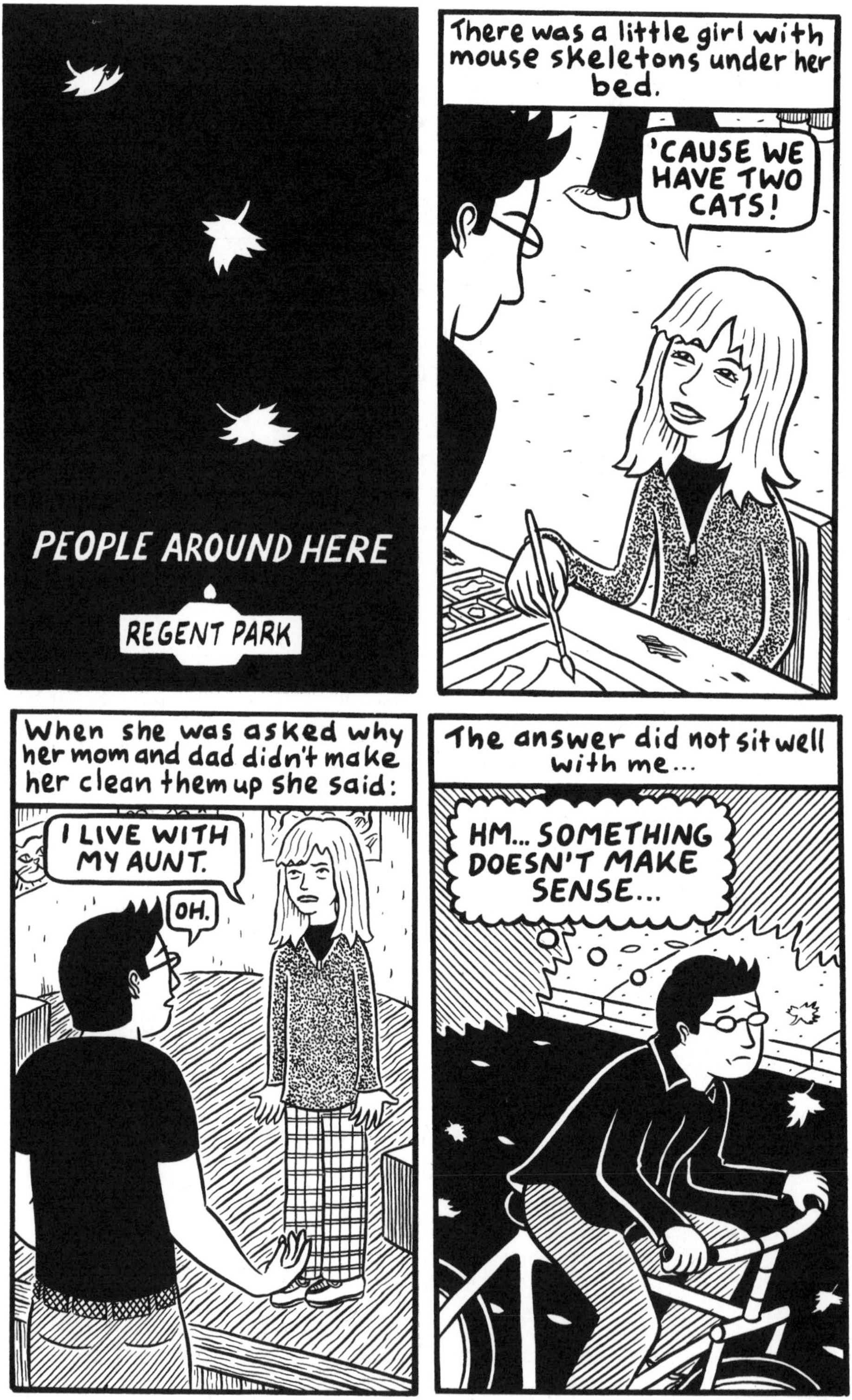
PEOPLE AROUND HERE
REGENT PARK
There was a little girl with mouse skeletons under her bed.
'CAUSE WE HAVE TWO CATS!
When she was asked why her mom and dad didn't make her clean them up she said:
I LIVE WITH MY AUNT.
OH.
The answer did not sit well with me...
HM... SOMETHING DOESN'T MAKE SENSE...

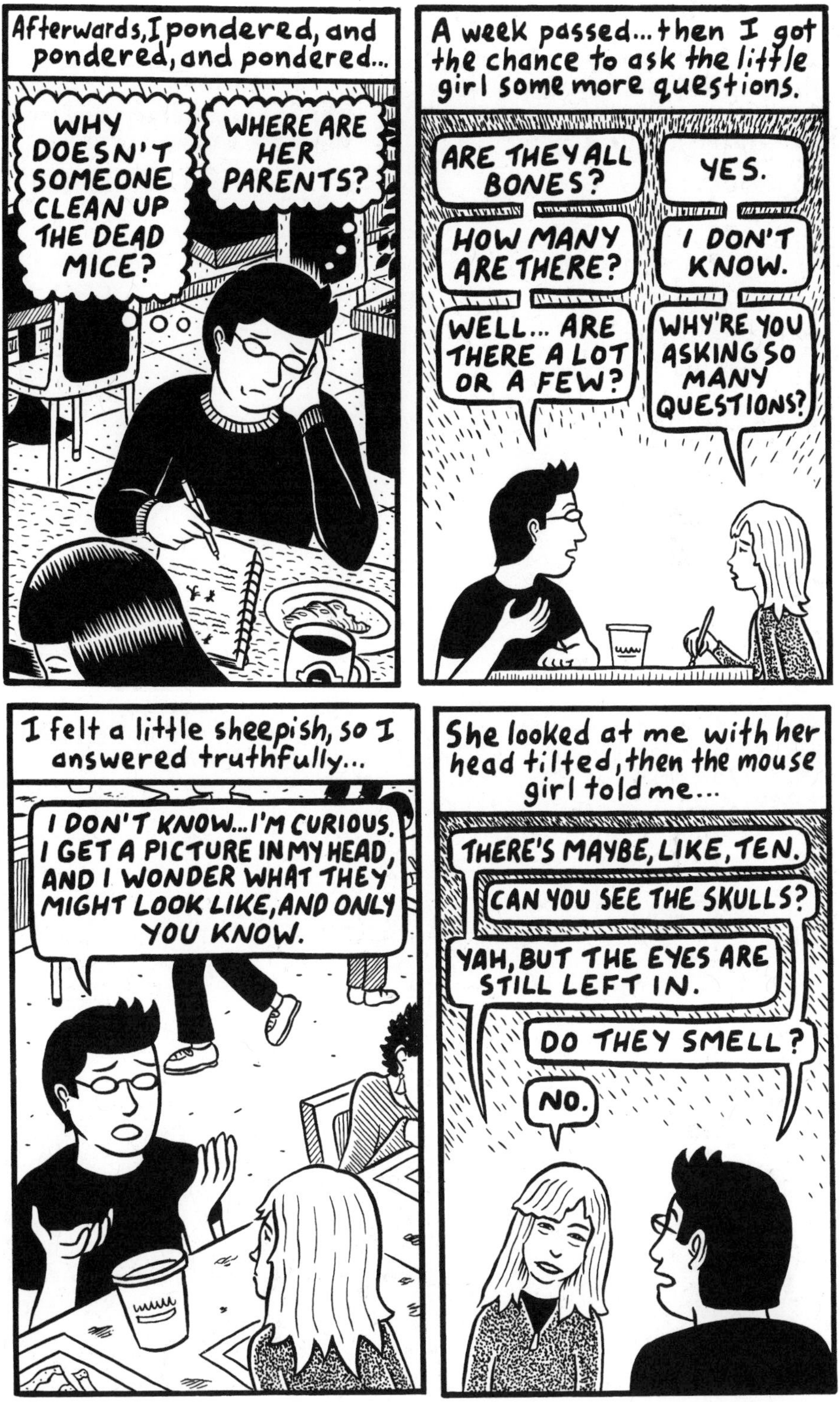
Afterwards, I pondered, and pondered, and pondered...
WHY DOESN'T SOMEONE CLEAN UP THE DEAD MICE?
WHERE ARE HER PARENTS?
A week passed... then I got the chance to ask the little girl some more questions.
ARE THEY ALL BONES?
YES.
HOW MANY ARE THERE?
I DON'T KNOW.
WELL... ARE THERE A LOT OR A FEW?
WHY'RE YOU ASKING SO MANY QUESTIONS?
I felt a little sheepish, so I answered truthfully...
I DON'T KNOW...I'M CURIOUS. I GET A PICTURE IN MY HEAD, AND I WONDER WHAT THEY MIGHT LOOK LIKE, AND ONLY YOU KNOW.
She looked at me with her head tilted, then the mouse girl told me...
THERE'S MAYBE, LIKE, TEN.
CAN YOU SEE THE SKULLS?
YAH, BUT THE EYES ARE STILL LEFT IN.
DO THEY SMELL?
NO.

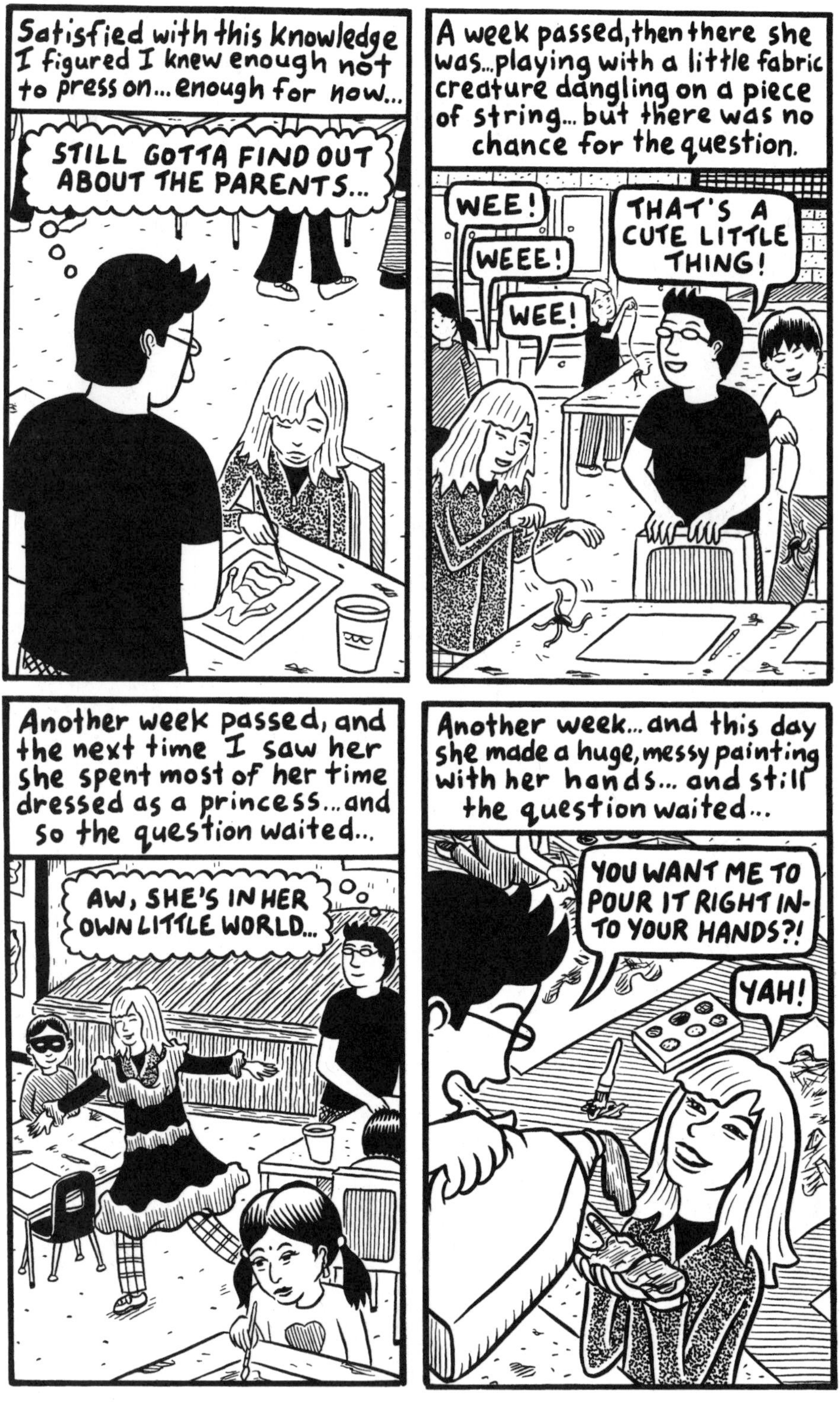
Satisfied with this knowledge I figured I knew enough not to press on... enough for now...
STILL GOTTA FIND OUT ABOUT THE PARENTS...
A week passed, then there she was... playing with a little fabric creature dangling on a piece of string... but there was no chance for the question.
WEE!
WEEE!
WEE!
THAT'S A CUTE LITTLE THING!
Another week passed, and the next time I saw her she spent most of her time dressed as a princess... and so the question waited...
AW, SHE'S IN HER OWN LITTLE WORLD...
Another week... and this day she made a huge, messy painting with her hands... and still the question waited...
YOU WANT ME TO POUR IT RIGHT INTO YOUR HANDS?!
YAH!

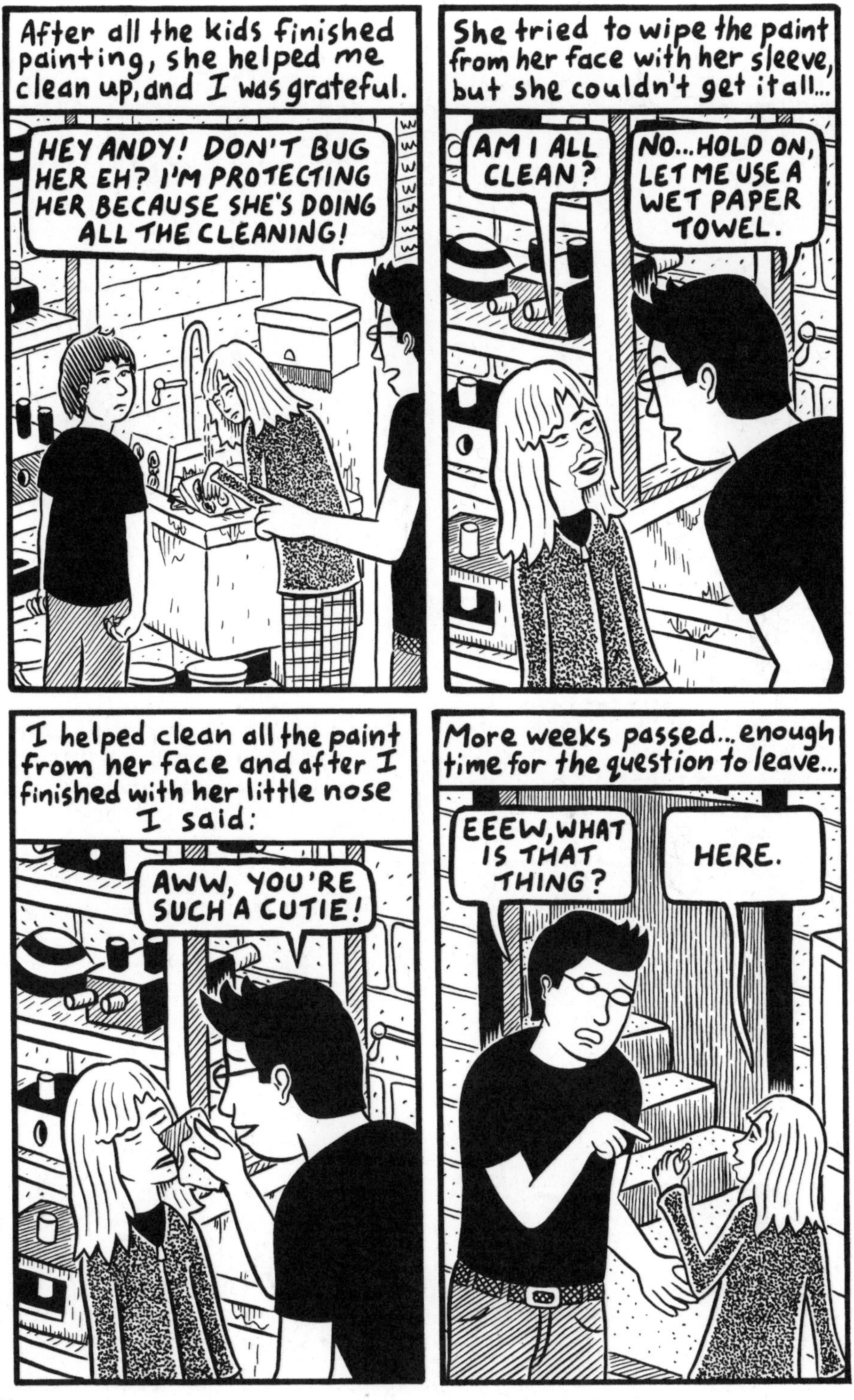
After all the kids finished painting, she helped me clean up, and I was grateful.
HEY ANDY! DON'T BUG HER EH? I'M PROTECTING HER BECAUSE SHE'S DOING ALL THE CLEANING!
She tried to wipe the paint from her face with her sleeve, but she couldn't get it all...
AM I ALL CLEAN?
NO...HOLD ON, LET ME USE A WET PAPER TOWEL.
I helped clean all the paint from her face and after I finished with her little nose I said:
AWW, YOU'RE SUCH A CUTIE!
More weeks passed...enough time for the question to leave...
EEEW, WHAT IS THAT THING?
HERE.

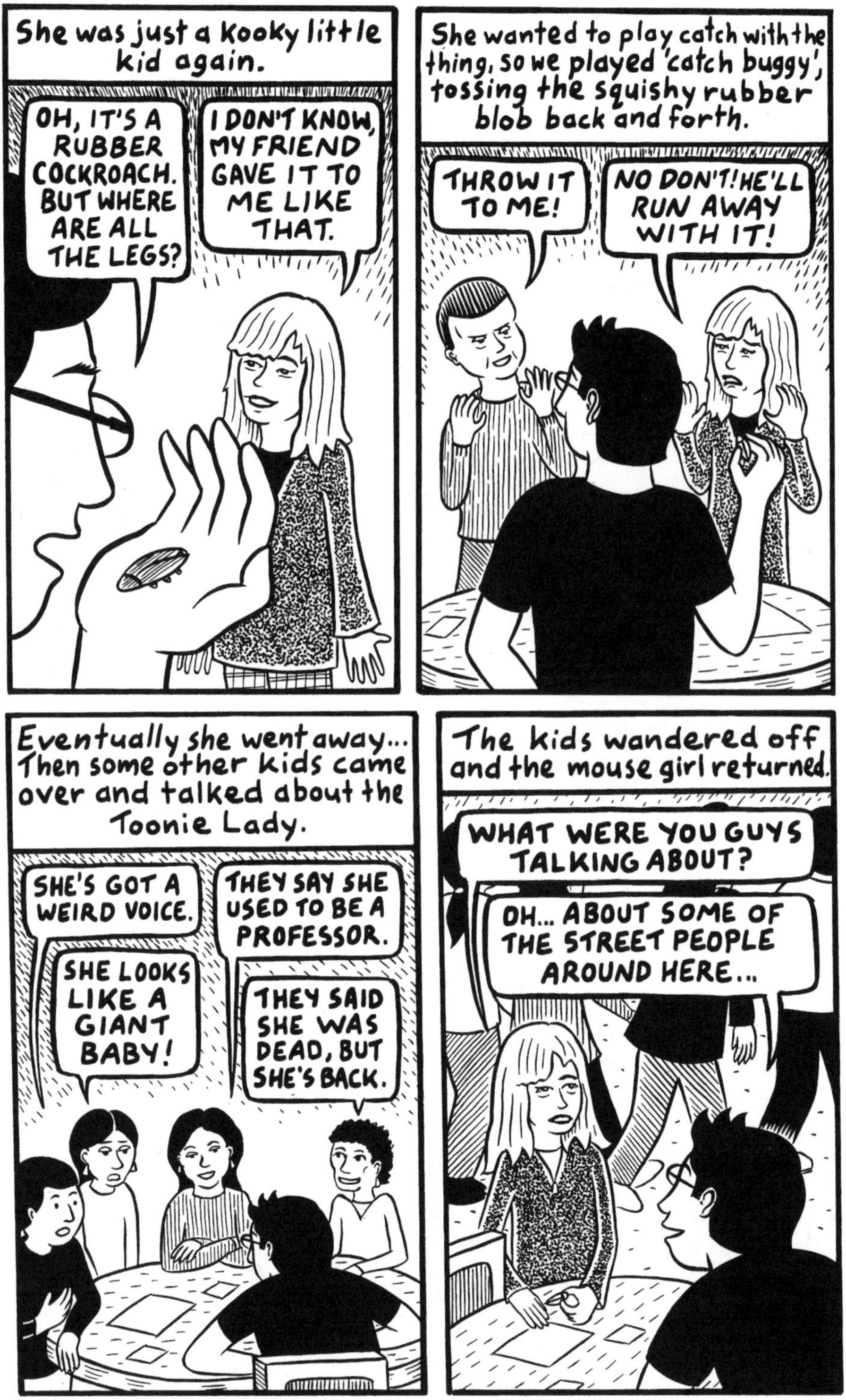
She was just a kooky little kid again.
OH, IT'S A RUBBER COCKROACH. BUT WHERE ARE ALL THE LEGS?
I DON'T KNOW, MY FRIEND GAVE IT TO ME LIKE THAT.
She wanted to play catch with the thing, so we played 'catch buggy', tossing the squishy rubber blob back and forth.
THROW IT TO ME!
NO DON'T! HE'LL RUN AWAY WITH IT!
Eventually she went away... Then some other kids came over and talked about the Toonie Lady.
SHE'S GOT A WEIRD VOICE.
THEY SAY SHE USED TO BE A PROFESSOR.
SHE LOOKS LIKE A GIANT BABY!
THEY SAID SHE WAS DEAD, BUT SHE'S BACK.
The kids wandered off and the mouse girl returned.
WHAT WERE YOU GUYS TALKING ABOUT?
OH... ABOUT SOME OF THE STREET PEOPLE AROUND HERE...

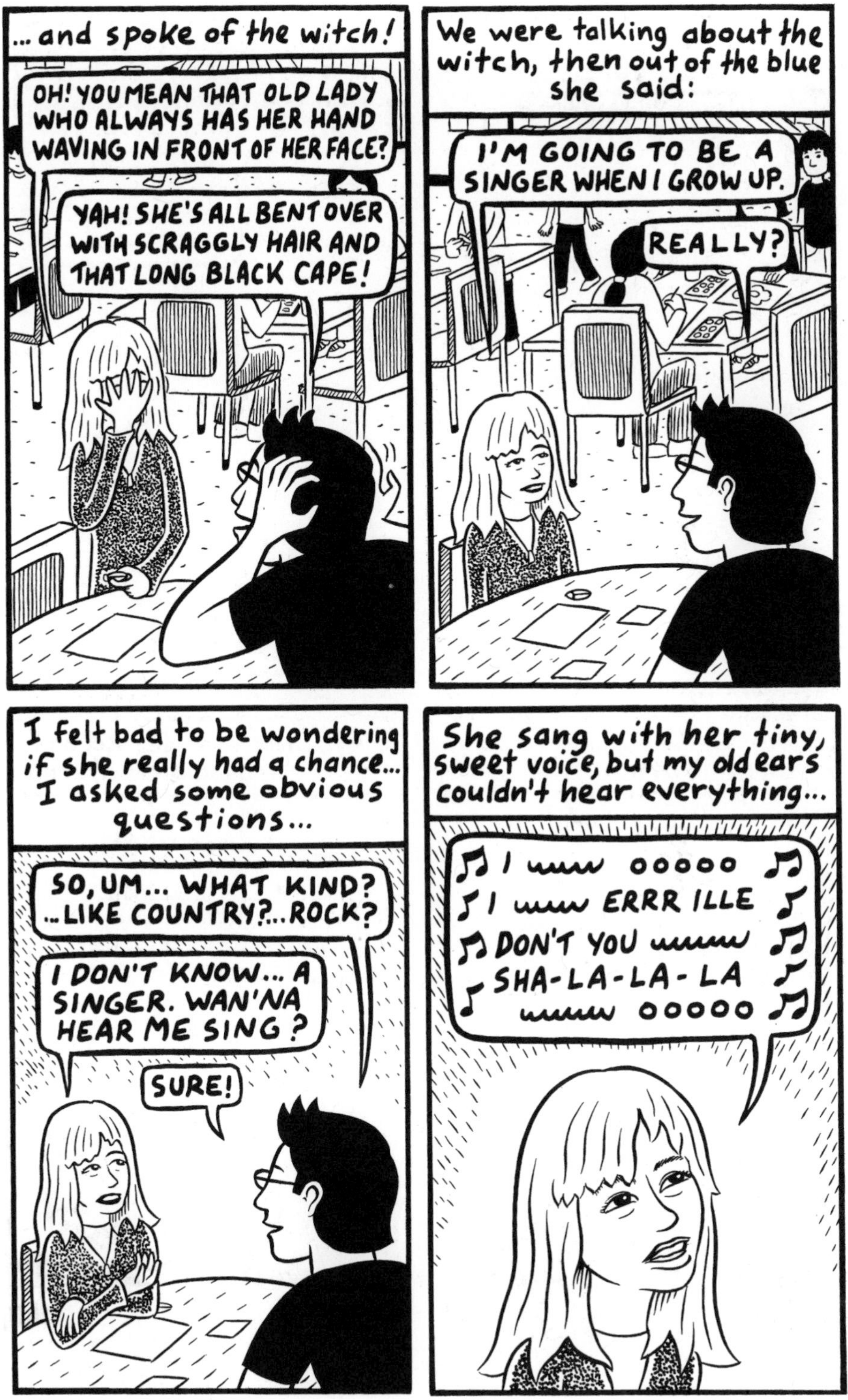
...and spoke of the witch!
OH! YOU MEAN THAT OLD LADY WHO ALWAYS HAS HER HAND WAVING IN FRONT OF HER FACE?
YAH! SHE'S ALL BENT OVER WITH SCRAGGLY HAIR AND THAT LONG BLACK CAPE!
We were talking about the witch, then out of the blue she said:
I'M GOING TO BE A SINGER WHEN I GROW UP.
REALLY?
I felt bad to be wondering if she really had a chance... I asked some obvious questions...
SO, UM... WHAT KIND? ...LIKE COUNTRY?...ROCK?
I DON'T KNOW... A SINGER. WAN'NA HEAR ME SING?
SURE!
She sang with her tiny, sweet voice, but my old ears couldn't hear everything...
I uuuu ooooo
I uuuu ERRR ILLE
DON'T YOU uuuuu
SHA-LA-LA-LA
uuuuu ooooo

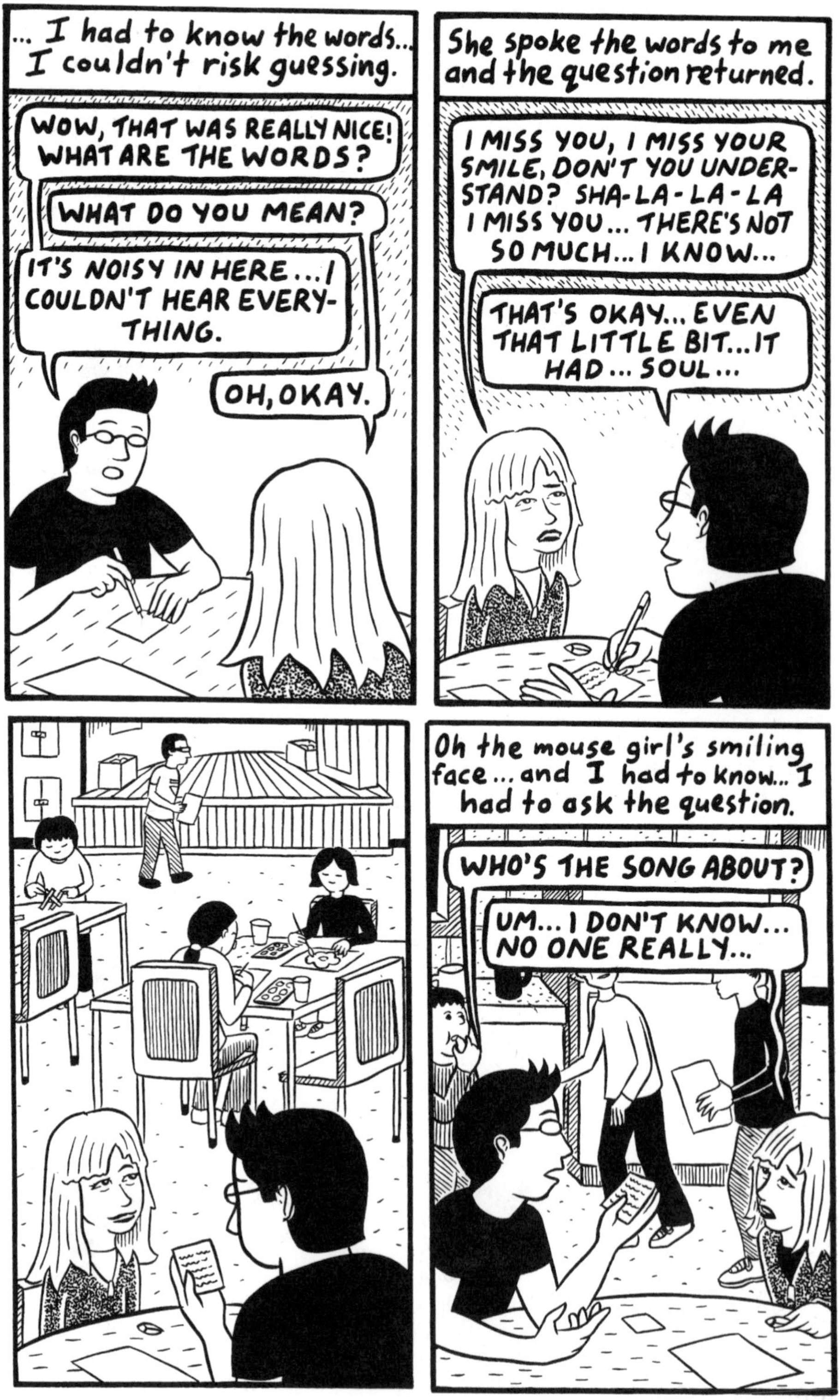
... I had to know the words... I couldn't risk guessing.
WOW, THAT WAS REALLY NICE! WHAT ARE THE WORDS?
WHAT DO YOU MEAN?
IT'S NOISY IN HERE... I COULDN'T HEAR EVERY-THING.
OH, OKAY.
She spoke the words to me and the question returned.
I MISS YOU, I MISS YOUR SMILE, DON'T YOU UNDER-STAND? SHA-LA-LA-LA I MISS YOU... THERE'S NOT SO MUCH... I KNOW...
THAT'S OKAY... EVEN THAT LITTLE BIT... IT HAD... SOUL...
Oh the mouse girl's smiling face... and I had to know... I had to ask the question.
WHO'S THE SONG ABOUT?
UM... I DON'T KNOW... NO ONE REALLY...

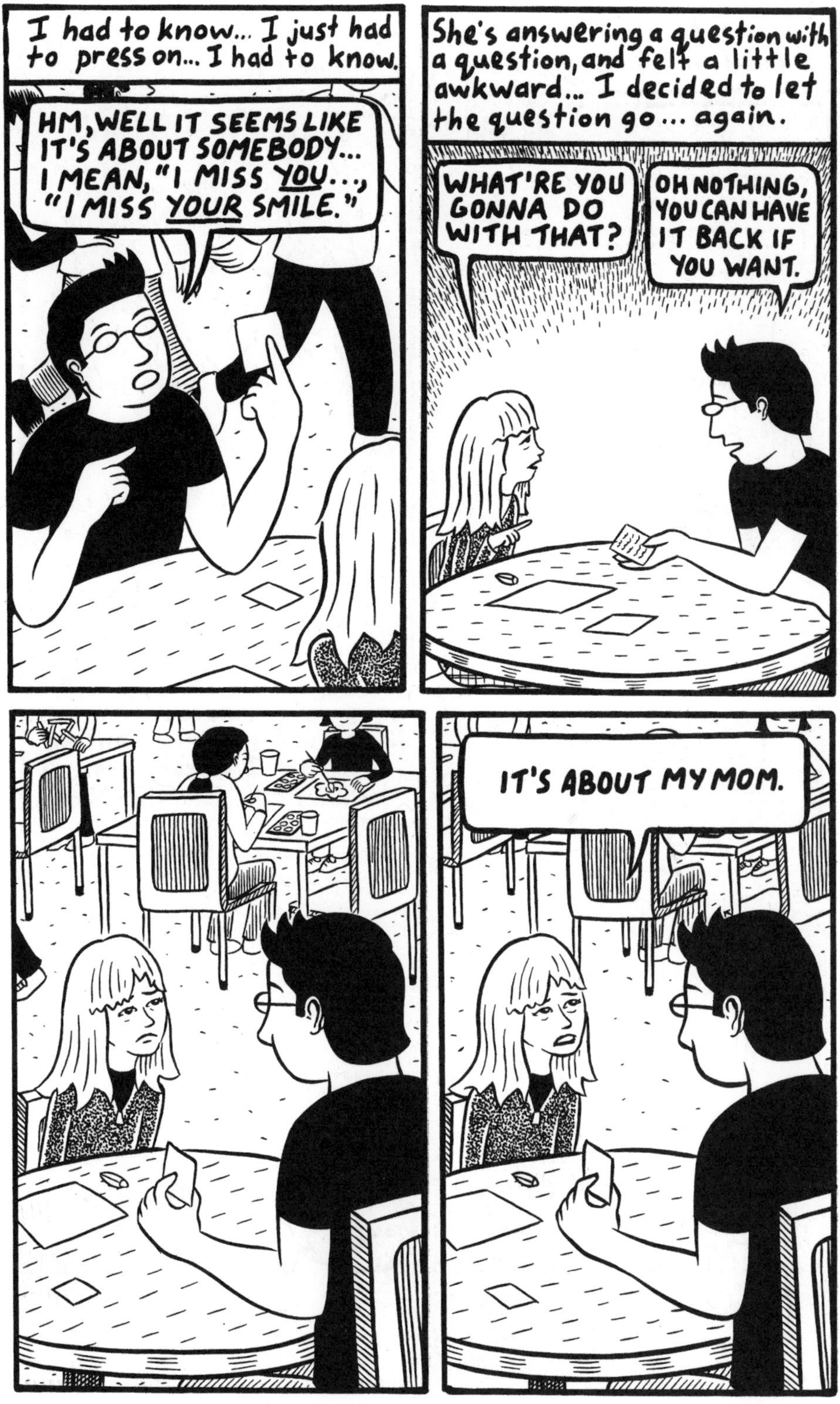
I had to know... I just had to press on... I had to know.
HM, WELL IT SEEMS LIKE IT'S ABOUT SOMEBODY... I MEAN, "I MISS YOU...," "I MISS YOUR SMILE."
She's answering a question with a question, and felt a little awkward... I decided to let the question go... again.
WHAT'RE YOU GONNA DO WITH THAT?
OH NOTHING, YOU CAN HAVE IT BACK IF YOU WANT.
IT'S ABOUT MY MOM.

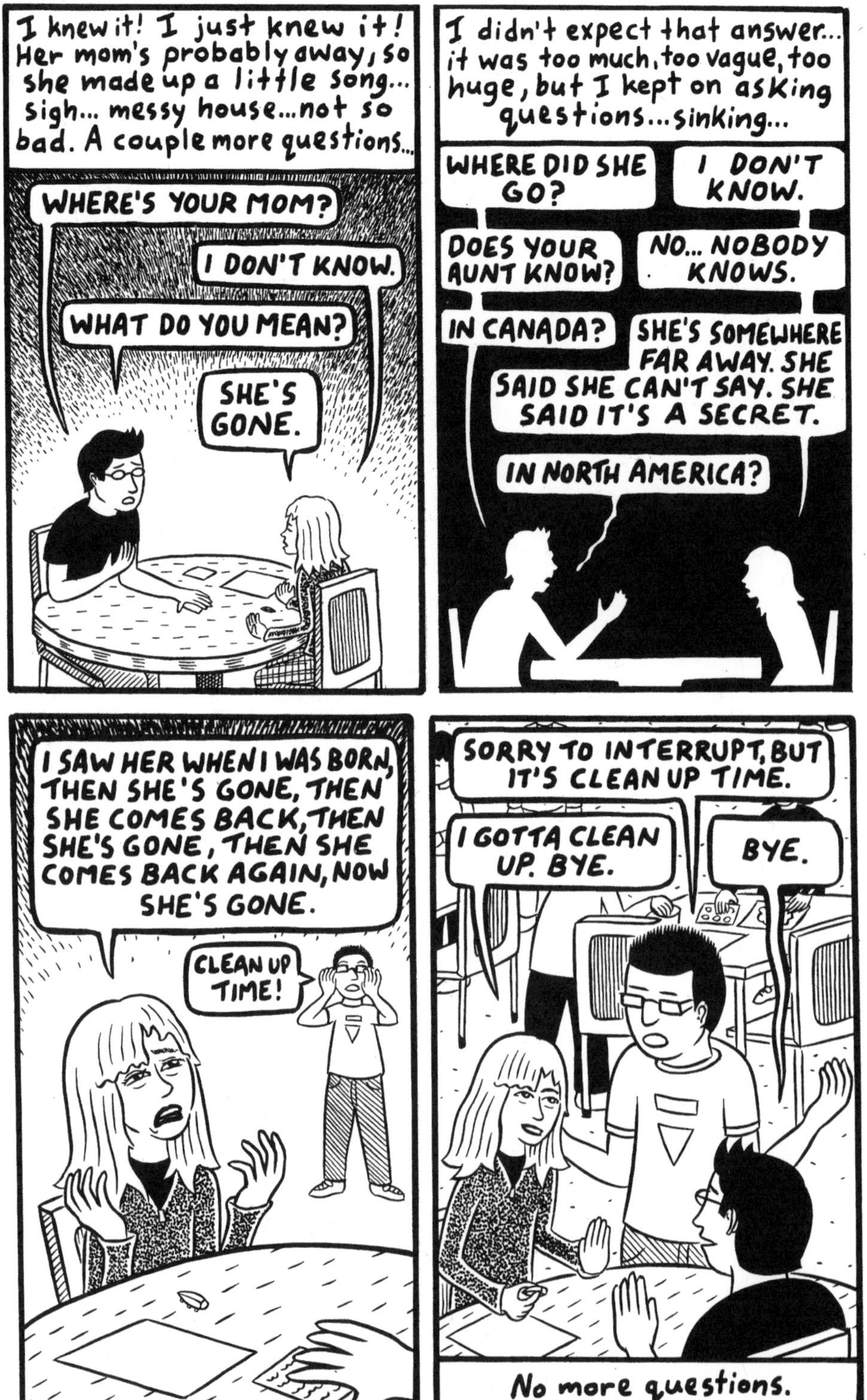
I knew it! I just knew it! Her mom's probably away, so she made up a little song... sigh... messy house...not so bad. A couple more questions...
WHERE'S YOUR MOM?
I DON'T KNOW.
WHAT DO YOU MEAN?
SHE'S GONE.
I didn't expect that answer... it was too much, too vague, too huge, but I kept on asking questions...sinking...
WHERE DID SHE GO?
I DON'T KNOW.
DOES YOUR AUNT KNOW?
NO... NOBODY KNOWS.
IN CANADA?
SHE'S SOMEWHERE FAR AWAY. SHE SAID SHE CAN'T SAY. SHE SAID IT'S A SECRET.
IN NORTH AMERICA?
I SAW HER WHEN I WAS BORN, THEN SHE'S GONE, THEN SHE COMES BACK, THEN SHE'S GONE, THEN SHE COMES BACK AGAIN, NOW SHE'S GONE.
CLEAN UP TIME!
SORRY TO INTERRUPT, BUT IT'S CLEAN UP TIME.
I GOTTA CLEAN UP. BYE.
BYE.
No more questions.

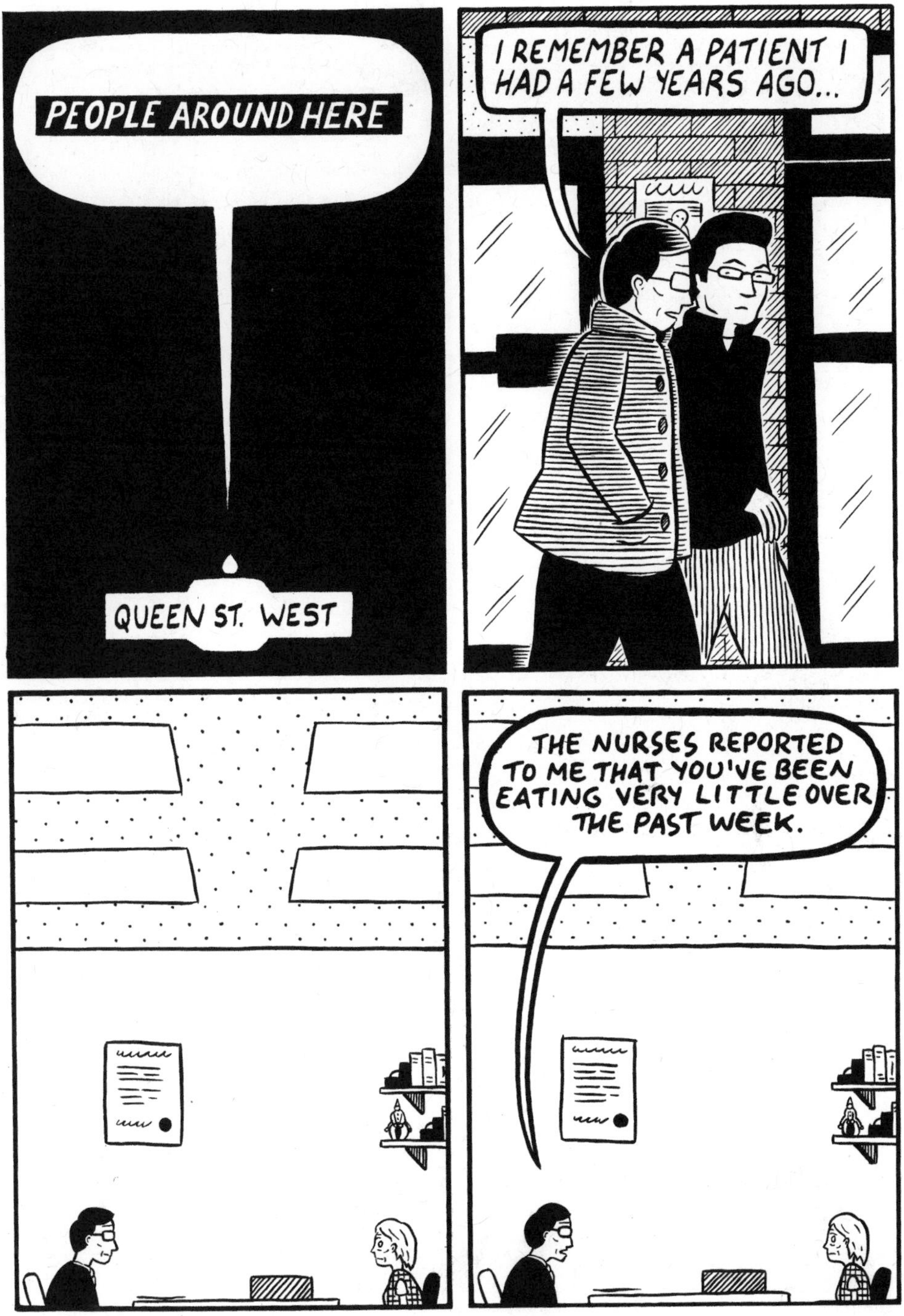
PEOPLE AROUND HERE
QUEEN ST. WEST
I REMEMBER A PATIENT I HAD A FEW YEARS AGO...
THE NURSES REPORTED TO ME THAT YOU'VE BEEN EATING VERY LITTLE OVER THE PAST WEEK.

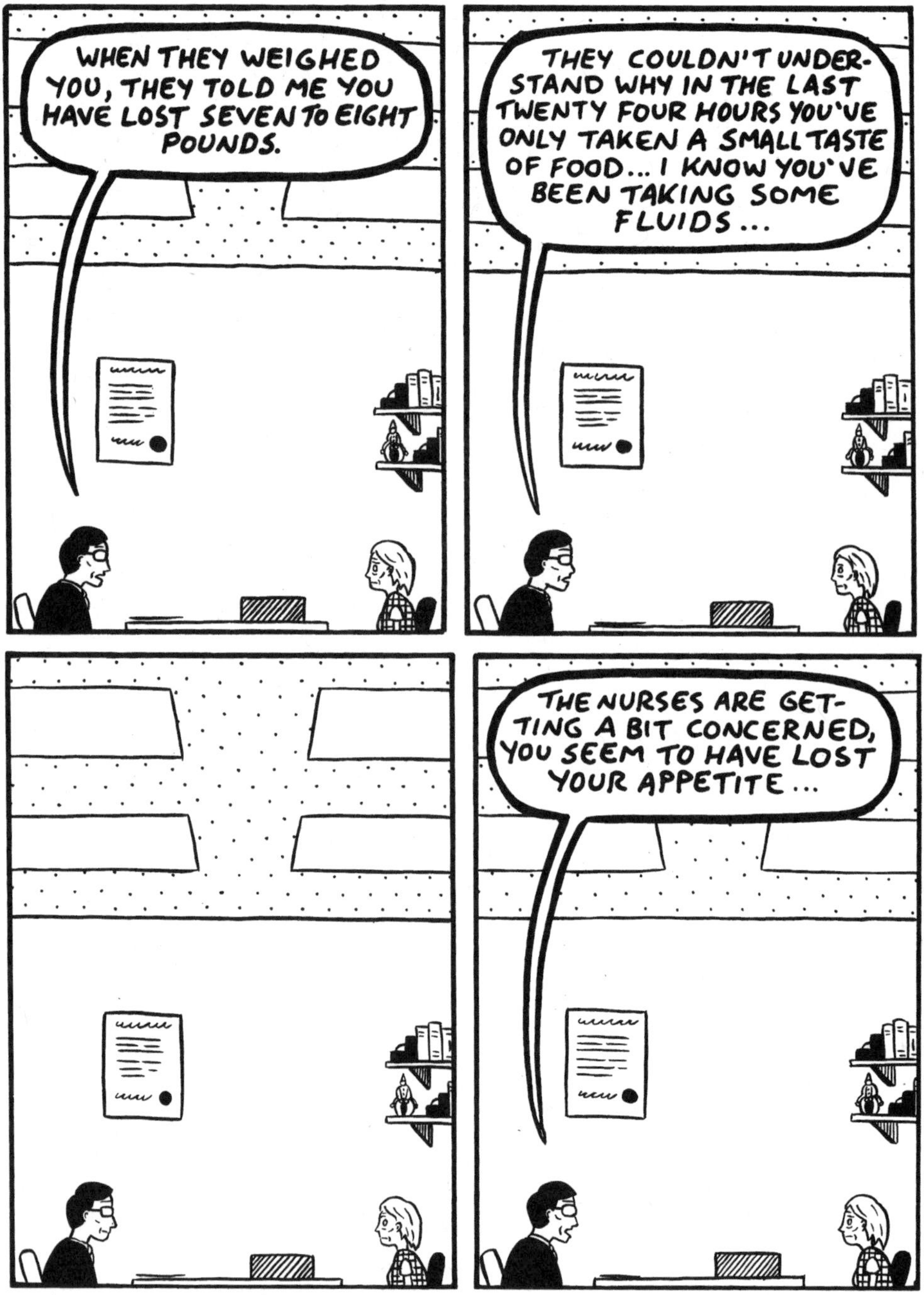
WHEN THEY WEIGHED YOU, THEY TOLD ME YOU HAVE LOST SEVEN TO EIGHT POUNDS.
THEY COULDN'T UNDER-STAND WHY IN THE LAST TWENTY FOUR HOURS YOU'VE ONLY TAKEN A SMALL TASTE OF FOOD... I KNOW YOU'VE BEEN TAKING SOME FLUIDS...
THE NURSES ARE GET-TING A BIT CONCERNED, YOU SEEM TO HAVE LOST YOUR APPETITE...

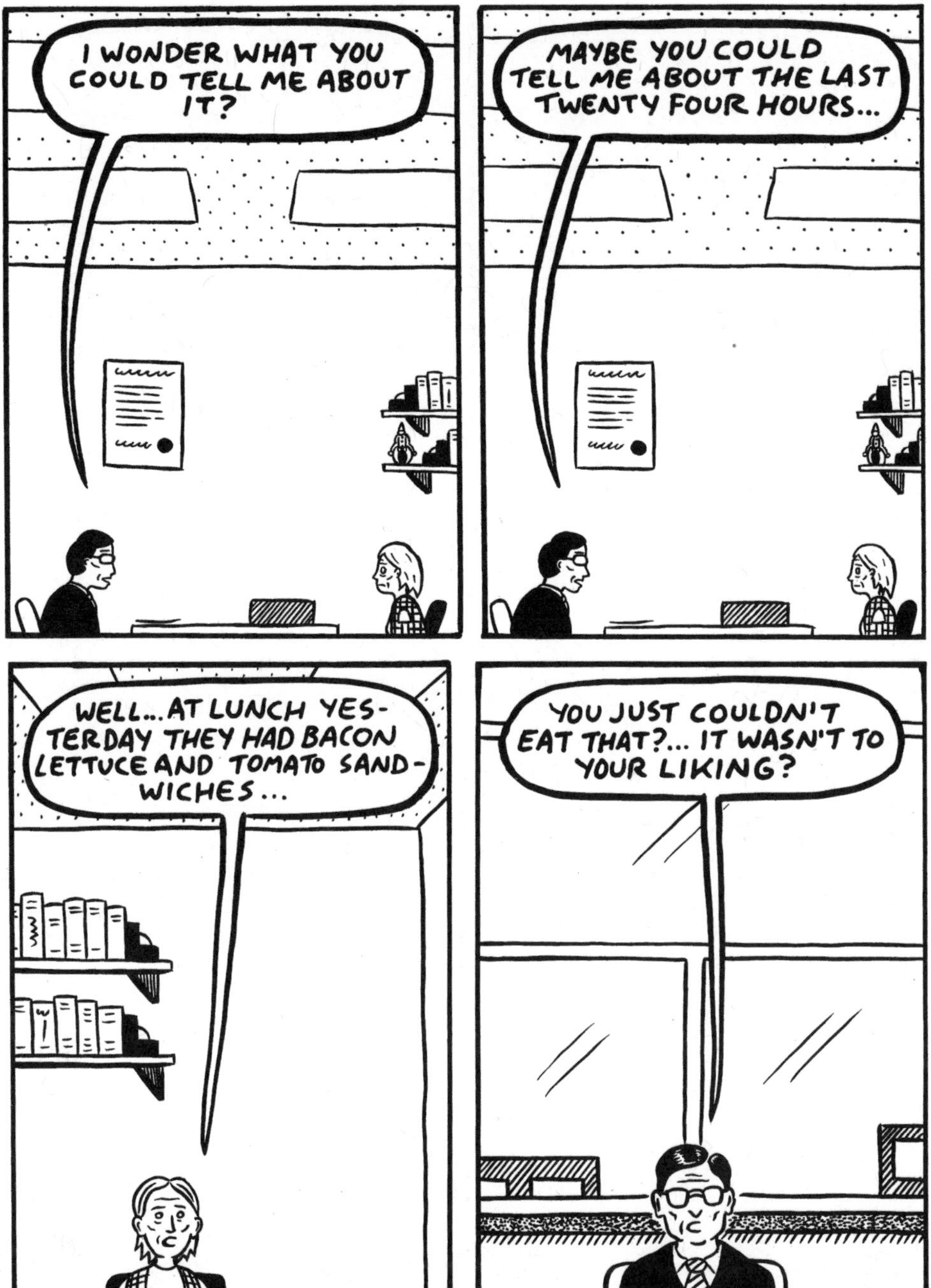
I WONDER WHAT YOU COULD TELL ME ABOUT IT?
MAYBE YOU COULD TELL ME ABOUT THE LAST TWENTY FOUR HOURS...
WELL...AT LUNCH YES-TERDAY THEY HAD BACON LETTUCE AND TOMATO SAND-WICHES...
YOU JUST COULDN'T EAT THAT?... IT WASN'T TO YOUR LIKING?

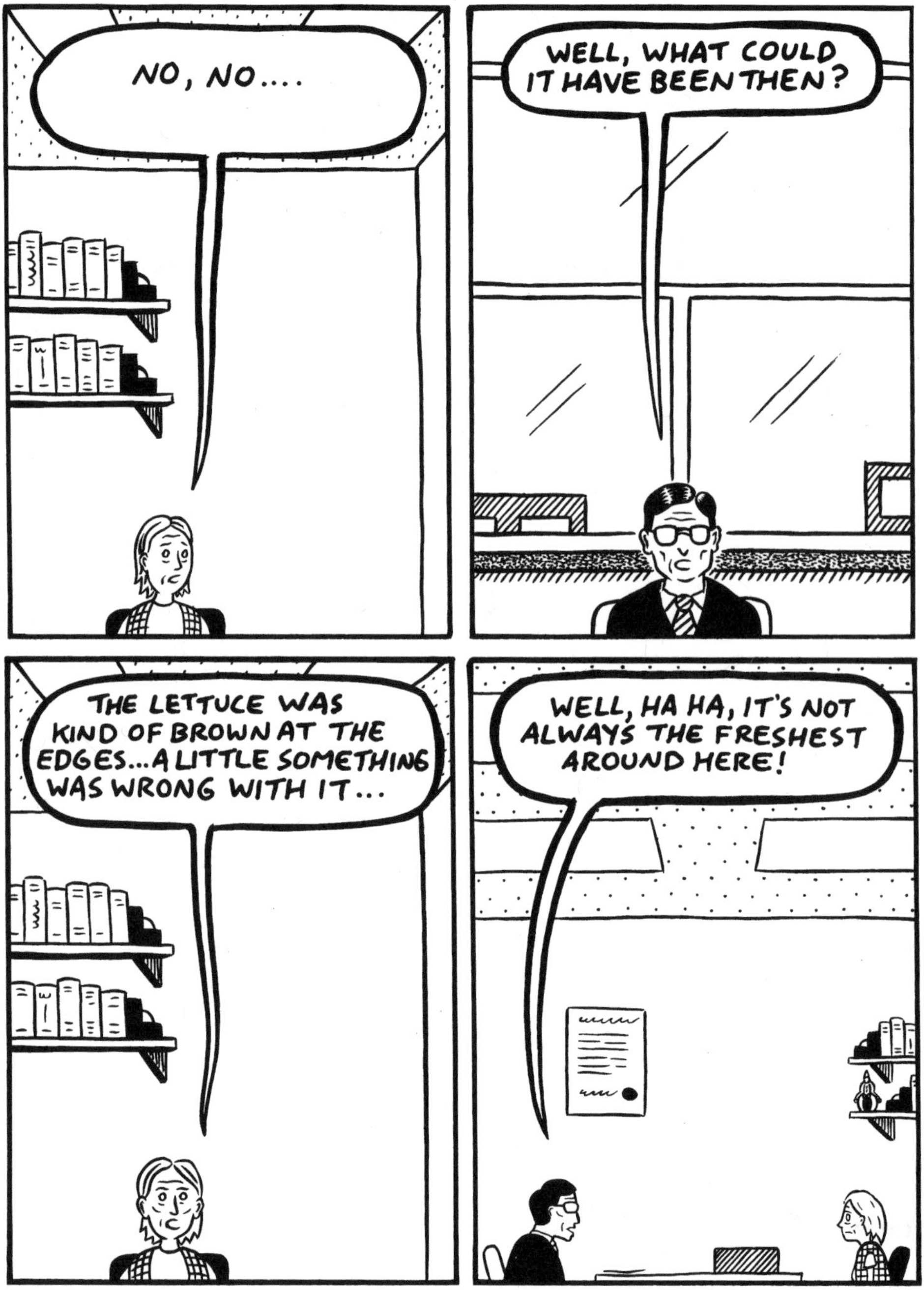
NO, NO....
WELL, WHAT COULD IT HAVE BEEN THEN?
THE LETTUCE WAS KIND OF BROWN AT THE EDGES...A LITTLE SOMETHING WAS WRONG WITH IT...
WELL, HA HA, IT'S NOT ALWAYS THE FRESHEST AROUND HERE!

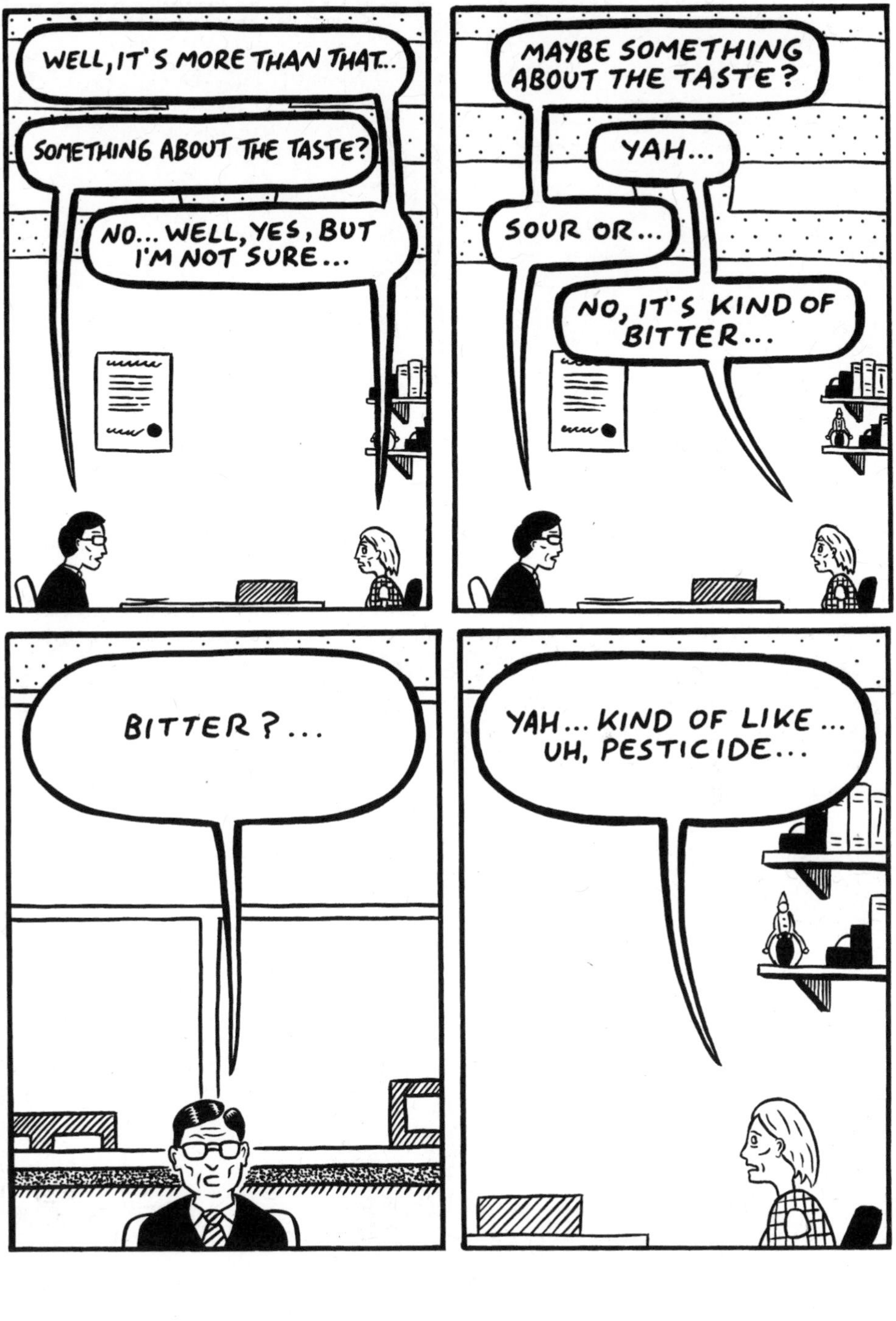
WELL, IT'S MORE THAN THAT...
SOMETHING ABOUT THE TASTE?
NO... WELL, YES, BUT I'M NOT SURE...
MAYBE SOMETHING ABOUT THE TASTE?
YAH...
SOUR OR...
NO, IT'S KIND OF BITTER...
BITTER?...
YAH... KIND OF LIKE... UH, PESTICIDE...

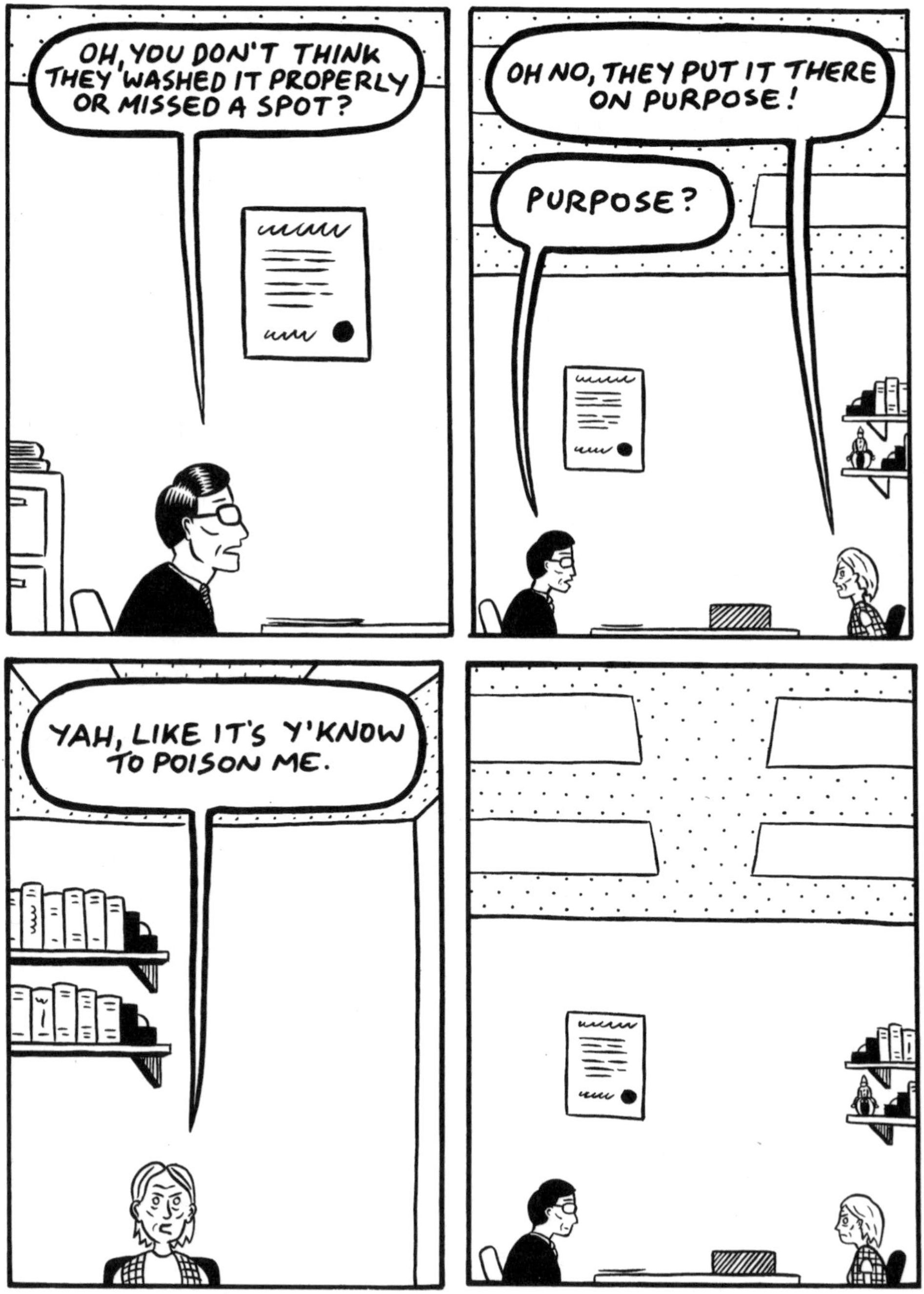
OH, YOU DON'T THINK THEY WASHED IT PROPERLY OR MISSED A SPOT?
OH NO, THEY PUT IT THERE ON PURPOSE!
PURPOSE?
YAH, LIKE IT'S Y'KNOW TO POISON ME.

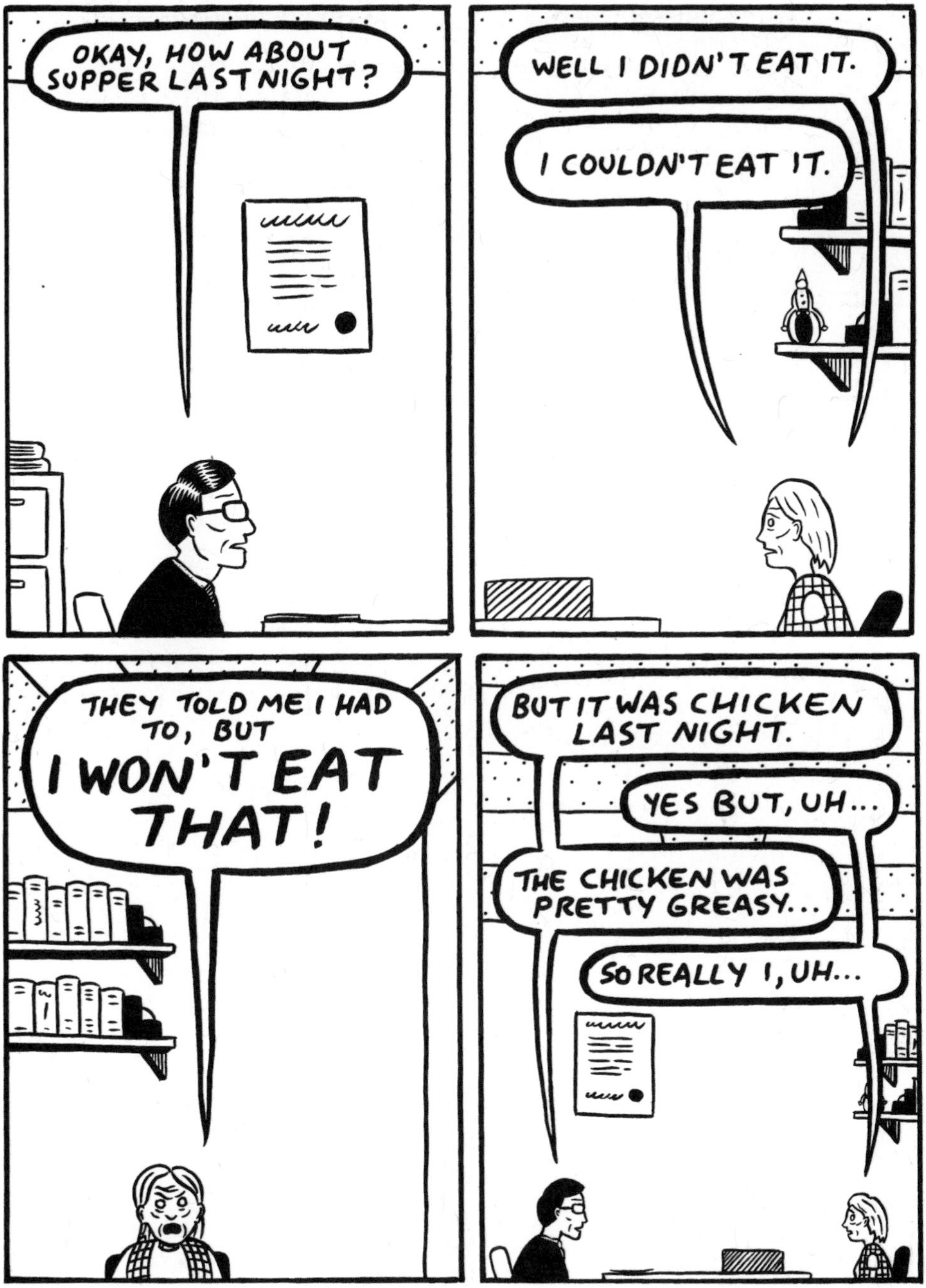
OKAY, HOW ABOUT SUPPER LAST NIGHT?
WELL I DIDN'T EAT IT.
I COULDN'T EAT IT.
THEY TOLD ME I HAD TO, BUT I WON'T EAT THAT!
BUT IT WAS CHICKEN LAST NIGHT.
YES BUT, UH...
THE CHICKEN WAS PRETTY GREASY...
SO REALLY I, UH...

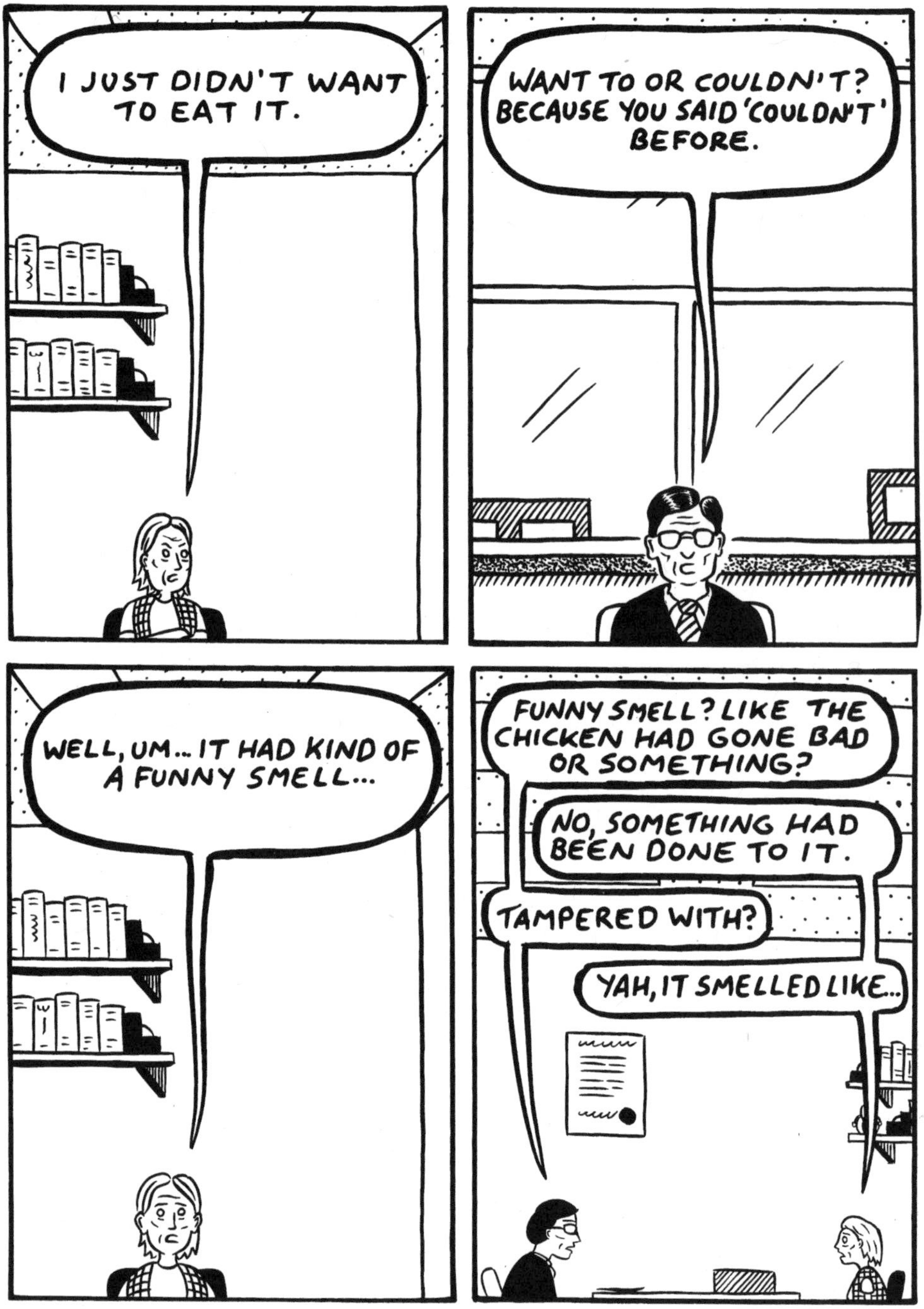
I JUST DIDN'T WANT TO EAT IT.
WANT TO OR COULDN'T? BECAUSE YOU SAID 'COULDN'T' BEFORE.
WELL, UM... IT HAD KIND OF A FUNNY SMELL...
FUNNY SMELL? LIKE THE CHICKEN HAD GONE BAD OR SOMETHING?
NO, SOMETHING HAD BEEN DONE TO IT.
TAMPERED WITH?
YAH, IT SMELLED LIKE...

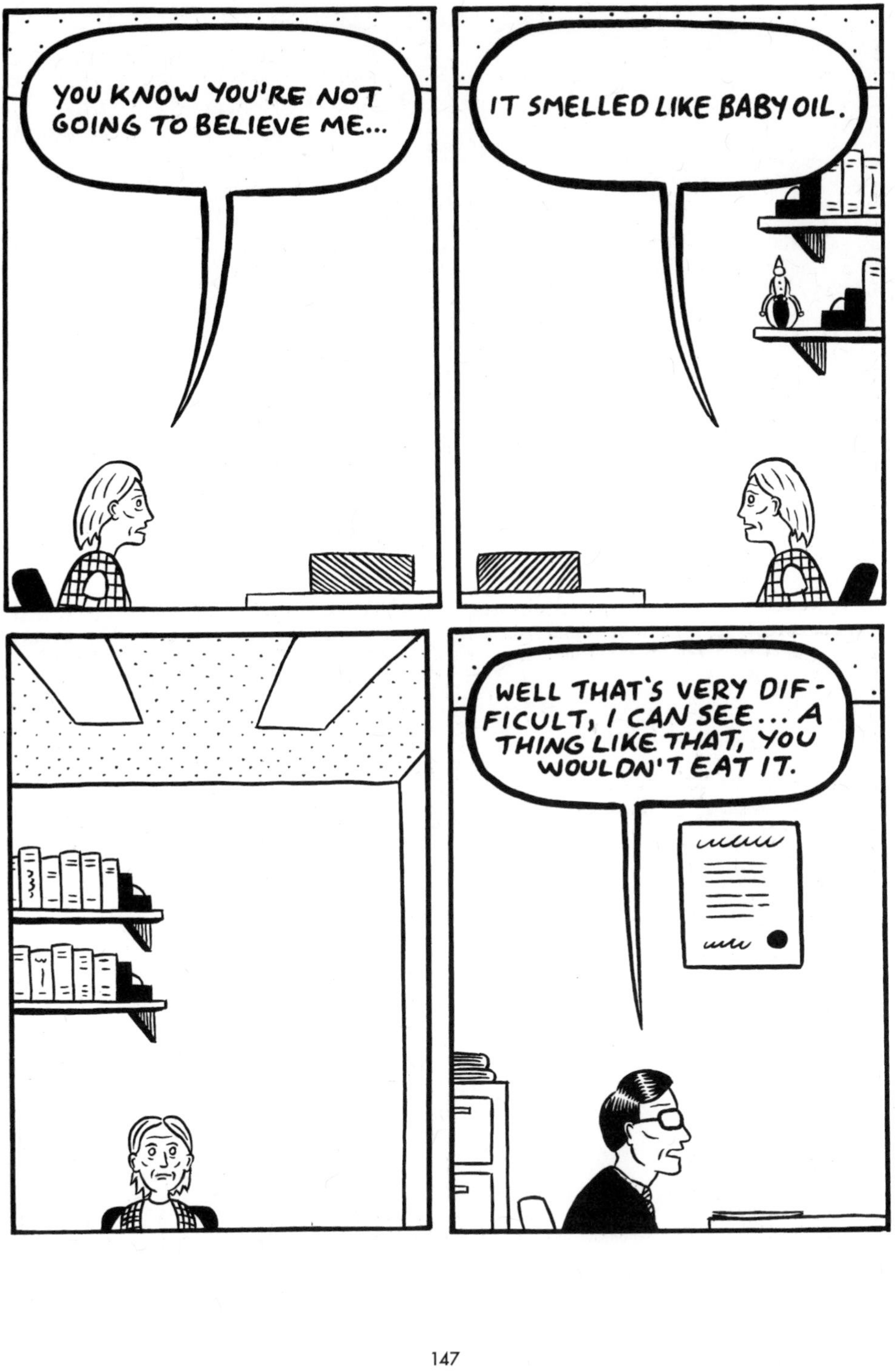
YOU KNOW YOU'RE NOT GOING TO BELIEVE ME...
IT SMELLED LIKE BABY OIL.
WELL THAT'S VERY DIF-FICULT, I CAN SEE... A THING LIKE THAT, YOU WOULDN'T EAT IT.

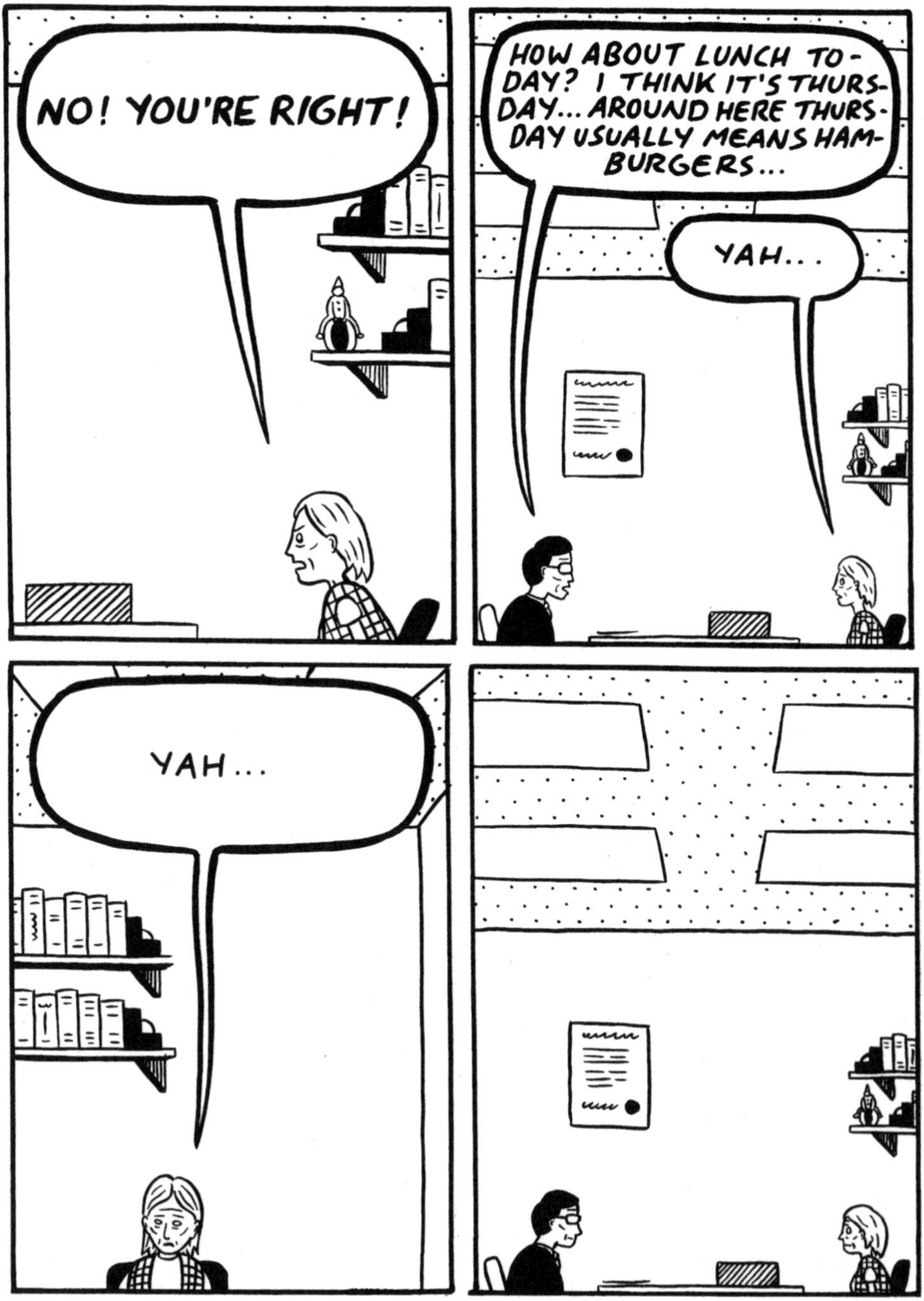
NO! YOU'RE RIGHT!
HOW ABOUT LUNCH TO-DAY? I THINK IT'S THURS-DAY... AROUND HERE THURS-DAY USUALLY MEANS HAM-BURGERS...
YAH...
YAH...

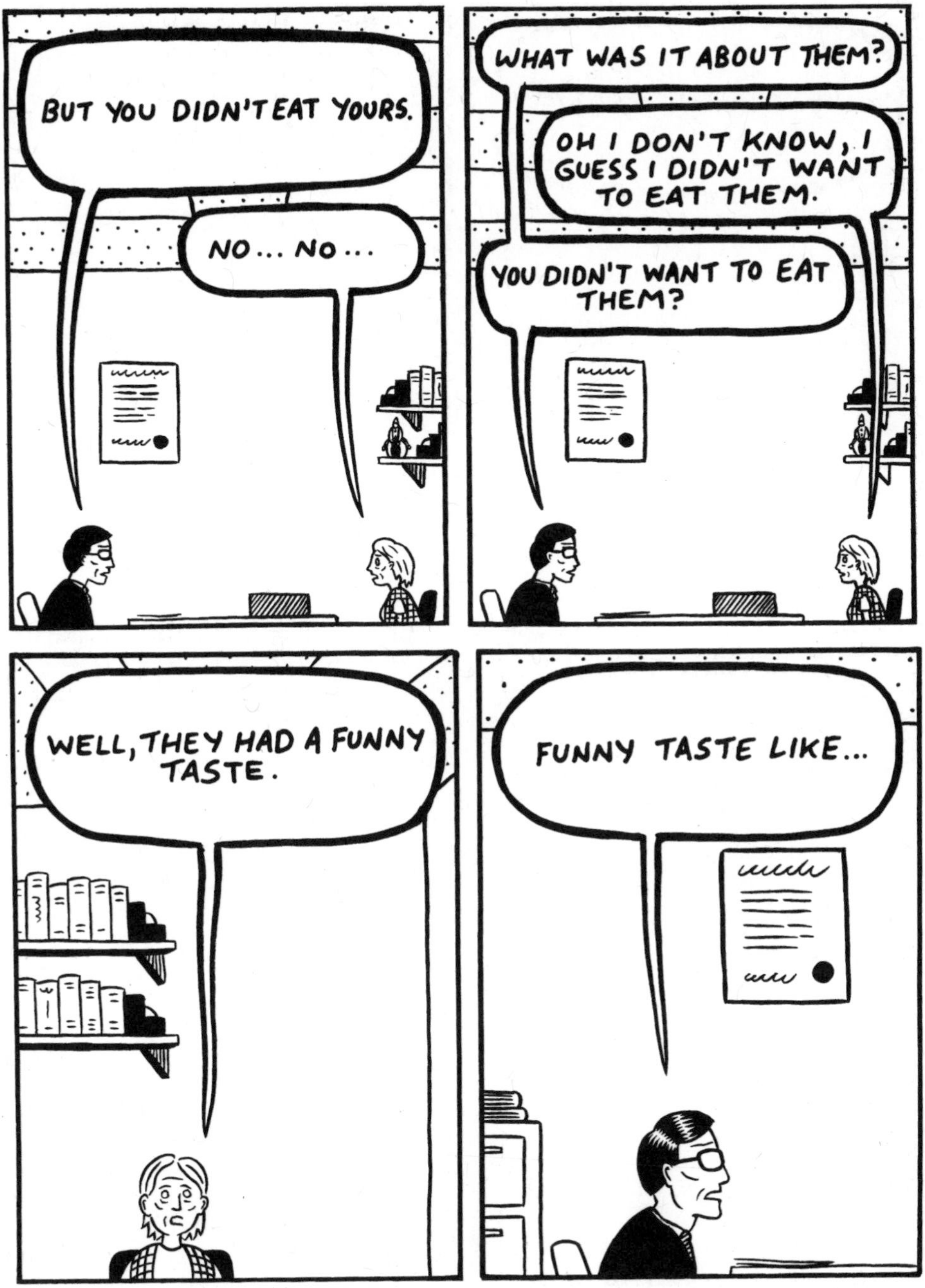
BUT YOU DIDN'T EAT YOURS.
NO... NO...
WHAT WAS IT ABOUT THEM?
OH I DON'T KNOW, I GUESS I DIDN'T WANT TO EAT THEM.
YOU DIDN'T WANT TO EAT THEM?
WELL, THEY HAD A FUNNY TASTE.
FUNNY TASTE LIKE...

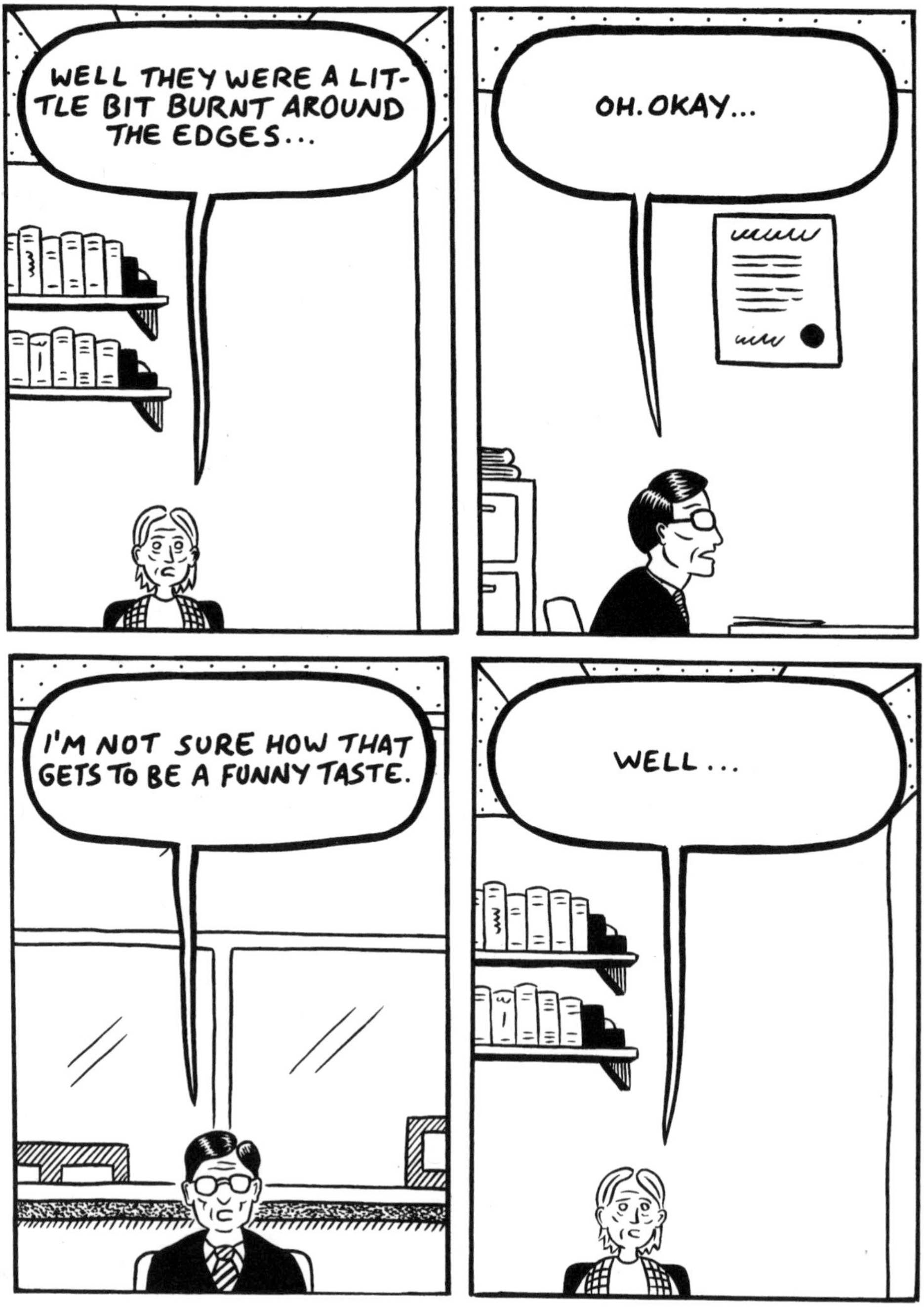
WELL THEY WERE A LITTLE BIT BURNT AROUND THE EDGES...
OH. OKAY...
I'M NOT SURE HOW THAT GETS TO BE A FUNNY TASTE.
WELL...

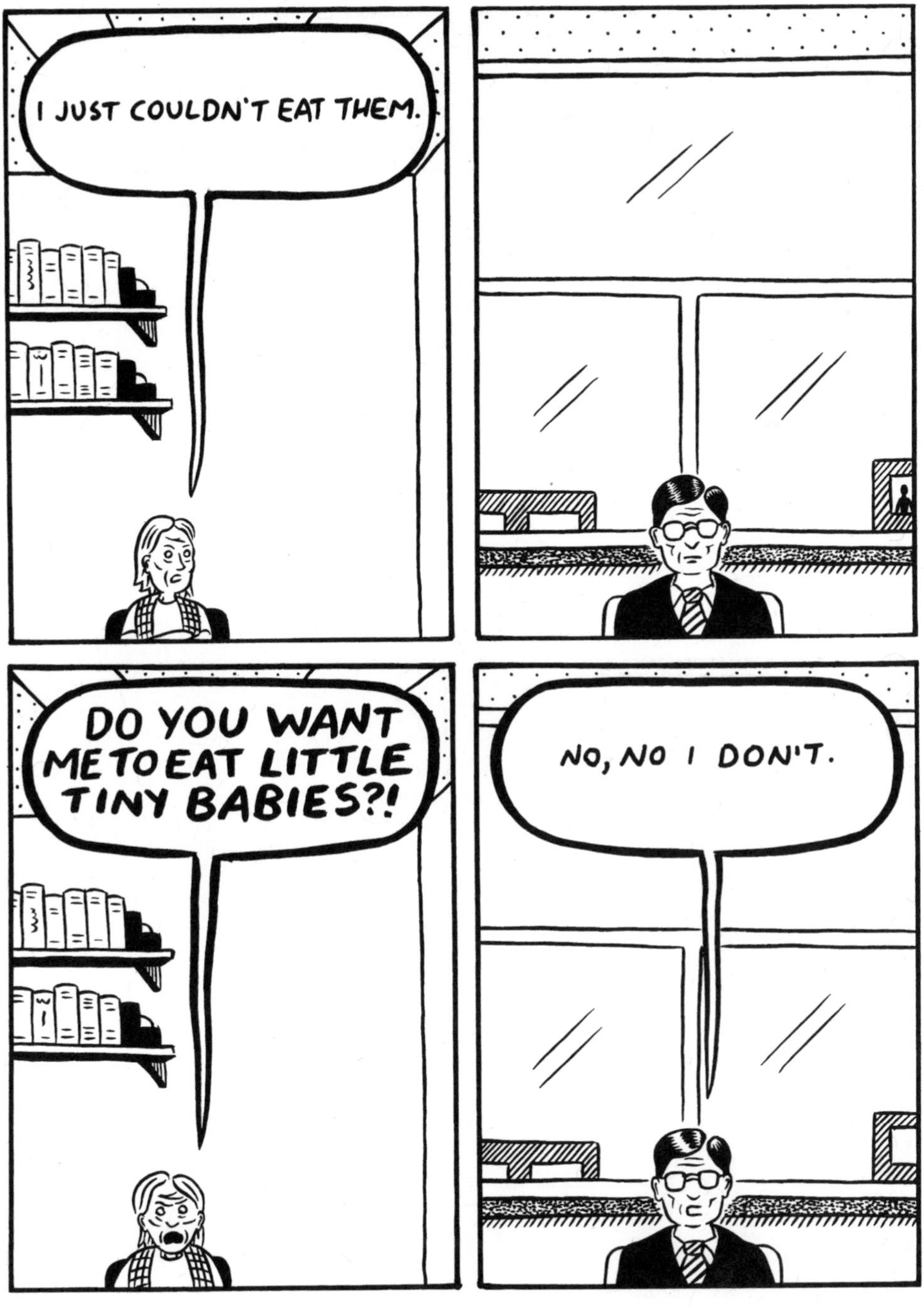
I JUST COULDN'T EAT THEM.
DO YOU WANT ME TO EAT LITTLE TINY BABIES?!
NO, NO I DON'T.

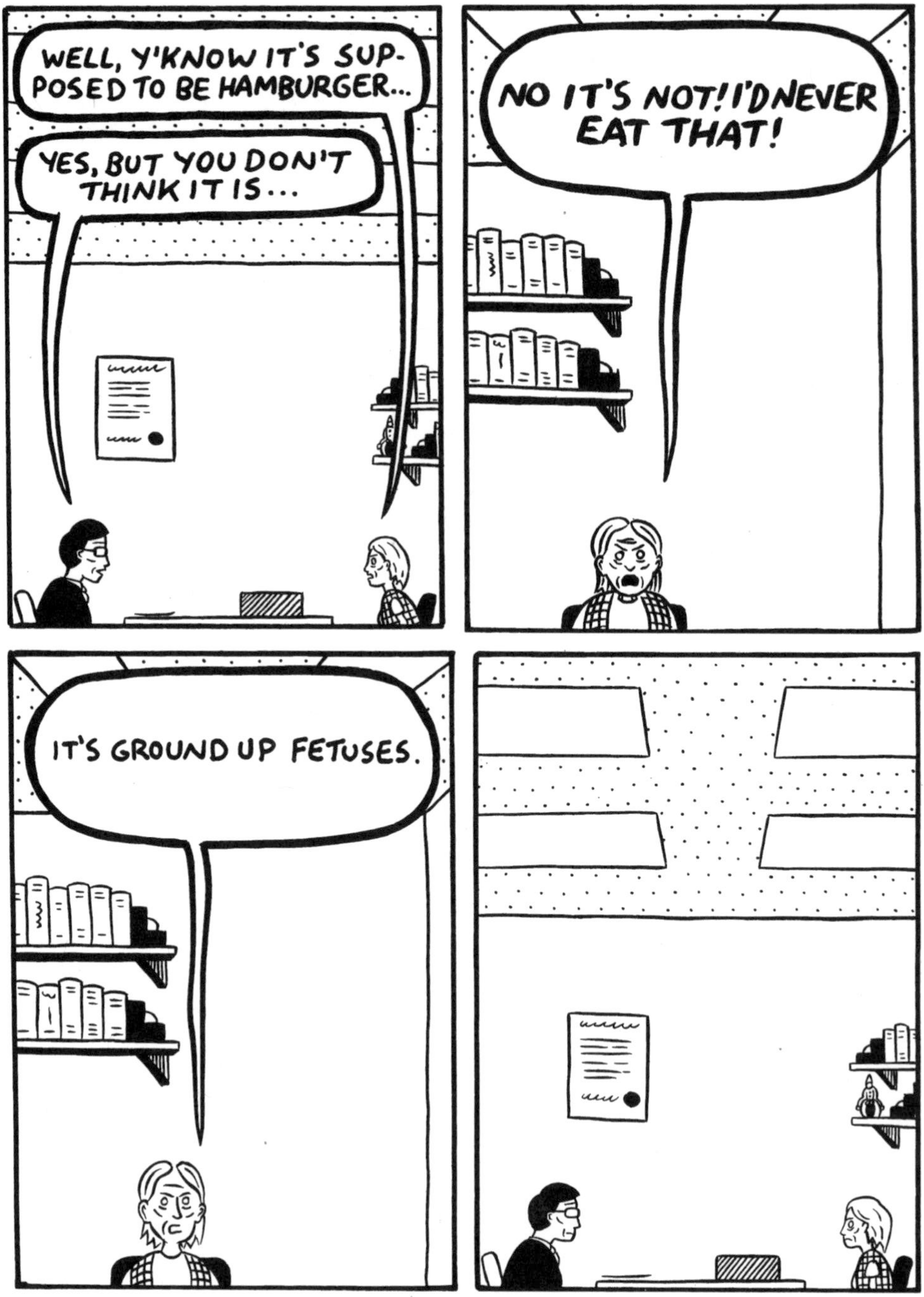
WELL, Y'KNOW IT'S SUP-POSED TO BE HAMBURGER...
YES, BUT YOU DON'T THINK IT IS...
NO IT'S NOT! I'D NEVER EAT THAT!
IT'S GROUND UP FETUSES.

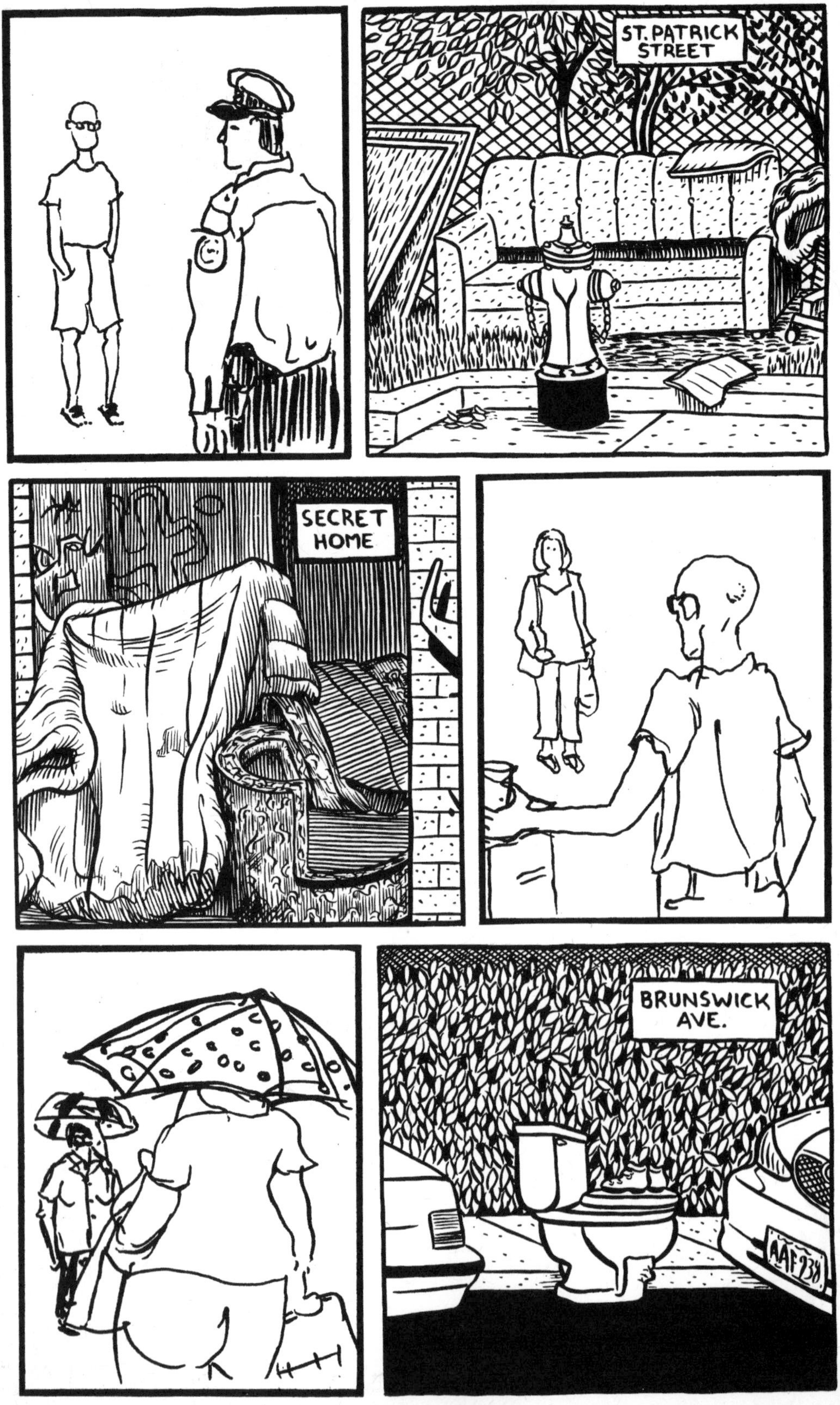
ST. PATRICK STREET
SECRET HOME
BRUNSWICK AVE.